M000299717

Sheepdogs
My Faithful Friends

Second Edition

ERIC HALSALL

Foreword by Phil Drabble

FARMING PRESS

First published September 1980 by Patrick Stephens
Reprinted June 1981, Patrick Stephens
Paperback edition September 1985, Patrick Stephens
Second edition October 1996, Farming Press
Copyright © Eric Halsall, 1980, 1985, 1996

All rights reserved. No parts of this
publication may be reproduced, stored in
a retrieval system, or transmitted, in any
form or by any means, electronic, mechanical,
photocopying, recording or otherwise, without
prior permission of Farming Press.

ISBN 0 85236 359 1

A catalogue record for this book is available
from the British Library

Published by Farming Press
Miller Freeman Professional Ltd
2 Wharfedale Road, Ipswich IP1 4LG, United Kingdom

Distributed in North America
by Diamond Farm Enterprises,
Box 537, Alexandria Bay, NY 13607, USA

Front cover photo by Richard Hinton
Back cover photo (bottom) by Marc Henrie
Cover design by Andrew Thistlethwaite
Typeset by Galleon Typesetting
Printed and bound in Great Britain by Biddles Ltd,
Guildford and King's Lynn

Contents

⦿⟫₀⟨⦿⟫₀⟨⦿⟫₀⟨⦿

There is a picture section between pages 310 and 311

This book is dedicated to the memory of Rhaq, Meg, Gael, Moss, Ken, Kyle, Gel, Hope and Rob, and their contemporaries in the high hills.

Foreword
to the Second Edition
by Phil Drabble

I was delighted to be invited to write the foreword to this new edition of *Sheepdogs, My Faithful Friends* because the book has become a rural classic since Eric Halsall wrote it, back in 1980. His head is still thatched with wool because his addiction now takes him 'sheep-dogging' every weekend and he spends his Sundays writing authoritative reports for the sheepdog world and specialist farming press.

We have much in common because I, too, feel half-dressed without my favourite dog, and Eric did the commentary for fourteen out of the seventeen years in which I presented the television sheepdog championships 'One Man and His Dog'. We naturally became close friends.

Our careers merged purely by chance. Philip Gilbert O.B.E., Head of the BBC's events programmes, which include sport, dropped in at a local agricultural show while on holiday in Northumberland, in the early 1970s. Here he watched his first sheepdog trial, out of pure curiosity. A minute television screen lurks at the back of Philip's mind which instinctively assembled shots of dogs driving sheep round a formalised, repetitive course. The montage he imagined was composed of dramatic pictures of stroppy sheep, defying men and dogs, and marvellous close-ups of soulful collie eyes, worshipping their masters, with whom they seemed to have a telepathic rapport.

To check his first impressions, Philip visited another show, where Eric Halsall happened to be giving a live commentary for fellow countryfolk already on his wavelength. Nobody who hears the torrent of sheer enthusiasm which spills from Eric's lips when he is describing the triumphs and disasters of what he is convinced are the wisest dogs on earth can fail to fall under his spell.

The planners were asked to provide a slot for one pilot programme about sheepdog trials – which could be stifled at birth if it didn't make the grade – but the planners themselves had fallen for the idea so that Philip Gilbert was lumbered with producing a whole series of eight forty-five minute programmes at peak viewing time!

He soon realised that, although Eric had forgotten more about shepherds and sheepdog trials than most of us will ever know, he had no technical experience of working on the box. Fitting commentary to film, after it has been edited and shortened to dovetail with available space, requires entirely different specialist skills from doing a live commentary as the trial unfolds.

I have been involved with a wide range of rural broadcasting since my first programme, in 1947, so I was invited to present the series, with Eric as my commentator. The dice were loaded against us but our mutual affection for working dogs impelled us to have a go. Neither has ever regretted it: millions of urban viewers have since been bitten by Eric's enthusiastic bug and are now as irrevocably hooked on sheepdogs as real countrymen are.

I am as proud of being invited to write the foreword for what will become internationally acclaimed as a classic as I was for the first edition, a generation ago.

Phil Drabble

June 1996

Preface
to the Second Edition

This book was originally written in 1980, but in this new edition the sheepdog scene is covered from its beginnings to the end of 1995.

After a lifetime in the Pennine hills I have come to know collie dogs so well and have spent so many happy hours in their company that it is as a tribute to them that this book has been written.

The book has a twofold purpose: to record the skills and the illustrious heritage of these collie dogs and to so interest my readers that they too will wish to know them. Not all are fortunate enough to be able to meet these dogs in their work-a-day lives, as I have done, but all are able to see them in sheepdog trials – there are over 400 trials annually in the UK – and so, while telling you of their home characteristics, I have written in detail of the background, purpose and aims of trials so that a knowledgeable and consequently greater pleasure can be derived from watching trials.

The book will therefore be of equal interest to the person who delights in the British countryside and enjoys the crafts of its residents – both human and animal – as well as to the farmer and sheepdog enthusiast.

After many years of agricultural journalism, of wandering among the shepherding folk of the countryside, the book also gives me the opportunity to say 'thank you' for the open hospitality which I always received. I have quizzed, nattered and undoubtedly inconvenienced many people over the years and yet I have always been met with the kindest response. Many will find themselves in this book, others will not, but only because of the necessity to keep within the covers. To all I acknowledge the help and the willingness to pass on so freely whatever information they could.

Only by such willingness to assist me, from the countless friendships which have followed our meeting, has this book been made possible so that in truth the finished project has many authors. This particularly applies to the pictorial section, which has been gleaned from many sources in order to present an outstanding collection of sheepdog pictures. Many are valued pictures in that they cannot be replaced and my sincere thanks go to all who have contributed. I have tried to credit and acknowledge the source of each picture but this has not always been possible so I apologise for any omissions and here record my thanks.

I should particularly like to thank Mrs Wilson, John Bathgate, David Moodie and Alistair McPhee for the majority of the historical pictures, and Barbara Carpenter and photographers Austin Bennett, Derek Johnson, Marc Henrie, Frank Moyes, Roy Parker and Tim Fearon-Jones for pictures taken especially for the book, and Claire Newbery and Kay Edge for their work on the manuscript.

I appreciate the encouragement of my professional colleagues, and thank the editor and staff of the *Farmers Guardian*, and in particular my good friend, Matt Mundell, recently of *The Scottish Farmer*.

My thanks also to Phil Drabble, the ideal partner in 'One Man and His Dog', for his Foreword; to Philip Gilbert, Ian Smith and their BBC television teams for giving me the opportunity to bring the skills of the working collie to such a wide audience; and to Norman Turner of BBC radio who really introduced me to a microphone.

Finally, but deserving of my premier acknowledgement, my thanks to my wife for tolerating all the inconveniences that dogs and writing so often create and, along with my sister and brother-in-law, for granting me 'leave of absence' from the outside jobs while the book was being written.

ERIC HALSALL
Cliviger, February 1996

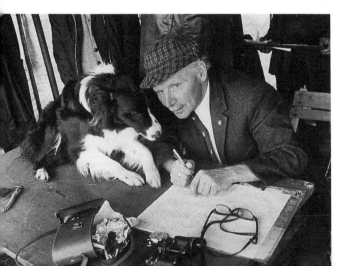

At this sheepdog trial not all my judging critics were human! Len Greenwood's Sweep checks my pointing at the Royal Lancashire Show (Burnley Express).

CHAPTER ONE

A Man and His Dogs

I set out to gather the hill with collies Rhaq, Meg and Gael, the finest companions a man could have, tell of their characters and qualities, and their vital role in farming sheep in high places.

A cold wet nose pushed into my hand. I looked down into liquid amber eyes, the most intelligent in the canine world. Rhaq, my sheepdog, stared back at me, adoration glowing in his deep soulful expression. He was waiting to go, waiting to receive my command to send him about his business, a mile-long sweep to gather the sheep from off the moor.

But I too waited – for the signal to tell me that Jim, my human partner in the gather of the hill, had reached position with his dogs and was also ready to go.

Cohesion, man with man, man with dogs, was essential, for the sweep of the moor had to be decisive and properly carried out, with all working to a successful and clean gather.

There were 1,000 sheep, ewes with their lambs and maiden ewes, known as hoggs, spread at their grazing over the bleak Pennine hill which rose before me, and they must all be collected in one operation. There was no time to be coming back for stragglers which had been missed.

It was the clipping gather. Mid-June and six o'clock in the morning and the whole flock of sheep to be taken from some 2,000 acres of steep, gullied, boggy and rock-strewn moor to the farm buildings in the valley where they would have their woolly fleeces removed by the shearers. It was the hardest round-up of the year, for though the lambs, born two months previously, were strong and fit, they still followed their mothers, who were possessive enough to face any dog which threatened their offspring.

It was cold at that height of 1,000 feet. The wind whistled across the rough bents and whins, its probing fingers chilling to the touch. I squatted with my back against a grey gritstone rock. Sheltered, I had time to light a pipe. Jim and his three dogs, Corrie, Spot and Glen, would still be some 15 minutes from their gathering point.

Rhaq settled beside me. He was not really impatient for, at six years old, he was an old hand at the gathering game. His kennel-mates, Meg and Gael, my other collies, joined us. Three years old and with the wasteful energy of youth, Meg emerged from among the rocks where the lingering scent of fox interested her. Gael came with her.

The youngest of the three, Gael, a beautiful sabled bitch, was little more than 18 months old, full of beans and keen for any adventure. Rhaq knew the hours of lung-bursting toil before us. He had the courage and stamina to run all day but the wisdom to conserve his energy. He was a specialist, like all his breed of Border Collie, doing a job in farming which no machine could ever do, for man with all his genius has never been able to invent a mechanical replacement for the shepherd's dog. No machine could ever fetch those 1,000 sheep down from that hill, and man alone would be utterly incapable of gathering them together from the vastness of the moor. The crop of these inhospitable Pennine hills is mutton and lamb for the table, and wool for clothing, and it can only be harvested with the aid of clever dogs.

Being close to these dogs I know their value to the individual farmer in the management of a sheep flock. As an agricultural journalist I realise their value to the sheep farming industry as a whole. Remove the expertise of the farmer and the working collie is probably the greatest single factor in the success of the business of sheep farming throughout the world.

In the United Kingdom, which has the biggest sheep flock in the European Community, there are 43 million ewes and lambs of which over 20 million produce in excess of £1,200 million worth of meat and 67,000 tons of wool worth about £30 million in the year. There are 93,000 farms with sheep in the United Kingdom. Multiply these figures to reach the world's population of almost 2,000 million sheep and you get some idea of the sheepdog's role in the farming community – and it also plays a great part in the herding of other stock. Its value in money terms is inestimable.

As long ago as the end of the eighteenth century James Hogg, known as the 'Ettrick Shepherd' and a contemporary of Sir Walter Scott and William Wordsworth, wrote, 'Without the shepherd's dog the whole of the open mountainous land in Scotland would not be worth a sixpence.' Thus the collie's job is vital to the agricultural economy of the hills, its role unique in the farming pattern of the upland grazings.

Rhaq, Meg and Gael stayed close by my side. They were relaxed, but ready for my command to send them to work. In that lonely place, where only the bleat of a sheep or the call of a wild bird ever join the scream of the wind, my collies were the truest companions a man could desire. Utterly faithful, tireless in their desire to please, of the mildest manners, they were temperamentally blended to companionship and hard work.

My dogs were typical of the modern working sheepdog which plays some part on every stock farm in Britain. Indeed, the collie dog has become so familiar that there is the danger of many farmers taking it for granted, undervaluing its worth and understanding very little of its true capabilities in stock management. They just do not bother to learn its ways, and it was the most successful BBC television series on sheepdogs, 'One Man and His Dog', which educated so many farmers to the true potential of the collie dog. The sheepdog will share its skills in partnership with any man who takes the trouble to know it for, always a willing servant, the intelligent working dog is never a bond-slave.

One of Yorkshire's finest sheepdog trainers, the late Mark Hayton, once said: 'The great qualities and powers of the sheepdog have been taught by dogs to shepherds, not by shepherds to dogs.'

It is the privilege of few really to know the collie dog; it is the privilege of many to thrill to its uncanny intelligence at sheepdog trials, now so popular at pastoral events in every part of the country. Sheepdog trials are held throughout the year, at Lakeland sports gatherings, at Dalesmen's sheep-meets and often in conjunction with agricultural shows during the summer months, and it is here, and on television, that the majority of people have learned something of the collie's art and thrilled to its clever skills.

But trials, although they have an important role in collie history and evolution, are the recreational side of a collie's existence; it is on the hill and fell where its true purpose in life is enacted, in the care of Britain's sheep flocks. For this purpose the collie has been bred with much more care and expertise than any Crufts show champion.

Sitting behind that boulder on the Pennine hillside, with the wind screaming past my ears, I looked with pride at my dogs.

Rhaq was black coated, long haired and handsome. He was about 18 inches to the shoulder, his ears were pricked and his tail was carried low in balance. Compactly boned and light on his feet, he was lithesome and fast as the wind. His eye was strong but flexible, and hill vigour and courage, coupled with his experience and knowledge of the ways of sheep, had given him power in his work. Supremely intelligent, he was the ideal shepherding dog. His line was the most illustrious of canine aristocracy, going back to Old Hemp, born at the turn of the century and the foundation sire of the modern working dog. Rhaq's ancestors had been sought for work on the sheep-runs of Australia, New Zealand and America.

His purpose in life was to shepherd sheep. His mother, Mossie, a gentle and efficient bitch, had given her life in an unsuccessful attempt to rescue a sheep from drowning in a moorland stream when she was ten years old. Her name has been roughly carved on a rock down in the

Rhaq, the best pal I ever had.

valley by this stream, as a memorial to her integrity. Such was Rhaq's heritage, and shepherding sheep with the maximum efficiency and minimum upset were his qualities.

Never was he happier than when working sheep and he excelled in his craft in a startling, if unspectacular, manner. More spectacular were his escapades among the rock ledges of the gritstone outcrops which dominate the moor top, and more than one ewe trapped on those narrow ledges and in danger of death by starvation or from a fall had been gently eased to safety by his gentle and persuasive yet dominant manner.

Sheep often became cragfast by browsing from ledge to ledge, easily jumping down onto tiny ledges yet loath to jump back unless persuaded. From some of the ledges the rock face fell vertically for 60 feet to the moor. Faced with such situations, Rhaq went calmly about his task of rescue, to him a routine job in his daily shepherding of the flock. He was good at his job.

Tough as he was, though, he showed the gentlest of natures when with newly born lambs and respected the strength of maternal spirit which turned their normally docile mothers into truculent adversaries. Yet he never flinched from their footstamping attacks when asked to herd them. Indeed, he put that mothering instinct to use when fostering an orphan lamb on to a strange ewe, bringing the inbred instinct to the boil by seeming to threaten the lamb so that the ewe took it into her protective custody – an old shepherd's trick.

Rhaq's nose was particularly keen for his breed and he was expert at scenting sheep buried under snow. When snow blizzards surprised the moor and sheep had been buried, he had saved many ewes from death by starvation, locating them by their thin scent rising through the covering snow.

Sheep he respected and knew as individuals, particularly the rams with whom he had many skirmishes around sheep mating time in November, when they were full of fire. Always he finished the master. Time after time he had leapt over a charging ram until it had spent its energies and was then content to be herded.

He was ruthless, too, in his pressure when forcing sheep towards the dipping trough or into the transport wagon, and could run lightly across the woolly backs of a yard-packed flock to chivvy their leaders into movement. Asked to separate a single sheep from a group for inspection, he was quick to cut it away from its mates and, by the strength of his eye, prevent it from rejoining the flock.

Perhaps his greatest value was his knowledge of sheep on the normal routine daily visits to the grazing flock on the moor, for he could almost sense if anything were amiss. A sheep cast on its back or trapped in one of the many peat bogs would die from suffocation or starvation, or would lose its eyes to the vicious beak stabs of crows if not discovered in time. Normally silent in his work, Rhaq, if unable to right the sheep by tugging at its fleece, would then bark for human assistance to meet the crisis. The moor was a treacherous place, with bogs of green-covered ooze which could suck in a sheep – or a man – and on more than one occasion Rhaq had saved me from the danger of such places, particularly when the mist had blotted out their whereabouts.

Rhaq also had humour. He would sell his soul for a chocolate biscuit or a drink of tea, and a favourite trick was to raid the kitchen vegetable basket and steal pea-pods. Then he would lie with the pod between his forepaws and split it with his teeth, pouncing upon and eating the peas as they rolled over the floor. When music came from the radio he would lift his nose skywards and, after one or two tuning notes, start to howl in tune with the music.

At three years old, Meg had not acquired Rhaq's extreme craft, though she was of equal calibre in the arts of shepherding and was still expanding her knowledge of sheep. She was tricolour – black, tan and white – and smaller in stature than the black dog, but she was able to work all day if required, whatever the weather, in cold but dry conditions, or in the pouring rainstorms, screaming winds or blinding snow blizzards of the Pennine hills.

Meg was a jewel in the lambing field. She had the patience of Job and would persuade and cajole a ewe and lamb to any place she wished. Orphan lambs were her pride and joy, and she would lie curled with them in the straw of their bed. She had even learned to feed them, holding the bottle of milk in her mouth while they tugged at the rubber teat.

Almost feline in her approach to sheep, and dainty on her pads, she was fast over the heather and quick in her turns. She was a ballet dancer among dogs, able to balance upright on her hind legs when peering out of long grass or over an obstruction. Naturally reserved, her friendship was abiding once the introductions had been made to her satisfaction. Her greatest fear was not of things physical but of being in disgrace. If she had sinned she would come before me and roll over on her back in absolute submission, ready to carry out whatever penance her crime deserved.

The youngest of the three, Gael, was the most lovable of collies, learning her craft well, if slowly, for she was very self-willed and had to know the reason for everything she was asked to do. She would never do anything if she could not understand the reason, and at times she seemed so useless that Rhaq lay down in disgust rather than work with her, and Meg looked the other way and increased her own efficiency,

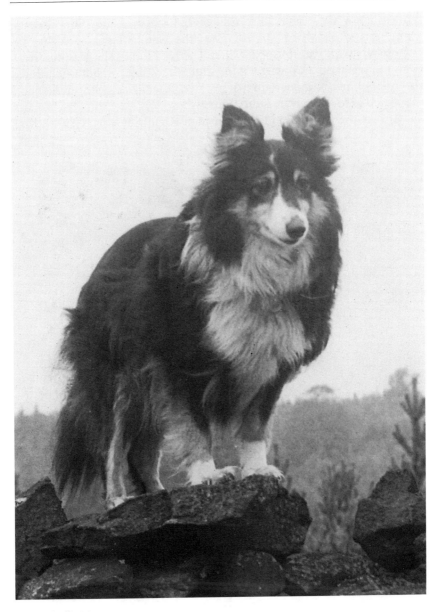

Eric Halsall's Meg.

carrying out out her work even more precisely, as though to balance her friend's misdemeanours.

Gael was a sporting dog. When at play she had a good sense of smell for the wild creatures around her, and if she put up a hare she could course it for well over 100 yards, so fast was her run. She liked her comfort and delighted in curling on the warm sheepskin of her bed when her work was finished. When I arrived home she was the first to jump into the car and, without the slightest inhibition, put one forepaw on each of my shoulders and lick my face. It was Gael who subsequently appeared before the television cameras.

Against the wisdom and experience of Rhaq and Meg, Gael was very

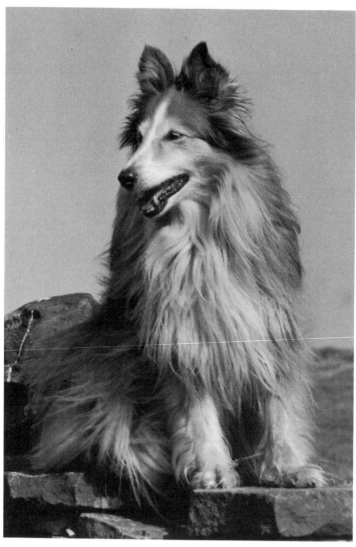

Eric Halsall's Gael (Country Notes).

much a novice – but she was learning fast. Her heart was in the right place, she had intelligence, and she had the muscle and sinew to keep going.

On that gather of the sheep from the moor Gael was to be kept in reserve, not used on the stamina-sapping outrunning of the round-up but put to work when the other dogs had bunched the sheep into a flock on the more leisurely walk to the farm.

Rhaq, Meg and Gael adored me and consequently their loyalty was not servile. We were a team of equals, each with a part to play and each dependent on the other for the success of the shepherding. The whole well-being of the moorland sheep, and so often their very lives in storm weather, depended on the success of our teamwork and the fidelity of the dogs.

Rhaq nudged my hand to lay his muzzle on my knee, a favourite trick when we rested, for it seemed he must always be sharing my thoughts. He gazed up at me. I tugged his ear. I loved that dog, and I envied the tranquillity of spirit which was mirrored in his soft gentle eyes. Only humans are said to have souls, but the deep warmth of spirit in the eyes of my dogs reflected what must surely be an inner contentment.

They were proud. They had character, each its own, developed by their calling and the skilful breeding of wise shepherds who, at the turn of the century, had realised the need for a specialised herding dog to manage their flocks. They were far, far different in every way from the first sheepdogs which had guarded the flocks of Job in the Old Testament days. The dogs of the Bible were lean, short-haired, quarrelsome brutes, used mainly as guard dogs to protect the sheep by fighting off wild predators and thieves. They were tough, in a ponderous way, and their strength was in their savagery. Though shepherds were present at the birth of Christ, their dogs were classed under the ancient laws of Moses as unclean animals, unworthy of mention.

Today's shepherding dog is loved by his master and is entirely different in stature and purpose, having no wild animals to guard his flock against. His vigour is required to intercept distant sheep which do not wait for him to approach. They begin to move away when they spot him and he may well have half a mile of rough country to make up to outpace them. Nor must he fail to catch those sheep, for if he does there may well be a day's labour lost in fetching them from the next valley. He is also far removed from the woolly-coated Old English Sheepdog of today's show bench which was once an active, alert dog capable of herding sheep. Nor does he bear much resemblance to the show collie, beloved of the 'Lassie' followers. They, together with today's Bearded Collie, which was a most efficient stock dog in its earlier years, are for

Tim Longton gathers Dalesbred ewes from Clougha Fell in North Lancashire with Bess and Dot (Derek Johnson).

the show ring where fashion dictates appearances and working ability is sacrificed to the detriment of the dog's true vocation.

Thus musing in the self-satisfaction of good companionship, in that wild but idyllic place, I enjoyed my pipe, snuggling a little deeper into my windproof jacket. The dogs were quietly stretched by my feet, the wind playing with their long hair. Gael, more restless than the other two, sat upright and pricked her ears to the bleat of a sheep. She watched a ewe, a lusty lamb at its side, biting the cotton sedges some 30 yards away. The cotton-grass spread like driven snow over the moor at that time of the year.

A tiny merlin, the lady's falcon, caught my eye as it sped low over the rough hags, and I listened to the wild bubbling cry of a curlew, the very spirit of my hills, which floated on downcurved wings through the thin air. The early morning sunlight glinted coldly from the waters of the reservoir in the valley; the narrow dirt track of the moor road skirted it like a twisting brown thread leading away into the distance of the tree-sheltered farm buildings, little larger than a matchbox in my vision. To the north-east, stretching away to meet the light blue of the brightening sky, were the wild and romantic Brontë moors; to the north-west I could see the tip of Pendle Hill, the hill of the witches.

The weather looked settled for a fine day, with the sun coming through, and that was important for the weather ruled every gathering day. Rain, with its poor visibility and low cloud, could put paid to any gather. On the June clipping gather the weather was all-important, not only on the day itself but during the days previous, for wet sheep would not shear and the wool must have risen with dryness to permit the fleece to be removed.

A thin whistle came down the wind. The three dogs pricked their ears and I knocked out my pipe. Jim was ready. His wise old Corrie and the strong black and white Spot had started to gather. I stood, tugging my hat down against the full force of the wind. The three collies jumped to their feet, their bodies suddenly tense.

Meg was on my left and a whispered 'come by' sent her on her way to meet up with Corrie at the extent of her run of perhaps a mile over the moor. Together the two collies would then sweep down the sheep towards the valley road. Jim's Spot and Glen would gather another sector of the hill. Suddenly surprised when Meg went bounding over the rough hags, the ewes near at hand lifted their heads from their grazing, called their lambs, and ran together in a protective little flock.

Rhaq stood to my right. He would hunt away to the extent of the grazing, and for most of the time would be out of my sight among the rocks and gullies of the steep hillside, working entirely on his own initiative. I could leave him to it; he knew the job better than I. He lifted his eyes to mine, reading my mind and, by the way I gazed towards the distant crest of the hill, become instinctively aware that I

The other way please. Bob Moore's Sally cuts off the escape route of Lonk ewes whilst gathering the hills above the Cliviger Gorge in Lancashire (Farmers Guardian).

wanted the full gather. 'Well away boy', and the black collie went, streaking away, belly to earth, racing across the rough ground to his task, taking a wide arc so that the sheep would move inwards and down from his line.

Gael became anxious, her youthful spirit craving action. 'What about me?' she said with her eyes. But whatever the temptation she was obedient and sat down as I ordered her. She was my reserve dog and her turn would come when the sheep were nearer at hand.

I sat on the rock and, a little disconsolate, Gael rested her head on my knee. 'Later lass', and she turned with ears pricked to listen for the working sounds of her kennel-mates. She felt thwarted, and I felt somewhat inadequate, for at that stage the success of the gather was entirely dependent on the skill of the dogs.

As the sheep moved down the moor I could watch progress and, whenever necessary, help the dogs with a whistled command – a command which informed them a lazy ewe was hiding behind a boulder, an artful ewe had taken her lamb into the shelter of a gully, a clever ewe had broken back on them.

Command is, of course, the vital link between man and dog for, while the dog must be capable of thinking and acting on its own when out of sight of the handler, shepherding is a job of teamwork. Basically four commands form the link, commands that are usually whistled over distance and spoken at hand. Stop, move on, go right, go left are conveyed with 'lie down', 'come on', 'away to me' and 'come by' in my language. In practice they are modified and enlarged to include such instructions as ease up, take time, steady, and get on, and by the inflection of voice or whistle. The final instruction is an almost universal 'that'll do' when work has been completed. By such communications I could help and advise Rhaq and Meg over a wilderness full of blind spots and places where sheep could be missed in the gather.

Ewes with lambs are always loath to move, even though the lambs are strong and agile. They move away from the dogs in fits and starts, dawdling whenever they have the chance, drifting down the hill, yet slowly coming together in small groups which grow into larger flocks, following their natural instinct to be together when under threat – even from the collies they know.

I saw Meg move quietly and unseen from behind a rock to encourage a lamb with a nudge from her nose – then skip lightly away as the mother charged towards her with butting head. Mother and daughter scuttled away to join the nearest flock. A bunch of four ewes and lambs, idly grazing among the cotton-grass, threw up their heads in sudden alarm when Meg, belly close to the ground, eyes fixed resolutely on the sheep, approached. They darted away, lambs bleating after their mothers, in the direction the collie desired. They were startled by the sudden whirring flight from the heather of a cock grouse which glided down the wind calling 'go-back, go-back'. Other wild creatures flew up before the gather – skylarks, meadow pipits, golden plovers and a black crow, the lambs' deadliest enemy. A hare went bounding away with long ears held high. Meg completely ignored it as she splashed through the bog, for her single thought was of sheep.

Of Rhaq I caught only occasional glimpses among the rocks on his ground. I watched particularly to see how he managed Flossie this time. Flossie was the name we had given to a particular old ewe who had reared six lambs and had shown such fertility that she had been retained in the flock while most of her sisters had been culled at four years old after raising three lambs, the normal length of time on the hill. Flossie was always to be found on the same bit of ground, a sheltered patch of good grazing between the rocks. Like all hill sheep she stuck to her own terrain, along with her remaining family and close neighbours, for the saying among hill folk is, 'Where grandmother lambed is good enough for mother and me.'

Flossie was wild and tough, a big black and white-faced ewe of pure Lonk breeding, the local breed of the east Lancashire Pennines, and she resented being ordered around by the dogs. Always she disputed their authority and, whenever she could, tried to dodge the gathering. Rhaq knew her of old, and as I watched he came face to face with her as she led her tribe towards sanctuary over the crest of the hill. For a moment dog and sheep stared at each other, each seeking dominance over the other's will. Flossie stabbed her forefoot at the ground and blew defiance through her black nostrils. Rhaq did not flinch. Muscles taut, he crouched low, tongue lolling from his mouth. Eyes unblinking, he gazed directly at the ewe, seeking a sign of weakness. Ears pricked forward, he lifted his forepaw and deliberately and slowly moved up to within two yards of the ewe's nose.

A flash of indecision crossed Flossie's mind. She faltered – and walking boldly up to her Rhaq won the tussle. Suddenly Flossie lost her nerve, shied away from the black collie and ran away downhill in the direction of the main flock. Rhaq had bossed her and her followers chased obediently after her. Of such incidents was the gather – and of such importance to its success were the dogs.

A moor gather is a carefully planned operation, with the dogs sweeping wide on the flanks to clear the ground and turn the sheep inwards to the dogs driving down from the centre. Hill sheep are wild and try to break away, but darting left, right and above, the dogs are always fast enough to turn them. Swinging away with tail balanced, leaping lightly across the rock boulders, splashing through bog water, the dogs are rarely beaten and, in a matter of minutes, do more than a man could accomplish in hours.

I walked across the hill to meet the thickening flock and Gael got her chance to play her part, sent to keep the sheep moving at a steady walk. I watched her closely, helping her when a straggling ewe and lamb had to be retrieved with whistled instructions which pierced the blaring noise of the flock. The flock was hustled along, not lingering, yet never unduly harried, for part of a collie's craft is the way it can drive sheep without causing them undue stress. Steadily the individual packets of ewes, lambs and hoggs flowed like grey streams down the moor to merge into a seething bobbing mass of bodies as they reached the valley drove road.

It took time, but the gathering of the hill was completed before the sun had reached its heat and the jostling, milling flock of sheep, unsettled and bleating their displeasure at the disturbance, with the warmth from their bodies and the dust from the track forming a cloud over their heads, swept into the grey walled yards by the farm buildings.

Peat spattered and wet, grimed with the mud and ooze of bog, and tongues lolling the heat from their lungs, Rhaq, Meg and Gael stretched their bodies on the cool stone setts by the door of the farmhouse kitchen, joined by Jim's Corrie, Spot and Glen, as he and I went in for food.

CHAPTER TWO

Magic of the Hills

I talk of the sheepdog trials, consider the wisdom, skill and dedication of collie dogs in the care of sheep, and trace their changing character from the birth of Christ to the present time.

Gathering sheep together and bringing them to its master, whether over rough hill or level pasture, whether a mile or two away or a few hundred yards, is the basic craft of the working collie. However, though perhaps the most important, it is only one of the skills of its daily life. It is a magic of the hills which few people other than shepherds and farmers are privileged to see, though thousands of town and city dwellers now thrill to the cleverness of the collie dog at sheepdog trials and millions found the appeal of these dogs compulsive viewing when the BBC filmed the trials series of 'One Man and His Dog'. A sheepdog trial is both a sporting and revealing competition in which man and dog test their skills in the craft of herding sheep against their contemporaries.

Clever working dogs, whether shepherding, gun or racing dogs, have always provoked argument as to their relative merits and it is an argument which can only be settled by matching dog against dog. This was so in 1873 when the first competition was run between ten dogs at Bala in North Wales, and when the shepherds and gamekeepers of north Derbyshire gathered on a bleak boisterous day in 1898 to settle their arguments – and thus started the famous Longshaw trials.

A trial is simply planned to assess ability and is obviously of great practical value in determining the qualities of the dogs taking part. Good dogs can – and do – delight in their prowess; human braggards – whose dogs perform wonderful feats on the hill! – have their teeth drawn; and the watchers choose their potential breeding stock. Trials are held wherever sheep are farmed, and in today's competition, when entries reach towards a hundred even at the remotest trials, it is a very good collie indeed which wins.

England, Scotland, Wales and Ireland each hold their National trials every year, choosing their champions and, by competition alone, their teams of collies meet each other in the International trials. These trials are governed by the rules of the International Sheep Dog Society and each country awards its greatest honour – its National championship – to the overall winner of the trials. The top dog handled by a farmer takes the Farmers' championship, the leading dog with a shepherd is the Shepherds' champion, the best dog at driving sheep across the course is the Driving champion and there is a Brace championship for the best pair of dogs working together.

These are the annual championships of the National, but the aim of every farmer or shepherd is to work his dog into the top 15 in merit at the event, for those 15 constitute the country's International team to meet the other countries at the International trials. The first two pairs of brace dogs and the best driving dog are also included in the International team.

These team numbers apply to all the four countries now, for although Ireland are relative 'newcomers' to the contest, having taken part for the first time in 1961 with smaller teams, their collies have made such great steps in ability recently that in 1993 they were classed on a par with the other three countries. So, with entries reaching the 150 mark at the Nationals, it is a very great honour to win a place in an International team, and the International 'cap' in the form of a badge for the handler immediately stamps a collie's quality.

At the International, held in September of each year and in rotation in England, Scotland and Wales (the International will be held in Ireland for the first time in 1997), the overall winner receives the Supreme championship, the blue riband of the heather and the greatest honour in the sheepdog world. Similarly to the Nationals, but irrespective of country, there are the Farmers', Shepherds', Brace and Driving championships, and the team shield is awarded to the country with the best overall standard of shepherding. It is a very great collie which takes the Supreme honour, for the road to the top is hard, long and very competitive.

After its basic schooling on the home pasture a collie will be taken to nursery trials for its first test where, as important as competing, it will learn to accept other dogs with strange men in strange places on strange sheep. Nursery trials are friendly gatherings of sheepmen and their dogs on Saturday or Sunday afternoons during the winter months.

Come the summer, and if it has shown promise, the collie will be entered at novice events where an average of 50 dogs will contest the awards. Having proved itself at this level of competition the dog will

The critics keenly watching their contemporaries at work in the Lancashire Pennines (Burnley Express).

then enter the open arena where the best in the land compete at the country's top trials. Then comes the 'big one' – the National – held over three days in England, Scotland, Wales and Ireland. Having won through to the International, the next obstacle is to win through the qualifying test of 60 collies (15 each from England, Scotland, Wales and Ireland) held on the first two days to finish in the top 15. These 15 collies compete for the Supreme championship on the third day. To win the Supreme championship is akin to a soccer team winning the European Cup or a racing driver the World Championship.

The many skills of gathering, bringing, driving, penning, singling and shedding sheep are tested at trials, all tasks which a collie meets in its daily life on the farm during the sheep farming year. Work is, of course, paramount. Trials are the show pieces, the shop-windows in which the shepherd proudly displays his craft.

So important is the bond of understanding and friendship which must develop between man and dog for efficient and profitable work that it is often said the perfect partnership resembles one mind shared rather than two separate minds.

Always an art, shepherding is fast becoming a science too, with modern agricultural technological methods, but the practical know-how of the man and his dog are the essentials of success. In this work a collie's intelligence and loyalty are never doubted by the men of the hills, though they seldom fail to wonder at it. Everyday shepherding is usually unspectacular, a job of work like so many others, and much is taken for granted. Yet these seemingly unspectacular skills are often the cleverest of canine acts.

Jim Wilson, whose name became a legend in sheepdog circles when he took his own skill and that of his dogs from the Border hills down to the trials fields, believed the cleverest thing he ever saw a collie do was to cajole a bereft ewe from its dead lamb and drive it two miles through a flock of other ewes and lambs to his farm buildings at Holmshaw near Moffat in Dumfriesshire. To the man who knows nothing of sheep this incident may sound trivial, but the collie, Nell, winner of two Scottish National trials championships, had to make the ewe overcome all the strong natural instincts of a mother to stay with her baby – its death not accepted by her – to prevent her from taking natural sanctuary among her own kind, and Nell herself had to counter the reactions of other mothers who felt their lambs threatened by her presence.

To deal with a single sheep is one of the hardest tasks that a collie can face for, being flock animals by nature, they tend to panic immediately they find themselves isolated or the sole centre of interest.

Tim Longton's Ken, Supreme International champion of 1966 and possibly the best collie Lancashire has known, could also bring one sheep right through a flock without being sidetracked. Strong and fearless if required (and he herded truculent bullocks at Rooten Brook Farm at the head of the Trough of Bowland), he was extremely gentle and patient in getting his way with sheep. During the *Daily Express* trials in Hyde Park in London, in front of 100,000 people, Ken, a handsome, rough-coated, black and white dog, was working his sheep round the course when one broke away into the crowd – an almost impossible position to be in – but Ken quickly followed the rebel and, to the incredulous gasps of the knowledgeable, brought it back on course.

Coming across a nervous ewe with the labour problems of her first birth and in need of human assistance to deliver her lamb, Hope, son of international champion Kyle, and a star of 'One Man and His Dog', from Field Gate Farm in Ribblesdale, stopped her ungainly and panic-stricken flight by heading her off. Then, planting his forefeet firmly on the ground in her path, as if to say 'Cool it, I'm here to help', he simply held her spellbound by the strength of his eye, his own confidence calming her and quelling her fear until his master, Michael Perrings, could help in the safe birth of her lamb. That act undoubtedly saved the

Quiet authority instils confidence in sheep. Michael Perrings' Hope at Settle in Ribblesdale (Roy Parker).

lamb's life; and for one animal to so instil confidence in another of a different and lesser order while under such stress and pain is something akin to genius.

My contemporaries have given many scientific reasons for this relationship between dogs and sheep. It is the hunter overcoming the hunted; it is the aggression of the dominant spirit causing abject fear in the lesser and weaker. I have lived in the countryside all my life and have seen a similar rapport between wild creatures as that between Hope and the ewe, and they have not been hunter and quarry as stoat and rabbit. As a naturalist I have tried to analyse this harmony for there is no doubt that animals can communicate, can instil confidence, can create fear, can casually pass the time of day. I prefer to enjoy the experience of witnessing it – and to wonder at the intelligence of these soul-less creatures.

Everyday tasks, exceptional tasks, a wise collie thinks. Initiative as well as intelligence is part of its make-up.

Mark Hayton's Pat was gathering sheep on the high moors between the two Yorkshire dales of the Aire and the Wharfe when one of the ewes slipped into a hill stream which was swollen and fast after a rainstorm. Realising the sheep was in danger of drowning, Pat dashed to grab the ewe's fleece in his teeth and so hold it above the flood. Confident that his master would come to see why he was so long on the gather, Pat held the ewe safe until Mr Hayton arrived.

Scottish shepherd Sam Carr will always remember his Moss with pride and affection. He was reading a book in the lambing caravan in the early hours when the lamp exploded, burning him and temporarily blinding him. Though naturally terrified of fire, like all animals, Moss took command and, rubbing against his master's legs to guide him, led him from the danger and down to the farmhouse and safety.

The intelligence and initiative, which is such a characteristic of the modern working collie dog, is the cultivated harvest of a family tree with roots in Biblical times. It is a family tree with many branches, each providing a sheepdog type for a specific purpose, such as the handsome Kuvasz flock guards of Hungary and the large Owtcharki drovers of Russia, but the most intelligently developed is the Border Collie, the dog which herds one-third of the world's sheep population. There are over 50 types of stock-handling dogs in the world, each with its pastoral role to play, but the working merit of the Border Collie has made it the universal favourite on the big sheep-runs of the globe.

Scientists tell us that dogs were domesticated, probably as hunting companions using the wild dog's natural instincts, by Britons in the Neolithic period, their remains having been found at Windmill Hill, near Avebury in Wiltshire. That domestication, probably by force and by keeping the dogs sufficiently well fed in the first instance, must have been quite an achievement – and probably at the cost of a few bitten limbs! The first mention of Britons as farmers came from a Greek named Pytheas around 330 BC and it is a fair assumption that farm stock needed to be guarded from predators so whatever dogs were around would be there in the role of guards.

This was their role in Biblical days, too, when they stood guard over the flocks of sheep and goats in the Holy Land. As such they were not required to be intelligent, just savage and strong, for their adversaries were wolves and other vicious attackers, and their presence would also deter robbers and thieves – the Biblical rustlers. Sheep and shepherds appear throughout the whole text of the Bible and even to this day the ewe-lamb is symbolic of a man's most prized possession. Not so the dogs – until modern times – for they were regarded as lowly creatures. This is obvious from the Book of Job in the Old Testament which quotes the farmer of Uz, who ran 7,000 sheep, as saying 'whose fathers I would have disdained to have set with the dogs of my flock'.

The first service that the dog did for sheep, then, was to guard them from attack, and this is still its purpose in life in some parts of the world. Such dogs as the Caucasian sheepdog of Russia, the Cao Serra da Estrêla – the mastiff-like sheepdog of Portugal, the generally white-coated Maremma of central Italy, its relative, the Pyrenean Mountain Dog of south-west France, and the Carpathian sheepdog of Romania are primarily guard dogs of the finest quality. These dogs are consequently of a different type to the Border Collie. They are much more solid in build, larger in stature, and capable of fighting off predators like wolves and even members of the cat tribe such as the lynx. Dogs of this type would have been guarding the flocks of the Cotswolds during the wool boom which started in the thirteenth century in Britain. In that period fortunes were made by the sale of wool to the continent and lives were lost for smuggling it out after Edward III placed a ban on its export. Sheep thrived and produced wool money, and though the dogs were necessary to ensure that income they received little attention.

There is little skill required to maintain savage traits in a dog. With the disappearance of such sheep predators as the wolf from England and Wales around 1500 (though it survived in Scotland until 1740 and in Ireland until 1770), it was no longer necessary to use dogs for guarding purposes, but the change in character could not take place overnight. For a long time British sheepdogs were somewhat savage creatures, of similar blood and habit to those of the main area of Europe. The problems of such dogs becoming sheep-killers must have been very real for our shepherding forefathers.

Sheep-keeping communities had spread from the south across England and Wales up to the Cheviots by the mid-fourteenth century. The difference between the dogs to be found among these communities must have been very great indeed, as their change to a more pastoral role took place. The overriding factors in stamping type, and certainly temperament, would rest solely with the way they were treated by their human masters. If a bad-tempered farmer thrashed his dog into submission it would become an untrustworthy, sneaking, snarling creature; the more affable man, on the other hand, would rear a stable, milder-mannered, friendly dog – this, of course, can happen today in regard to temperament.

Many different families of dogs with diverse capabilities and characters were scattered around the country. Breeding was a very haphazard affair, with natural selection little better than in the wild prevailing, and it took over a century before a dog, smaller than the guard dog type, was capable of work that involved actually herding. The book *De Canibus Britannicus* by Dr Johannes Caius, of Cambridge University, and translated from the Latin around 1570–75, refers to the driving of sheep by dogs. 'This dog, either at the hearing of his master's voice, or at the wagging of his fist, or at his shrill and hoarse whistling and hissing, bringeth the wandering wethers and straying sheep into the self-same place where his master's will and work is to have them, whereby the shepherd reapeth this benefit, namely, that with little labour and no toil or moving of his feet he may rule and guide his flock.' In this book the

Ever alert, a collie dog is interested in every happening. Glyn Jones' Bracken, Gel and Glen (Derek Johnson).

English sheepdog of Tudor times is said to be 'not huge, vast, and bigge, but of an indifferent stature and growth, because it hath not to deal with the bloodthyrsty wolf, since there be none in England'.

James A. Reid, the man who, as its secretary, was greatly responsible for the initial growth and strength of the International Sheep Dog Society, claimed that the Border Collie as a breed could be traced from around the year 1600 and that Scotland was its place of origin both in name and breed. He believed that its introduction to northern England did not take place until the eighteenth century when, with sheep well established on the hills, stock were walked south in the great droving days before the building of the railways. The passage of stock from the Borders of Scotland to the lands of Northumberland, Cumbria, Lancashire and Yorkshire thus widened the use and distribution of the dogs which handled them. With such time-consuming work involved, farmers really became interested in improving the efficiency of their dogs for this task.

Oliver Goldsmith had his *Animated Nature* published in 1774 – the year of his death – and drawing much upon the opinions of the French naturalist, Buffon, wrote of the dog: 'Supposing, for a moment, that the species had not existed, how could man, without the assistance of the dog, have been able to conquer, tame, and reduce to servitude, every other animal? . . . The flock and the herd obey his voice more readily even than that of the shepherd or the herdsman; he conducts them, guards them, keeps them from capriciously seeking danger, and their enemies he considers as his own.'

Goldsmith describes the shepherd's dog thus. 'This is that dog with long coarse hair on all parts except the nose, pricked ears, the long nose; which is common enough among us, and receives his name from being principally used in guarding and attending on sheep.' He goes on: 'This sort of dog is to be found in the temperate climates in great abundance, particularly amongst those who, preferring usefulness to beauty, employ an animal that requires very little instruction to be serviceable. Notwithstanding this creature's deformity, his melancholy and savage air, he is superior to all the rest of his kind in instinct; and without any teaching, naturally takes to tending flocks, with an assiduity and vigilance which at once astonishes and yet relieves his master.' It is noted from this description that the dog was still regarded as somewhat savage – whatever his deformity was!

Goldsmith's sheepdog story is most revealing and traces what I have already assumed to be the case in the Border Collie's evolution, his story further making the shepherd's dog 'the stem of that genealogical tree which has been branched out into every part of the world'.

Indeed Goldsmith, or Buffon, whose opinion he really quotes, goes so far as to infer that the shepherd's dog in different characters is the foundation stock of most other breeds: 'The shepherd's dog, transported into the temperate climates, and among people entirely civilized, such as England, France, and Germany, will be divested of his savage air, his pricked ears, his rough, long, and thick hair, and from the single influence of climate and food alone, will become either a matin, a mastiff, or a hound. These three seem the immediate descendants of the former, and from them the other varieties are produced.'

Every breed of dog in the world has its champions and they in turn hold often conflicting views as to the ancestors of their fancy, so I hasten to add that I do not hold Buffon's views that the sheepdog is the 'father' of all dogs, particularly as the mammal family of Canidae to which the dog belongs has about 38 species. But it is an interesting conjecture!

A most authentic record of the early dogs used by shepherds for work with their flocks in Britain is in a book published in 1790 by Thomas Bewick, the Northumberland engraver, entitled *General History of Quadrupeds*. By this time sheep husbandry had progressed rapidly, with flock owners having established such individual breeds as the Blackface, Herdwick, Cheviot and Clun, in addition to the original Romney Marsh and Cotswold types. Suffolks were being evolved and Robert Bakewell, the famous breeder of Dishley in Leicestershire, had carried out his programme of improvement on the Leicester Longwool sheep. It is consequently understandable that sheepmen with

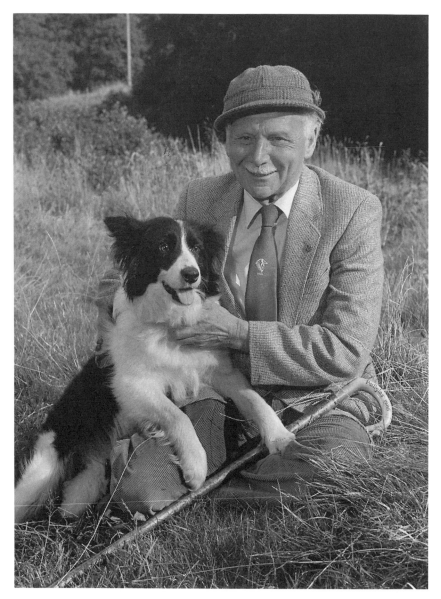

Eric Halsall, commentator of BBC2's 'One Man and His Dog', in the Wye Valley (BBC).

this knowledge and interest in improving their stock were finally show-ing some interest in the better breeding of their dogs. Bewick's drawing in his book of a black and white shepherd's dog is very similar to the

Border Collie of today, and his comments of its work so like the duties of the modern collie.

Bewick writes: 'This useful animal, ever faithful to his charge, reigns at the head of the flock; where he is better heard, and more attended to, than even the voice of the shepherd. Safety, order, and discipline are the fruits of his vigilance and activity. . . . In driving a number of sheep to any distant part, a well-trained dog never fails to confine them to the road; he watches every avenue that leads from it; where he takes his stand, threatening every delinquent, and pursues the stragglers, if any should escape, and forces them into order, without doing them the least injury.' Significant is a remark in his text of this dog being 'preserved in the greatest purity in the northern parts of England and Scotland', which shows that at this time men of wisdom were recognising the value of sound breeding to produce the dog they required for their helpmate.

When naturalists and historians fail to record the times, poets and writers can usually be relied upon to supply some information about events and fill the gap, and during the early nineteenth century the shepherd and his dog received some literary reference. Most famous of all, and undoubtedly most reliable because he was a shepherd himself, was the work of James Hogg, the 'Ettrick Shepherd'. It was he who first recorded the great value of the shepherd's dog to the farming community of the Borders. He wrote: 'A single shepherd and his dog will accomplish more in gathering a stock of sheep from a highland farm than twenty shepherds could without dogs, and it is a fact that without this docile animal the pastoral life would be a blank. Without the shepherd's dog the whole of the open mountainous land in Scotland would not be worth a sixpence. It would require more hands to manage a stock of sheep, gather them in from the hills, force them into houses and folds, and drive them to market than the profits of a whole stock would be capable of maintaining.'

James Hogg, knowing from personal experience the value of the working collie, did much to educate the outside world of its virtues. He lived from 1770 to 1835 and time has proved him a good, honest and truthful recorder.

It is interesting to note Hogg's reference to men without dogs gathering sheep from the hill, for it is recorded in the late eighteenth century that men actually did this. *A History of British Livestock Husbandry* of the time tells of men in Wales dressing in running costumes for the task of gathering sheep from the mountain. What would those lads have given for a good dog!

Shepherds were by now beginning to care for their dogs and a report by Dr John Brown in 1810 reveals the high regard of a Border shepherd for his bitch, as well as illustrating the wisdom and intelligence now being bred into working dogs. Dr Brown wrote of Jed as 'a very fine collie, black and comely, gentle and keen', and of her master's comments, albeit in the Border tongue, 'Ay, she's a fell yin; she can do a' but speak.' Asked about whether Jed's kind needed much training her master replied, 'Her kind needs none. She sooks 't wi' her mither's milk.'

The Old English Sheepdog, of a lither and less bulky stature than its present-day form familiar in the show ring, has been recorded as a working dog in England, particularly in the south where it was probably not ousted by what was to become known as the Border Collie until around 1900. Together with the Bearded Collie, the Old English had some part in the evolution of the modern working dog. While the Old English Sheepdogs were strong and intelligent they were somewhat slower in movement than the North Country collies which were being bred to work lively hill sheep over the roughest terrain.

These were becoming much lighter and speedier creatures, adept and suited for fell work, and by 1857 their skills were reported 'to arise from an intuitive disposition in the animal, rather than from laboured training'. That intuitive disposition for working sheep was finally established in the modern collie dog by the breeding of one dog, Old Hemp, at the end of the nineteenth century.

Old Hemp, born in September 1893 in Northumberland, is today regarded as the foundation sire of the present highly skilled working dogs of Britain and the world. He stamped his character and ability so forcefully on the shepherding scene of the Borders that his bloodline became favoured almost to the exclusion of all others. Adam Telfer, who farmed near Cambo in the Morpeth area, bred Old Hemp and said of him, 'He flashed like a meteor across the sheepdog horizon. There never was such an outstanding personality.'

A sturdy, well-coupled black and white dog, he turned out to be a genius at shepherding sheep and none who saw him ever forgot him. Consequently his progeny were eagerly sought and his dominant line created.

Almost faultless in this work, Old Hemp was rough coated and broad headed with flop ears and liquid amber eyes which were pools of wisdom. He was born with such knowledge of his craft that he never required training and went to his work naturally. He ambled after sheep when only six weeks old. Father of the breed, he was created by the intuitive skill of a wise and experienced breeder of shepherding dogs, for on the face of it his parents were of no outstanding calibre.

It could only be experience in the ways of collies which made Adam Telfer decide to mate the light-coated, tan-marked black and white

Roy with the shy, almost black-haired Meg. Roy was an easily handled, good-tempered dog, not too strong in the eye, and Meg was an entire contrast, stiff eyed, self-conscious and reticent, but very upper class and stylish with the pedigree of the Old Rookin White dogs. Only Adam Telfer knew they were made for each other.

So, after a long and fascinating history, starting in Biblical times, the story of the present-day Border Collie really starts at the end of the nineteenth century.

Old Hemp, father of the modern working collie.

A collie of 1850 at Ramsden Farm, Walsden, in the Lancashire Pennines.

CHAPTER THREE

Shepherding the Dales

I recall my early days with collies in Wharfedale, tell of a great Yorkshireman and his methods of training, and consider the mystique of command words. I see the results of sound training at lambing time when motherly love in parent ewes gives collies a rough time, and I meet the most efficient family of collies in Yorkshire.

My story begins in the 1920s, in Wharfedale in the Yorkshire Dales, where my mother's family had lived and farmed for many generations with various interests around Burnsall, Appletreewick and Barden Tower. It was here, in the most beautiful countryside, that I came to love collie dogs as companions and to admire their expertise of craft, for they were as much a part of my family as my cousins, aunts and uncles.

As a youngster the dogs were my great pals, old Moss in particular, for he was honourably retired from work and we spent many happy hours chasing voles in the beck, running rabbits or nosing for moles by the Wharfe. We saw otters in those days, too. They were carefree days when, in the warmth of a summer's sun, Moss and I climbed to Simon's Seat to play hide and seek among the grey rocks. Resting, to share Aunt Polly's sandwiches, with the whole dale spread like a map below us, I would point out various objects in the distance, old Moss blinking his dimming eyes with vision no further than a few yards.

Moss was gentle and kind, and at his retirement age of ten years a bit overweight for, beloved of us all, he was given the best of titbits. He was a wise old dog, as knowledgeable in the wiles of rabbits and voles as in the ways of sheep, and the perfect companion for my wanderings in the open countryside.

In later years, when I realised just how indispensable the dogs were to the running of the farms, I came to admire their skills and their expertise at handling sheep thrilled me. To see Spot and Glen pushing a bunch of white-nosed Swaledale ewes across the fell when we were changing grazing was to see canine intelligence and understanding at its very best. The two dogs linked together, and with whoever was handling them, with precision-like action, and the sheep rarely eluded them. Here were dogs, descendants of the Border breed of Old Hemp, which could tackle every sheep job on the farms – they were 'Jacks of all trades' – the gather of the flock from the fellside, the concentrated work of driving the sheep from one place to another, and the shedding-off of individual sheep for veterinary inspection.

Looking back, some of those dogs – indispensable tools of the sheep farmer's trade – were bought as pups for only a few shillings yet their value to the farm must have been hundreds of pounds. Though labour was cheap in those days, and time had not geared to the hustle of today, the dogs, measured in work capacity, were really the most valuable animals on the farm. It is only in recent times, with money values soaring and sheep production measured in millions of pounds, that the collie dog has at last reached the £1,000 mark of value, and that only for the very best. Most pups are still obtainable for around £50.

My love and regard for working sheepdogs grew from those early days in Wharfedale. We did not go much further than the local Dales shows and saw few sheepdog trials but I remember the talk often got round to shepherding competitions, for Wharfedale had one of the best handlers of the period in Mark Hayton, who farmed over the fells in the well-known Ilkley Moor area. He had represented England in International trials and in 1926, when I was six years old, had won the Supreme championship of the International Sheep Dog Society with Glen at York.

Mark Hayton, who died in September 1948 at the age of 76, was a real gentleman and much respected in the local community and in the sheepdog world generally. He became English President of the International Sheep Dog Society and won countless trials, including the International Farmers' championship in 1936 and the English National title in 1937, in addition to his 1926 Supreme victory. His dogs were always dogs of the fell, schooled with understanding and a profound knowledge of their individual characteristics to the finer skills for trials work. A solid Yorkshireman who proved by results his common-sense approach to breeding and training sheepdogs, his methods were followed almost religiously by the folk of the dale.

To discuss methods of teaching a collie dog to make the best use of its inbred talents would require a book in its own right and others – Tim Longton, Glyn Jones, John Templeton, Matt Mundell and Tony Iley – have written them, but I think that it is well worth remembering some of Mark Hayton's advice, which is as applicable today as when I first heard it as a teenager in the dale. He was against what I now call the 'yo-yo' method of training, by which a dog is made to learn and obey the commands of its master whatever the situation. This is usually taught to a dog by making it carry out one act time and time again while giving it a whistled or spoken or gestured command until it associates one with the other. When being taught by this method, usually inside a barn or within the confines of a paddock, the dog is held on a long lead – the wife's clothes-line is ideal – so that the reaction to command can be encouraged physically by pulling on the lead. Mark Hayton believed that this method, the popular method of the time and still very widely followed today, taught the dog the implicit obedience of a slave and destroyed its initiative and self-confidence. Although disciplined and willing, the dog relies entirely on the master at the helm to give the instructions – to pull on the string of the 'yo-yo'! It is a training method which can begin early, however, for the trainer need not wait for the pup to develop character, and it does produce some good dogs, albeit dogs requiring guidance throughout their lives.

Watchers at trials should bear this in mind when assessing collie quality. Mark Hayton's method of training was, I suppose, somewhat unorthodox and revolutionary in his day. He believed in dogs as individuals, in that each had its own characteristics and dignity, and that each would need different treatment to bring out its finer shepherding qualities.

Hayton was a wise and kindly man who understood animals and he did not believe that mass-production training methods gave the best results. His basic argument was that if man had gone to all the trouble, patience and skill to implant shepherding wisdom in the collie brain by breeding, why ruin it all by dominant treatment? He always said that before you could improve on nature you must study nature, and above all things you must be patient. 'Wait upon nature,' he used to say, giving a pup plenty of freedom to learn by play and considering mischief a promising sign while checking outright misbehaviour and teaching the basic compatibility rules, he allowed a puppy to reach the age of understanding before taking its sheep training in hand.

Nine months old was the age he considered a pup old enough to think for itself. By that time you should know plenty about the pup's temperament and nature and that is the time to introduce it to sheep. This first introduction should be by walking the pup up to the sheep, not by sending it for them, so that you would be on hand to check any misdemeanour it might get up to. Mark Hayton always counselled patience, and when taking a young dog to sheep for the first time he advocated the relaxed, almost leisurely introduction.

In one of his few published articles he wrote, 'Light your pipe and keep an eye on your pupil. If he is ready, he will begin to set or eye the sheep, or he may walk stealthily round them.' The first time I followed that instruction to the letter I got thrashed for smoking before I was considered old enough! Mark Hayton went on, 'Do not interfere. Just steady him, according to what he can bear. If he eyes the sheep and walks them away, follow him as closely as you can. Pursue this natural method, and, as he learns to wear the sheep, leave him alone. Never put him further for his sheep than he cares to go; he will run out when the need arises. If he does not start naturally, come away and try again when he is a little older. Wait on nature, for man's creation, where it cuts across nature, is a mere freak.' From this it will be seen that he let the natural ability of the dog blossom into action and in its own good time, and then its work on the hill under his command extended that very basic ability into the skill of a craftsman.

Mark Hayton was wise in the ways of sheepdogs. He sent many dogs abroad and he devised a unique technique of passing on his commands which were, of course, vital to a dog's new owner if the animal was to be really efficient. Remember, this was before the days of tape-recorders, on which a voice can now easily be sent with the dog, so

Mark Hayton of Ilkley Moor, and his collies (Barbara Carpenter).

Mark Hayton had his whistled commands set to violin music and it worked admirably.

Writing of command, I am often asked today why such apparently queer phrases as 'away to me' and 'come by' are used for 'go right' and 'go left' instructions to the dog. I believe that they have been derived down the years from 'come away round to me', with a corresponding wave of the hand to denote the direction, as in the older training methods referred to earlier, and 'come by here to me' with a wave of the other hand. Similar commands were 'come by an head' and 'come by an hint' which meant 'come to the head' and 'come behind' the sheep.

Now the commands have been shortened for both the man's and the dog's sakes, and for speed of reaction the first command word is different so that the dog can move immediately as desired without really waiting for the full message. Incidentally, not all shepherds use 'away to me' and 'come by' for the same instruction of right and left. Some handlers reverse the meaning. (The words used in command are actually immaterial. 'Right' and 'left' will do equally well, provided the dog is trained to these commands, but country traditions die hard and there is something much more colourful in the present commands.)

The one essential point in teaching a dog its commands is that you *always* use the same phrase or word to request the same action. Similarly, it is advisable to keep to the whistled commands to which a dog has been trained, and while it can be done, it is not always satisfactory to change them – as sometimes happens when a dog changes ownership. Whistled commands are the musical intonations of short and long notes, sharp and drawn, and are based on the variations that the mouth can produce. The plastic mouth-whistle with its wide scope of pitching notes is now commonly used.

Tom Gumbley shows the type of plastic mouth-whistle most commonly used by handlers (Derek Johnson).

Temperament is never better tested than in the lambing field. Michael Perrings' Hope (Roy Parker).

Once a young collie had started to work and learned to obey command, I remember Mark Hayton saying that the best experience a dog could have to learn the vital lesson of controlling its temper was to take it among ewes with lambs. As lambing time in the dale was always a time to be visiting my relatives, I have particular memories of that time of the year and of the work which the dogs had to contend with when herding ewes which were over-boisterous in the defence of their young.

Wharfedale has always been my second home, and in later years, with all my relatives gone, I filled the need to stay part of this lovely place by visiting friends, in particular Michael Perrings who managed beef and sheep projects at Throstle Nest, a little higher up the Wharfe than my old haunts. There, among the Swaledales, on the 1,700 ft heights of Conistone Moor towards Whernside and across from the famous Kilnsey Crag, I enjoyed the lambing as much as ever, for it is the loveliest time of all for the sheep farmer. It is also the hardest and most vital time of the whole year for him, though, as his whole livelihood depends on the success or failure of the lamb crop.

Much depends on nature herself, for the weather can be so vital; much also on the farmer's previous planning and preparation of the ewes for motherhood; and everything on their careful shepherding at the time of giving birth. Most of the ewes will lamb without trouble and are best left alone, but many will be better with some attention so that constant vigilance of the flock is absolutely necessary and time as measured by the clock ceases to exist. Compensation is in assisting in the miracle of new life, the fascination of seeing the birth of a new generation, and even the most unromantic and hard headed of farmers feels some stir of emotion – if only at the satisfaction of reaping his just reward. In spite of having seen it all before, lambing never fails to bring its own special excitement – provided you can stay awake long enough to enjoy it!

Every April, when the white dots appear over the lower moor to which the ewes have been brought for easier inspection, there is a freshness in the air. Though cold winds often sweep across the land, carrying heavy rain and sometimes snow, with every day the sun is gaining in strength. As you walk round the flock your spirits lift to the wild music of the curlews. A snipe drums, its tail feathers extended, high above the moor; a lapwing rises from its nest and dives to mob the dogs who harmlessly nose the eggs; and the wheatear, bobbing and curtseying from the top of the stone wall, has just arrived from Africa.

Lambing time is the crunch time for any collie, particularly a young collie, for it makes or breaks him – just as Mark Hayton said. If you think you have a good dog before lambing time, you will certainly know for sure afterwards. It is the one time of the year when ewes will really test a collie's character. Some dogs are born great, others attain stature.

One of the few youngsters I recall which proved his claim to the first category in the lambing field was Michael Perring's 2½-year-old Bran at Throstle Nest. Ewes must be herded quietly and without harassment when their lambs are due and Bran, black and smooth coated with a white ring round his neck, could control a ewe, however wild and tetchy she was, without upsetting her. Many collies, experienced ones included, get so frustrated at this time of the year that they tend to use their mouths a little to impress their authority. Bran never had to resort to this physical approach. He was of an illustrious line, the son of Davie McTeir's Ben, the white-headed dog which won Scotland's National trials championship and the International Shepherds' championship in 1972, and mothered by Thomson McKnight's Dot, the International Farmers' champion and reserve Supreme champion to her mother Gael in 1967. Gael, Bran's grandmother, was seven times in the Scottish International team and was the greatest sheep bitch of all time.

Bran, on his first trials outing when two years old, won the Yorkshire nursery event at Chipping in the winter of 1972 by forcing the sheep – strong Swaledales – backwards into the pen, such was his power. He was eventually exported to work in America.

Michael Perrings later farmed at Field Gate near Settle in Ribblesdale, but while at Throstle Nest Farm in Wharfedale he lambed some 600 ewes of the Swaledale breed, tough, lively hill sheep which numerically are the most popular breed in Britain. With ewes and lambs kept as high up the fell as possible in their natural haunts this was hill lambing at its best, but every flock inspection meant a hard slog. It was a task for a stout heart because the Land Rover could only pitch and roll its slow upward crawl over limestone outcrops for part of the way. The rest of the inspection had to be done on foot, whatever the weather.

On one particular evening inspection, when I joined Michael and his two collies, Kyle and Gael, snow from the previous month's blizzards still lay in drifts ten feet deep in the gullies. Upwards across the rough bents, over limestone ridges and between lichened boulders we walked. Below, the Land Rover, left lonely in that great expanse of fellside, was the size of a toy, and a sudden glint of sun reflection marked the course of the River Skirfare on its way to the parent Wharfe. All along our route over the high ground there were ewes and lambs to be inspected, either from a distance when all was well and the least interference the better, or from close by when either Kyle or Gael brought a wayward mother to its forsaken lamb. Odd gimmer ewes, sheep with their first lambs, found motherhood frustrating and their parental instincts had to be roused.

Sometimes a ewe or a lamb showed signs of distress and had to be dosed with veterinary medicine. One ewe, crouched in the shelter of a limestone rock, required Mike's manual assistance to deliver her lamb. In a normal birth the lamb literally dives from the mother's womb, its head between its forelegs. Malpresentations take various forms: the legs may be bent under the body, the head may be bent back, the whole body of the lamb may be upside down or turned around. In such instances the ewe will require assistance from the shepherd to deliver her lamb safely. Fortunately most ewes lamb perfectly satisfactorily on their own. One ewe or one lamb saved made our inspection completely worthwhile.

A lamb bleated in confusion and the collies pricked their ears to the discordant cry of loneliness in that wilderness of land space. Caught up, the lamb was placed in Mike's bag until its mother could be located. The shepherd's bag at lambing is a portable veterinary surgery containing such an assorted collection as antiseptic lambing cream, tonic medicine, serum and syringe, soap and towel, knife, aerosol marking dye and rubber rings for castration. There is also the hip-flask of spirits for weak lambs – and weak shepherds!

Twins skipped from the path of the dogs. Like the lambs of the lowlands they were full of the joy of life, and cold and bleak as their

The typical poise of a champion. Michael Perrings' Kyle, 1970 International Shepherds' Champion (K. & J. Jelley).

home felt to my human senses, they had even better shelter among the hags and rocks than lambs on the bare, flat, windswept lowland pastures. They could crouch snugly to shelter from the icy wind. Up here, too, were the succulent mosses for nibbling and between the brown bents were shoots of green grasses.

Inevitably some of the lambs would die, for though primroses were blooming yellow on the banks of the Wharfe in the dale, the snow still lay white in the ghyll. Yet they were hardy sheep, those Swaledales, and they did not surrender easily. Starting life up on the high hill those lambs would be stronger to face the rigours of their future, and there was less risk of disease to the flock in general. It was in that inhospitable land that they actually got the best start in life, though an extra vigilance was required of the shepherd and his dogs.

Down the wind came the anxious voice of a ewe, a lonely, heart-rending bleat. Mike pointed towards the top of the fell where, on the white, exposed rocks, I spotted her. 'Fetch her, Kyle,' and the dog bounded to his bidding. Lightly leaping the deep weather-cut fissures which sliced open the limestone, Kyle circled the ewe and moved on to her. Seeing him, she threw her head up and moved away. But something drew her back, even into the face of the collie, and as I watched I saw from Kyle's attitude that he too had ceased to press her. His ears were forward and his head was angled in a quizzical, alert attitude: his manner seemed to have a calming effect on the ewe. Though she bleated and ran around a little there was less distress in her voice and actions. Whatever her problem, Kyle's presence had suddenly reassured her. Then Kyle lifted his head, yapped once, and disappeared from sight.

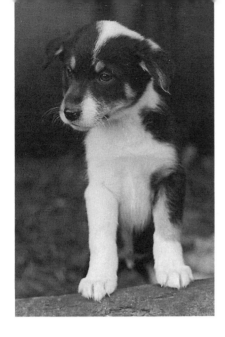

Did you say sheep? Keenness is promising (Derek Johnson).

'He's calling us. There's something wrong. He's gone into one of the crevices,' Mike said. And the reason was solved quite simply when we climbed to the rocks. In the 3 ft deep fissure a white-woolled lamb was nuzzling into Kyle's thick coat, the tip of its nose seeking a non-existent milk supply from a slightly embarrassed-looking collie.

Lifting the lamb from its prison it was reunited with its mother and trotted away, none the worse for the little adventure. Had Kyle not used his own initiative, not called Mike, and had forced the ewe away as commanded, the outcome would have been much different. Those limestone cracks on the top of Conistone Moor could be death traps for lambs.

The initiative of the handsome three-year-old collie had saved another lamb's life earlier in the week. The top of a 2 ft square stone-built drain which ran water from the lower moor had collapsed at one place in the field and a lamb had fallen into this trap. It was unable to get out and when Kyle heard its cries of distress and scented at the hole, the lamb, breasting water to its tiny chest, fled frightened into greater danger in the blackness of the drain. Again calling Mike with his yapping bark, Kyle summoned help. There was only one way. Kyle would have to play the role of ferret and bolt the lamb. Entering the drain lower down the dog splashed against the running water, squeezed his body past the obstructing earth fall and nosed the lamb back to where Mike was waiting at the hole to grab it to safety.

Kyle's intelligence in his daily work on the moors of Upper Wharfe-dale was reflected in his competitive shepherding on the trials field, as also was that of his fell-mate and litter-sister, Gael.

Kyle and Gael were of the most illustrious of sheepdog bloodlines. They were the son and daughter of Thomson McKnight's Gael, the

Supreme International champion of 1967, and sired by his Jaff, also of International calibre. In a gruelling double-gather test of 20 unseen sheep at half a mile over Kilmartin's difficult course of bog, dyke, burn and trees at the 1970 International championship in Argyll, Kyle won the most coveted Shepherds' honour in the world. His work on that September day proved the vigour and stamina, controlled power and supreme intelligence of the modern working collie. Buffeted by wind-driven rain and tested by strong, wilful Blackface sheep, he shepherded with calm assurance, adding to the glory of his line by finishing his task 33 aggregate points in front of his nearest challenger. The previous month, at the English National trials, he had won the English Shepherds' honour and, of 146 shepherds' and farmers' dogs, finished reserve overall champion.

Pedigree of KYLE (47050) 1970 International Shepherd's Champion with Michael Perrings

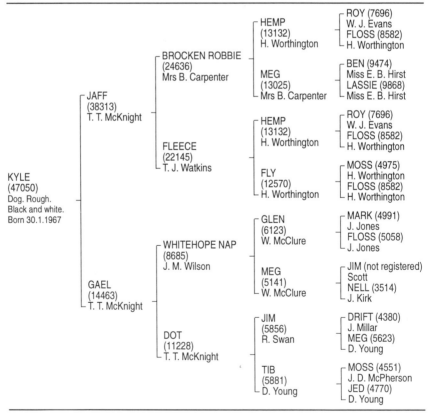

The numbers in brackets are the Stud Book numbers of the International Sheep Dog Society

Gael played her part in that great international victory. Kyle and Gael had always worked and played together and Gael made the journey to Kilmartin just so that her brother would not fret for her company. Her victory was the psychological one! Kyle respected her greatly and always, when travelling in the car, allowed her to occupy the seat while he lay on the floor. A trim little smooth, black-coated collie, she had her own moments of glory on the trials field. She partnered her brother to third place in the English Brace championship, but her greatest success was the winning of the coveted Fylde trophy in the spring of 1971, a mini-international triumph over 127 entries including 31 English, Scottish and Welsh internationals.

As with Kyle's major victory, hers was also taken in the vilest weather, and the more spectacular in that she had to overcome a sickness which kept her from the lambing fields that year. Yet on the trials day her work was only faulted half a point. Sadly Gael never recovered from her illness and later in the year, before she was five years old, she was buried on the hillside where she had spent her working life. I missed her almost as much as Mike, for she was a particular favourite of mine. She had such nice ways, and I always thought she would eventually prove a better collie than Kyle, who was to win further honour for England and in the BBC television trials.

By the time Mike left the management of Throstle Nest to farm in his own right at Giggleswick, in the adjoining dale of Ribble, Kyle had won many honours, including the Yorkshire championship, and had seen five lambing times on the bleak hillside of Conistone Moor. At Field Gate, where lusher lands run close to the Ribble, he had an easier life, quickly adapting to the herding of dairy cows and Dalesbred ewes.

Beyond the hospitable door of the old stone farmhouse, whose date stone is 1684, and where everyone was greeted with that friendly welcome so accepted among countryfolk, grew an efficient agricultural unit geared to dairying.

A delightful place, looking out across the wide river valley to the white escarpments above Settle and the familiar outline of Ingleborough, it became perhaps even better known as a place of quality dogs. Although Mike had left the high places, dogs were equally as important to the management of his stock.

Here Hope, son of Kyle, came to learn his craft when he was little more than a puppy. He was born on the slopes of Pen-y-Ghent, at Newlands House, mothered by Adrian Bancroft's bonny-looking Anne, a winsome clever bitch, always ready to please, who twice won England's Shepherds' championship. Hope took much of her delightful character, grew into a big strapping collie, and had a double dose of the best brains in the collie world.

To some extent he replaced Gael in my affections, for he was easy to know and willing to please. While his father was a one-man dog, he would herd the sheep, bring in the cows for milking or put the hens to roost for everyone, even the children, Alison, Isobel and Jill. Margaret, Mike's wife, even ran him with confidence in trials.

The ideal collie, in my opinion, I used him to explain the basic qualities of his breed to four million viewers in the 'One Man and His Dog' series, and I remember him standing patiently and unworried on a dinner table in a crowded, smoke-filled room while I used him for the same purpose at a Luneside Farmers Club meeting.

Unfortunately, as does happen in disputes for the 'leadership of the pack', he had a difference of opinion one day with his father and suffered a damaged eye which on occasion caused him double vision and spoiled his trials potential. However, he still won the open championships at Malham and Kilnsey in the Yorkshire Dales.

But Hope did not miss the glamour of crowd adulation for he was happiest at home, staying among the folks he knew and loved and quietly going about his job. He could not escape fame altogether, though, particularly after becoming a television star, for he was used in a television commercial and, more importantly, he became respected as a breeding sire, his sons doing particularly well in competition. Hope and his father, Kyle, became known throughout Britain and it is their successes and those of his other dogs that caused Michael Perrings to say, 'They have made me a lot of good friends all over the country' – another, if unusual, tribute to the working dog.

Although Michael Perrings, who died prematurely when he was England's President of the International Sheep Dog Society in 1993, won an International and an English Shepherds' championship, he never won a National title although he came close to it, being reserve three times.

In 1970 the clever black and white Kyle was second by only two of 200 aggregate points from two judges to Tim Longton's rough-coated Glen from Quernmore in north Lancashire, shepherding testy and wilful hill sheep over the flat lands of Houghend on the fringe of Manchester. Kyle also ran third at the 1975 National.

In 1985 Mike's black-coated Dryden Spam was second to Thomas Longton's courageous Bess, also from Quernmore, only three aggregate points of 220 down, on wily Mule shearlings at Ferry Meadows outside Peterborough in Cambridgeshire; and over extensive land near West Heslerton outside Malton in north Yorkshire in 1988 his forceful Craig was only two aggregate points behind the winner, Brian Dodd's rough-coated Laddie, again from Quernmore.

Spam won the prestigious Holme championship over 64 rivals at the

Two International handlers, Mel Page of Wales and Michael Perrings of England, with collie Dryden Spam, have a chat.

entrance to the Cliviger Gorge in 1981 when he was only 2½ years old and the course was flooded; and in 1986 he shepherded five Welsh Mountain hoggs to win the Shropshire and West Midlands Show trials for England over Welsh and Scottish opposition.

Craig, a son of John James's international Fly and of bloodline to Supreme champions John Thomas's Craig, Gwyn Jones's Bill and Alan Jones's Roy, won many trials but his best run was perhaps in winning the Yorkshire society's qualifying trials by one of 90 points over 77 rivals in 1991, running out of time in the final.

The successful merging of the bloodlines of Michael Perring's Kyle and Adrian Bancroft's Anne, both of which went back over common ancestors, provided north Yorkshire with some good herding dogs. In commentary over the public address system on the Great Yorkshire showfield at Harrogate, when Michael and Adrian were handling their dogs in exhibition work, I described them as the most efficient family of collies in the country. This family comprised the two older dogs, Kyle and Anne, who, though of different parentage, were grandson and granddaughter of Jim Wilson's Whitehope Nap, known as Scotland's power dog and winner of the Scottish National championship. They were partnered by Hope, Jaff and Gwen, their two sons and daughter, proving, if ever proof were needed, that working pedigree counts for an awful lot. All five were first and foremost dogs of the farm. Trials and exhibitions were a pleasant relaxation.

At Newlands Farm, tucked away at the end of a track under the top of Pen-y-Ghent above Ribblesdale, Adrian had four generations of his home-bred collies helping him to manage a flock of Swaledale ewes and a herd of beef cows. But Anne, who died naturally and contentedly after 13 years of happy partnership with her master, was special. 'I don't think I'll ever again work with as good a dog' Adrian once told me, and in justification of her master's faith she won four English International 'caps'.

From Far Dean Farm on the Brontë moors, Adrian was brought up with Lonk × Dalesbred halfbred sheep, sheep that with their stoic and determined nature taught him the necessity for more strength and determination in his collies, and having found the right blend of blood-lines he has stuck to breeding his own helpmates.

Anne was sired by Sam Dyson's Mac, a collie from the Brontë sheep-runs which had a great influence in improving the working dogs of the Lancashire–Yorkshire Pennines, and she was mothered by her master's Maddie, whose bloodlines went back to one of the greatest of Welsh collies, Hughes's Jaff, the winner of three International and six National championships, and to one of the best-ever hill dogs, Jim Wilson's Cap.

Adrian has now left Newlands Farm and lives in Settle, from where he manages stock near Lawkland.

Sheep and lambs are instant weather prophets. See them scattered across the grazing, grey and white dots spotted over the lower hill, and the weather and prospects are set fine; see them lying in the shelter of the rocks and field walls and the clouds are down with rain threatening. Hill ewes are good mothers and will protect their lambs from driving rain with their bodies, couching their babies close where they will be sheltered.

If they are fit and well after a good birth, ewes will produce around

Adrian Bancroft's Anne, twice England's Shepherds' Champion, from the slopes of Pen-y-Ghent.

three gallons of milk a week in the first two weeks of suckling and are constant providers. From docile, timid creatures parent ewes become belligerent, protective mothers – to be avoided when their babies are born, as any collie will tell you, for it is a dog's roughest time of the year when knocks from irate mothers are commonplace.

Yet I find that ewes are almost pathetically trusting with some of their contemporaries on the hill, particularly with crows. Ewes are prepared to challenge a dog and usually one which they know has never harmed them, yet they will allow the black-hearted crow to get within striking distance of their lambs. There is nothing deadlier than the hard, ebony-like beak of a crow. Gruesome though it is, many lambs, particularly if they are weak and tend to lie around, lose their eyes and tongues in this way and subsequently die.

Crows – and foxes – troubled the flock of 1,000 Welsh Mountain ewes which Selwyn Jones ran on the rocky Migneint Mountain from Bron Erw near Ffestiniog in North Wales. Their ravages on the young lambs, particularly those which were a little slow to find their legs, were only countered by the extra shepherding of Selwyn and his three dogs.

The most experienced of his collies, Jill, an eight-year-old smooth-coated tricolour daughter of a Welsh National trials champion, Alan Jones's Lad, had a remarkable mouth, so soft and gentle that she could catch and pick up lambs without hurting them. This ability was of great practical use to her master when he wanted to give a veterinary injection against disease. Jill was a wise collie in many ways, understanding all she was told, and she even knew what would be accepted on the home farm and what would not be accepted on the trials course. For instance, there are times in the lambing field when a slight nip from the dog will do a truculent ewe a power of good without harming her, but such action will very often lead to disqualification at a trial. Selwyn used to tell Jill, 'Don't do what you do at home, don't get hold of the sheep – please,' and she always obeyed.

There you have the difference between a normally intelligent work dog and a highly intelligent dog whose master has taken the trouble to encourage and develop its inbred wisdom. There also is the answer to those who disparagingly and sneeringly claim 'trials dogs' as a race apart, soft, pampered creatures, unfit for real work. They are indeed different – in that they have masters who admire them and take pains to encourage the best in them, and to polish their natural sagacity.

Selwyn Jones has represented Wales in International competition more than a dozen times. He won the National title in 1963 with Vicky, and he is greatly respected in sheepdog circles, both as a member of the International Sheep Dog Society's council and as a judge of the International trials on four occasions. He has spent all his life at Bron Erw, on

1,000 acres of mountain and 500 acres of hill land, where he farms
130 Welsh Black cows, sturdy and robust animals with splendid beef
qualities, in addition to the sheep flock.

Beloved of the Welsh hill men, their lambs appreciated by the
butcher for the high quality, tenderness and flavour of their meat, the
small, white-faced Welsh Mountain sheep are, with their skippy, flighty
ways, far from popular with the collies of England and Scotland when
visiting Welsh trials. Used to pressing the heavier breeds of their home
lands, they are often startled to see the Welsh ewes bolting from their
approach.

But you can never be certain when assessing the ways of sheep, and a
dog has to be quick to adapt to whatever it meets at the end of its
outrun.

I well remember Welsh Mountain ewes proving very stubborn at the
Centenary International at Bala in 1973, though hot sunshine contributed to their cussedness. Sheep – indeed any stock – are normally
moved around in the cool of the morning or evening, but trials have to
proceed whatever the weather and then the collie with sheep wisdom
emerges.

At Bala, for instance, on ground by the River Dee and just a few
hundred yards from where the first-ever sheepdog trials were held in
1873, the Welsh ewes did not run at all true to pattern.

They were in no mood to hurry, wanting, if they had to go at all, to
take their own time and course, and they disputed every authority of
dogs which had expected immediate and even a too speedy response to
their approach. This surprised some of the dogs in the final: they were
thrown out of gear and they were found wanting.

But Glyn Jones's Gel, from the mountain above Bodfari in the Vale of
Clwyd, and a bonny-looking youngster who grew into one of the
finest collies Britain has known, won the championship by virtue of
his herding intelligence and stamina. Then only three years old, Gel
worked at Bala with a firm kindness, guided in his finest hour by a man
who knew sheep absolutely, and he finished the exacting test with a
mighty 29-point gap over dogs which, though experienced, did not
adapt quickly enough to the truculent ewes.

It was interesting to see in that heyday of the Wiston Cap bloodline,
which had become so dominant since the Scottish dog won the 1965
International, that the two dogs in front at Bala, Gel and Jim Cropper's
prick-eared Clyde from the Lancashire moorlands, were from John
Bathgate's Rock, a collie which won every major trial in Scotland
except the National.

CHAPTER FOUR

The Wisest Dog in the World

*I consider the adaptability of the modern collie in dealing with a
varied sheep population, realise that it can never be mechanised,
and list the qualities which make and keep it a master of its craft.*

Today's collie dog is the finest piece of farm machinery that man has
evolved from God's creation, and the greatest friend that any shepherd
could desire during his long lonely hours on the hill. No mechanical
contraption can ever be devised – as with so many other farming jobs –
to do the work of the collie dog in stock herding, and its ability is
directly linked with the success or failure of any sheep enterprise.

The Border Collie is the ideal dog for herding farm stock, sheep in
particular. It is inherently intelligent, of a good temperament, strong,
well built and relatively free from disease, and it has the stamina for its
arduous task on the sheep-runs of Britain and the world. In short, it is
the master of its craft.

But within that basic make-up is also a complex character, for more is
expected of the modern working collie than of any other breed of dog.
It is expected to master virile Scottish Blackface ewes, as wiry and fleet
as deer, over the almost perpendicular slopes of the Cuillins on Skye; it
is expected to run without hesitation over the sharp screes of the
limestone hills of Yorkshire to outpace the flighty Swaledale flocks; and
it is expected to have the power and patience to drive heavy Longwools
over the sweeping downlands of the South Country. Given time it will
adapt to any of these conditions and to whatever stock herding it is
faced with.

Typical of this adaptability to varying shepherding tasks was Tot
Longton's dour, medium-sized tricolour Rob. He was reared from four
months old to work Dalesbred sheep and Friesian milk cows at Lee End
Farm on the good land of the Conder Valley at Quernmore in north
Lancashire, yet in eight seasons on the trials fields matched his ability

and intelligence against over a dozen different breeds of sheep, across hillside bents and lowland pastures, to write one of the finest success stories.

His record of 40 open championships, one International and two National championships, and five appearances in the English International team is such an incredible one in these days when entries reach towards the hundred mark at every trial that no writer of fiction would dare to credit one collie with such success. Of him, Tot once told me, 'He is ever willing to work and whatever he goes for he brings. No stock can overcome his intense concentration and forceful command.'

Ken Brehmer's black-coated Ben, a strong determined dog, left one of the bleakest of Blackface herdings on the Northumbrian Cheviots to win three International 'caps' for England, on fit Mule ewes over the parklands of Chatsworth in Derbyshire, on testy Blackfaces at Chathill by the north-east coast, and in 1978 on stupid white-faced Oldenberg×Cheviot halfbreds over the lush fields of Welbeck Abbey by Sherwood Forest in Nottinghamshire when he won the National championship.

Now shepherding in the wilds of Sutherland, Kenny runs his dogs in Scotland's National trials, and has represented that country three times in International competition. In 1991 his seven-year-old Bute was the International Driving champion, and in the 1994 trials of television's 'One Man and His Dog' at Hallbankgate in the Tindale Fells of Cumbria he was only beaten in the final. In 1995 he judged Scotland's National trials.

Adaptability to the task in hand is thus one of the prime assets of the shepherd's dog, but obviously one strain of collie blood is better at a specific task than another. A dog bred and reared on smooth lowland pastures can hardly be expected to cope with the near-perpendicular mountainsides of the Scottish Highlands as well as the native dog. Consequently the working collie is almost a breed within a breed, a specialist at its own type of shepherding, yet versatile enough to master other conditions when given time. It is because of this adaptability that British dogs are in constant demand in Australia, New Zealand and America.

It is good stocksmanship to breed to an ideal for maximum efficiency, to use bloodlines that are proven for the specific purpose required of the end product be it milk cows, bacon pigs, lambs or working dogs. The hill farmer will breed from lines of proven fell dogs, dogs with extra stamina and speed; the lowland farmer will seek his ideal among collie families which have been reared and blooded to strength on heavy stubborn sheep.

There are around 50 pure breeds of sheep in Britain and perhaps

300 crossbreds, all suited to the land they graze, and each has some individual trait, however slight, which a good collie will come to know.

Watching Drift, his 6½-year-old brave and forceful medium-sized dog, working reluctant Blackface ewes into the dipping bath at Hallmanor Farm in the Southern Uplands of Scotland, six miles from Peebles, John Bathgate said: 'He's as good as two men here because he knows he has to get in and lay into them if necessary. For this work a dog must be powerful, really powerful.'

In the Lake District Chris Todd, who farms 450 Swaledale sheep and 40 suckler cows on nearly 1,000 acres of rough fell and 200 acres inbye at Loweswater, likes a long-legged dog among the crag and bracken. 'You can see it better, it can move faster, and it is generally more agile than a smaller dog,' he says.

Litter-brothers Bob and Pete, two tough Lakeland dogs which were always squabbling between themselves yet developed into perfect working partners on the fell, earned recognition by the Stud Book committee of the International Sheep Dog Society on the merit of their

Agile and fit like all her breed, George Scott's Gael takes the fence in her stride (Frank H. Moyes).

ability, always more convincing than that of pedigree alone. They went on to win the English Brace championship for Chris in successive years in 1976 and 1977, and in 1977 at Austwick in the Yorkshire Dales they represented England in the 'One Man and His Dog' television trials. Also in the television trials were Chris's home-bred litter-sisters, the smooth-coated Pat and the rough-coated Belle, born in May 1989, who were reserve champions in the Brace class of the English National in 1994. In 1995 the tricolour Pat was in England's singles team.

Chris, a modest man who says he couldn't earn a living without his dogs and credits all his successes in 40 years of trials to them, believes that 'A clever dog recognises different types of sheep, moves more forcefully on heavy sheep which need pushing and lies back off light sheep which are more flighty.'

Down in north Herefordshire, just about ten miles from the Welsh border, which makes him a keen Welsh rugby fan and a choral songster, John James farms 120 acres of sweet grass and arable land from the picturesque timbered farmhouse of Shirleath at Kingsland. He rears around 200 early lambs, mating the smart and attractive Kerry Hill ewes to the black-faced Suffolk rams, in addition to rearing 60 bullocks for fattening, and he likes a powerful dog for this kind of stock.

The black, white and tan Mirk, taken to Shirleath when he was 12 months old, was typical. Though a little shy of strangers, he was strong, well built and of a good temperament, and proved his skill on heavy sheep in winning, at four years old, the 1975 English National championship on Mule ewes over the downland country near Wantage in Oxfordshire. Also on Mule ewes in Chatsworth Park, Derbyshire, he won the English Driving title the following year. His was the wisdom of good breeding, for he was line-bred to Supreme champion Wiston Cap. The same year that he won the National trials, his father, John Richardson's Mirk, won the Scottish National and International Shepherds' championships.

John James's black and tan Ben, home-bred out of Nell by John Thomas's Don, who earned three International 'caps', was also a big, classy collie with plenty of balance who wasn't afraid to face up to sheep.

Jimmy Shanks, known for his portly manner and smiling character, ran his stock on the braes which climb to Ben Vrackie from the eastern shore of Loch Lomond at Auchengyle, where in summer the bracken stood tall enough to cover even a man of his stature. He wanted dogs which would use their voices, barking to startle his sheep from this hot jungle. It was hard graft for a man to care for stock under those conditions and he had to have dogs with guts, which would give their maximum effort.

I have seen collies work under all sorts of varying conditions. I have also judged them over vastly different trials courses, and always the common factor has been their high intelligence and strength for the job.

It is thus up to man to develop these basic qualities for his own particular farming needs. Many farmers and shepherds are already doing this by selective breeding for the specific points they want, and in this work properly run sheepdog trials are invaluable for they are the shop-window of the breed, where wise men can note the dogs which show the qualities they are seeking for their breeding programmes.

I make the point of emphasising 'properly run' trials for there is a tendency with some trials organisers to accept too many entries – justified by the increased revenue to themselves, but pure greediness in most cases – resulting in tests being omitted, courses being far too small in area, time factors for the work reduced to an impractical minimum, and tests made easy so that dogs can finish their task as quickly as possible to enable the excessive entry to be completed.

Trials which follow this pattern are no good for the future efficiency of the collie, indeed they can do much harm to the breed. They are not even a spectacle for the watching public, who have rightly come to expect skilful entertainment after the success of sheepdogs on television. Good trials over varying terrain of the correct size, and incorporating all the herding tests in a workmanlike time, will improve the working collie by bringing out the qualities to be fixed and by showing up the faults to be bred out.

Nor were the National trials prior to 1982 to be commended. Too many entries in too short a time promoted a hustle and bustle which was intolerable to good shepherding. In this respect the International Sheep Dog Society was defeating its own object of improving the collie dog until the Directors made rules to keep entries to a manageable level.

The modern Border Collie has been carefully bred for generations and, in many cases, inbred to stamp its herding qualities. Sheep are far from being the stupid creatures most people believe; they are at least equal in intelligence to a horse. So the dog which herds them must be no mug.

But sheep and dogs have always been involved with each other and time, evolution and man have lifted that relationship from the predator and his prey, the hunter and the hunted, to the herder and his flock. The urge to hunt, tempered by man to the urge to herd, is still instinctive in the most skilled collie, as it was in the primitive dog, but the relationship between man and dog has grown – the leader and his minion – so that the present highly efficient system has resulted.

Yet man is a fool in many ways and his desire for absolute dictatorial dominance over lesser creatures and his greed for easy financial profit can, and does, spoil much of nature's handiwork. Collies are now big business, with top class workers bringing over a thousand pounds, competent workers £500, and barely trained dogs still in the hundreds. With a booming export trade to the sheep-runs of the world as well there can be a temptation to push a collie's basic training to the utmost, for immediate, if short-lived, results instead of complementing and assisting nature's own time.

Such legendary dogs as Jim Wilson's Whitehope Nap and his rough-coated Mirk, and Dick Hughes's Jaff, were all over four years old before they had really settled down and tuned to their handlers. All three had 'a year under each paw' before they reached greatness – Nap to win the 1955 Scottish championship and subsequently become the founder of one of the most successful lines of shepherding dogs; Mirk to take both the Supreme and Scottish titles in 1950; and Jaff to become the greatest driving dog of them all with three International and three Welsh National Driving championships.

In the same pattern, Bob Shennan's mottled Mirk, from 1,000 upland acres in the Carrick district of Ayrshire, was 7½ years old when he won the 1978 Supreme championship; John Thomas's clever Craig, with Speckle-faced ewes at Llandovery, was over seven years old when he took the title to South Wales in 1977; Thomas Longton's indefatigable little Bess from the Conder Valley in north Lancashire was almost ten years old when she won the 1986 Supreme championship; Gwyn Jones's strong rough-coated Bill from Penmachno in the Mignaint range of Snowdonia was 6½ at his Supreme success in 1974; and Gwyn's white-headed Shep was 4½ in 1976, and in 1990 his black and white Queen was 8½ years old when she won the top honour.

Dual Supreme champion Bobby Dalziel's handsome white-bibbed Wisp from ground which rises to the 2,270 ft Ettrick Pen in the Scottish Borders was rising four when he won his first championship in 1989; another dual Supreme champion, John Wilson's black and white Spot from Ettrick Forest was 5½ years old when he won the first of his two championships in 1991; the other dual Supreme champion, Raymond MacPherson's rough-coated Zac from the Tindale Fells of Cumbria was close on five when he took his first title at York in 1975; and the 1995 winner, Stuart Davidson's good-looking Craig from a Blackface herding by Loch Fynside in Argyll, was 5½ years old.

Nature can never be rushed, as all countrymen know.

In addition to quick sales of half-competent work dogs, there is the easy market of the show bench, but that is another story – devoid of sheep!

Mutual respect is essential for the perfect partnership. Glyn Jones and Gel (Mel Grundy).

Fortunately there are not many professional breeders and few practical men are so thick-headed as to crush a collie's thinking powers, nor so tempted by easy money, well knowing that a collie dog under the right hands is a marvel and in the wrong hands a cringing slave fit for nothing but automatic and robot control.

A collie takes after the man who teaches it, yet the wisest retain their own individuality, and I agree wholeheartedly with John Holms's opinion that 'to describe any dog as almost human is the greatest insult one can bestow on the canine race. . . . Anyone with doubts about this', he says, 'should try to do what any dog does in a sheepdog trial. A dog is man's best friend, not because of any human traits but because he can do so many things better than us – and a whole lot which we can't do at all.' No other friend would ever be expected willingly to work the long strenuous hours over the roughest of land in the vilest of weather conditions for the simple reward of affection, food and shelter.

The choice of collie is therefore of the greatest importance; man and dog must be temperamentally suited. You must like it, it must like you. Indeed, choosing a collie is as important for a shepherd as choosing a wife! At certain seasons, such as lambing, he will spend more time with his dog and every day it is his companion for hours on end.

Today's collie dog is undoubtedly the wisest dog in the world. Its inbred intelligence is proved daily on the hills of Britain, its purpose in life is to shepherd sheep, it has been bred for it, and its knowledge of the ways of sheep is almost uncanny. It is strongly muscled and lightly boned and fast as the wind over the most rugged ground. In nature and temperament it is a most placid creature, yet assertive and forceful in handling awkward stock. It likes nothing better than to work in the service of man.

Balanced and compact in form, around 45 pounds in weight and standing about 22 inches to the shoulder, it has a box-head with plenty

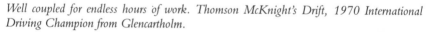

Well coupled for endless hours of work. Thomson McKnight's Drift, 1970 International Driving Champion from Glencartholm.

The head is the brain-box, broad across the skull. Len Greenwood's Cap at Ramsden Farm, Walsden (Farmers Guardian).

of skull width for brains. The ears, either pricked or flopped, are well set on the corners, open and clear to receive its master's instructions; its nose is blunt with wide and open nostrils, allowing a quick and good passage of air. The clear, dark eyes reveal a calm light of wisdom, the alert keenness of interest and the contented nature of a placid temperament. They change like the weather, softening to a word of approval, hard and wilful in the mastery of a truculent sheep, steady and oftimes baleful if tested to extreme or questioned in authority, but always reflecting the glow of loyalty to their ancient craft.

A collie is a proud dog, its head and shoulders well set on a supple body. Its back is firm and strong, sloping slightly to the withers, and the spine is particularly flexible, allowing the quick and decisive movement in turning after bounding sheep. The spine runs sweetly into the long feathered tail, which is so vital to the dog in the form of a rudder, balancing and complementing its supple speed of turn and flanking. When in repose the tail is carried low with a proud upward swirl at the tip. So perfectly balanced and co-ordinated for effortless movement, its deep chest, strong bent stifles, and short and powerful hocks add the necessary physical qualities to cope with its demanding life.

Fast enough to give the speediest sheep a fellside start, it runs light on oval feet padded well enough to stand the tear of rocky ways. An all-weather, outdoor dog requires the protection of a good coat and whether long or short haired the collie's coat grows in two layers. The top coat is the umbrella, which drains off the water, and the undercoat the warm, waterproof cladding.

Purely a utility dog, where efficiency based on brains and stamina is the only yardstick, the modern collie has lost none of its beauty of appearance. Its thick silky coat or close smooth cover, if properly groomed, gives it a handsome look, and in outline it is pleasing with no factor overemphasised as in so many dogs of the show bench.

Long haired or short haired is really a matter of preference. It is generally accepted that a rough-coated collie will stand the winter's cold better, but in deep snow its feathering can collect snowballs to hamper progress, while a smooth-coated, bare-skinned dog is better in the heat of a summer's day. My friend Dick Fortune, who reared the famous Canterbury lambs in New Zealand for over 20 years and who won many sheepdog trials in New Zealand and Australia, exploded this myth, at least as far as the hot weather argument is concerned. He said, 'A smooth-haired dog has a very dense coat and the air doesn't get through it, whereas the air can get through the looser hairs of a longer coated dog.'

Length of coat has no bearing on the dog's working ability. Of the last 20 Supreme champions 17 were rough coated and 3 smooth. Nor does colour affect a dog's performance with stock, other than that a predominantly white dog seems to require extra power. Both sheep and cows can be very inquisitive and a white dog attracts their attention, making them turn to see what strange creature it is that chivvies them.

Of the strongest constitution, today's collie is remarkably free from disease, and with the right care and attention will have an effective working life of up to ten years on the hill. It is naturally healthy but its work makes immense demands upon its physical resources.

George Hutton, who farms top quality Swaledales on 2,000 acres of the bleak 3,000 ft high Helvellyn range of the Cumbrian fells, estimated that his Nip, a stout-hearted black-coated hill dog of the finest calibre, would cover towards 100 miles in a ten-hour day during lambing time. All that Nip and his contemporaries ask for such devotion to duty is nourishing food and a dry lodging.

A turn of speed to outrun the fastest sheep over the roughest ground. John Squires' Jaff from the Yorkshire hills (Derek Johnson).

Energy is provided by proper food and it has been estimated that for a day's work a collie requires 1,600 calories of energy. A dog is a carnivore and should therefore be given meat – cooked rather than raw – with cereal, vitamins and minerals to make up a concentrated meal. The amount depends entirely on the dog's work-load, its age, its sex, its conditions, and generally an amount that can be consumed in two minutes is a guide. Variety of offering should prevent the meals from becoming monotonous. Collie dogs are particularly fond of salt in their food. Clean water should always be available for the dog. The meal is best fed at night after the day's work is over and there is time for quiet digestion.

The energy derived from the meal should not be wasted by having to produce warmth in a cold housing so that a dry, draughtproof bed is essential. The kennel should be weatherproof, with plenty of fresh air and light. Bedding should always be clean and preferably laid down on a raised boarded platform, never on concrete or stone.

One of the accusations levelled at farmers is that on the whole they tend to care little for their dogs and treat them badly. Once the cows have been brought in for milking the dog is tied up and there it stays until the next milking time. There is some truth in the accusation, for I have seen dogs living in conditions of appalling filth – but then the whole farm concerned reflected the bad husbandry of its owner.

I have also seen dogs tied on the end of chains which were strong enough to hold the liner *Queen Mary* in dock. I have seen dogs which had barrels for homes, or draughty packing-cases which leaked rain-water like sieves. Outside such kennels the earth has been padded solid with the relentless, bored pacing of these captives. Under such

Dry, draughtproof and healthy housing for three champions. John Richardson's Mirk, Sweep and Wiston Cap (Matt Mundell).

conditions it is not surprising that dogs become bored and savage, yapping, barking and snarling at any man or beast which enters their domain. Never should a collie, or any dog for that matter, be permanently chained. It must feel wanted, not neglected. A moment's thought by the guilty and they would realise that they are shortening the dog's working life by their lack of interest – and that should wake them up. At today's prices a working dog is a very valuable asset.

Nothing will awaken a farmer quicker than to touch his pocket, and I am constantly baffled by the attitude of some farmers to their dogs. Having said that, I do not believe a working dog should be coddled, but it should be cared for properly.

As so often happens in society the whole farming community tends to be judged on the deplorable actions of some individuals, for few shepherds and farmers whose dogs are virtually an extension of their right hand in the management of their stock are guilty of this neglect. So little time is required to make a dog comfortable – a quick wash-down to remove the dirt at the end of a working day, the removal of any vegetation such as bracken or thorns from its coat, and a brisk rub-down to dry it off, particularly around the ears – followed by its feed and retirement to a dry, warm bed. Grooming of the coat should be carried out as necessary to keep it free from vermin and fit and well – and proud. Never should a collie be put through the sheep-dip – it does happen – for this is senseless, thoughtless cruelty. Simply, a collie dog should be treated as you would a good friend.

CHAPTER FIVE

Preparing the Trials Stage

*Tells of the aims as well as the trials and tribulations in the
staging of the top sheepdog events, and of the national downpour
which led to a television success.*

A collie dog is a healthy dog. It has to be fit to meet its arduous calling.
Its only defect sometimes is its eyesight, for some collies are subject to
fading eyesight, Progressive Retinal Atrophy, when they are around five
or six years of age. By taking this problem in hand by selective breeding,
however, the International Sheep Dog Society has more or less stamped
out this defect.

Before a collie is allowed to run at the trials of the Society it has to
pass a rigorous health test, and rightly so. It is as much for the collie's
sake as for the watchers – particularly the so-called 'do-gooders' who
often know little of the subject they complain about. A veterinary
surgeon examines each dog, mainly for Progressive Retinal Atrophy or
PRA as it is known, at the top trials. This test used to be carried out
before the dog was allowed to run but nowadays, because the eyesight
test could impair its work, the PRA test can be done after the dog has
run.

When I was course directing for England every competitor had to
hand me a form from the veterinary surgeon to say that their collie was
sound in eye and limb. This led to the comment, 'What is that mysterious piece of paper which every competitor gives to you when he
walks on to the field to start his trial?' I can assure you it was not a
'fiver', or any other amount of bribe.

Some competitors offered the certificate with a cheery word, others
had to be asked for it. Some competitors enjoyed a brief chat, some
welcomed a word of encouragement, some were so wrapped up and
concentrating on the job before them that they just didn't want to know

you. You came to recognise and accept the various temperaments without insult or rancour. All that was technically necessary was to ask the competitor if he knew the course he had to run and to collect the vet's certificate.

I knew competitors who virtually went into retreat for a short period before they went on to compete, their nerves so stretched that a few minutes away from it all, walking behind the grandstand or in the car park, was their preparation for the big test.

Once the Course Director had welcomed the competitor on to the field and flagged the instructions to the shepherds at the far end of the field to release the sheep he would fade gracefully into obscurity and let the trial proceed.

Talking of course directing, each country used to have its own Course Director at the International, whose job quite simply was to 'mother' the team, to ensure that the trial was fair, that nothing interfered with it and that everything went according to plan.

Nowadays, and wrongly in my opinion, the Directors of the Society have decreed that the host country for the International provides the Course Director, with an assistant. Granted, this decision does save some money in hotel bills, but the welfare of the competitors should come first. The Directors have also decided that Course Directors at Nationals should only act for three years – it takes that long to become really efficient at course directing!

I have made many friends – and a few enemies – over the 40-odd years I have been involved with sheepdog trials and during my judging duties, as a Director, and as Course Director with the International

The trophy table of the International Sheep Dog Society. Philip Hendry announces the results with assistant, Dorothy Martin, and the Duchess of Devonshire waits to present the awards at Chatsworth 1978 (Marc Henrie).

Sheep Dog Society. The friends are numbered in hundreds, the enemies counted on one hand – I hope – and only temporary dissidents at some judging decision I have made.

Weather plays such an important role in the Course Director's 'private life' at National and International trials because he is out in the open all the time. If you are roasting in shirt-sleeves, as at Chatsworth in 1976, you have plenty of visitors, both official and unofficial, vying for the two or three chairs in the Course Director's plum viewing spot in front of the judges; if it is raining 'cats and dogs', as at Leek in 1974 or at the great Kilmartin downpour in the same year, you huddle in waterproofs completely alone and unwanted.

In the first case there were times throughout the three days when you got just a little fed-up with the many questions asked; in the second you would welcome a little company. It is amazing, too, just how lonely it can feel sitting but 20 yards from a crowd of people but entirely without company. But, like the wicket-keeper in a cricket team, you are always in the action. Every competitor has to be met, every trial has to be watched, every sign of tension has to be smoothed – and you have to protect the judges from a lynch-mob!

Basically a Course Director's job is simply to make sure that every competitor gets the same chance of success, that every sheep is sound, that every group of sheep on release from the holding pen is left in a position to gather which makes no greater demands on one dog than another, that nothing interferes with a trial while in progress to jeopardise its outcome.

The Course Director's most thankless task is to walk out to a competitor and tell him that his dog's work has fallen below the standard required by the judges and that he has to retire. This is the judges' decision and the Course Director is only the messenger; most handlers are sporting enough not to object to this enforced retirement.

Apart from the practical duties I've outlined, we each used to offer a word of encouragement to members of our team at the International, trying to relieve a bit of the tension in the less experienced handlers, and keep the hubbub of the grandstand crowd from swamping a handler's commands to his dog. Unless you've been in front of that grandstand you cannot credit the amount of noise that comes from people's voices in normal conversation. While behaving scrupulously fairly to all taking part, there is more to course directing than just waving a flag as a signal to the stewards for sheep.

Take Kilmartin in 1974, for instance! Her Royal Highness Princess Anne was visiting, even in that long-remembered downpour. Would I go half-way up the course to the quarter-mile mark where the gate through which the royal cars would enter on to the course was sited –

and if there was a trial being run when the Princess arrived at the gate would I stop her! Hopefully asking the policeman who was on security duty by the gate if he would stop the royal entourage, I was left in no doubt as to his feeling, even in his broad Scottish accent: 'I'm too young to go to the Tower.' Fortunately the Princess arrived just when a collie had completed its work and I was able to open the gate immediately. A beaming royal smile was my reward.

Course directing is stage-managing and I was tutored by some most efficient men. Among them were Ernest Dawson of my local society at Holme, who could get through the biggest entry in the minimum time and without any complaint; Jim Wilson, who after retiring with nine Supreme championships course directed for Scotland; Frank Tarn, who worked so hard for the International Sheep Dog Society's success; and Will Fife, the mild-mannered Northumbrian who was my predecessor with England. I also learned much from my two colleagues in the International trio, Willie Hislop for Scotland and Bill Jones for Wales – we used to 'share' Ireland in those days. Willie and Bill were the two most willing and co-operative blokes I could ever wish to work with and added tremendously to the efficiency and good spirit of the International trials.

One of my most quizzical companions on the Course Director's bench at an English National was a tall, good-looking young man who introduced himself as a television producer from the BBC. This was at Leek in 1974 where it rained solidly for the full three days and Philip Gilbert, whom I came to admire and respect for his quality of craft, sat with me throughout, for much of the time huddled under a large umbrella.

Philip had the germ of an idea that sheepdog trials might make good television, but you had to have a vivid imagination to think that the drab, featureless playing-fields landscape of Leek could ever be transferred to the television screen with any success. I had always held the opinion that to the casual spectator sheepdog trials were not spectator sport for they were repetitive and the finer and vital points between good and bad were difficult to follow, nor were they explained to the watcher.

Fortunately Philip Gilbert subsequently ignored my warning and I was never happier to be proved wrong than by the 'One Man and His Dog' BBC2 television programmes – but they were produced by an expert. It was the subsequent genius of production which spurned the distances and captured close-ups of both dogs and sheep and which stamped its class and ensured its success.

When Philip Gilbert said goodbye at Leek I thought, 'That's the end of him and his ideas,' but Leek was really the start of 'One Man and

That'll do. Philip Gilbert, BBC producer of 'One Man and His Dog', and assistant, Gerry Cole, in the mobile control room (Derek Johnson).

His Dog', though it was over 12 months before the first series was produced. It was the beginning of three hectic years of planning, preparing, filming and studio pressure, and a genuine friendship which I value very much; and the end product was so worthwhile.

With the first eight-week series of programmes in 1976 Philip Gilbert lifted sheepdog trials in general, and the International Sheep Dog Society in particular, from obscurity to national interest. Almost overnight the collie dog became famous and popular and its craft became known to the four million viewers to whom it gave pleasure – the most important result of all. Four million people is 40 times the number of people who attend the Soccer Cup Final at Wembley and, ever since that first series of pro-grammes, the working technique of sheepdogs is no longer a mystery and trials have reaped the benefit by becoming one of the most popular of pastoral events, rivalling the hitherto unchallenged popularity of show-jumping.

The whole story of the making of 'One Man and His Dog' has been recorded so admirably by my partner-in-crime, Phil Drabble, in his book of the same name, and the television story is told in detail in my book *Sheepdog Trials*, that it is sufficient to say that all the trials were run under International Sheep Dog Society rules based on the National layout.

Competition was the keenest possible between the top collies from the four countries taking part – and the Television Trophy is very high on the list of coveted awards. Grafting though the programme-making was at times, it was successful due to the happy understanding which developed between the competitors, the trials organisers and the technical experts of the BBC, to whom no praise is high enough for their tolerant acceptance and appreciation of canine temperament. No prima donna is more trying than a star-struck collie bitch, as producer's assistant Gerry Cole found out when one adopted her!

The quality of the technicians' craft was recognised where it mattered most, by their own contemporaries, when the British Academy of Film and Television Arts twice nominated the programme for their coveted award, the equivalent to the film Oscar, and the programmes have since been shown in many countries around the world. Out of the series the collie came supreme and finally received its accolade as the wisest dog in the world.

Quick to see the impact of collie appeal to the viewing public, commercial television immediately used working sheepdogs for advertising programmes. Michael Perrings's Hope from Giggleswick, George Hutton's Nip from Threlkeld, Maurice Collin's Spot and Derk from Skeeby, and Alan Jones's Spot and Craig from North Wales appeared as advertising agents.

I tell the story of 'One Man and His Dog' in a chapter of another of

'One Man and His Dog' in Wales. Commentator Eric Halsall with judges Eurwyn Daniel and Ray Ollerenshaw (BBC).

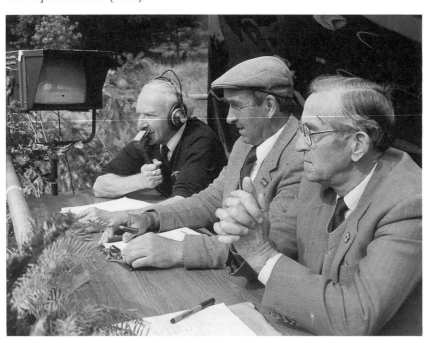

my books, *Sheepdog Trials*. The programme was first produced by Phillip Gilbert and taken over with equal success by producers Ian Smith and Joy Corbett. In the space of a few weeks the programmes did more for sheepdog publicity than had hitherto been done in 70 years. Membership of the International Sheep Dog Society increased and people came to understand something of the vital role of the working sheepdog in the agricultural economy of the world. 'The value of this series to the Society is immeasurable,' said Philip Hendry, the ISDS secretary, in his 1979 annual report to the Directors' meeting at Carlisle.

Sheepdogs had received only sparse publicity in the past. The writings of John Herries McCulloch and Sydney Moorhouse were dedicated works, and now of historical importance to the breed. Following the success of television trials there have been a number of published books in the past few years, and the *Farmers Guardian*, *The Scottish Farmer*, *Yorkshire Post* and *Working Sheepdog News* record current happenings.

Though I had seen many of the country's cleverest collies working on the northern hills and competing in trials at North Country shows, it was not until International trials were resumed in 1946 after the war that I became involved in the newspaper reporting of these major events. It was a period of double wins at Supreme level, with Glen winning for Jim Wilson in 1946 and 1948, and David Daniel's rough-coated Chip winning in 1949 and 1952, but I particularly recall Lancashire's first post-war International at Blackpool in 1951 when Ashton Priestley's Cumbrian-bred Pat, son of Joe Relph's Fleet, won

Do you see any sheep, miss? David Daniel's Chip, 1949 and 1952 Supreme Champion (Scottish Illustrations).

England's first Supreme after the war. It was 16 years later in 1967 that I was to judge the English National in partnership with Ashton.

The judging of the International Society's trials is over a course which has virtually taken the same pattern since James A. Reid, an Airdrie solicitor and secretary of the International Sheep Dog Society for 32 years from 1915, evolved the layout to stand the test of time in its practicalities for assessing the qualities of working dogs. Today, with little change, it is the best in the world and all trials in the United Kingdom are based on the International course. James Reid had implicit faith in his course to improve the working standards of collie dogs and he saw animals which had been graded on it oust all other breeds of working dog. They and their progeny have been preferred to the local breeds on all the great sheep-runs of the world.

James Reid was the architect who built the International Sheep Dog Society and during his time in office he organised 57 National and 21 International trials, putting British collies at the top in working ability and letting the rest of the world know it. How he would have welcomed the television interest after all his labours to make known the great qualities of the Border Collie! It was one of his successors as secretary, Lance Alderson, who did.

If trials have a fault it is not to the dogs or their handlers but to the spectators, the host of town and city dwellers who annually visit the countryside and enjoy the relaxation of country shows. To them trials, or the competitive reasons why one dog is better than another, are a bit of a mystery. Apart from the obvious requirements of the dog to guide the sheep between the hurdles and finally into the pen, the reason why one dog is deemed to have done it better than another is not clear to most – or at least it was not until the BBC series removed much of the mystique by explaining the basic facts of sheepdog trials.

A sheepdog trial is simply a series of practical herding tasks designed to test the working ability of a collie dog in the management of farm stock, the tasks being arranged to form a continuous series of tests in gathering, driving, shedding-off and penning sheep, into which is introduced the competitive element. All the tests are practical ones which a collie is expected to master on the home farm – there are no gimmicks or circus tricks involved – and the judgement is given on the collie's ability to handle the stock in a workmanlike manner and without creating undue stress and strain on the animals herded. Add to the competitive interest the oftimes cussedness of sheep, the loss of a dog's patience, the human failings of judgement, the craft of singling a separate sheep from its own kind, the struggles at the pen mouth and the satisfaction of watching a perfected art, all in the pleasant relaxed atmosphere of the open air, and the appeal to the spectator is apparent.

CHAPTER SIX

The Moment of Truth

◦⟫∘⟨◦∘⟫∘⟨◦∘⟫∘⟨◦

*In which I go through the National and International trials tests
stage by stage, describing the good points and the faults in a
collie's work to the judge's standard, and I talk of the men who
evolved the high standard.*

Join me on the judge's bench and we'll work through a trial. This is the
National course used by each country to decide its champions and
choose its team for the International.

It is run over a minimum of 30 acres of ground with a distance of
400 yards between the collie's start – the post where the handler stands –
and the five sheep to be fetched from the top of the field.

At the start when the handler, a few butterflies in his stomach, and the
collie, tensed and eager for the command to go, stand waiting they have
the maximum 110 points from each of the two judges, for the method
of marking a trial is for the judges to *deduct* points for faults in the work.

The dog may be sent away on either the right- or left-hand side of
the course to gather the five sheep at the top of the field. He should run
out quickly and quietly, and without further instructions from his
master, in a nice arc which will bring him to a position to cover his
sheep and block their escape without disturbing or scattering them.
Should he cross the course before reaching the sheep and gather them
from the opposite side to that which he was directed he will be heavily
faulted, losing at least half the 20 points allotted to this section of the
work. He will also lose points for requiring extra commands to find his
sheep, for stopping on his way out, for going out far too wide in the line
of gather, for coming too tight and scattering his sheep, and for failing to
cover his sheep at the end of the outrun.

The lift – when he moves up to take control of the sheep to set them
on their way down the field towards his master – is a most vital point in
the trial. It is the collie's first contact with the sheep and it is here that he

National Championship course

Sheep

Dog can gather
either side

400 yards fetch

Gather

Drive | 150 yards

Drive 150 yards

Shedding ring

Pen

must immediately assert his authority and show that he is the boss and
will stand no nonsense. Quietly moving up, he must dominate them
and send them trotting on the way he dictates for the maximum ten
points. There are two extreme faults to be down-pointed at the lift, one
for weakness in controlling the sheep, usually requiring whistled and

The holding-pen. Derbyshire Gritstone sheep awaiting their turn at the Deerplay Hill trials in Lancashire (Derek Johnson).

shouted commands of encouragement from the handler, and the fault of over-reaction, the brash tearaway dashing approach which scares the sheep into panic flight.

Fetching the sheep down the field to the handler is possibly the easiest section of the trial, the natural action of the collie to bring his charges to his master, and is tested on the dog's ability to keep his sheep in a straight line – bringing them through a pair of gates set seven yards apart – and to keep them moving at an easy steady pace for 20 points. Faults here are for loss of control resulting in the sheep straying off line, weaving about on their course, stopping to graze, and the other extreme of rushing and chasing the sheep. Failure to guide the sheep through the gates is, of course, faulted.

At the end of the fetch of 400 yards the five sheep, nicely bunched and comfortably moving without panic or fear, are turned round the back of the handler in as tight a line as possible for good marking, to start driving away for 150 yards.

Driving is not easy and has to be taught to a collie, for it is against his natural instincts of always bringing sheep to his master. Again he will be tested on his control: a firm steady mastery of the sheep at the right pace on a straight line through the first set of drive gates will give him full

Course director, Raymond Wild, flags for sheep to be released at the Deerplay Hill trials, a true test of a collie's ability, with the sheep to be gathered on the topmost ridge (Derek Johnson).

marks. Commanded to flank his sheep – move round to turn them – he will next cross-drive for 150 yards, moving the sheep across the field in front of the handler, some 130 yards from where the man stands, and through the second set of gates. The drive gates are set seven yards apart. The final stint of driving, another 150 yards to complete a driving triangle, is the simplest, really back to the art of bringing sheep as the dog drives them back to his master. Driving points are marked out of 30 and faults are lack of push or power to keep the sheep going in the desired straight lines, too much power or lack of restraint resulting in a galloping race, going too wide on the turns and, of course, missing the hurdles.

Two of the five sheep are marked with red collars and the next test, for ten points, which takes place within a 40 yd diameter circle marked on the ground with sawdust, is one requiring absolute and instant cohesion between man and dog. Two of the three unmarked sheep have to be shed off, or separated, from the remainder.

Shedding is a test of temperament, for after the complete flow of movement of the trial to this point, the collie is asked to become almost immobile as he holds the sheep steady with the strength of his eye for his master to manipulate. Then the dog must spring into action to come between the two and the three sheep. There must be no hesitation when the collie comes through the gap – and he must not waver for a second. This stage tests quickness of decision in the handler and immediate reaction from the dog for, as throughout a

David Carlton's Tony 'lifts' his sheep on the top of the moor – his master (circled) a mere dot in the distance (Derek Johnson).

really successful trial, both must work as one. Faults in the shedding ring are fear and cowardice in facing the sheep, ragged and rash work, failure to act on instruction, too much work left to the handler and opportunity lost.

The shedding test completed, the five sheep are united and herded into a 9 ft by 8 ft pen constructed of hurdles, with an 8 ft hinged gate. Again close teamwork is required for the full ten points, the collie taking one side, the handler the other. The handler controls the gate by holding the end of a 6 ft long rope fixed to the gate. The collie should again be quietly in control, watching to prevent any breaks – any escapes – by the sheep, holding them steady by the strength of his eye, applying or easing off pressure to settle the sheep so that they have no alternative but to enter the pen. Points will be lost for harrying the sheep, for any unsteadiness or slackness in holding them, for rash moves, loss of concentration or interest, and for the cardinal sin of loss of temper resulting in gripping or biting the sheep.

Finally, for ten points, a test of courage. The collie is asked to single off – or take away from its fellows – one of the two sheep with a red collar. Sheep being essentially flock creatures tend to stick together and it is also a test of patience – in both dog and man – to force a gap into which the dog can speedily move to cause the separation. Then comes the trial of strength of will: the dog must 'wear' the sheep, prevent it by dominance of mind from rejoining the other four sheep. This is often a very testing and tense situation and the collie must show his absolute dominance over the sheep until the judges are satisfied with the shout

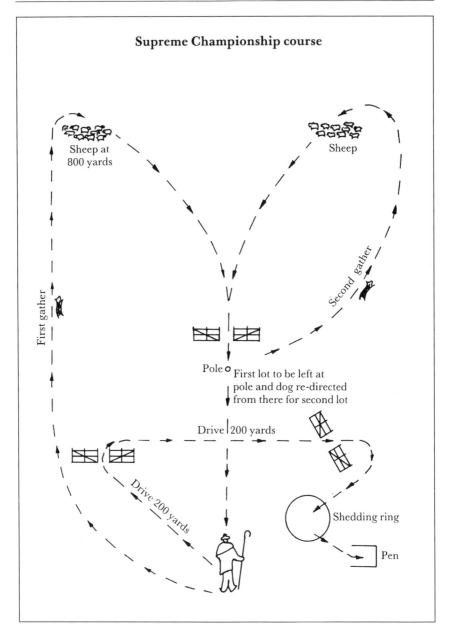

Supreme Championship course

Sheep at
800 yards

Sheep

First gather

Second gather

Pole o First lot to be left at
pole and dog re-directed
from there for second lot

Drive 200 yards

Drive 200 yards

Shedding ring

Pen

'that'll do' to end the trial. Failure to respond to his master's call to
'come through' and cut off the sheep, cowardice in facing up and lack of
power to dominate the sheep are all down-pointed.

Throughout the trial the man and dog should work as a partnership,
with total understanding and confidence in one another, each carrying

The fetch – Harford Logan's Jim from Ireland brings his sheep through the gates in the television competition at Austwick (Derek Johnson).

out his specific role, the handler guiding, the dog answering while using his own intelligence in the method of his contact with the sheep.

Quiet control without undue commands, absolute mastery of the sheep without pressing dominance, and all the work completed within the allotted time of 15 minutes will bring good points. Only in exceptional circumstances – a particularly stubborn ewe facing up to a dog may need a sharp lesson by a nip on the nose – is gripping tolerated. The handler is not allowed to touch the sheep.

Pure, practical, sensible shepherding, where the sheep are treated with respect, will win sheepdog trials.

As you now see from our judging, all the tests incorporated in this National trial are practical ones which a collie dog will be asked to carry out in his daily duties on the home farm.

Outrunning for lifting and fetching stock constitutes the gathering which is the first and most essential part of a collie's job, the gathering of sheep from the moor to bring them home for dipping or shearing, or the cows from the lowland pasture·at milking time. Driving is often gathering in reverse, putting the sheep back on the moor, moving them to a different pasture, sending the cows back to grass. Shedding and singling-off sheep is necessary at almost every inspection of a sheep flock, when sheep are sorted for the tupping, lambing, marketing and for veterinary inspection. The penning is a facsimile of the work of

Twenty sheep are herded in the International Supreme Championship test – Alan Jones' Spot reaching the end of his fetch at Chatsworth 1978 (Marc Henrie).

putting sheep through a narrow gate opening into a byre or yard, or when sheep have to be loaded into the trailer. Indeed, a trailer was actually used to take the place of the accepted hurdle pen in 'One Man and His Dog'.

We have just run through the National type of trial, and this is the test which is also used for the qualifying round at the International.

The big one, the International Supreme, which is the stiffest trials test in the world, is extended to include two separate gathers by the dog. The first for ten sheep at half a mile distance, and the second – after the dog has brought this first flock half-way down the field and through the fetch gate – away a quarter-mile to the opposite corner of the course for another ten sheep.

This second flock is also brought on the fetch through the gate to join the first ten sheep, and then all 20 sheep are taken on a driving test of 600 yards similar to the National layout. Five of the 20 sheep are marked with a red collar and in the shedding ring the dog has to separate these five, and the final test is to put these five into the pen.

Steady pacing as Jean Bousfield's little prick-eared Taff starts to drive his sheep away at Chatsworth, 1978 (Marc Henrie).

Judging methods are exactly the same as we have discussed, with the total points increased to 170 per judge and the time allowed for the work increased to 30 minutes.

The same qualities and faults apply to brace work, when two collies work ten sheep, except that here you are particularly looking for a partnership with each dog doing its full share of the work.

In the Driving test at the International the dog should muster the 50 sheep he has to work and keep them going away from him at a steady trot, nicely bunched, and on the line he is asked by his master. He must show that he has the power and authority to drive the sheep without faltering wherever he is commanded to. They must not be allowed to stop, graze, break away or straggle out of control.

At a National event two judges, both marking out of the total points and aggregating them for the verdict, make the decisions; and at the International four judges, one each from England, Scotland, Wales and Ireland, sit on the same basis of aggregate points. Ireland, with their calibre having increased in stature, had a representative in the judging corps for the first time in 1984.

It is not an easy task to judge these big and important events, and is probably an equivalent honour to a football referee taking charge of the Wembley Cup Final. For three days you are on your toes for some ten hours a day to give an honest decision – and that decision is of the utmost importance to the handler involved. It is the difference between representative honours – and International 'cap' – and failure.

Judging varies – human nature varies – but the basic principle of what is good and what is bad in a collie's work does not. It is just a matter of interpretation. For instance, when I judged the National with Ashton Priestley our only difference of opinion was in the degree of command – I took off more points for excessive use of whistle and voice in controlling a dog. Ashton had a remarkable memory – he could remember in detail exactly what the first dog in a three-day entry had done as well as the last dog at the end of the event. Although it is often said that you are on 'a good hiding to nothing', judging, at times exacting, is very rewarding for you see every detailed move of every dog and come to know its temperament and skills – and failings.

I have known of only two dogs who were adjudged perfect in trials work – Jim Cropper's big upstanding Fleet from the Rossendale Pennines on Rough Fell hoggs at Shap trials in June 1968, and Maurice Collin's 3½-year-old Spot from Skeeby in north Yorkshire on Swaledale gimmers at Sutton, Thirsk, in 1975. The only collies that I've judged almost faultless in trials, being only half a point from perfection, were Timothy Longton's rough coated Rob, and Tim Longton's tricolour Becca from Quernmore in north Lancashire at the 1995 Royal

Lancashire Show's three-day trials at Chorley, where Mule shearlings were most amenable to shepherding, and Evan Hopkin's little tricolour Fly in the championship tests of the British Subaru contest in the Vale of Clwyd in North Wales.

I wasn't alone in my judgment of faulting Fly just half a point of 100, for my co-judge, Gwynfor Pritchard, was of the same opinion.

Small in stature, Fly was big in heart. The Welsh Driving champion of 1983 and winner of television's 'One Man and His Dog' trials in 1983, she was almost perfect in the final of this prestigious trial which had 220 entries, only my critical judging deducting that half-point over the Ffynnogian Fields near Ruthin.

Fly was 8½ years old at the time, had learned her craft with Speckled face ewes and crossbred beef cows at Pengwernydd near Aberystwyth in Mid-Wales, and was utterly reliable in every section of shepherding. In her quiet yet undisputable way with sheep, Fly ran a trial which will long be remembered in Welsh sheepdog circles. She was sired by the quietly efficient, unassuming Craig, winner of the 1977 Supreme championship for John Thomas, out of James's Fly, and she had Griffith's Craig and Gilchrist's Spot in her line.

My first judging stint was for the Hayfield Sheepdog Society at a

Big in heart – one of the best Welsh collies, Evan Hopkins' little tricolour Fly which won the 'One Man and His Dog' televised trials in 1983.

Shedding sheep. Alan Jones and Spot cut away an unwanted ewe, Chatsworth, 1978 (Marc Henrie).

nursery trial, the lowest standard of competition, and I have since travelled northern England, Scotland and into Wales, making lots of friends and deciding some of the top awards. I have found that most of a judge's critics are people who have never been in the 'hot seat' themselves.

Trials are friendly occasions, though, informal for the most part, with prize-money never high enough to encourage nastiness. There is no betting allowed on a trials course. Sufficient is the honour of winning and defeating your neighbour's dog.

I've judged well over 100 open trials and had some happy times, even when I was accused of 'bringing the game into disrepute' when I fell into the River Wenning during judging at Hornby in north Lancashire in 1973 while retrieving sheep, and had to judge for the rest of the day without pants – hidden in the car I hasten to add! I've also judged a trial alongside the famous Bechers Brook at Aintree racecourse when the Royal Lancashire Show held its trials in Liverpool.

The only gripe I have with being invited to judge, which I try to accept for I know how difficult it is sometimes to find a judge, is the time one has to leave home to get to a trial in a faraway place – it could start at 8 am – and the long journey back when the trial could finish as late as 7 pm. Trials organisers should bear this in mind when choosing a judge.

You have to learn to lose before you can become a good winner, and the competition spirit takes men and dogs in different ways. Some handlers are tense and the butterflies dance in their stomachs, their dogs

Two minutes before the supreme victory. Bob Shennan and Mirk ease the sheep into the pen – the final test – to win at Chatsworth, 1978 (Marc Henrie).

catching the mood and straining every nerve and sinew to go into action. Others are relaxed and go to the starting post unmoved, their dogs equally relaxed and ready to please 'the boss'.

Luck is a word often heard in competitions of every kind but a sheepdog trial based on the standard of the International Sheep Dog Society allows little chance of luck playing too great a part. Rarely does luck so favour a badly trained or incompetent collie that it finishes at the top. Luck must undoubtedly enter in some degree, however slight, into a competition of any sort, particularly when five sheep, one man and one dog, possibly of completely differing temperament, are involved.

Some sheep can be particularly trying. An odd one may have been taken from its mates, which are left in the holding pen, and try to break away and return to them. Weather conditions throughout the day's trialling often change, and sheep don't like pushing in the heat of the day – and nor does the dog. Wind and rainstorm upset sheep and add to the shepherd's difficulties of command. But a good dog and an alert handler make their own luck at trials. That is to say, a good and efficient partnership of man and dog can meet all the problems with confidence, capitalise when everything goes right, and use practised ability and experience when difficulties arise. Making full use of good sheep separates the masters of their craft from the not so good and produces champions.

All the good trials throughout the United Kingdom are based on the International layout, the distances for outrunning and driving being fitted to match the terrain of the land. The International Sheep Dog Society, since its inception in 1906, has done a great job in improving the ability of working dogs by its guidance and rules for trials.

The International, as well as being the event at which the best dogs are identified, is also a big social occasion – and a lot more effective in uniting the United Kingdom than any parliamentary act, organisation or decree. For four nights the hotels around the trials course, and especially if the residential area is a small town or village, are subjected in the nicest possible way to impromptu ceilidhs and sing-songs where the Scots, the Welsh, and the Irish vie in voice with each other. We English are mere lookers-on.

The Society also holds its annual dinner during the event. Old friends are greeted, once-a-year meetings enjoyed, old memories awakened and many new friendships made. There is an overall atmosphere of good spirit when the sheepdog International comes to town. Overseas visitors – there are always farmers from Australia, New Zealand, South Africa and America visiting – add spice to the gathering and many a dog grows in stature over a wee dram in the refreshment tent.

The dogs, too, have a relaxed and easy three or four days with 'just those queer-looking sheep to be taught a lesson in front of those cheering people'. Most of the top dogs are fully aware of the occasion and while their main concern is sheep, they are not above the adulation of the watchers and the petting from small children with gooey sweets. But the business is the most serious in the world and the rewards the most valuable in merit.

It all started in July 1906 when a few Scottish and English sheepmen gathered for a meeting at Haddington in East Lothian. Under the chairmanship of George Clark of Eaglescairnie Mains they formed the International Sheep Dog Trials Society with a committee of ten and James Wilson of Lauder Place, East Linton, as secretary. Their avowed intent was to stimulate public interest in the shepherd and his calling and to procure the better management of stock by improving the sheepdog.

Quickly into action, they held their first trials the following month at Gullane Hill by the Firth of Forth, east of Edinburgh, and the 27 entries were all dogs which had won a prize or commendation at a local show and they came from both sides of the Border. In the light of the big rise in present-day entry numbers their 'qualified dogs' rule was a wise one, to make sure that only the best went to the International course.

Gullane was won by Richard Sandilands from Dundas Mains, South Queensferry, with Don, a rough-coated black and white son of James Scott's Old Kep. The Society showed a financial profit of £9 at the end of the day, and the response to the new venture from the farmers and shepherds of the Border region and from Northumberland encouraged progress so that the trials were held annually up to the start of the Great War. Nine one-day trials with one overall championship were held, with five victories going to Englishmen and four to Scots.

Sweep, a grandson of Old Hemp, won twice, once under Adam Telfer of Cambo, the breeder of Old Hemp, and then with Thomas Armstrong of Otterburn. Completing his 'hat-trick' of success, Thomas Armstrong won in 1911 and 1914 with Don, a grandson of Tommy and exported to New Zealand.

James Scott, the famous 'Troneyhill' from Ancrum, won twice with Old Kep, a grand dog, not of the direct Old Hemp line, and in fact the sire that prevented Border dogs from becoming too inbred to Hemp. Kep was a cool, well-balanced collie and won 45 prizes in trials.

James Scott was greatly respected as a handler and in 1929 he wrote, 'It is rather unfortunate that the majority of sheep farmers in this country at least, are not alive to the importance and value of a well-trained collie. If they were, they would encourage in every way possible all attempts to make their canine friend more valuable, serviceable, and efficient. But they don't; few of them are so disposed.' I think that still applies today, even though the International Sheep Dog Society has made great strides.

In 1915 James Reid, who had been a member for three years, took over the secretaryship of the Society, which then held no trophies and had only £5 in funds, but his enthusiasm, hard work and love of working collies was to make the Society world famous in farming circles. He kept interest alive during the dormant war years and wasted no time in gathering his resources so that when the Society was able to recommence activities in 1919 with trials at Lanark he had obtained three trophies and instituted three separate classes of competition.

Hired shepherds had always argued that they were at a disadvantage to self-employed farmers in as much as they had no stock of their own on which to train their dogs and had not the same facilities for attending local trials. So Mr Reid formed separate Shepherds' and Farmers' classes in addition to the general championship. These separate classes continued until 1975 when it was felt that, under modern circumstances, shepherds were no worse off than farmers in both training and time facilities. Nowadays the Shepherds' championship is awarded to the highest scoring shepherd's dog in the same classification of competitors as farmers at both National and International level.

In 1921 Wales showed interest in the Society and E. Jones Jarrett, of Corwen, was invited to be one of the judges at the Ayr International that year. The following year Wales joined the Society and, to mark the occasion, the International was held at Criccieth, and the organisation as it runs today, with the Society divided into national sections, was evolved.

The first time that National events were held as one-day trials was in 1922. Alex Millar won Scotland's trials at Lanark with the rough-coated Spot, a young black and white dog which went on to win three more National championships and the International championship in 1925. At York Ernest Priestley of Hathersage in Derbyshire was England's winner with the four-year-old Moss, winner also the following year and a collie of Dickson's Hemp line, as was the Welsh winner at Llandudno, John Pritchard's black and tan Laddie, the son of Hunter's Sweep, winner of two International Shepherds' championships before being exported to New Zealand.

In 1927 the first team contest – won by England – was introduced, and in 1929 the first Brace contest – won by Alex Millar for Scotland – and in 1937 the first Driving championship – won by J. M. Renwick of Alston – were added to the International programme, which in 1926 had become a three-day event, as it is today. Brace competitions were included in the National events in 1931 and Driving competitions in 1938.

Northern Ireland entered the International in 1961 and sent a team of

Thomas Gilholm and Lord Mostyn watch the International trials at Ayr in 1933.

three single dogs, and from 1965 when Eire joined the entry was known as Ireland, with four single dogs and one Brace entry. Collies from the Isle of Man are classed as part of the Irish section which, in 1979, to match a rapidly growing membership and improvement in collie quality, had an International representation of eight singles, two Brace and one Driving entry. By 1993 Irish dogs were considered good enough to have a full team of 15, like the other three countries.

James Reid retired from the Society's secretaryship in 1946, having created an organisation which had brought the working collie out of obscurity and fulfilled all the intents of that meeting at Haddington in 1906. He had framed a set of rules for trials work which are basically unaltered today, and in this materialistic world, where money is the criterion of achievement, had increased the modest 'fiver' of 1906 to £2,695. His foundation was built upon by T. H. Halsall of Southport, who produced the Society's first written constitution and inaugurated the Stud Book which lists the pedigrees of all registered working collies and to the end of 1994 included 216,113 dogs.

Three subsequent secretaries who each left their mark were Wilfred Dunn, who handed over more of the actual trials work to practical men; T. J. W. Evans, whose main contribution was in ministering the Society's finances; and Lance Alderson, who instigated the first major sponsorship for the Society. Today the secretarial work is in the capable hands of Philip Hendry, who has greatly streamlined the Society, fostered sponsorship and general good relations with kindred associations,

The first of the best – Richard Sandilands's Don, the first collie to win the International Championship in 1906 at Gullane.

The site of the first ever International Trials as it is today – Gullane 1906 (Frank H. Moyes).

and obtained the acclaim and publicity which was lacking and which has greatly increased membership to around 6,300.

In addition to its secretaries many men have served the International Sheep Dog Society well, and none better than Archie McDiarmid, its chairman from 1968 to 1974 who, almost single-handed, revised the constitution to cater for the growing interest in sheepdogs. A wise man whose knowledge of collie dogs was profound, he was always fair and fearless in his leadership of the Society. He died in 1994, having been a member of the Society since 1920, a Director since 1926, and he was the Society's International President in 1976. I spent many happy and tuitional hours in his company, which lightened for me the often tedious hours in the public announcer's van at the English Nationals.

There are many people who have nurtured the growth of the Society

Isaac Herdman's Tommy, a dog which had a great influence in improving the standard of working collies throughout the world.

Left: *Dr Keith Barnett who did so much to control PRA in the Border Collie.*
Right: *Alan Leak's Roy, from Gaisgill, gets his eyes tested before competing in the 1979 International trials at Stanraer* (Marc Henrie).

and whose work behind the scenes in all the four member countries is often overlooked. Since 1965 Dr Keith Barnett has been a popular visitor to National and International trials and his work for the Society was of the utmost importance. In conjunction with the Society's Stud Book committee and with the full co-operation of members Dr Barnett has steadily been working towards the eradication of Progressive Retinal Atrophy (PRA) from the collie, and examined all collies which competed at International level – the top stud dogs – over 20 years. The majority of cases of PRA can be diagnosed at two years old, and the progeny of affected dogs are now refused entry to the Society's Stud Book. Since the Society came to recognise the defect of PRA and Dr Barnett started his examinations in 1965 the incidence of the disease has been reduced in dogs examined from 12 per cent to less than two per cent and the condition is now under control.

CHAPTER SEVEN

Caps Off to the Master

Jim Wilson, the master of sheepdog handling, proved that breeding counts by the almost mythical skills of his collies which became sheepdog legend. I linger down memory lane, savouring their greatness.

Scottish farmer James McMorran Wilson, MBE, who died in July 1975 following a road accident at the age of 74, is still regarded as the master of the art of collie handling, and rightly so if his successes on the trials fields are any yardstick. In 19 years of competing at National and International trials JM, as he was known throughout the world, won 55 trophies including nine Supreme championships, a record as fantastic as the intelligence of his dogs.

From Jim Wilson I got much encouragement as an agricultural journalist, for he was always constructively critical, wise in his counsels and the undoubted authority on sheepdogs. I listened to his every word with respect. He became master of competitive shepherding through-out Britain but he was primarily a breeder of pedigree Blackface sheep in the Southern Uplands of Scotland and it was for their management that he needed wise dogs.

Blackface sheep, the pride of Scotland with their tasty lean lamb meat and Harris tweed wool, need moving around a lot to get the best pasturing, and assisting JM in the management of sheep which made record prices at the Lanark ram sales was the collies' prime purpose in life. In the autumn of 1955 a Blackface ram lamb from Jim Wilson's Whitehope Farm at the head of Leithen Water, some five miles from Peebles, was sold for £2,600 – well over £10,000 by today's prices – to create at the time a price record for any breed of sheep in Britain. The sheep entrusted to the care of his dogs were of high quality and the standard of that care spread their reputation throughout the farming world. Two weeks before the Whitehope lamb made that record price,

Wilson's Bill and Nap had run first and second in the International Supreme championship at Edinburgh.

Was there ever a better example of man and dogs working as a team for the welfare of a sheep flock than the incident during heavy snow-fall in 1937 at Whitehope Farm? Just before the start of March bliz-zards which were to sweep the Borders and cause heavy sheep losses, hundreds of the Whitehope ewes, all heavy in lamb, sensed the coming storm and moved down the hill to lower ground over a mile from the farm buildings. When the snow came they were sheltered and screened from the brunt of the storm by a clump of woodland and the stone dyke, and all were safely pastured.

But though the snowfall ceased the driving winds continued to blow for days afterwards and soon sheep were being covered by drifting snow to become buried from sight. Even so the situation was under control. Jim's six-year-old Roy, a black and white rough-coated dog who, though he only had the full sight of one eye, was compensated with a good nose and the wisdom to scent out buried sheep. With Roy finding and Jim digging, the sheep were released from their icy tombs. Later in the year Roy was to win his third Supreme International Trials Cham-pionship at Cardiff to create a yet unequalled trials record.

Life for the sheep in the pasture only began to get desperate when there was no break in the weather. The hard labour of digging out sheep and carting food through the mile of deep snow-covered track was becoming too onerous and exacting to continue. Jim decided that the sheep must come to the food. Taking little Nell, Roy's seven-year-old half-sister and so wise in the ways of sheep, to shed-off ten of the strongest ewes in the flock, he used them to batter down a way through the snow over which the rest of the flock could follow to the farm.

With Jim digging away the deepest drifts in front, Nell, knowing exactly what was required of her, drove the ten trail-breakers into the snow, pushing, forcing, willing them on. It took over five hours to reach the farm buildings and Nell, her coat white and frozen with snow, was physically exhausted though her spirit was undimmed. Jim called that 'her finest hour' – far outclassing her winning of two Scottish National trials championships – for that was essential, indeed life-saving, practical shepherding. Behind her trail-blazing the sheep flock was driven along the trampled route by her kennel-mates, Roy and his famous sire Craig, the two dogs working entirely under their own initiative until every ewe was safely delivered.

On the trials field Roy won six International and five National cham-pionships, Nell won two International and seven National championships, and Craig won two International and three National championships – but their true value was really shown on that cold snowy day in March 1937 in

Jim Wilson's Roy – the most famous dog in the world.

the Scottish Borders. By their deeds Roy, Nell and Craig, and their equally successful kennel-mates and successors at Whitehope, Fly, Nickey, Cap, Glen, Mirk, Moss, Tib, Bill and Nap became part of collie history and were used extensively for breeding purposes so that their bloodlines have played a major part in collie evolution. Of these 12 dogs, and there were others, six of them won the Supreme International trials championship. Roy won the coveted honour three times, in 1934, 1936 and 1937, for an all-time record, and Glen, remembered for his brisk and controlled driving, became only the fifth collie ever to win more than one International and only the second to win two Supremes, in 1946 and 1948.

Probably the greatest trials dog of all time, Jim Wilson's handsome one-eyed black and white Roy was equally good on the hill. On the competitive field, in addition to his three Supremes, he won three other International titles and five National championships, and on the uplands of Whitehope he brought an uncanny skill to the shepherding care of one of the finest Blackface flocks in the Borders.

Undoubtedly he had the quality of genius, that little extra to his absolute knowledge of the ways of sheep. He was confident in his manner, purposeful in his shepherding and decisive in all his actions. He coupled solid ability with initiative, he had speed of action with gentle but assertive control, and his method made sheep respect his presence.

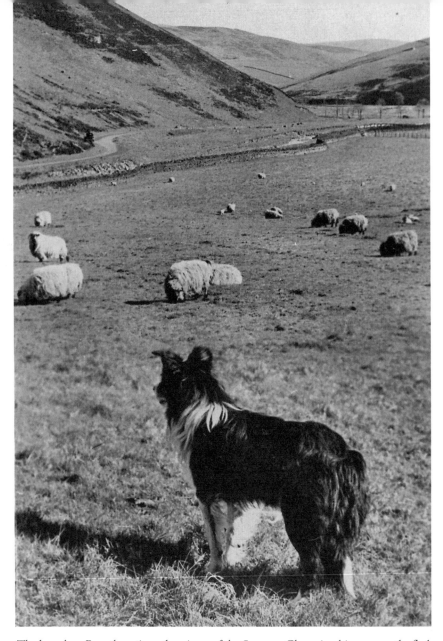

The legendary Roy, three times the winner of the Supreme Championship, surveys the flock he herded at Whitehope in the Scottish Borders.

In turn he respected the man he worked with and enjoyed the easy grace of a true craftsman. He was never servile and enjoyed a romp with his fellmates, just as any young dog when off-duty, for Jim Wilson was never a harsh disciplinarian. He controlled his dogs rather than commanded them and Roy knew the limits of his tolerance.

Roy was fortunate to have a master with such profound knowledge of the canine mind, for at times he displayed a shocking temperament, a sulkiness inherited from his father, Craig, winner of the 1930 Supreme championship. In less knowledgeable hands Roy would never have become a sheepdog legend. Indeed, he may never have risen to such great heights had he not had a sulky dispute when he was only a youngster with his half-brother Jix. He was beaten by the taller Jix and lost the sight of one eye. Hitherto almost useless as a worker and physically retarded by a dose of distemper (though JM still had faith in him), Roy had shown little promise of things to come but the fight with Jix stirred some latent instinct and he started to work seriously. It was almost as though the physical defeat by Jix became a challenge. 'If I can't lick him in a fight, I'll lick him at his craft.' Though his sight improved Roy was virtually a one-eyed dog after the fight, but this defect never appeared to handicap him. He grew in stature with experience and training and developed into a shepherding genius.

Roy would move up on a packet of sheep in a quiet, forthright manner, his approach direct but never hurried, his gaze intent on their eyes, demanding submission to his will. He drove with a balanced easy grace, controlling his speed to the nature of the ground and the strength of the sheep. He knew his master's Blackface flock on the Moorfoot Hills intimately as individuals, for no two sheep are exactly alike. He knew their hefts, where each one grazed, their strengths, their weaknesses – knowledge of immense value to any shepherd.

This ability to identify sheep, which is well developed in the minds of most good collies, served Roy well in trials. It is just not possible to expect any dog to assess the personality of a sheep in the short space of a trial, but Roy was quick to know the leader, the stronger willed, the awkward one, and he reacted accordingly, using either gentle or more assertive power to master it.

On occasion at home he had to use force to control a particularly obstinate ewe. This he did by a quite deliberate grip of his teeth. Such gripping – without anger – is the final resort to mastery and, though one of the great bones of contention in trials work, a collie which cannot be trusted to grip a sheep without harming it is of little use on the farm. A collie's only weapon of defence against a charging sheep is its mouth. The finished, complete Roy, winner of three Supreme International championships and canine protector of the pedigree Blackfaces of Whitehope, was the product of good breeding and skilful training.

Handsomely black and white, and rough coated in appearance with the typical white ruff of his kind, Roy was the son of Craig, himself renowned as a hill and trials dog, out of the legendary Loos, reputed at the time to be the greatest sheep bitch that ever lived and the 1925

Pedigree of ROY (1665) 1934, 1936, 1937 Supreme Champion with Jim Wilson

The numbers in brackets are the Stud Book numbers of the International Sheep Dog Society
— Indicates that this dog is not known

International Farmers' champion with William Wallace of Fingland, Dalry, in Galloway.

Craig, who left his influence on Border shepherding in a reputed 900 pups and won two International and three National titles on the trials field for Jim Wilson, was mothered by Alistair Craig's Mist, another great breeding bitch on Arran whose great-grandsire was Don, winner

Jim Wilson of Whitehope, nine times winner of the Supreme International Championship, with Whitehope Nap and Bill at the Edinburgh International in 1955.

of the 1911 and 1914 International championships and subsequently exported to the New Zealand sheep ranges.

Craig's father was Thomas Dickson's black and white rough-coated Hemp who, though slightly bowed on his front legs, was a sturdy animal. The son of Fenwick's Jed, another collie which went to New Zealand to James Lillico, whose imported dogs set a collie standard in that country, Hemp won the 1924 International Farmers' title but really earned his place in sheepdog history as a stud-dog. Mated with Wallace's Loos, he sired some of the greatest sheepdogs in the Borders and stamped quality on the working dog.

Perhaps the most successful breeding pair of all time, Hemp and Loos were the parents of Jim Wilson's two clever bitches, Fly and Nell. Fly, a bonny alert bitch born in 1926 in a Scottish byre, was only 2½ years old when she won JM his first Supreme title at Llandudno, and those Welsh sheep seemed to suit her for when the International returned to Llandudno in 1931 she won the Farmers' championship. At the Scottish National trials she in turn partnered her workmates, Craig, Nell and Roy, to three Brace championships. Keen eyed and ever watchful, she had a white chest and white forelegs and she was pictured by the

Fly, Jim Wilson's Supreme Champion of 1928.

Wallace's Loos, a famous brood bitch.

Scott's Old Kep, International Champion in 1908 and 1909.

Dickson's Hemp, the greatest stud dog of his day.

International Sheep Dog Society after her 1928 victory sitting proudly by the Supreme championship shield which dwarfed her in size – and which her master eventually won outright after his third success in 1934 with Roy. Fly cost Jim Wilson a mere £4 when he bought her for his herding, then at Holmshaw, Moffat, in Dumfriesshire.

Little Nell was born in 1930 and she won three Scottish National titles, all at Helensburgh. Rough coated and black and white, the most delightful of collies, she struck up a great partnership with Roy, one year her junior, and together they won three successive Scottish Brace titles and two successive International Brace championships between 1936 and 1938. In feminine terms she was pretty, but not just a pretty face for she had brains to match her beauty. A lovely sensitive bitch, she was keenly intelligent with an alert poise and commanding manner.

Winner of the 1935 and 1936 Scottish National titles, she was beaten by half a point from earning a true 'hat-trick' by Roy for the 1937 championship. When Roy had his tantrums on the home farm it was either Fly or Nell who invariably stepped in to mitigate his sulky mood.

Nickey, the winner of the 1933 International Farmers' and Scottish National championships, made a big contribution in lifting the skills of herding sheep in Australia. Her own skill so encouraged the Queensland sheepmen to improve the standards of their own dogs that her importation to Edgar Ferrier was an important milestone in Australian collie history.

Jim Wilson had great faith in Loos blood which produced consistently good and amazingly intelligent sheepdogs, able to cope with the daily rigours of shepherding the Border uplands. All his post-war champions were of the line, and Glen, son of John Kirk's good-natured Nell and Willie Hislop's Glen, earned the distinction of being the first-ever collie to win the Supreme and the International Farmers' championships at the same trial, at Worcester in 1948. He had two years previously won the Supreme at Edinburgh.

Mirk, grandson of and line-bred to his master's great hill dog, Cap, was the winner of the Scottish National and the International Supreme in the same year, in 1950.

Loos herself was bred by James Reid, the secretary of the International Sheep Dog Society, in May 1921, sired by Telfer's Laddie out of Loos I, and her bloodline ran back through the 1907 International champion Moss to Herdman's Tommy and Old Kep. She went to William Wallace at Fingland in Galloway when she was only eight months old and ran her first international trial in 1924. In 1925 she won the International Farmers' championship at Criccieth in Wales but her fame eventually came from her qualities as a brood bitch. Blue blooded

The legendary Loos.

herself, wisely mated, and the most diligent and gentle of mothers, Loos produced and reared the most successful collies of her time.

Loos was a little stocky brood bitch, well built, rough-haired, with a white chest and forelegs, and her left ear flopping below her right giving her a jaunty appearance. The mother of collies which won 11 International and 16 National championships, she died on 7 January 1937 at the ripe old age of 15½ years, described as 'one of the most amazing animals the world has ever known'.

In every branch of livestock breeding there are sires and dams which can be said to have stamped a great influence in moulding the ideal. Loos was one of those dams and her great breeding partner, Dickson's Hemp, was one of those sires. Different in line to Loos, Hemp was also of Old Hemp breeding through Herdman's Tommy, and their progeny were, consequently, line-bred to Tommy, a dog whose influence in improving the standard of working collies throughout the world has not been truly acclaimed.

Hemp was a strong dog bred during the Great War by Adam Telfer in Northumberland. His shepherding skills were nurtured by Walter Telfer at Fairnley between Otterburn and Morpeth before he went over the Border to Thomas Dickson at Crawfordjohn, with whom he won the 1924 International Farmers' championship. His sire was Yarrow, his dam Fenwick Jed, both of whom were subsequently exported to New Zealand. Hemp and Loos were thus of the Tommy bloodline – Hemp through Telfer's Yarrow and Herdman's Tyne, and Loos through Reid's Loos I, Tom Gilholm's Lille, and the 1907 International champion William Wallace's Moss, a dog with Scott's Old Kep influence and sent to New Zealand as Border Boss.

Inbreeding can produce genius or idiocy and Tommy, who was the product of a mating between a bitch called Gyp and her brother's son from Old Hemp, was close to genius, yet fettered with unwanted traits. In spite of this, or perhaps because of this, due to his breeding qualities he actually became one of the greatest sheepdogs of his time and he gave great strength to the Border Collie breed. He was clever on sheep but much too strong willed to be handled with effective control. Always he wanted to do things his way – which was so often the right way.

But wise breeding with bitches gentle enough to dilute the strengths to manageable amounts without sacrificing his intelligence produced sons and daughters with most of his best herding qualities and few of his faults. Two of his sons, Moss and Lad, out of James Scott's Ancrum Jed and Andrew Brown's Old Maid, reflected his tempered skills to win the International championships of 1907 and 1913. Tommy was not a good-looking dog, with his wolf-like head, albeit filled with brains, and perhaps it is because of this that historically he has not received the recognition due to him, though in 1938 John Herries McCulloch, the most discerning of sheepdog historians, wrote: 'Tommy was a most prepotent dog and the best representatives of the modern breed are descended from his progeny.'

Even so, it is doubtful if Tommy's impact on the Border Collie breed has been truly accepted. His grandsire, Old Hemp, is always regarded as the foundation sire of the modern Border Collie and it is true that apart from Tommy, Old Hemp created outstanding work-lines through Sweep, the 1910 champion, and through William Wallace's Hemp. But when John Herries McCulloch did a genealogical chart of international champions from 1906 to 1951, showing that the 29 collies which won 35 championships were all descendants of Old Hemp, only two of them were actually free of Tommy's blood. And the influence continues, though obviously with the passing of years other dominant animals have made their mark. Every one of the 36 Supreme champions from 1960 to 1995 were descendants of Tommy, including Wiston Cap, winner of the 1965 title when he was only 23 months old. He has left his own particular stamp on the present-day Border Collie.

Other great collies in this honours list are Gwyn Jones's Bill and his black and white Queen from a herding in the Mignaint range of Snowdonia; Glyn Jones's super-intelligent Gel from the hill of Bodfari, champion of the International Sheep Dog Society's centenary trials at Bala in 1973 and reserve champion in 1975; Thomson McKnight's most reliable Gael from the Borders, the greatest sheep bitch of all time and the 1967 champion; Tim Longton's clever Ken from a Dalesbred flock on the gale-lashed Pennines of north Lancashire, winning in 1966.

The list is so extensive – Bob Shennan's mottled Mirk from a Black-face herding in Ayrshire; John Thomas's 7½-year-old Craig from work in the Eppynt Hill range of Mid-Wales; Gwyn Jones's big white-headed Shep with a flock of Welsh Mountain ewes at Penmachno in North Wales; Raymond MacPherson's handsome Zac from watching over horned ewes on the Cumbrian fells; John Templeton's 4½-year-old Cap from Fenwick Moor by Kilmarnock and now in America; John Murray's tall black and white merled Glen from Sanquhar in the Borders; Davie McTeir's tricolour Bill from a Blackface herding in Manor Glen in Peeblesshire; Harry Huddleston's trim little Bett with Dalesbred sheep and pedigree Friesian cows in Lancashire's Lune Valley; and Llyr Evans's four-year-old Bosworth Coon with 300 halfbred ewes and beef cows in the lowlands of Northamptonshire.

All were Supreme champions, as were John Mackenzie's smooth tricolour Don from a Cheviot sheep herding on the hills above Oldshoremore on the north-western seaboard of Britain; Lancashire's Thomas Longton with the little Bess, so confident in her herding of the most unruly sheep over extensive rising grassland on the island of Anglesey in 1986; Sydney Price's six-year-old Davy from Cressage in Shropshire, winner at Woburn in Bedfordshire; Meirion Jones's hand-some Spot from managing 400 halfbred ewes and 60 beef cows above the Vale of Cwlyd; Alasdair MacRae's 3½-year-old rough-coated Nan from work on Blackface and Cheviot ewes near Loch Leven; and Stuart Davidson's black and white Craig with Blackface sheep on Loch Fynside in Argyll.

Dual champions in recent years Bobby Dalziel's white-bibbed Wisp from ground which rises over 2,000 ft above the Ettrick Valley in the Borders, and John Wilson's rough-coated Spot from Ettrick Forest were both descendants of Tommy. Tommy was described as an ugly-looking dog and it is interesting that one of his most famous descendants, Alan Jones's Roy, winner of the 1961 Supreme championship at Ayr, would have won no honours for beauty when he was a puppy. In fact Roy was an ugly little pup who grew into one of the greatest collies that Wales has known, working with Welsh ewes and Welsh Black cattle on the home farm of Pontllyfni on the Lleyn Peninsula and winning seven National and three International championships on the trials field.

Always Jim Wilson sought to keep the bloodlines of Tommy, Hemp and Loos in his collies and one of the best was a dog which never had its skills reflected on the trials fields. Because of the abandonment of trials during the Second World War, Cap, a big white-headed collie who herded the Blackfaces while the German bombers flew the Border skies, never came to the public eye, though his ability as a herding dog was known throughout the locality.

Home-produced food was of the utmost importance for a beleaguered nation during Cap's finest years, and with meat finely rationed every ounce of flesh which could be kept on growing lambs by quiet handling was vital. Cap was master of his craft. On windswept hills which rise to 2,000 ft no other food could grow and good management, always essential to produce the best, was of even greater importance in wartime. To this end Cap gave his whole energy and skills, never lonely in working with the man he respected and loved, faithfully following a daily routine which produced prime food for the nation, and oblivious of the fame and renown of his forebears which was equally his right.

I wonder if anyone ever assessed the value of the working collie to Britain's war effort in terms of food – and also in wool for clothing? Involved in the wool trade in Galashiels, 15 miles from Whitehope, at

Wilson's Cap who created a line of champions.

The black and white Glen, Supreme Champion in 1946 and 1948 with Jim Wilson.

the time, I certainly realised its great contribution to the Border production of garment wool and sheep-meat.

Fame did come to Cap, though he never enjoyed its glory, for it was
through the success of his sons and daughters that this supremely intelligent dog eventually became renowned. Descended from his master's
Craig, the 1930 International champion, and from seven other International champions, Cap, born in July 1937, passed on his skills to the
puppies he sired. The most renowned of these was Nell, his daughter
from McCaskie's Moss, who came to be known as the mother of
champions and who earned her place in trials history when three of her
sons finished in the top three placings at the International trials at
Worcester in 1948.

Jim Wilson's five-year-old Glen was first and his older brother Willie
Hislop's Sweep was third, both sired by Hislop's Glen, and Wilson's
Moss, a 2½-year-old son of the 1950 Supreme champion Wilson's
Mirk, was second. Willie Hislop's Sweep had earlier won the Scottish
National title, and he added the International Driving championship to
his honours at Worcester. Sweep was 15 months older than his brother
Glen and they were great contenders on the trials field, their matching
skills never better demonstrated than two years previously in the Scottish National at Stirling when they tied for the championship on 96½ of
100 points and Glen won the title on a run-off. Later in the same year,
at the International, Glen won the Supreme and Sweep the Farmers'
honour for Scotland. They were two consistently good collies.

Their mother Nell, with John Kirk at Shoestanes by Heriot Water in
Midlothian, was prevented by the war years from showing her own

skills at trials though she was happiest and most efficient on the hill. She had plenty of power with a flock and was very wise in sheep lore. Gentle by nature, she had a method and style characteristic of her line, and she was so easy to handle, always biddable and willing to please, for she took a pride in doing the right thing. A healthy black and white bitch, she produced fit and wise puppies twice a year for nine years, and even when she was 12 years old was still able to run out a mile to gather sheep.

Jim Wilson's Moss was one of Nell's 44 puppies and he was a most unlucky dog when it came to the big trials, though he contributed a lot to the working bloodlines. One of his sons, John Evans's Tweed, carried on the tradition of winning Supreme championships in 1958.

Moss, by his master's Mirk, the grandson of Cap, never won at National or International level though he came close, running reserve champion at the Internationals of 1948 and 1949. Born in 1946, he developed the ability of his clan, won his first trials prize over the novice course at Lakeland's famous Rydal 'dog-day' when two years old and, less than two months later, was second at the International in competition with the cleverest collies in the land.

Jim Wilson left the International Trials scene with a flourish in 1955 at Edinburgh, winning outright his third Supreme championship shield and his second Farmers' championship shield with the handsome four-year-old Bill, a great-grandson of Cap. For good measure he also took the reserve honour in both the Supreme and Farmers' contests with another great-grandson of Cap, Nap, the smooth-coated 4½-year-old collie which he had handled in the Scottish championship and his fourth outright win of the National trophy the previous month.

Bill's sire was Anderson's Garry, a proven work dog of wide acclaim, and he was bred by John Kirk from his Nell line. In his winning of the Farmers' title on Blackface ewes he dropped only 3½ of 165 aggregate points from the three judges with an almost perfect stint of trials shepherding.

Bill was sold to America, to Ray Parker, but Nap stayed at White-hope to become one of the best known breeding sires in the world of sheepdogs. Nap, with a broad head, strong muscle and good bone, was compact as a coiled spring. A medium-sized black and white bare-skinned dog, he became known as Scotland's power dog. His matings replenished and strengthened Tommy's bloodlines and influence as Cap's had done, and shepherding in the Borders and the north of England, where he was extensively used as a breeding sire, showed a marked improvement from the influence of his progeny.

An example of Nap's influence and improvement of general shepherding standards, and the interest shown by farmers in his proven

Pedigree of CAP (3036) with Jim Wilson of Whitehope in the Scottish Borders

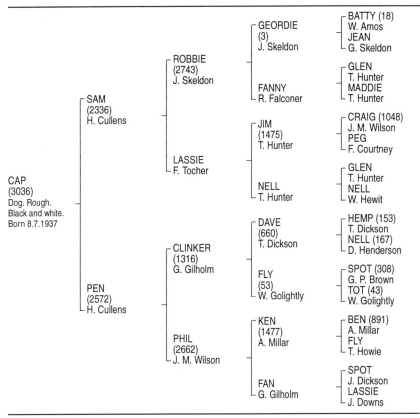

The numbers in brackets are the Stud Book numbers of the International Sheep Dog Society

ability, was reflected in the statistics of collies taking part in Pennine nursery trials, the starting level of trials competition at which many farmers with no aspirations for open trials work compete during the winter months. The collies taking part more accurately reflect the general standards of an area's working dogs than the open trials. In three seasons which I analysed in the 1960s, eight Nap-bred collies won 20 per cent of the total awards in the first season; another eight 'Nappers', seven dogs and one bitch, earned 53 awards or 40 per cent of the total in the second season; and in the third – the 1965–6 season – 12 Nap-bred collies, seven dogs and five bitches, won 72 awards, 41 per cent of total awards.

A review of the International championships over recent years shows

Pedigree of WHITEHOPE NAP (8685) 1955 Scottish Champion with Jim Wilson

The numbers in brackets are the Stud Book numbers of the International Sheep Dog Society
— Indicates that this dog is not known

the immense influence of Nap blood on working dogs, an influence carried on by his great-grandson Wiston Cap in recent years. Of the last 20 Supreme champions, 12 are of the Nap bloodline. In 1974 all the five champions in the Supreme, Farmers', Shepherds', Driving and Brace contests were of Nap line; in 1971 the leading seven collies carried his blood; and in 1965 when Wiston Cap won the top honour, four of the five champion collies were of Nap breeding.

In the 16 years from 1971, when Jock Murray, a 66-year-old Dumfriesshire shepherd from Sanquhar, realised a lifetime's ambition when his tall black and white merled Glen won the Supreme championship at Cardiff, three sons, three grandsons and one granddaughter of Wiston Cap have won eight Supreme championships.

Little Nell, three times Scotland's champion.

Collies of the Whitehope Nap line are good in the right hands, which I suppose is true of any strain, but they are so quick witted and strong that as my old friend Len Greenwood used to say, 'If the handler can match their speed of thought and action they are the best in the world, if he can't and his mind is one split second behind the dog's, they are the worst.' Generally they are very fast, quick to change direction and keen to work, and consequently they can become very hot tempered if not handled firmly. Nap's most famous daughter was Thomson McKnight's Gael from Glencartholm in the Valley of the Esk, the winner of the 1967 Supreme championship and for seven successive years in Scotland's International team.

Nap was perhaps the most controversial breeding sire of them all. You either liked his progeny or you hated them – there were no half-measures – and much depended on your own ability as a handler.

He was born on 2 January 1951, one of a litter of two dogs and one bitch sired by William McClure's Glen out of McClure's Meg at Maidland, Wigtown. His maternal grandam was Kirk's Nell, showing that right to the last of his great dogs Jim Wilson was correct in his assessment of the fine quality of Tommy–Hemp–Loos bloodlines.

All Jim Wilson's dogs were first class, equally skilful in working the Border hills without putting undue stress on the Blackface ewes or the relatively confined trials fields where small packets of sheep could be extra flighty. Canine enough to be playful and boisterous when with their contemporaries at competitive events, they settled immediately to the serious job of working sheep when their turn came. They seemed to sense the big occasion and blended perfectly with a man who never really petted them yet never raised his hand to them and always treated them with respect.

JM was, of course, a remarkable man and when he won his ninth Supreme championship at Edinburgh in 1955 it was not only the Border men who rejoiced. Sheepmen from all parts of Britain and from several countries overseas took off their hats to 'the master', as they called him. Yet despite his great successes and his newsworthiness, he was in a way rather a shy man and shunned publicity.

His is a record which will probably never be beaten, for no other man has won the world's greatest sheepdog honour more than three times. And it started almost by accident. When he was farming at Holmshaw, Moffat, he was entered for his first trial by his father and he won a limited class prize with an unregistered bitch called Nell. His first International was at Ayr in 1921 when he was 20 years old. The climb to the top had begun.

Jim Wilson had natural skills with collie dogs, but he worked hard at learning the handler's art. He had great powers of patience and concentration and he developed a will to win, so essential in all competitive ventures. Every trial was important and long before it was his turn to run he studied the work of his contemporaries, the layout of the course and the whims of the sheep. When he did go to the post he handled quietly and speedily, keeping his dogs on their toes and the sheep on the move.

Jim's knowledge of dogs was profound and he had a way with animals, anticipating the actions of both dogs and sheep. Above all he had faith in his dogs, they knew it and responded to form a perfect partnership. First and foremost JM was a practical sheep farmer, and he had plenty of work for his dogs so that their skills were naturally developed. Roy, bringing sheep from the 2,000 ft heights of Whitehope Law, Glen driving ewes at a brisk walk across the slope of the hill, or Mirk swinging away on the whistle to collect a wayward group were everyday happenings and rarely did the dogs need what may be termed as 'trials tuition'.

JM trained collies which won 12 Supreme International championships in all, handling six of them to win his own nine titles. In addition to these nine Supremes he won six International Farmers' and two

International Brace championships, and 11 Scottish National and six Scottish Brace titles, but perhaps his most treasured trials memento was an inscribed gold watch which King George V gave to him after a 'command performance' at Balmoral. He was known world-wide as the greatest sheepdog handler of all time, and honoured by his country when he received the MBE for services to agriculture.

Thorough in all he did, he took over the duties of Scotland's International Course Director when he retired from competition, and he taught me much when I subsequently took the job of Course Director for England. It was always a revealing privilege to discuss collies with JM, for his experiences were so wide and his knowledge so practical.

CHAPTER EIGHT

What of Today?

❧❧❧

I ponder on whether today's collies are as good as their predecessors, consider the evidence in the lean and bountiful years of International trials, and the results of breeding from the Supreme champions, including the great Wiston Cap.

Jim Wilson and his magnificent collies have passed into the annals of sheepdog lore and, with such memories as they left to stir the mind, it is a common enough topic to compare the dogs of today.

Much depends on one's age, for the dogs of yesteryear grow in stature with the passing of time. But make no mistake, they were good, and the names and qualities of earlier champions, both on and off the trials field, stay fresh in the mind. And let us not forget that they were the foundation stock of the dog which we know today.

Can today's collie match the power and balance of Northumberland shepherd Bob Fraser's rough-coated Nickey, of the famous Mindrum line, in the control of a packet of Cheviot ewes, or the combination of intelligence and stamina which made Jim Wilson's white-headed Cap master of the Border sheep-runs? Recall the uncanny understanding of Spot, one of Scotland's most successful champions, with Alex Millar; the ballet-like balance of Jimmy Millar's smooth-coated Speed when penning sheep; the easy movement of black and white Vic under David Murray from Glenbield near Peebles when lifting sheep at the start of the fetch. Remember Priestley's Hemp, faultless to the end when at 12 years old he ran his last trial to perfection at Cawthorne near Barnsley in 1937? So temperamentally sound, he won the English National title for Ernest Priestley in 1930, and three years later was one of the English Brace-winning pair for Ernest's son, Ashton. Remember Chip, the rough-coated black and white dog from Henglyn Farm, Ystradgynlais, near Swansea, and the businesslike way he went about winning the 1949 and 1952 Supreme championships for David

The end product of trials encourages a collie to use its inbred skills where it matters most, in the management of the home herd on the hill. Ray Ollerenshaw's Shep above the Ladybower Reservoir in Derbyshire (Marc Henrie).

William Danial? What of the qualities, the temperament and brains of Joseph Relph's Bright, Harry Huddleston's Maddie, Bill Sanderson's Vic, Thomas Roberts's Jaff, John Gilchrist's Spot I and David Dickson's Ben? All showed us that power is allied to balance and is so essential in the good stock dog.

Such individuals of the past were indeed unsurpassable, but even they never faced the many and varied trials tests on so many different breeds of sheep over differing courses as there are today; and undoubtedly the breed as a whole – the dogs used for everyday farm herding – cannot possibly have reached today's general standards, though there is always plenty of room for further improvement under the conditions of modern farming.

To win an open trial today a collie has to better perhaps 100 contestants, often triple the number of 30 years ago. Conversely, there are more losers to face criticism for their failures!

Collies today are big business, dogs often changing hands for over a thousand pounds, and there is a flourishing export market to the sheep-runs of Australia, New Zealand, South Africa and America, so that the progeny of current champions can command high prices.

Perhaps the danger here is that by using only dogs which may have had a flash of success the bloodlines are dangerously narrowed down. This is not the fault of trials, but of the men who cannot properly use the results of trials. Skilful breeders are, of course, aware of the danger and know when to infuse a new source of brain-power, of stamina, vigour and stature. The more a breed – or family of dogs within the breed – becomes purer in blood, the more weaknesses will develop, but judicious outcrossing will rectify those faults. This is, of course, the fundamental rule in the breeding of all pedigree stock – knowing when an outcross of hybrid vigour is required and to what degree to revitalise the bloodline.

Every dog which wins a Supreme championship gets more than its fair share of bitches to mate, and to a lesser or greater degree every one of them has made some impact on the Border Collie breed, but in recent years none has continued to have more of an effect than John Richardson's Wiston Cap, winner of the 1965 championship. In 1978 41 of his sons and daughters were competing in the four National trials and three of his sons, three of his grandsons and one of his grand-daughters have since emulated his success in winning the Supreme title – a remarkable example of the value of pedigree breeding to a proven line. Of collie blue blood himself, a great-grandson of Whitehope Nap back through Kirk's Nell, Wilson's Cap, Dickson's Hemp, to Tommy, whose influence I have already recorded, Wiston Cap arrived on the sheepdog scene almost like a saviour.

For some years prior to 1965, with very few exceptions, there had been little to enthuse over in the performance of collies of international status. The standards of general practical work, the quality of outrun-ning, the controlled mastery of sheep were not up to what could be classed as hill standards. This is a general comment, of course, but did apply to the rank and file and consequently reflected the decline in shepherding qualities on the farmlands of Britain.

A glance at the records of the International championship for the years 1962, 1963 and 1964 shows the poor quality of the work. Of the 12 top dogs – the finalists for the Supreme – seven failed to complete their tasks in 1962, five in 1963 and six in 1964. In the vital test of gathering their sheep – the basic requirements of any work dog – four scored only half the possible points in 1962 and 1963, and three in 1964. Reading my newspaper reports for these three years the one recurring comment is 'poor running'.

Among the outstanding exceptions were such individuals as Tim Longton's clever Ken, the 1964 International Farmers' champion from Quernmore in north Lancashire, and Thomson McKnight's Gael, the wholly reliable bitch and 1964 Scottish National champion from Glencartholm in the Borders, both of whom were to win subsequent Supreme championships.

Alan Jones's black and tan Roy from Pontllyfni in North Wales had lost none of the skill which won the 1961 championship and he almost repeated his success in 1962, losing by failure to take his second gather instructions immediately to finish in reserve place, 13 aggregate points behind Alfred Lloyd's long-haired black and white Garry from work with 160 Kerry Hill crossbred ewes on 113 acres near Builth Wells in Breconshire who, though he won the day at Beaumaris, showed that he could lack power on truculent sheep. Similarly in 1959, Supreme and Farmers' champion Meirion Jones's rough-coated Ben from North Wales showed that, even at 8½ years old, he was still a great dog by winning third place in the 1964 championship.

Davie McTeir's white and black Mirk, with 600 Cheviots on 1,000 hill acres at Shiplaw, Eddleston in the sheep lands of Peeblesshire, was the outstanding dog at the 1964 International at Drymen by Loch Lomond, winning the Shepherds' and Driving championships and reserve Supreme with reliable and workmanlike skills that really caught the eye. A smallish 8½-year-old dog, Mirk made up for his size by pure guts and his outbye herding was excellent.

Herbert Worthington's smooth black and tan Juno, in her first International from contract herding on the mountainside around Mardy, Abergavenny, became the first bitch for 25 years to win a Supreme title

Correct pacing is essential. Speed runs off the meat from sheep! Geoffrey Billingham's Jan on Cheviot sheep in the Borders (Frank H. Moyes).

Fast off the mark to prevent the sheep escaping. Geoffrey Billingham with Wiston Wattie (Frank H. Moyes).

in 1963 and her work on manageable Dalesbred ewes over the flat lands of York racecourse was sound. But the great success of that year was Tot Longton's Rob, then only two years old and fresh from the nursery fields who, in spite of being hampered by the poor visibility of morning mist during his trial, finished third and in the next eight years won 40 open trials championships.

In addition to McKnight's Gael and Worthington's Juno there were four other bitches whose mastery of sheep and dedication to their craft were a delight to watch, Tot Longton's experienced Nell and Tim Longton's great-hearted Snip – thwarted by one sheep from taking the

Never should a collie give way, even to the most truculent sheep or cow, and a nip on the nose is often the only way to assert authority. George Scott's Gael on Suffolk rams at Lady Rigg Farm, Kelso (Frank H. Moyes).

1962 victory – from north Lancashire; John Templeton's mottle-nosed Maid from Blackbriggs Farm, Mauchline, in Ayrshire; and Gwilym Rhys Jones's seven-year-old Nell, the pride of South Wales when she finished sixth in 1962 and Wiston Cap's closest challenger three years later at Cardiff, on both occasions beaten at the pen.

Also among the few to remember were John Evan's Don, English and International Farmers' champion in 1962, and Ben, the 1963 English and reserve Supreme champion, from Tidenham on the west bank of the Severn in Gloucestershire; Tom Bonella's smooth, prick-eared Ben, the 1962 Scottish champion and 1963 reserve Scottish champion, from Tillyochie Mains, Kinross; Jim Brady's red-coated Buff, the best of Irish collies from Ballynure in County Antrim; Eric Elliott's four-year-old Pat, with Whitefaced Woodland sheep in the Derbyshire Peak, whose gathering in the 1964 test was impressive; Len Greenwood's strong-working Moss, England's Driving champion in 1964, from the Lancashire–Yorkshire Pennines; and if you could control a fast tricolour worker, Bob Seaton's 5½-year-old Glen from the lush lands of Thornby in Northamptonshire.

These were the exceptions to a bunch of very mediocre collies.

And then along came Wiston Cap!

At the Cardiff International in September 1965, when still under two years old, he showed us how shepherding should be carried out. He showed us how Supreme championships should be won – by authoritative and precise skills and as the outworking half of an immaculate partnership with his master. Remember the sheer rhythm of that return for his second gather when we all sat up to take notice? Here at last was

Tim Longton's Roy faces an awkward cow at Quernmore (Derek Johnson).

something to enthuse over. Yet when the pulses had calmed we realised that Wiston Cap had only done his job correctly, like many before him. Assessed calmly, his work had faults. He dropped points on his first gather and a touch on the fetch, he missed the cross-drive hurdle and was round the pen once – yet there were few major shepherding faults, for he just settled to the practical job of herding 20 Welsh Mountain sheep over the two-mile test as his nature, his breeding and his training had taught him. We had been so starved of the real thing for too long that, good as it was, his ability could have been – and was in some shepherding circles – over-exaggerated. It was good that he came back a year later and won the Shepherds' championship over the big course.

From 1965 the name of Wiston Cap was on every sheepman's lips and he has probably mated more bitches than any other dog before or since. But fame has its price and, like his great-grandsire Whitehope Nap, he had his severe critics. He was too keen, he turned away in the face of an extra-obstinate ewe, he was too weak at the pen – he was too good to be true! Wiston Cap proved them wrong, adding for good measure the fruits of his sirings to emphasise the outstanding qualities of his bloodline. His own make-up was predominantly from Jim Wilson's great hill dog Cap, and he inherited similar skills, which thrilled the trials spectators and got through all the herding work at home with the easy grace of a born professional.

John Richardson refers to him as a tremendous herding dog, equally

John Richardson's Wiston Cap, Supreme Champion of 1965, and the logo of the ISDS.

impressive in yarding sheep as on the open hill. Wiston Cap had a great temperament, he was always consistent, and he believed utterly in the partnership with his master, with whom he had a unique understanding. This to a great extent was the secret of their trials successes, the implicit faith that each had in the other and the communication that developed between them.

Wiston Cap, born in September 1963, was the tan-marked black and white son of his master's Cap, a half white-headed dog which John had bred to carry some 16 crosses of Wilson's Cap. His mother was Walter Hetherington's smooth-coated Fly from Innerleithen, the gentle but authoritative daughter of Jim Wilson's Bill II, the son of Whitehope Nap.

Pedigree of WISTON CAP (31154) 1965 Supreme Champion with John Richardson

The numbers in brackets are the Stud Book numbers of the International Sheep Dog Society

On his father's line, Wiston Cap was the great-great-grandson of two Supreme champions, Jim Wilson's Glen and John Evan's Roy, the grandson of the great Welsh collie Hughes's Jaff, which John Richardson greatly admired. In Cap's immediate maternal pedigree, apart from Whitehope Nap, was another of Jim Wilson's great dogs, Moss.

John Richardson was shepherding South Country Cheviots on 700 acres at Lyne near Peebles when he weaned Wiston Cap at five weeks old, and the pup immediately impressed the tall, good-natured shepherd with its willingness to learn. Cap proved to be a natural, born to shepherd sheep, and he was working at the age of three months and had taken his place in the farm duties when six months old. At ten months he earned his first trials prize.

When he entered the Scottish National trials on touchy Blackface ewes over the green lands of Bught Park at Inverness, in August 1965, he had grown into a strong prick-eared dog, well built and supple in movement, nice in the eye and extremely intelligent. He stood on his feet well and his work was balanced and pliable. He was competent and unafraid, and he was reliable. His stance and outline are known throughout the world as the insignia of the International Sheep Dog Society.

Wiston Cap proved his ability by earning an international 'cap' at Inverness at his first attempt, finishing seventh in the merit-selected then 12-strong Scottish team. Three weeks later, at Cardiff, and still under two years old, he made history – the youngest collie ever to win the Supreme championship in its present form – and the Wiston Cap legend had begun. Since that Supreme victory the sheepdog world has acclaimed a great collie, and has perhaps overlooked the tremendous part which John Richardson played in the dog's success.

John Richardson, whose interest in collies started when he used to herd the cows in his dairying days, is one of the best handlers that Scotland has produced, and he's proved that he was not just a one-dog man by training and handling two of Cap's sons, Sweep and Mirk, to Scottish and International championships. The intelligence and ability of Sweep and Mirk, and others who were to win high honour in other hands, were a credit to the family of collies which John had so patiently developed.

Sweep and Mirk were full brothers of different litters and though they both had the basic skills of their father, were quite different in appearance and character.

Sweep, born in June 1965 at Townhead, Lyne in the Peeblesshire hills, was a black-coated, rough-haired dog who was happiest on the sheep-runs where he had the freedom to run big gathers and the power to move large droves of sheep. This was particularly reflected in the

International Driving contest at Towyn in 1968 when he drove the flock of 50 Welsh Mountain ewes to victory for Scotland.

Mirk, born in April 1968, was a big, rough-coated black, white and tan collie who enjoyed the finer skills of his craft, and he was very much at home on the trials course where he won the 1975 International Shepherds' championship at York. Both dogs were mothered by Jackie McDonald's Lassie, a great-granddaughter of Jim Wilson's dual Supreme champion Glen, so that once again the blood of Cap and Loos was proven.

John Richardson won his first Scottish Shepherds' title with Sweep working North Country Cheviots at sunny Dornoch in 1968, and he added two more with Mirk in 1973 and 1975. Mirk's first National success was in mastering a particularly awkward batch of Blackfaces in Camperdown Park, Dundee, for the 1973 Shepherds' championship, and he went forward to the International to finish second in the Shepherds' class. His best year was 1975 when he was seven years old and earning his keep on the uplands at Johnscleugh, Duns. Over a testing course at Loan's, Crossburn, on the outskirts of Troon by the Firth of Clyde, the tricolour hill dog needed all the skills and power of his line to boss Blackface ewes for the overall success of the National, Shepherds' and Driving championships. The following month he travelled to the flat green Knavesmire racecourse at York to win the International Shepherds' title on heavy Mule ewes.

In the same year Mirk's son, John James's four-year-old Mirk with a Kerry Hill flock at Shirleath Farm, Kingsland, in the north lowlands of Herefordshire, won the English National championship at Wantage in Oxfordshire.

What were these collies worth? In 1965 John Richardson was offered £500 for Wiston Cap, and when his Mirk showed his worth he was priced at £700. Change that into current values and the prices soar, but to the man who lives with them, respects them and needs them to do his job of work they are priceless.

Wiston Cap retired from the International scene in 1973 but by then he – and his progeny – had proved the absolute supremacy of his blood in the craft of herding sheep. Three of his sons have since won the International Supreme championship, 66-year-old John Murray's blue-fronted four-year-old Glen, home bred at Southgateside, Sanquhar, in Dumfriesshire, on lively Welsh Mountain ewes at Trelai Park, Cardiff, in 1971; Ayrshire farmer John Templeton's 4½-year-old Cap from the 300 acre milk and sheep holding at Fenwick, near Kilmarnock, working on Blackfaces on Town Moor at Newcastle in 1972 before running fifth in the American World Championship and being sold to Fred Bahnson for work on the plains of North Carolina; and Gwyn Jones's upstanding black and white Bill, at 6½ years old one of the finest working collies, from home work with Welsh Mountain ewes in Snowdonia, mastering the strong Blackface sheep and ruggedness of Kilmartin's gale-lashed test in 1974.

Wiston Cap's three grandsons, who were to take the greatest sheepdog honour in the world, were Gwyn Jones's big, white-headed Shep from Penmachno with excellent herding of strong North Country Cheviots at Lockerbie in 1976; Robert Shennan's strong, rough-mottled Mirk from Turnberry in Ayrshire, working Mule ewes at Chatsworth in 1978; and Wyn Edwards's good-looking Bill from the Vale of Clwyd in North Wales, only the second collie in 60 years to win the Supreme twice in successive years, 1981 and 1982, boss of Swaledales at Armathwaite and master of Blackface ewes at Blair Atholl.

Wiston Cap also had a granddaughter, Thomas Longton's little Bess, who when she was almost ten years old won the Supreme championship in 1986 over the extensive rising grassland of Anglesey in Wales to crown a near-perfect career on the trials fields, and take England back to the top. Intelligent and assured, her shepherding of the most unruly sheep enhanced the dominance of her line and won the praise of every sheepman, concluding her career in the best possible way. She had spent her days herding hill ewes and black and white milk cows at Lee End Farm in the Conder Valley of north Lancashire, and her weekends winning trials awards in every part of the country.

Having written so much of the qualities of the collies of yesteryear the question which naturally arises is 'what of the future?'

I see a sheepdog trial on every Saturday, open trials in the summer and nursery trials in the winter, and I have often discussed this topic with farmers and shepherds and for the most part they are optimistic.

There is a tendency, however, to breed the lighter type of dog to cope with the conditions of working a small packet of sheep at trials, but not many farmers can afford to keep a dog purely for trials work. It has to earn its keep on the home flock, and wise breeding and the demand for what may be called purely 'farm' dogs will keep the collie strong and fit. Unfortunately, as James Scott said in days gone by, the majority of sheep farmers are not interested in trials which can make collies more valuable, serviceable and efficient.

Many farmers today are just not interested, and I call them lazy farmers for I believe that a dog which is good at trials is only a 'polished' farm dog, with which the farmer has spent more time on making its work more precise.

One now officially retired farmer for whom I have a great respect and whose opinions are worth listening to is Sydney Price, who won the Supreme championship in 1987. He feels that dogs don't get the same

None must be allowed to slip away. George Scott's Gael takes a packet of Suffolk rams right up to her master for inspection (Frank H. Moyes).

amount of practical experience they did in earlier days. Although he believes that there's nothing wrong with the dogs of today and that they are equally as good as the earlier dogs, he thinks that they don't get the same experience as dogs of yesteryear for, in his opinion, and he has bred some of the finest in the country, sheep are not as good under modern farming methods as they used to be. He is of the opinion that sheep don't get shepherded as much as in the old days.

Sydney earned an impressive reputation throughout the country for his ability to breed and show pedigree sheep of the Kerry Hill, Clun Forest and Suffolk breeds to Royal Show championship standards. He told Austin Bennett, whose writings are much appreciated in sheepdog circles, 'Years ago we'd be looking at the sheep every day and hill men would take the sheep up the mountain at night and bring them down in the morning, and consequently the dogs got plenty of work.

'Nowadays people are breaking dogs to cope with the circumstances and too many are only good for trialling.

'I know things have to change, but we must never lose sight of the purely practical side of shepherding. It is very important that trialling never loses sight of that.'

He is, of course, right for it is indeed very important that sheepdogs don't get bred too soft for their work of shepherding sheep on the home farm – that is far more important than running competitively at trials, although trials do have a part to play in their evolution.

CHAPTER NINE

Method is Genius

In which I seek the qualities of genius in a generally clever and hard-working breed of dog and discover that it comes from the gift of method. I see it on my visits to Glyn Jones in North Wales, and discuss the other collie trait – 'eye'.

Wise, hard working and tolerant as a race, we have seen that there are individual collies which stand out above their fellows by their extra, almost fantastic ability in the art of herding stock. In addition to the high intelligence and stature of their kind they have that something special that is best described as method, the ability to blend in sympathetic understanding of the stock they herd. It is really an indefinable quality, yet it marks the difference between first-class ability and genius.

'It is very rare and it is precious,' said the late Mark Hayton of Otley in Yorkshire, one of the finest of sheepdog handlers, farmer on the Wharfedale side of Ilkley Moor, and the winner of one English and two International championships, including the 1926 Supreme with Glen. He described method as the intangible bond of confidence which some collies created with their sheep.

I have seen dogs whose quiet but firm control over their sheep removed any aggravation, without frustration, without tension and without loss of temper. Remove stress from sheep, or any livestock, and you have a longer living, quicker developing, more docile animal. In this age of modern and streamlined farming methods not enough emphasis is placed on the often disastrous effects of stress on livestock. Nothing upsets sheep more than to be moved around, to be jostled and bustled, and the good collie herds with the minimum of fuss or disturbance, saving its master a deal of financial loss.

Unfortunately method cannot be implanted in a dog, for it is something which comes from within. Perhaps it is the sixth sense of the collie world, the trait of genius, but while training will develop a collie's

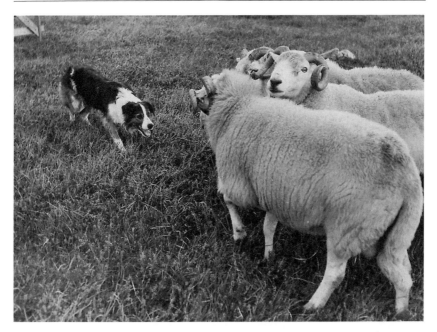

Determined and unflinching power. Strong Welsh Mountain rams give ground before Eurwyn Daniel's Ken, 1960 Supreme Champion (News Chronicle).

wisdom to the extreme, no amount of training will instil method. In fact Mark Hayton did refer to method as 'an attribute of genius in a sheepdog', the gift of the greatest.

That the quality is a gift is seen when two collies faced with a similar shepherding problem approach it in the same intelligent manner, yet one accomplishes its task with far less excitement and flurry than the other. This is best seen on a trials course when conditions are virtually the same for each contestant. To the observer both collies can make identical shepherding moves, running at the same speed, flanking at the same angle, moving up or laying back the same distance in control of the sheep, yet one keeps a sweet and flowing progress while the other scatters and frightens the sheep.

Mark Hayton, who was a great student of nature and firmly believed that a collie's natural attributes of intelligence and character should be fostered and encouraged, not supplanted by man's ideas, recognised the quality of method. Others less wise failed to see its importance and were intolerant of the 'slow developer' or the 'too clever' dog. They failed to learn from their dogs and quelled whatever initiative was in them. They wanted the dog to respond implicitly and unthinkingly to their commands. It must do immediately whatever they told it to do. They won trials, for on the trials field the dog could always be under their eye and command and so their dogs gave a false impression of their quality – and were sought for breeding by the unwise.

Such trainers of these 'yo-yo' dogs, pulled hither and thither on a whistled command, have much to answer for in the evolution of working dogs. Their creations were false for when taken to the moor and running out of their sight, and consequently out of their command, they were lost. The power to think for themselves had been taken from them. This type of collie has no future and does not last, but its use in badly planned breeding programmes retards the overall status of the breed.

A wise man learns from his dogs, and when the natural intelligence of tested bloodlines coupled with sympathetic training and handling are fortunate enough to have a dash of that mysterious quality known as method, the result is canine genius. You could see it in the work of most of Jim Wilson's champions on the Border hills, in the orderly ease with which Roy dominated sheep, the initiative of little Nell, the sensitive understanding of Fly, the crouched expectancy of Craig, the complete calmness of Cap, the brisk efficiency of Glen and the precise moves of Whitehope Nap.

There was method, too, in the way that Dick Hughes's Welsh Jaff could keep a flock of sheep bunched and trotting away at a steady pace; in the unspectacular class of Tim Longton's Ken, master of every situation on the heights of Clougha Fell in north Lancashire; in the steady balanced watchfulness of Michael Perrings's Kyle when gathering Swaledales on the fells of Wharfedale; and in the stylish purposeful rhythm of Thomson McKnight's Gael on either dairy cows or lambing ewes in Eskdale.

Again, it showed in the cool confidence of Alan Jones's Roy during his remarkable record year of winning four Welsh titles and two International titles in 1961; in the unflurried authority of Tot Longton's old Rob over whatever breed of sheep he was faced with; in the honest competence of David McTeir's Mirk in the control of 600 breeding ewes at Eddleston; in the matchless and natural instincts of John Richardson's Wiston Cap, both on the trials field and on the Peeblesshire hills; and in the commanding personality of Glyn Jones's Gel, who so thrilled four million television viewers that he earned 'star rating' in the BBC's 'One Man and His Dog' series.

Method was in the ways of Thomas Longton's little tricolour Bess from north Lancashire, calming the most unruly sheep at Anglesey in 1986; in Bobby Dalziel's 3½-year-old prick-eared Wisp, with 400 South Country Cheviot and 450 Blackface ewes on the bleak hills of Potburn above the Ettrick Valley; in Gwyn Jones's handsome Queen from Snowdonia; in the confidence of Alasdair MacRae's rough-coated tricolour Nan from Loch Levenside; in the wise movements of John Wilson's black and white Spot from Headshaw in Selkirkshire; and in the forthright and controlled shepherding of Paul Turnbull's Nap, a grand type of collie from a hill herding of Blackface sheep in Northumberland. All these collies had that mysterious flash of genius which made sheep happy to accept and trust their authority.

Glyn Jones, who farms up on the mountain at Bwlch Isaf above Bodfari in North Wales, knows the quality of method for he, like Mark Hayton, believes in teaching not training, and there is a subtle difference. Teaching shows a collie not only how but *why* it should do something; training insists that it do something whether or not it knows the reasons. Training, or the word 'breaking' which is so often used, implies that man is responsible for implanting the working ability in the collie dog when in fact its ability is inbred and just waiting to be brought out and developed.

James Hogg, the shepherd poet of Ettrick in the early 1800s, once wrote, 'I declare I have hardly ever seen a shepherd's dog do anything without believing that I perceived his reason for it.'

Glyn Jones's Gel had such wisdom and won the Supreme championship for Wales in 1973 when he was only three years old, but Glyn knows that Gel was a much better dog in 1975 when he was adjudged second in the Supreme at York. By then, at five years old, he had exploited his wisdom to the full, helped and encouraged by a master who could almost get inside his mind. Together Glyn and Gel were supreme in the art of shepherding, the one complementing the other in a partnership of equals.

Whether it was on the steep slopes of the mountain where the wind blew cold over the Clwydian range and Welsh ewes had to be tended, in the stockyards of the auction mart where Glyn also works and where speed in moving stock is of the essence to keep business flowing, or in the comparatively relaxed atmosphere of the trials field, Gel showed that mark of sheepdog genius which Glyn Jones nurtured.

To have seen this Welsh dog in action was to have seen perfection, and the most satisfying sight in the world is to watch a master at his craft. One waxes lyrical at the pleasure and I remember with a touch of embarrassment my own commentary on Gel's work in the 'One Man and His Dog' trials. Not until I saw the completed film as viewers saw it did I realise how fascinated I had become with the dog's skill. Watching Gel working ten Swaledale ewes in partnership with his kennel-mate Bracken, to win the television Brace championship over the grassy course by Loweswater Lake, I remember saying 'Glyn's superfluous', so immaculate was their teamwork. It was an unfair comment on their lord

Some collies are born with it. The quiet commanding authority of method. Glyn Jones' Gel, 1973 Supreme Champion.

and master, but like all good handlers Glyn kept his own guiding presence very much in the background and let his dogs show off his skill by simply showing their own.

There is such a comradeship between Glyn Jones and his dogs, and this was particularly so with Gel, though they sometimes disagreed on who was boss, a trait the farmer did not disapprove of for he must have spirit in his dogs. 'Gel had guts,' he said. 'Though we have never actually fallen out he tested me all the time and that's how we got the best out of each other.' Gel had guts in other ways also. When he was seven years old he suffered a serious ligament strain which threatened his active life and put him out of the Welsh National yet, showing the stamina and courage of his breed, he came to my local trials in the Gorge of Cliviger at the end of the year and took the championship against 83 of the best collies in the land. On that September day the quality of his shepherding of Gritstone ewes over a course split by the Lancashire Calder and watched over by grey crags was faulted by only two of 90 points.

Gel, handsome in his long black and white coat and strong in nature, was a dog in a million but though he took all before him in the competitive world his true value was on the mountainside, at home. For all his fame he still had a job to do on the farm. Often his weekend trials romp would not come until after he had driven out the cows after the evening milking. His main job was with a flock of Welsh and cross

Pedigree of GEL (63023) 1973 Supreme Champion with Glyn Jones

The numbers in brackets are the Stud Book numbers of the International Sheep Dog Society

Cheviot ewes over the 800 acres of bracken-faced mountain in the Clwydian range above Bodfari in North Wales. He came here, to the homeliness of Bwlch Isaf farmhouse, tucked into the mountainside, when he was only ten months old and it was on this mountain where he 'learned to listen' – a factor which his master believes is one of the very basic lessons of collie instruction. 'So often you can see more of the sheep ground or the trials course than the dog, and if he will listen to you, you can help him with instructions,' says Glyn, adding with his usual cheery sense of humour, 'If a dog doesn't listen to you on this mountain, he'll run himself till he's glad to listen.'

Gel soon learned to listen – and to realise that in some things at least 'the boss knew best!'

From that moment the partnership blossomed and bore fruit very quickly. When Gel was only three years old, in 1973, he won the highest accolade in the sheepdog world, the Supreme International championship, fittingly at the International Sheep Dog Society's centenary trials at Bala, to the vocal appraisal of his human countrymen, into whose hearts he restored some of their lost pride for it had been nine years since Wales had previously won the top title.

It was not Gel's best trial – his return up the field for the second packet of sheep lost a lot of points – but Glyn takes most of the blame for a rare misunderstanding of handling and Gel ran many better trials after that day. But Gel beat the cream of English and Scottish dogs, who were much better fancied, and victory was won with the determination and guts which were to stamp his character.

He almost repeated his Supreme victory in 1975 over the flat lands of York, finishing in second place with a better trial than his Bala run. Finishing third in the qualifying trials, which gained him entry to the Supreme contest, he completely mastered the grey-faced Halfbreds, being unfaulted by the three judges in the gathering, shedding, penning and singling sections of his test. On the final day the overall work was to be outstanding and Gel went quietly about his task in front of the packed grandstand to score 387 of the possible 450 aggregate points, only beaten on the last run of the day by Raymond MacPherson's white-headed Zac on 388 points. Gel's points on that day were 23 more than his victory run at Bala.

Gel's education in the art of shepherding began at ten months old when he went to Bwlch Isaf from Bob Jones, who had reared him at nearby Denbigh. He was an intelligent pup and of that illustrious line we have already considered back through Wilson's Cap, Dickson's Hemp to Tommy and Old Hemp. His mother was W. T. William's four-year-old black and white Nell and he was sired by Elwyn Griffith's Craig, a collie of some stature and reputation in North Wales. Gel's paternal grandsire was John Gilchrist's Spot and his work showed the great driving lope of this dog, which twice won Scotland's National championship and the reserve Supreme honour. Other influences in his line came from Wilson's Moss and Mirk, Kirk's Nell, Watson's Shep and Walker's Craig, and he had the hill and trials qualities of John Bathgate's Rock who won most of Scotland's leading events.

Unfortunately Gel could pass his characteristics on to but a very few sons and daughters, for some quirk of nature made him a bad breeder. In a good home, with a caring family, Gel matured into a handsome, rough-coated collie with brains to match his beauty and the road to stardom opened up.

Gel was to have the most understanding and efficient of handlers, for

Glyn Jones is a man who knows and loves collies, even their individual flaws, and he cares that each has its own characteristics – a point that many sheepmen fail to appreciate when choosing a partner for their work. Glyn found that in Gel he had the ideal partner, a dog which would figuratively extend his own arm to reach every sheep on the mountain in the most efficient way. I recall the emphasis that Glyn placed on good gathering one night when we were talking 'dogs' in the cosy farmhouse kitchen at Bwlch Isaf. It was after the poor efforts of the Welsh dogs at the previous year's International at Cardiff and Glyn was rightly critical of their failure to get to their sheep in a proper manner. Three of the four Welsh dogs in the Supreme test had retired.

I was at Bodfari to judge Glyn's local trials, held the following day on the undulating pastures by the village, and to a great extent the work of the Welsh collies in those trials proved his point. I marked all the leading Welsh dogs in an entry of 100 over a 350 yd gather of Welsh lambs and it was a collie from Yorkshire, John Squires's blue-coated Mirk, then four years old and recently in England's International team, which won the championship. On another night in Glyn's company – when we were in London together for 'One Man and His Dog' – he showed his own speed in the gather by outrunning a taxi, but that's another story!

Bwlch Isaf is renowned throughout the sheepdog world as a place of genial hospitality, supplied in typical warm-hearted country style by Glyn, his wife Beryl, and daughters Ceri and Rhona. It is famous too for the calibre of another of its collies, the little prick-eared Bwlch Bracken, a daughter of the 1965 Supreme champion Wiston Cap. When Bracken was only 18 months old Glyn said: 'You'll be hearing about her.' How true, and what a perception of collie quality by the Welsh farmer, for she won International recognition nine months later at her first attempt at the Welsh National, partnering Gel to the winning of the Welsh Brace championship.

Since that time television viewers have thrilled to the artistry of those two collies and the matchless understanding they had when working together in three series of 'One Man and His Dog'.

More temperamental than Gel yet with a matching skill, Bracken had her own successful method on sheep. She was an alert bitch and had the intelligence to counter the wayward actions of sheep before they really materialised. Bred by Glyn's wife, Beryl, who is an English girl, Bracken was English-speaking so that Glyn had to be bilingual, working Gel to Welsh spoken commands and Bracken to the English.

Bracken, sleek and feminine, black and white and medium coated, had many of the winning ways of her mother Sheba whose gentle nature made her the ideal brood bitch. From Sheba, Bracken's bloodline went

The non-stop bustle of the auction-market where strength and authority are really tested. Glyn Jones' Glen and Bracken put Welsh Mountain sheep into the pen at Ruthin (Derek Johnson).

back through much of Glyn's and his father's breeding on the maternal side, and to Wilson's Bill, the 1955 Supreme champion, on the paternal side. Thus Bracken, of the Wilson's Cap lineage on both sides of her pedigree, was yet another champion to prove the outstanding quality of the Border hill blood. The little bitch won two 'caps' for Wales and with Gel was undefeated in three series of the television trials. She died in January 1988, having shown much ability in shepherding sheep both on the mountainside and on the trials fields, and having given a great deal of pleasure to all who knew her.

Perched high on the mountainside, we cannot leave Bwlch Isaf, a place which city folk dream of in summertime but don't care to know in winter, when snow cuts it off from civilisation, without talking of Glen. Glen's claim to fame is that he is the only collie in the world to have been taught his craft under the fascinated eyes of a television viewing audience when being used as the 'guinea-pig' in the second series of 'One Man and His Dog' to show the amount of time and patience that goes to the making of a skilled working collie.

A self-assured, tall-standing youngster with the almost cocky attitude of one ear up and one ear down, Glen, 11 months old when the cameras first saw him, quickly followed the tradition of his more famous kennel-mates, making the grade on the television trials course at

Glyn Jones with Bracken, and Eric Halsall with Gel at Rannerdale in the Lake District (BBC).

17 months old, on the mountain at home, and winning his first 'cap' for Wales at two years of age.

Over the National course at Aberystwyth in August 1977 he worked Speckled-face sheep to 180 of 200 aggregate points to finish eighth of 171 entrants in the 15-strong Welsh team at his first attempt. A month later at the International he won through from the qualifying trials to the final 15 in the Supreme contest which just proved too much for his inexperience.

Glen was a particular favourite of Ceri, the Jones's 17-year-old daughter, who could handle the smooth-coated dog almost as well as her father and she won local trials competitions with him. Sadly, and with a hint of mystery, Glen was killed in May 1979 when he was four years old. He was found dead on the mountain above the home farm and veterinary examination showed that his death was due to multiple fractures of the skull. Subsequently his character was totally exonerated by the Flint Magistrates Court of a charge of sheep worrying which was brought against him. The esteem in which he was held by a great number of people was shown in the number of letters which arrived at Bwlch Isaf when the news became known, and reflected his immense popularity as a television 'star'.

Glyn Jones has that natural, unassuming quality that dogs get along with. They trust him, they listen to him, they can work with him and they know where they stand with him, and even if they don't make the grade, they leave him with respect. Few can have the star quality of Gel, Bracken and Glen, but Glyn starts many collies for farming folk who respect a good dog for their work.

Glyn won the Welsh National in successive years at Tywyn in 1980 and at Llansawel in 1981 with one of the best young collies ever to be seen on a trials course, Bwlch Taff, a son of Glen out of Bracken. Tricolour and rough-coated with the alert ears of his mother, Taff was only 16 months old when he mastered the most awkward of Mountain ewes to win in 1980, and his smooth and controlled work over the big, flat course at Llansawel in hot sunshine the following year reflected the understanding and the respect he had for his master. When, in 1982, he finished second on a run-off in the Supreme championship at Blair Atholl, his story reached the realms of fiction.

Taff was a particular favourite of mine, and when he went blind in later years whenever I was at Bwlch Isaf, where I have always been more than welcome, I used to take him for a walk, guiding him round the field by pointing him in the right direction.

Always the breeding must be right, for Glyn Jones is a perfectionist and is always striving to improve the skill of his dogs, along with that of himself, thriving on the competition of top class trials and enjoying the good companionship and friendliness of these events. He is a man of immense fun, the twinkle is never far from his eye, yet he is also a realist and knows exactly the capabilities and the limitations of each of his dogs. 'If you treat dogs with respect and encourage them, they'll reward you with diligence' is his philosophy.

Glyn has judged the International, travelled the world judging trials and giving advice on sheepdog handling, has written what I consider the best book, *A Way Of Life*, on sheepdog schooling, and I have been privileged to be involved with him in the production of three videos on sheepdog training. He and his wife Beryl were asked to gather together and prepare consignments of young collies for Bulgaria, before the Iron Curtain came down, and for the Falkland Islands after the war there. On a visit to Bwlch Isaf I met Gunter Piepenbrock of Bielefeld in Germany, who had hitherto been a correspondant and telephone friend, who translated into the German language and published the 1985 version of this book under the title *Meine Treuen Freunde*.

In recent years Glyn's collies, Cap, a tricolour son of Bwlch Taff, and Taff, an intelligent dog to cross with the Bwlch bloodline, have won the Welsh National Brace championship and, keeping the tradition set by Gel and Bracken in Brace contests, television's 'One Man and His Dog' trials.

Cap, bred by Stuart Wilkinson at Thurgoland near Sheffield in Yorkshire, ran in the Welsh International team in 1990. A rough-coated dog born in February 1984, he is by Bwlch Taff out of Mist, and on both sides of his pedigree is Wiston Cap. His maternal bloodline goes back to Tim Longton's Ken which won the 1966 Supreme championship and Harry Huddleston's Bett, winner of the 1969 Supreme.

Taff, by J. G. Edward's Tweed out of J. E. Roberts's Judy at Llanfyllin, was in the Welsh International teams of 1991 and 1995. His bloodline includes many proven Welsh collies and goes back to John Murray's Glen which won the 1971 Supreme championship at Cardiff. Also in his line is Alan Jones's Craig, the winner of the Welsh National title in 1976, and for three successive years, 1975, 1976 and 1977, was the Welsh Driving champion. In 1975 and 1976 Craig won the International Driving titles.

Together, Cap and Taff won the Welsh National Brace title on Welsh Mountain sheep at Llandinam in the centre of Wales between Newtown and Llanidloes in 1993, and the 'One Man and His Dog' championship at Derwent Valley in Derbyshire in 1989.

A practical man farming 800 mountain acres which rise to 1,400 ft above the Vale of Clwyd, Glyn Jones must have a practical dog to assist him, but he wants a practical dog with a bit of class in him. This is perhaps the simple explanation of the difference between an ordinary farm dog and a successful trials dog.

Method in a collie's character leads, as we have seen, to something akin to genius; the correct amount of 'eye' – the eye of control – in a collie dog stamps its style. Indeed, the power of eye in the right amount gives a collie the confidence to move sheep with the quiet authority which leads to a graceful flowing action. Too much eye and the collie stands transfixed on its sheep, willing them without movement to a state of stalemate; too little eye and the collie has to rely on a brashness of action which is often rowdy and far from stylish. Control is at its best and strongest when it is carried out quietly.

Fortunately the quality of eye, unlike the gift of method, can be bred into a dog. Adam Telfer bred it into Old Hemp, the foundation sire of the modern dog, when he mated his 'stiff-eyed' Meg to the 'free-eyed' Roy. The two blended to perfection.

The quality of eye was one of the collie traits which sheepdog trials really highlighted, though it was a characteristic known way back in the days of James Hogg's father, around the year 1750, for the Ettrick shepherd records it in his writings.

Trials, the first of which was held in the Borders at Byrness in upper Redesdale near Carter Bar in the Cheviots in 1876, emphasised the importance of eye power. Two men who realised its quality were William Wallace, a Scotsman farming at Otterburn in Northumberland, who handled eye with an artistic touch and won the 1907 and 1922 International championships with Moss and Meg, and James Scott of Overhall, Hawick, the first man to work-exhibit collies in America.

James Scott believed that eye originally belonged to a select strain of dogs and his own Kep, one of the best-ever breeding sires, did much to

Ewe shall not pass. David McTeir's Ben shows courage and initiative in stopping a breakaway Blackface in Manor Valley (Frank H. Moyes).

stamp the quality. An extremely clever, cool and calm-natured dog, Kep won 45 trials awards including the 1908 and 1909 International championships. He was another of the great dogs in the shaping of the modern Border Collie, for with all interest centred on Hemp-bred collies in the early 1900s it was he who widened the dangerously narrowing bloodlines. Quoting James Lillico, one of the best-known sheepdog men of the period, 'The advent of Scott's Kep as a popular sire saved Border dogs from drifting into a race of highly strung and closely inbred Hemps.' Kep was far enough removed from Old Hemp to prevent this threat, though his dam, Turner's Cleg, was the granddaughter of Shotton's Pose, the grandam of Old Hemp.

The quality of a dog's eye is still one of the controversial talking points at today's trials. Many people liken the holding power of eye to hypnotism, for that uncanny power which a collie can exert over a sheep by just staring at it does appear of that nature. But the collie's power is not akin to the trembling influence which a hunting stoat casts upon a rabbit or the paralysis with which a snake holds a mouse. In the collie's case it is a concentration of will power to dominate the thoughts of the sheep so that it comes under control. The sheep does not suffer the fears of the rabbit or the mouse, but is resigned to the authority of the collie. This characteristic is one of the most striking traits bred into the modern collie.

Like every characteristic in every breed of animal, particularly in one whose development has involved man, the eye appears in varying degrees of strength in different breeds of dog. Some are too strong in eye and, immediately they see a sheep, stand transfixed like a statue staring their power over the sheep. A state of immobility ensues, and not all the whistling, shouting – and cursing – of the shepherd will persuade the dog to move the sheep. The dog has truly mesmerised itself and plays the staring-out game, much to the frustration of its master who invariably has to walk up the moor to move both dog and sheep. Such a dog can make life very tedious for its master.

Eye must be allied with movement to be practical. To have seen Glyn Jones's Gel come quickly to a packet of ewes at the end of an outrun and, creeping forward with his muzzle low to the ground and his eye steady and demanding, move them quietly on their way without scatter or fear was to see the correct eye of control in the Border Collie. Similarly, when Gel cut out a sheep in the shedding ring he moved up to it, facing it, with every muscle tensed to prevent it turning back on him, eyes so commanding that the sheep willingly accepted his authority. The value of eye is entirely a matter of strength, not too much, not too little, the ideal being just sufficient concentration on the sheep to keep them at ease and moving freely.

Allied with the power of eye must be the quality of courage, the courage to face up without flinching to the most wilful sheep or the strongest bullock. This is tested in many ways during a collie's day on the hill and in the stockyards, particularly when dealing with the protective instincts of ewes for their lambs or when the dog has to force reticent sheep or cows into a narrow gateway or into a transport wagon.

Often strong measures are called for to master a stubborn animal, especially to turn one which is bolting. In extremes the collie's only weapon is its mouth. It is also its only defence against a charging sheep or cow and the collie with courage will bite, or grip to use the sheepdog term, with deliberation and decision to control the sheep or cow. All other biting is a display of weakness, frustration and anger, and not to be tolerated. On the trials field the courage of a collie is put to the test when it is asked to single off and wear one sheep from the small flock – to separate one ewe from its companions and prevent it from rejoining them. Then we sometimes see a collie grip – and another great controversy of the trials field arises. More often than not the collie is disqualified, for that is the easiest decision to make. Gripping is at the very least frowned upon, so that it usually needs a brave judge to say that the gripping was justified. But if trials are to have any value in sorting the 'dogs from the pups' they must truly measure the practicalities of everyday shepherding. Whenever a gripping takes place on the trials field, especially at International level, the arguments rage for and against and are often very heated.

Is a collie at fault if it uses its teeth to show that it will stand no

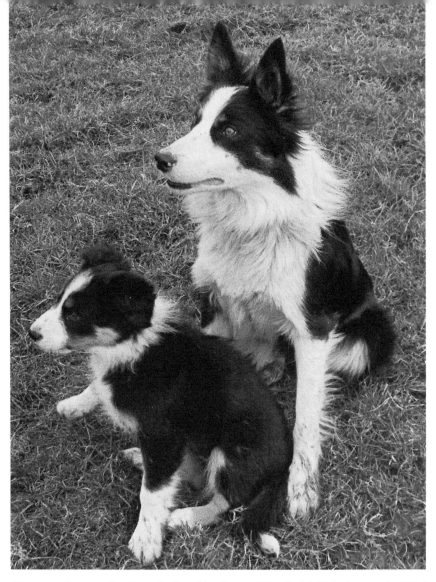

The puppy Lyn proudly sits at the feet of her famous father Bwlch Taff who won the Welsh National Championships in 1980 and 1981, and the reserve Supreme title in 1982, for Glyn Jones of Bodfari.

nonsense from a stubborn and wayward sheep? It is a truly practical trait for a collie to grip – accepting, of course, that it is not a worry, or the sneaking, cowardly bite of weakness on the back end of the sheep, but a face-to-face confrontation. If a sheep charges a collie, is it not practical for the dog to stop it, even with its teeth? So the arguments go.

I recall two particular decisions which changed the whole outcome of International results. At Bala in 1973 William Cormack's little four-year-old June from Caithness, another clever bitch of the Loos line and

Scotland's National champion that year, was disqualified at the final phase of a great qualifying trial when cutting off the single sheep and turning it with her mouth. One shepherd in my hearing called it the most decisive piece of shepherding of the whole event.

At Stirling in 1967, when very possibly on his way to his second successive Supreme championship, Tim Longton's experienced seven-year-old Ken from Quernmore near Lancaster leaped up to grip and stop an extremely rebellious ewe which was bolting from the shedding ring and was called off.

Both were great collies, wise and experienced in the ways of sheep and not prone to fits of temper. Both knew that the sheep they faced had to be bossed by a decisive act of authority that would leave no doubt as to who was in charge. Both acted coolly and deliberately, and without anger. In both instances neither collie did more than momentarily grip the sheep to turn it and, as I saw it, the disqualification act was practical work. Indeed it showed courage, initiative and decision in the dog.

'I would have thought a lot less of the dog if he had let the sheep go,' said Tim Longton about Ken's act. 'Failure to stop that sheep at home would have meant a long trek to re-gather it.'

Whatever, according to the trials rules of the International Sheep Dog Society disqualification or not rests with the judges, invariably practical men with years of experience, but it is a point which causes much discontent every year.

CHAPTER TEN

Harvest of Champions

I laze through the harvest in the sun with Tony of television fame while his master clips the sheep in Bowland's Forest, my paternal home, and watch Lancashire's first Supreme champion at work on Clougha Fell.

Clipping time and the midday sun was hot from a cloudless sky over the fells of north Lancashire.

I sat on the concrete yard, resting my back against the grey stone of the barn, my fingers gently tickling the ears of Tony, the big rough-coated collie at my side. Both of us were lazily watching a sheep being expertly parted from its woolly jacket by David Carlton, manager of breeding ewes and beef cows at Lickhurst Farm in the Forest of Bowland, the area where the most skilled of England's bowmen learned their trade before Agincourt. I was hot, but enjoying the sunshine; Tony was hot, panting the heat from his lungs, though he had the sense to lie in my shadow. But it was good clipping weather.

Conditions were right to bring a rise to the wool, to lift it from the body of the sheep so that the shearing clippers could cut the straight fibres as clean as a mowing machine cuts grass stalks.

Never more than at clipping time is the weather important. Hill sheep are clipped in June when the fleece is fully grown, and when the ewes will least feel the cold at the loss of their warm jackets. If left the sheep would moult naturally, like other mammals, and as primitive sheep still do, but taken at the right time the wool is a valuable harvest. It is one of the products of the collie dog's labours.

David clipped his sheep in the shade of the barn with swallows zipping in and out to feed their youngsters in the rafters. Strong, fit hoggs, the progeny of the crossing of two pure breeds, Lonk and Swaledale, and known as 'country-bred' in the locality, the sheep were being clipped for the first time in their lives and needed handling firmly, with some degree of gentleness to reduce the stress to their nervous system. They were quite a handful, but like all good shearers David handled them correctly and quietly so that after the initial protest each one laid without struggling while the work was done.

Each sheep was caught up under the throat by the left arm – the automatic clippers being held in the right hand – and brought to a sitting position, its back resting against David's legs. Then his work was decisive, taking the opening-up cut across the short coarse wool on the exposed belly of the sheep and carefully sweeping round the teats of the udder and over the crutch on to the back leg.

Moving up to the neck, David said 'This always frightens me. I have visions of cutting the throat.' Next round the face, the curly wool of the neck, on over the shoulder for the long sweeping cuts right along the body of the sheep up to the spine. The fleece peeled away like a doubled-back cloak over the spine and one side was shorn.

David stepped over the ewe and repeated the procedure. Far side of the neck, diagonally across the body to leave those lovely quilted pattern marks on the under-wool, then cutting out the shoulder wool and down to the back leg, the shears glided smoothly over the sheep's skin without hesitation or jerkiness. The final threads of wool cut through, the whole woollen bundle fell to the ground after a skilled and efficient operation which inside five minutes left each sheep clean and fresh.

Only when it was released was a sheep unsure of itself. It was bewildered. Its new lightness of weight felt strange. It looked naked and skinny and a little undignified in its white underwear. While thus bemused, David took the opportunity to mark it with his flock sign, a quickly applied dash of red raddle down the left flank of the ewe which would enable him to pick it out at a distance when it went back to the moor. A more permanent flock mark had already been burned into the horn of the sheep. Tony saw each sheep off down the yard into the paddock, then returned to lie by my side.

The shorn fleeces were rolled and set aside ready to be packed into sacks for transport to the grading factory. Each fleece weighed around 5–6 lb and when it was processed its finer quality would be used for the manufacture of tweeds, rugs and the thicker hand-knitting wools, but most of the wool of coarser quality would be ideal for the production of carpet yarns. By prices current at that time the value of each greasy fleece was around £3 – hardly an overpayment for the work of production and winning. Wool is such a varied commodity and the 67,000 tonnes of greasy wool straight from the sheep, then worth around £30 million and produced by about 50 pure breeds of sheep and at least 300 crossbred types each year in the United Kingdom was and still is graded into 300 different classes – there is a wool appropriate for every purpose. David's labours on the Pennines were just over the hills from the West Riding towns where the major concentration of the woollen textile industry was situated, and over 90 per cent of all the worsted cloth and more than 50 per cent of the woollen cloth made in the country was and still is produced there.

Incidentally, the word tweed is said to have resulted from a clerical error in a Scottish order book when twill – the Scotsman's tweel – was mistakenly written as 'tweed'. It is not associated with the famous river.

On the sheep's back the fleece simply protects it against the weather, the outer long fibres running off the water like thatching and the inner close soft wool retaining the body warmth. Though the 'golden fleece' of the past is perhaps not quite so bright and sheep are now farmed primarily for their meat, fortunes have been made out of wool and dynasties established.

During the Middle Ages wool was the principal industry of western Europe, with big longwool flocks of sheep in Lincolnshire and the north of England, the shortwools of Herefordshire and the Merinos of Spain supplying the wealth of England, the Low Countries and Italy. Some of the churches and merchants' houses of East Anglia and the Cotswolds still remind us of the sheep's importance in that period. The big houses of Yorkshire bear witness to the affluence of the wool trade at a later date.

David Carlton, harvesting his wool clip in the Forest of Bowland, worked hard. He had to with 250 breeding ewes, 130 beef cows of the creamy-skinned French Charolais type and a lively packet of Ayrshire dairy heifers to manage on 200 acres. His only help came from his three dogs, Tony, Meg and Joss; without them he could not have coped with the work-load.

Tony, at six the oldest and most experienced of the trio, was his right hand. The most intelligent of collies, he was always capable and willing and, most importantly, he thought the world of his master so that a happy efficient partnership resulted and the work became a pleasure. On moorland rising over 1,300 ft, where at clipping time heat haze often shimmers the rounded outlines of the Bowland fells, Tony, big and strong, ranged the rough ground with the easy lope of the sika deer he sometimes surprised. It had not always been so, for Tony had to overcome the painful handicap of delicate pads which nearly ended his working days before they had really begun.

Taken by David to Lickhurst from his birthplace in Scotland when he was under 18 months old and priced at only £18, he was so quick to learn his craft that after only three months he was winning prizes on the winter nursery fields of the Pennines – trials organised to test and grade

David Carlton's Tony, strong and reliable, in the Trough of Bowland.

young collies. In only his second trial on Lonk ewes over the cold moor of Deerplay in the Rossendale Pennines he won fifth prize in an entry of 33. Then things began to go wrong. Tony developed sore feet which made him lame and it looked as though he would spend his life as a yard dog. For months, while veterinary skills sought a cure to his troubles, his wistful eyes looked out over the grey sheep-dotted stretches of sweeping fell he loved to roam.

But Tony was made of stern stuff and David is a patient man. The measure of their determination and understanding was reflected three years later when together they finished fifth of 190 entries in the English National trials of 1976 to represent their country at the International where they won the Shepherds' aggregate trophy. The following year they won the English heat of the television series and finished fourth at the Ruthin mini-international. More important was the fact that they were together again in their daily work on the Lickhurst sheep-runs. The malady, discovered to be an allergy to hookworm, was cured.

David classed Tony as an exceptional work dog – 'Plenty of power yet calm with sheep, cattle, pigs, geese, anything that moves' – yet accepted his minor faults on the trials field. 'He tends to pull up sometimes on his outrun just short of his sheep,' he says.

Yet in spite of this Tony had an impressive trials record which enhanced and reflected the quality of his breeding line. By John Richardson's black-coated International champion Sweep, the son of Supreme champion Wiston Cap, Tony was bred by Tony Iley out of his Jace, the daughter of another Supreme champion, Llyr Evans's Bosworth Coon. With the further bloodlines to such great collies as Jim Wilson's Nap and Cap, Hughes's Jaff, Fraser's Nickey, Dickson's Hemp and Kirk's Nell, his pedigree was blue blooded.

Tony again won an international 'cap' in 1978, but I reckon his best piece of trials' shepherding was one which earned no reward. Competing in the English National trials, he showed a quality of ability and determination which resulted in one of the best-ever stints of trials' shepherding I've ever seen. Tony had one quite wicked ewe in a packet of five Mule sheep which was absolutely intent on going her own way, irrespective of her four companions and in spite of the dog. She stuck her head in the air and dashed around like a creature gone quite mad. Often she fled at full speed in entirely the opposite direction to her companions.

Accepting, with what looked like a canine shrug of his shoulders, the apparently hopeless task of getting the renegade along with the other four ewes round the course and through the hurdles, Tony settled to his job. First he guided the four, then went off to retrieve the wayward ewe, back to the four, off to the defaulter, so it went on. And Tony, by dint of his speed, courage and simple refusal to be beaten by the odd sheep achieved the impossible, getting through all the hurdles success-fully and, even more remarkably, succeeding in penning the sheep and finishing his final shedding. It was a great piece of shepherding where the bad luck of receiving bad sheep to herd was overcome by pure skill. It deserved a better reward and showed that a collie's best shepherding is not always his winning performance.

Tony was winning his international 'caps' while David Carlton was farm-managing at Lickhurst; he has since moved to Loud Scales Farm, below Beacon Fell, to farm in similar country in his own right.

Since Tony, David's most successful collie was the tricolour Slim who won four open trials in the 1994 season, winning at Hesket Newmarket and Crosby Ravensworth in Cumbria on the same day in August of that year. Slim, whose pedigree went back to Supreme champions Wiston Cap and John Thomas's Craig, was in sound competitive form on that day, immediately answering his master's commands and dropping only 17 of 180 points in the two trials.

Bowland is a place I know well and equally as appealing to me as the Yorkshire Dales, for both have childhood memories which are the best in the world. My father came from a little village on the southern fringe of the Bowland area, my grandfather was the water-bailiff on the Ribble, and my uncle, Tom Hayhurst, with whom I spent many happy times, farmed in the beautiful village of Waddington two miles from Clitheroe. I have many friends farming the Forest, which is not the vast area of trees its name suggests but around 150 square miles of northern hunting forest of high fells and deep-cut cloughs. It is sheep country at its bleakest, tempered by the tranquillity and contrast of peaceful and sheltered river valleys of green pastures where the twenty-third Psalm could have been written. It is a land of hardy sheep, productive cows and good collie dogs, and produced Lancashire's first-ever Supreme champion, Tim Longton's clever Ken in 1966.

Ken came from work with a large Dalesbred flock at Rooten Brook Farm above the village of Quernmore, three miles from Lancaster, and to see the handsome six-year-old dog and his son Cap herding the sheep on Clougha Fell was something quite special. Working in

Tim Longton and Ken, 1966 Supreme Champions at Chester (Daily Express).

absolute co-ordination, their talent was so natural and easy that it bordered upon perfection.

The sheep, hill ewes with plenty of spirit, moved quietly, steadily, almost flowing down the hillside. There was no sudden bolting, no breaking back nor faltering. They were under the complete control of the two black and white dogs. What is more, the sheep trusted those two dogs to guide them safely over the bleak, gully-cut and rock-strewn land where the wind whipping in from the open expanse of Morecambe Bay on the west buffeted their wiry bodies and tugged at their long fleeces. It is always a cold job, this shepherding of high places.

Ken and Cap had so many shepherding qualities that it would have been invidious to isolate any one of them. They made shepherding on the fell easy, and they made shepherding on the trials field a series of successes. They enhanced a Longton tradition of three human generations which is world famous, and though Lancashire is well known for the quality of its sheepdogs and sheepmen, it was Ken who first brought the world's highest shepherding honour to the county.

There have been many excellent collies, including five National champions, working over the 1,500 ft high sheep-runs of Rooten Brook. The most recent was the red-coated Tweed, winner in 1981 at Bolton Abbey; Glen, a grandson of Wiston Cap, was England's champion over the flat lands of Houghend on the fringe of Manchester in 1970, and herded the Dalesbreds until exported to Australia. The white-headed Roy was champion of the English National in the Leek downpour of 1974, and another Cap, the grandson of Ken, won England's Brace championship for three successive years. Roy and Cap became so efficient and camera-conscious when we were making the 'One Man and His Dog' programmes that no one would have been surprised if they had asked to join the actor's union!

And there was little Snip, winner of the 1965 National championship, four times in England's International team and perhaps the most loved of all for she was the greatest-hearted collie ever. When failing in eyesight at nine years old she still insisted on going to the fell, though Tim had retired her on veterinary advice.

Ken won the English National at Blackpool in 1966 and was the supreme collie in more ways than on the trials field. He was naturally intelligent, and solved problems with his brains and experience; he was strong in stamina and assertive in mind; and he was practical in his handling of sheep and always respected them. He had the ability to adapt to the situation, to conserve his energy by anticipating the moves of his sheep, to gear himself to the right speed and power for the sheep under command. He was so quiet, simply and naturally powered, that at times he looked almost idle. He was truly one of Britain's great collies.

He was such a good all-round dog, either with the Dalebreds on the open moor or with the black beef cows round the yards, that he was very often taken for granted. Not until his untimely death, due to complications after being kicked by a cow when he was 8½ years old, was his value really appreciated by the outside shepherding world. His full potential as a stud-dog was never realised for he had no pretensions to outstanding style. His was the practical approach in everything, the frills were for others. Yet his contribution to practical shepherding techniques was appreciated by 'officialdom' when Tim was invited to take him as the ideal collie to a shepherds' symposium. Was it the Englishman's modest nature to decry his own champions and persist in the fallacy that all good collies must of right come from north of the Border that affected Ken's use as a breeding sire? It was left to an Irish handler of renown to acclaim openly Ken as the best collie in the British Isles, and that was before the Lancashire dog won the Supreme championship, the greatest competitive measure of a working dog.

Whatever, Ken carried his shepherding to perfection, accepting the plaudits and fame of his successes on the trials field but really never happier than when working the open moor.

He was born at Rooten Brook on an April day in 1960 of true North Country heritage, with the world's finest working blood in his veins. His mother was Spy, then five years old and a daughter of David Dickson's Ben and Bill Jolly's Spy. She was a black and white bitch of Loos blood and the granddaughter of Wilson's Cap. Ken's father was Philip Mason's Chip from Goosnargh, a 6½-year-old dog whose lines went back to John Holliday's international Roy and Dickson's Hemp.

He was descended from Tommy and Old Hemp, pioneers of the modern breed, and included in his pedigree were dogs whose names and exploits were legendary in the sheep country of the northland. Ken was the twelfth of his direct line to reflect his ability by winning the Supreme title.

During his early life he spent a time of learning with Norman Woods at nearby Abbeystead, and Norman encouraged his natural abilities for shepherding. Well grown and with the basic skills of his craft he returned to Tim Longton at Rooten Brook. He was a handsome dog. Tall in stature, strong and fit, he was the typical black and white rough-coated Border Collie, and he carried his right ear down and his left ear pricked which gave him a jaunty devil-may-care attitude. He had the three important qualities of good temperament, good gathering sense and pluck which Tim Longton looks for in his dogs.

Ken entered the International scene boldly. On his first England singles appearance he won the International Farmers' championship at

Drymen on the shores of Loch Lomond after winning the English Farmers' championship in 1964. Two years later he reached the peak of trials perfection, winning the English National and Farmers' championships and the great Supreme International title. This accolade was won after three testing trials against 438 of the most experienced dogs in the British Isles, and won the trophy for England after a lapse of eight years, giving English shepherding prestige a timely and much-needed boost in International competition.

Ken's Supreme victory at Chester was a great stint of shepherding. Over the half-mile gather of rising and undulating ground he was always in control of the Welsh Mountain sheep and in harmony with

Pedigree of KEN (17166) 1966 Supreme Champion with Tim Longton

The numbers in brackets are the Stud Book numbers of the International Sheep Dog Society
— Indicates that this dog is not known

his master. His one blemish was at each of the lifts of the two separate groups of ten sheep, but his forceful action at these first contacts with the ewes left no doubt in their minds that he intended to call the tune. This he did right to the end. Indeed, Tim tells how the dog saved the day in the shedding ring.

'I was getting a little impatient with time going on and two of the seven remaining sheep left to shed and I moved forward to part a sheep that was in the course of changing its mind. Had Ken not realised that I was trying the impossible and himself remained steady as a rock I could have spoiled the whole job.' Ken's final score was 425 of 450 aggregate points from three judges, the best score for ten years and 12½ points in front of Scotland's champion, John Gilchrist's Spot, the clever and stylish white-headed dog which in successive years won the Scottish National championship.

Spot was another collie who proved during that International at Chester just how highly developed is the collie brain. Coming to the first gate of the driving section John, his vision impaired by raindrops on his glasses, whistled Spot to turn the sheep too soon. Spot hesitated and looked back at his master knowing that the instruction was wrong, and then reluctantly and obediently did as he was told and the sheep missed the gate. 'He knew I had made a mistake,' said John.

Tim Longton's Ken represented England on four occasions and his long list of trials successes included the famous Longshaw championship twice, the Royal Lancashire, the Yorshire and London's Hyde Park.

It was really Ken's dedication to his craft which finally stopped his winning ways. Part of his duty at Rooten Brook was the herding of beef cows and he never flinched from the most aggressive cow. When he was just over eight years old he developed an abscess on his back, thought to be the result of a kick from a cow, and in spite of the best of veterinary care he never got over the surgery.

One of his greatest trials was without glamour though of the realms of fiction when, after his operation, he ran fifth of 55 entries on Swaledales at Fearby Cross near Masham in Yorkshire's North Riding. Three-and-a-half points behind the winner, Ken showed that he had lost none of the skill and courage that had made him famous. But his 'comeback' was not to be. He died four months later.

Ken's partner in so much of his shepherding in the pouring rainstorms, screaming wind gales and blinding snow blizzards on the heights of Clougha Fell was Snip, one year his senior and a little bitch who never flagged whatever the conditions. She had the courage of a lion and once completed the half-mile double-gather course with 20 sheep at the 1965 Cardiff International in 27½ minutes after a mistake at the sheep pens had misled her on the second gather and resulted in her having to outrun again. The victim of human error, she could not possibly win that trial but she proved to all who saw her the indomitable courage, perseverance and stamina of the modern shepherding dog.

She had happier moments. She won the English National and Farmers' championships at Leicester on strong white-faced halfbreds in 1965 after twice being runner-up for the National title in 1961 and 1963, and she graced England's International team with honour on four occasions, though eventually she was to go blind, which caused her retirement. No more faithful collie ever lived. Snip was of Jim Wilson's bloodlines through her mother, John Bathgate's Meg, and her father was the Irish National champion, Whitehope Corrie.

The prick-eared black and white Cap was the son of Ken and Snip, and the breeding showed when, at two years old, he won his first English International 'cap' at his first attempt, going on to a story-book International when he finished fourth in the Supreme championship and won, with his father as partner, the reserve Brace championship. Sadly he was to be affected by his mother's complaint of blindness, but at a much earlier age.

Tim Longton has always been one of England's most consistent handlers both in singles and brace competitions and he took his fourth English Brace title in six years to Rooten Brook in 1978 with the

A successful trio. Tim Longton's Ken, Supreme Champion; Snip, English Champion; and their son Cap, fourth in the Supreme test, at their Rooten Brook home in North Lancashire (Keith Taylor).

3½-year-old Bess and the 2-year-old red-coated Tweed. It was rather a fairy-tale success for Bess for she was only five days old when her mother Nell died, and she reached maturity only by the devoted care of long, tedious hours of hand-rearing from her breeder Norman Woods of Ortner House in Over Wyresdale.

Bess was not the first weakling to reach stature under Tim Longton, for he won his first International representation at his first attempt in 1951 with Nell, who at birth had been the weakest of a litter of nine pups. She, like Bess, was a small bitch with a strong heart and was helping Tim in his work as shepherd to the Blackburn Corporation Waterworks with their flocks around Dunsop Bridge in the heart of the Trough of Bowland. Nell won the English Shepherds' championship in the rains of Grange Park, Wetherby, when she was three years old. She had gone to Tim from his father at nine months old and, quick to learn, she was winning trials at 15 months.

So dedicated to her craft was Nell that on one occasion, having been left at home to nurse her young family, she squeezed through a narrow window to arrive on the hill when everything was going wrong with the shepherding of ewes and lambs by her less experienced kennel-mates. Quickly she put things right, retrieving two lost lambs to their mothers from a flock of strange sheep before returning to suckle her pups.

Tim remembers how she taught him to keep his temper. 'When she herself was getting annoyed at some stupid sheep she would twitch her tail slightly and when I went to help her, she would give me a look which warned me to go easy. It was a lesson I benefited from in later years, particularly on the trials field.'

Nell contracted the dread disease of hard-pad and, though moved to the warmth of the farmhouse kitchen for constant attention, she died, to be mourned by the whole family.

Tim Longton is not given to exaggerated praise. He is a practical farmer who conceals his feelings, but there is affection in his voice when he talks of his collies. He of all people knows just how much those dogs meant to him. Of all the dogs he has handled, he says, 'I like to think always that we're practically two of a kind, thinking alike, doing alike in everything.' Working long and lonely hours in wild country Tim looks to his dogs for companionship. 'They're tremendous pals, they never seem to let you down. . . . There is little said between us. But often when I sit down the dog will come and lay his chin on my knee. His attitude says, that's grand mate, I'm still here with you, and it's a great relationship.'

A sheepman's life by its very nature breeds independence and self-reliance and Tim Longton has a natural aptitude for handling collies.

Even on the big occasions of the Internationals, with thousands of critical eyes watching, he is a cool customer – as one would expect of a former glider troops sergeant who was at the fateful landing at Arnhem in the Second World War.

Two of Tim's good companions were Tweed and Clun Roy. The red-coated Tweed, a grandson of Wiston Cap and Gilchrist's Spot, who ran for England in 1978, 1979, 1980, 1983, 1984 and 1985, partnered the big upstanding Clun Roy to the English Brace honour in 1985. Clun Roy had a great respect and feeling for sheep and treated them with consideration. He was a rough-coated tricolour dog bred at Craven Arms in Shropshire, the son of his master's white-faced Roy, the English National champion of 1974, and back to Lionel Pennefather's Irish champion of 1962 and 1966, Bess, and John Evan's Supreme champions Roy and Tweed. He ran for England in 1980, 1981, 1983, 1984 and 1985.

More often than not Tim Longton starts his collies in competitive work on the nursery fields of the Pennines. These nursery trials are the beginning – training grounds where a collie gets used to travelling in a car, meeting different people, hearing new sounds and coping with all breeds of sheep.

On these winter fields, where you often have to huddle from snow, rainstorm and biting wind in the shelter of a stone wall or farm vehicle, everybody is equal – it doesn't matter if you've just won the Supreme championship. All the collies are starting on what may well be an illustrious international career or just better work on the home farm.

Glen was one of Tim Longton's dogs which started its competitive career on the nursery fields of the 1987–8 season and went forward to win two single and two Brace representative honours for England.

In March 1988 the black and white Glen, who was good to handle and was a natural worker, won the Pennine Inter-Club trials between the Fylde, Holme, Meltham, Trawden and Yorkshire societies when he was 15 months old. Field work which was immaculate on lively Mule hoggs over wide, level and soaking pastures at Goosnargh gave Glen the individual championship, and his Fylde team third placing in the team contest.

Two months later, with convincing and forthright shepherding of pedigree Swaledale hoggs, he won the coveted Yorkshire open championship over the ups and downs of the high pastures of Hallam Hill above Earl Crag at Sutton, near Keighley. In fact, 1988 was almost a fairy-tale year for Glen: he won the fiercely contested Penton trials in the Borders, and was only a single point from victory at Holme's Deerplay Hill trials.

West of the Cheviot Hills at Penton trials, which are contested by many of Scotland's leading collies, the black and white Glen imposed his authority on Blackface hoggs which were never easy, negotiated the outwork successfully, and completed his shed and pen for an impressive victory. At Deerplay, after he had run the rough moor and climbed 260 ft in an outrun to gather three shorn Gritstone ewes on the 1,450 ft contour in a most practical way, he slipped a little at the pen to lose the vital point.

A year later he won the Lake District championship and his nice, easy ways were to win the Yorkshire and Macclesfield titles, and partnered by Becca, the Royal Lancashire, Longshaw and Nidderdale Brace titles. He partnered Becca into the English teams of 1991 and 1993. In 1993 their partnership won them reserve Brace title.

Glen was a son of Davy, the Shropshire collie that won the 1987 English National and Supreme championships for Sydney Price, and his paternal ancestry went back to McTeir's Ben, the 1972 International Shepherds' champion and to Supreme champions Wiston Cap and McKnight's Gael.

Becca, who partnered Glen to her first representative honour in 1991, won the Royal Lancashire championship in 1992, the Peak title in 1992, Longshaw in 1991 and 1993, and has represented England six times. She is a dependable medium-sized rough-coated tricolour bitch who always runs her heart out and gives of her best. She started her competitive shepherding career on the nursery fields of the Pennines when she was just over 12 months old, and immediately showed that she could handle any breed of sheep, taking 15 awards and the Fylde Sheepdog Society's championship in the 1988–9 winter season.

After shepherding on the bleak moors above Rooten Brook Farm at home, she lapped up the comparatively easy grasslands of the valley, and she herded Mule hoggs with confidence and style to win the Fylde nursery championship at Goosnargh in February 1989. Chosen in the seven-strong team to represent the Fylde Society in the Inter-Club championship later in the year, she helped them to victory with the second-best run of the day. She didn't let the grass grow under her feet and in the following open season she won at Macclesfield in Cheshire and Hope in Derbyshire.

In seven years Becca has won 24 open championships which include such prestigious events as the Peak and Longshaw championships, Holme, Moorcock and the Royal Lancashire. I judged her on the third day of the three-day Royal Lancashire trials in 1995, and her shepherding was almost perfect – I only had half a point of 100 off her in the gather of Mule shearlings.

Becca is a granddaughter of Syndey Price's Davy, the winner of the 1987 Supreme championship, back to Wiston Cap and McKnight's

Gael. In her maternal pedigree are Supreme champions Gwyn Jones's Bill, John Thomas's Craig and Alan Jones's Roy.

Rob, whom I always found to have a lovely temperament, blended with her to win eight Brace championships including those of Nidderdale, Macclesfield and the Royal Lancashire. In 1995 he partnered her to win representative honours for England.

When he was only 2½ years old, in 1994, he was so composed that he kept six Mule shearlings trotting on the correct lines after two faultless outruns and decisive lifts to win the double-gather championship of the Royal Lancashire over the flat close-cropped grasslands of Astley Park at Chorley. That year at Chorley was a great triumph for Rob for in partnership with Becca, he also won the Brace championship.

Starting his trials career by winning the novice title at Crosthwaite in 1993, he has since won six open championships in two years.

A rough-coated black and white dog of handsome appearance, born near Preston in Lancashire in 1992, Rob is of the best of breeding, a paternal grandson of Wyn Edward's Bill which won the 1981 and 1982 Supreme championships, and a maternal grandson of Michael Perring's Dryden Spam which was the reserve English champion in 1985.

Tim Longton, the son of a farmer who believed in having a good dog, was born in Littledale in 1919, and believes that temperament is all important in a collie dog. When he's breeding he's not thinking about trials, but about a dog that can drive 600 sheep off the moors and fells.

Tim has represented his country over 30 times in International competition, winning three International titles and 17 English championships. He has won the county championship at the Royal Lancashire Show trials twice in the last five years, the Yorkshire championship five times, the Peak championship of Derbyshire, and the famous Longshaw title seven times.

On behalf of the International Sheep Dog Society I presented Tim Longton with the Wilkinson Sword which the Society give annually to a person who has made an outstanding contribution to the Society, sheepdogs or sheepdog trials, at the Armathwaite International. On that occasion I said that, in spite of Tim's elevated stature in sheepdog circles, he was always willing to help any newcomer to sheepdogs with advice. Even though he had won most of the top trials, was a past English National President, a Council member, and a Director of the Society, he was never 'big headed', though he has every right to be, and was always prepared to assist the beginner.

He has helped to make the name of Longton famous thoughout the sheepdog world. When we have appeared together on television, he has never let the side down. Collie work is an inborn trait in the Longton family. Tim's father, also named Tim, won the English National in 1949

Handling skills inherited. Thomas Longton, son of Tot Longton of Quernmore, wins the English Brace Championship at his first attempt, at Penrith in 1979, and is congratulated by Ray Ollerenshaw, chairman of the International Sheep Dog Society (Marc Henrie).

with Dot at Morecambe, and his brothers, Tot, Will and Jack, his son Timothy and his nephew Thomas have all represented England in International competition. It is a family skill which is continuing.

Tot won the Supreme championship of the International Sheep Dog Society in 1983 with Jess at Aberystwyth, and his son Thomas won the Supreme title with Bess in 1986 at Beaumaris. Both Will and Jack have represented England. Timothy won the English Brace championships with Gel and Cap in 1988 and 1990; and Tim's grandson Michael represented England in the Young Handler section of BBC2's 'One Man and His Dog' competition in 1994. Will's son Bill has won open, novice and nursery honours.

CHAPTER ELEVEN

Wise Dogs of the North Country

⊶⊃o⊂⊶⊶⊃o⊂⊶⊶⊃o⊂⊶

I recall the winning of the Supreme championship in the most atrocious weather in 1983, the wisdom of Rob, and the story that started in the mist of early morning; I consider the blue bitch that brought Lancashire's second Supreme championship and meet the first lady to captain England's shepherding team.

Tot Longton won the Supreme championship of the International Sheep Dog Society in 1983 at Aberystwyth in Wales with the 8½-year-old Jess in the worst weather conditions in which an International has ever been held. The weather, with gale force winds which blew down parts of the grandstand, marquees and caravans, and littered the field with debris, was so bad that the officials considered cancelling the event. This was a purely human decision for the safety of spectators, for collies often meet such conditions in their daily lives on the home farms. But the blustery wind blowing straight in from the Irish Sea made it impossible, for the most part, for dogs to hear the commands of their handlers and much had to be left to their own intelligence.

Jess was equal to the task and her own skills, coupled with the commands she could hear from her experienced handler, made a winning partnership. On that day, 3 September 1983, collies as a whole showed their supreme traits with determined and authoritative shepherding of Welsh Halfbreds – mettlesome and often wilful – that has made British dogs the best in the world.

Pointings from a competitive point of view were understandably low, but the medium-coated Jess scored 23 more than her nearest rival, John Thomas's prick-eared Cap, the 1982 English Shepherds' champion. She had implicit faith in her handler, taking his instructions immediately when she could hear his commands, and Tot had implicit faith in her ability. She worked well, ignoring the fierce wind which tugged at her body, driving steadily and quietly, and keeping firm control all the time. The winning of the Supreme title in such atrocious conditions was her 28th open championship.

A mottle-legged clever little bitch, always happy at her work, with a forthright style which held the initiative, Jess won 35 open championships in nine years, including the Royal Lancashire, Yorkshire, Fylde, Peak and Longshaw titles. Of the Whitehope Nap bloodline, she was by her master's black and white Ken out of Bill Rockcliffe's Jill from Kendal.

Tot farmed in the valley of the River Conder below Tim Longton's Rooten Brook. There, on the 95 grassland acres of Lee End Farm, he milked the 'Marydale' pedigree Friesians and reared quality fat lambs from a Teeswater × Dalesbred sheep crossing. To herd such stock Tot always had collies of the finest calibre, collies which down the years since around 1945 had earned for their master a trials record second to none and, when it seemed that it was never to happen, that final accolade of the Supreme championship in 1983.

Tot Longton's Supreme championship was a popular win for, irrespective of country, he was a respected handler everywhere, and the win was acclaimed by all. Twice before Lee End collies had been reserve Supreme champions, the black and white rough-coated Bute in 1956, and Gyp in 1971, while Spot in 1960 and Rob in 1963 ran third in the contest.

The classical rough-coated Nell won the 1959 International Driving championship, and Gyp the same honour in 1971; and the wise old Rob and the younger Lad together took the 1969 International Brace title, but Tot classed these as minor International honours in his quest for the supreme accolade.

Tot took the misfortunes which seemed to arise at his Internationals, indeed he took all set-backs in his usual philosophical and cheery way, with a smile on his face. He once said to me, prior to 1983, when he thought he would never win the Supreme title, 'It's just one of those things.'

Nevertheless, since he started competitive shepherding in 1945 when he was 28 years old he had a most enviable record on the trials field – two English National championships with the prick-eared Mossie in 1950 and 1956, three Driving championships and nine Brace titles. Not until 1983, at the gale-lashed International at Aberystwyth, did things finally come right for him, with the Supreme title. He had won most of the major trials in England and had represented his country on 20 occasions, helping England to seven team championships. Yet one of Tot's greatest trials brought no material reward – but great satisfaction.

It was on a September morning in 1963 when, off into the dawn mist of York racecourse to seek 20 unseen hill sheep, his young tricolour Rob raised the supreme international victory hopes of English supporters higher than they had been for over five years. Though only two years old, one of the youngest collies ever to reach the Supreme championship test, the rough-coated Rob did not fail those hopes. He finished the exacting test of this greatest of all sheepdog trials to a great cry of English approval, adjudged third in the championship at his first attempt. Though his shedding was almost perfect, his youthful lack of experience reduced his pointing against the most experienced collies in Great Britain. Yet his success was of the realms of fiction, for only eight months previously he had been competing in Pennine nursery class trials.

At the end of that trial I remember saying to Tot, 'If only he could have won.'

He replied, 'Yes, but you've got your story anyway.' At that moment Tot was a better journalist than I, for of course I had a story.

Rob's performance on that morning in the hard matter-of-fact atmosphere of farming contest had a touch of romance about it. He was only a youngster; he had run first while the other collies and their masters were flexing their muscles in preparation; and he had gone away into a blanket of ground mist which made it impossible for either him or Tot to see their sheep target. To finish third against such odds was a remarkable achievement.

But as we came to know Rob it was quite understandable, even expected, for he was of noble breed, a dog of tremendous heart and skill, and he just didn't know the word defeat, either in facing an awkward cow at home or the flightiest of sheep on a trials course.

He went to Lee End when he was four months old, the rough-coated tricolour son of John Gilchrist's Bob from Midlothian and Bob Fraser's Nell, the 1955 English Shepherds' champion, and of the Northumbrian farmer's famous Mindrum line, and his initial trials practices came on the cold rainswept winter nursery fields of the Pennines in 1962–3. His first experience of open trials and their stiff competition came when he was still only 21 months old at Hayfield in the Derbyshire Peak and he finished second of 66 entries and then only beaten on the time factor. This was something he was quick to put right in following trials, for power and speed of control were to become his characteristics.

At his peak, when intelligence and experience combined to produce a great working dog, he was capable of anticipating the moods of stock and was dominant in his mastery of their whims. This ability was amply reflected on the trials field where, after his romantic and immediate rise to fame at York in 1963, he continued in almost fictional vein to close

Tot Longton's wise old Rob, winner of 40 Open Championships and five International caps (Farmers Guardian).

his career with 40 open championships and five International 'caps' in eight years.

Rob adhered himself to the affections of North Country sheepmen by his dour refusal to be beaten, and he inspired and tempered his younger partner, Lad, to the sense of occasion to win the 1969 International Brace championship at Chester to give Tot Longton his best International success to that date. Twice Rob was a partner in the winning of the English Brace title, with Lad in 1969 and with the trim little Nip in 1968.

Of aristocratic line, he was a half-brother of John Gilchrist's Spot, Scottish National champion of 1965 and 1966, and also of his master's Nell, of English pride, and his origins were the best in the world, back to Old Hemp. On both sides of his pedigree he went back to Wilson's Cap of the Borders; on his sire's side he was descended from John Gilchrist's Spot, the 1947 Supreme champion, and from Jim Wilson's Glen, the 1946 and 1948 Supreme champion. In his list of 40 victories were the leading trials of Longshaw in Derbyshire; the Royal Lancashire, Holme and Fylde in his home county; the wild Moorcock event in Upper Garsdale; Patterdale and Threlkeld in the Lake District; and, further south, of Husbands Bosworth and the Vale of Evesham.

True to reputation he left the trials scene as he had started – in a blaze of glory. Tot intended to retire him at the end of the 1970 season, when he was almost ten years old, but Rob's fitness and spirit eschewed inactivity and in May 1971 he won his fortieth open championship at Penton on the Scottish Border.

The shadows were lengthening over the slopes of the Cheviot Hills and 81 collies had that day failed to master completely the strong and wilful Blackface hoggs as the wise old dog went to his task. His approach was the typical, confident surety of purpose which had become synonymous with his name. He mastered his sheep at the lift and they accepted his authority so completely over the course and in the penning that when he came through to take the final shed-off – with decisive action – he had completed a masterly stint of shepherding of exhibition quality. It won him 59 of 60 points, three points in front of the best of English and Scottish dogs, and as he loped off the field, tongue just lolling a little with exertion, it also won the spontaneous acclaim of the crowd of Border farmers. He ran some great trials in his career but none better than his finale at Penton.

Rob went to Lee End Farm late in 1961 at the tragic death from distemper of Spot, the smooth-coated collie who, at five years old and in his prime, had earned a reputation as one of Lancashire's best. In 1960 Spot ran third in the Supreme championship and was reserve in the Farmers' championship at the International.

Spot's kennel-mate was Nell, winner of the 1959 International Driving title, and together they formed a great partnership, winning England's Brace title twice in three years. In Spot's last season before his untimely death he partnered Nell to 11 victories and one second placing in 13 Brace contests. Both were of Jim Wilson's Cap line of breeding and as fine a pair of collies as one man ever handled. They were ideally matched and in three years became part of the Longton tradition.

But perhaps Tot Longton held a little prick-eared bitch, Mossie, in most esteem. With her in 1950 at Bakewell he won his first National title, the year after his father, Tim senior, had won the honour.

Mossie, Lancashire born and bred, eventually won her second National championship at Hereford in 1956, and the National Driving championship in the same year. With Bute, a black and white daughter of Bill Jolly's Bute, sired by Wilson's Supreme champion Glen, Mossie won the 1954 English Brace title. Bute ran reserve Supreme champion in 1956.

Mossie was the first of the great collies of Lee End, and she was home bred out of her master's Fan and sired by Bill Jolly's Glen whose pedigree went back to Ben, handled by the great Alex Millar to the International Farmers' championships of 1928 and 1930 and the Scottish National championship of 1930, and subsequently exported to New Zealand. One of Mossie's ancestors, Vim, was lost at sea while returning to Scotland from an Irish trials event.

England never had a more faithful servant than Tot Longton in her international cause, and his consistent prowess as a handler played a big

Tot Longton's Bute and Mossie, Brace Champions of England in 1954.

part in building Lancashire's reputation in sheepdog matters. Efficiency was the stamp of Tot Longton's collies, style was incidental. They had the ability to work to command, to work with speed and control, to fear nothing – and the will to win in competitive trials work.

Extending this reputation into the 1970s, the 3½-year-old tricolour Lad, a grandson of the 1967 Supreme champion McKnight's Gael, worked hard on Suffolk halfbreds which tested his patience to the extreme over the downlands of Berkshire to win England's reserve National championship in 1969, and he later partnered Gyp to win the 1971 and 1972 English Brace titles.

One of Lee End's best-known bitches was Gyp, who inherited the forthright manner of her grandsire Whitehope Nap, and it was this strength of character which gave her a place in collie history at the Cardiff International in 1971. She was 6½ years old at the time and won the right to compete in all the four sections of the International – one of the few collies to do so in the story of the International.

Apart from intelligence and ability, she showed an outstanding degree of stamina – and with an injured leg – for she ran a total of 5½ miles of concentrated competitive shepherding in hot weather, covering Driving, Farmers', Brace and Supreme courses, for because of a rerun ordered by the officials, due to a marking fault in the sheep, she covered the Supreme course twice. To this was added the wearing task of shedding, singling and penning sheep, all within a time limit.

She won the Driving championship on 50 Welsh Mountain sheep for a drive of half a mile; she was reserve Supreme champion; she won third placing in the Farmers' championship; and with kennel-mate Lad she ran fourth in the Brace contest. Gyp was mated to the 1968 Supreme champion Llyr Evans's Bosworth Coon and one of her pups born in February 1969 was Jed.

Jed grew into a handsome black and white rough-coated bitch and, schooled at Lee End and on the nursery fields in the winter of 1970–1, where she was the most successful youngster of the season with 13 awards including six victories, she became good at her work, though sometimes a little temperamental – which was not always a bad thing. She took her place in the farm duties alongside her mother and started to make her own reputation in competition.

Her first victory was in November 1970 in a nursery contest of the Yorkshire Sheepdog Society at Utley near Keighley when she was 22 months old, but I particularly remember her work a fortnight later when she ran the windswept Deerplay Moor to win Holme Association's event with the loss of only one point. The following season she was on the novice circuit, where she won three events, and in April 1972 she really 'arrived' on the trials scene, winning the coveted Fylde open in fine style. She went on to win 35 open contests in seven years, and leave her own mark on the Lee End honours list.

Born of Jed's sister, Bill Rockcliffe's Jill, the medium-coated Jess also won her first major championship at Fylde in 1977 when she was only 2½ years old. She was 8½ years old in 1983 when she proved herself Britain's top collie by winning the Supreme championship. Clever and happy at her craft, small in stature and forthright in manner, Jess had her finest year in 1983. She was reserve English champion, and she won her 30th open championship at Whitworth in the last trial of the year. When she retired from the trials fields in the following year she had won 35 open championships.

Tot died suddenly in October 1990 at the age of 73 and the esteem with which he was held was reflected in the number of farmers overflowing from the chapel and the schoolroom into the grounds at his funeral at Quernmore in north Lancashire. His memory will never be forgotten, for the gates of the burial ground bear his name and two shepherds' crooks, and into the headstone of his grave is carved a sheepdog.

They talk a lot in north Lancashire of a blue bitch called Nell, an almost mythical character it would seem at times for she is reputed to have been faultless on the fell and unbeatable on the trials field. In fact, according to Harry Huddleston of Snab Green, Arkholme, Nell was owned by his father and won 45 prizes in 50 trials before the First World War. That blue bitch was where the Huddleston quest for sheepdog's top honour really started, a quest not to be fulfilled until September 1969 when Harry's clever little 6½-year-old Bett became

Lancashire's second Supreme champion and only the third bitch to win the title in 31 years.

For Harry, who had handled his first dog in trials soon after leaving school and was then 53 years old – and known by all as 'light Harry' to distinguish him from his cousin 'black Harry' Huddleston of Brookhouse – the victory was charged with emotion. Years of planning, striving and hope had finally borne fruit. A tall, mild-mannered man, none nicer, he gave much of the credit to the collie Bett. 'She is not much to look at but her head's screwed-on right' was his pointed appraisal of the little bitch.

But if ever the International has been won by teamwork it was on that September morning at Chester, for with obstacles fringing the field on the line of the outrun, Bett needed all the guidance her handler could give her to reach the unseen sheep. Using a lifetime's sheep lore in assessing the problems himself, and the trim little bitch doing everything that was asked, theirs was a triumph for sound practical shepherding.

Bett was by nature and breeding a dog of the farm, where her main task was the careful herding of the 'Grassgarth' pedigree Friesian milk cows and the 150 Dalesbred ewes on the 230 acre Snab Green holding in the Lune Valley. She was a kindly dog, black and white and rough coated, small in stature yet big in spirit, and I had held a great admiration for her ever since I judged her National trial at Dovedale in 1967 when she ran second, the barest half-point from victory.

She worked quicker than most collies, keeping her charges on the

The gentlest of bitches, Bett, Supreme Champion of 1969, always tried to please her master, Harry Huddleston of Arkholme in the Lune Valley.

move all the time, and it was a practical art which won merit registration by the International Sheep Dog Society. She was not registered on pedigree at birth and she earned entry to the Stud Book the hard, but the most satisfying way, on performance. Work was in her blood and her skills came naturally. She went to Harry when she was about 12 months old and he recalls, 'I could do almost anything with her when I had only known her for three weeks.' Checking her breeding, it is in no way surprising that Bett was worthy of the Supreme accolade.

Her sire's line reflects all that is good in north Lancashire breeding, back to that blue bitch of Harry's father. Her grandam was Joe Gorst's Bett, the 1953 English National, 1953 and 1954 English Driving, and 1953 International Driving champion. It is interesting that, beyond her paternal grandsire, Bett had blood common to Tim Longton's Ken, Lancashire's other Supreme champion, and their kinship blood took in Supreme champions Wallace's Moss, Scott's Kep, Armstrong's Sweep, Armstrong's Don, Batty's Hemp, Telfer's Haig, Brown's Spot, Roberts's Jaff and Wilson's Craig.

Famous Lancastrian ancestors in Bett's pedigree are Maddie I and Maddie II, handled to International status by 'black' Harry Huddleston, and 'lile' Glen, also worked by 'black' Harry, which in 1939 earned 12 prizes in 15 trials. Their ancestry was from Mossie, a bitch owned by Tim Longton senior, of Quernmore, which was mated to T. C. Martindale's Ken, the greatest sire in the North Country at the time. Bett's maternal pedigree blended the best of Scottish blood, with Wilson's Cap appearing over half a dozen times, and to Wilson's one-eyed Roy, the great collie which won the Supreme title three times.

Bett honoured England's International cause on three occasions and, previous to her, Harry had represented his country many times with such dogs as Jim, Gem, Glen, the blue-coated Duke, Kep, the reserve Farmers' champion in 1961 at Ayr, and the white and black Laddie whose shedding of the 15 unwanted sheep one after another in a matter of seconds at Towyn in 1968 will long be remembered.

Since Bett and Laddie, the strong, experienced Coon, and the friendly Cap, both of the Wiston Cap line, have been successful under Harry's control; Coon represented England in 1974, and Cap in 1979, 1980 and 1981.

'Black' Harry, Harry Huddleston of Brookhouse, is also a name synonymous with successful sheepdogs and he has handled many great dogs for England, including Udale Sim, winner of the National championship and the reserve Supreme title in 1972.

A smooth four-year-old collie which showed his enjoyment in his work, Sim had an easy and decisive action, controlled with complete power, and he was also of that famous blue bitch line of the Huddlestons.

He was bred by his master, who himself reared eight generations of Sim's forebears, and his temperament was so good, his eye without nastiness and his heart so keen for work that he was included in Britain's team of three collies to the New Zealand championship in February 1973. There he made such an impression that Harry was eventually persuaded to return him to New Zealand for stud purposes. Sadly he died while making the trip.

Travelling the Lune Valley, as I have so often done, especially in August when dogs are tested at some of the top trials in the North Country, it is the contrast of mood and countryside which makes the area so pleasant. That hedging and walling competitions are held side by side at the local shows emphasises the mixture of upland and lowland farming. On the fells where the adaptable Dalesbred ewes, the lively Swaledales and the handsome Rough Fells vie with each other for popularity among the Halfbreds, the wind is always on the verge of a scream and the grey rain clouds muster, but the valleys are lush and green and the hedgerows bright with wild flowers. It is a land where the three old counties of Lancashire, Westmorland and the West Riding of Yorkshire meet and it garners the best of each county.

Its dogs are proved over some of the most exacting trials courses, over Barbon's steep fellside where Rough Fell ewes, if ruffled at the top, leap downhill like mountain goats, over Moorcock's windswept bents in Garsdale, at Hill Top above Dentdale, and on the lusher lands of Caton, Lunesdale and Hornby.

I think my marathon judging stint would be Cautley near Sedbergh where I marked 120 collies in the day. It was from Hebblethwaite Hall at Cautley in August 1977 that 25-year-old Miss Jean Hardisty – now Mrs Alan Bousfield – took the heather-fringed route to Northumberland with Flash and Taff to make collie history. With really authoritative shepherding Jean handled her little 4½-year-old black and white Flash to become the first-ever woman in the four international countries to win a National title when she beat England's most experienced handlers in the country's three-day trials at Swinhoe on the north-east coast.

Her success, in her first National, also gave her the honour of being the first woman ever to be included in an English team, and though little short of a fairytale win for Jean, was well merited, purposeful and worked for with a skill from both handler and collie which was acclaimed by all her older, wiser contemporaries. This slip of a girl, after only three years of open competition, handled with the calmness and competence of a veteran, and her success was the result of a dedicated partnership and mutual understanding with the collie bitch which mastered testy Blackface ewes over the large National course to a sound 186 of 200 aggregate points from the two judges.

As we have already seen in North Country tradition, her success also came from an inherited ability in both handler and collie, for Jean, though by profession an accountant at the time, was the daughter of Wilson Hardisty, a highly respected handler of working collies, and Flash was the great-granddaughter of Mr Hardisty's Jim, winner of the 1961 English National. The hours and hours of patient schooling while helping her father with the Swaledale flock in her spare time and at weekends and in the evenings at Hebblethwaite had been rewarded, for Flash's timing in winning her first open trial was perfect. It brought the 'lile lass and the lile bitch' an armful of trophies as National and Farmers' champions and technically gave them captaincy of the English team for the 1977 International.

At Libanus in the Brecon Beacons in South Wales the following month they failed to qualify for the Supreme event, but to show that her success was not just good fortune on that Friday afternoon in Northumberland, Jean worked her other collie, the tricolour Taff, into the English team the following year, finishing sixth in the National at Welbeck. Further, she won through the qualifying round to the Supreme championship that year at Chatsworth – beaten in the shedding ring – but proudly leaving the field to the biggest ovation of the day from the packed grandstand.

She was the first woman handler ever to reach the Supreme championship. It needed more than just ability for Jean to compete at this level in a predominantly man's world and the crowd responded to her pluck.

The only other lady handlers to win a trophy in National competition and represent their country at the International were Mrs Julie Deptford, an English girl shepherding in Morayshire, who won the Scottish National in 1991 with Gwen, and Mrs Annie McCormack from Kingussie near Inverness, who won the Scottish Driving championship in 1958 with Swan.

Julie won the Scottish Brace titles of 1991 and 1992 with Bess and Nell, and Mrs McCormack was again in the Scottish singles team in 1962 with Ness, a daughter of Swan. Julie represented Scotland with Gwen in 1989, Mrs Jean Thompson of Portpatrick, with Wullie, in 1980, and Mrs Viv Billingham and Garry from Swindon, near Yetholme, in 1982. Viv was also in Scotland's Brace team with Holly and Glen in 1990. Mrs Barbara Sykes from Perlethorpe, near Newark, had her Meg in the 1983 English team, Mrs Rhos Edwards and Don from Partridge Green near Brighton on the south coast were in the 1993 English team and Katy Cropper, then at Hardrow in Wensleydale, had her half white-headed Trim, the lovely tempered bitch which won the 1989 singles championship of the 'One Man and His Dog' trials, and her 3-year-old Max in England's team in 1990.

CHAPTER TWELVE

Efficient Dogs for Efficient Farming

I describe how the collies of the Lake District are essential to the efficient farming of the high lands, salute the 'Nipper' on his fell beat, and meet a Highland Scot whose collies have won two Supreme and two American championships.

The rimy-faced Herdwick of ancient origin is the queen of the Lakeland fells, from Skiddaw in the north to Ulverston in the south. No tougher sheep exists to turn the dry and rocky grazings of the hard land of the Cumberland range of mountains into meat and wool. Stocky and dour, they graze the ledges of the vertical crags, their coal-black lambs at foot.

That they are descendants of sheep cast ashore from a wrecked Spanish vessel on the coast near Drigg many generations ago is more romantic tradition than fact, for they are unlike any Spanish breed and more closely resemble sheep of the northern climes from Sweden or Denmark. The word 'wick' is an old Scandinavian term for a district and the name Herdwick comes from the sheep farms of monastic days, such as the Herdwick of Furness Abbey at Butterilket in Eskdale, recorded in 1180, long before the Spanish galleon ran ashore on the west coast.

Herdwicks are hardy and lively sheep, comparable to a mountain goat on the rocky pastures, and living in the wettest part of England are clothed in wiry fleeces whose kemp keeps out the rain. It is the wool from which John Peel, the famous huntsman, made 'his coat so gray'. With that wool titivated a lot with red ruddle, the Herdwick ram is a bonny-looking sheep when he parades the local dales show rings and his pride carries the fame of his breed to the Royal of England and the county shows of the northland.

Men who recognise good sheep recognise good dogs for the two are linked, and nowhere more so than in Lakeland where fitness and stamina are paramount. To match the wily Herdwick among the rocky crags and crevices requires the highest intelligence as well as the toughest character. Vigilance over the flock is essential in man and dog in this wild terrain, and especially so at lambing time when foxes are a threat to the sheep.

In keeping the marauding fox at bay the shepherd also looks to another dog, the hound, to protect his sheep. There is no other way than hunting with hounds to keep the fox population within sensible limits in country like the Lake District – and those who say otherwise do not know the facts. The 'anti-foxhunting brigade' have never had to earn a living with sheep, or they could not advocate its banning. Because hunting foxes with hounds is enjoyed it appears to be wrong and cruel to some people, but one doesn't have to be miserable in the carrying out of a necessary job. Because the skills and thrills of the chase – on foot don't forget – and the satisfaction of breeding good hounds are enjoyed and acclaimed, it is condemned. Countrymen take so many of their pleasures seriously, and where the knowledge and expertise of their crafts are involved they do right, for these have not been come by overnight.

Shepherding is one of the crafts at which the Cumbrian farmer excels, and linked with it is the quality of his dogs. He was so interested in improving the quality of his dogs that in 1878 he formed the North Western Counties Dog Trials Association to hold annual competitions for working dogs. In 1891 this society was re-formed into the Lake District Sheep Dog Trials Association which ran the famous trials test over the high rock-strewn and bracken-covered fell of Applethwaite Common above Windermere up until 1978. This would appear to be the oldest trials society in Britain, though Longshaw in north Derbyshire, who started in 1898, claim the honour.

In recent years the native Herdwick sheep has suffered the expansion threat of the Swaledale, particularly into eastern Lakeland and, while acknowledgeing that the Herdwick is still the best sheep for the harder areas, the steep ground where there is a lot of rock and scree and not a lot of grass, many farmers now prefer the Swaledale on their fells. The Swaledale is possibly a better mother to rear a larger lamb, while Swaledale wool holds a better price than the Herdwick and the draft ewes will be easier to sell at the back end. Two of my good friends who are of this opinion are George Hutton, whose Swaledales run on bleak fell rising to 3,000 ft across from Saddleback near Threlkeld, and Chris Todd, with 450 Swales on the cone-like Melbreak which juts to 1,670 ft above Crummock Water.

It is quite possible that the three of us know every reasonable and accessible piece of ground in Lakeland on which a dog trial can be held. Seeking sites for the 'One Man and His Dog' series of television trials, we have looked at small flat fields at the heads of the lakes, the up-and-down fields to be seen everywhere in the valleys and the rock-strewn areas of the larger stream passes in an attempt to combine practical shepherding tests with the beauty of the area. We've sat to plan the tests by deep grey waters, by clear bubbling streams splashing down from the heights, and on grey lichened rock, and I think our sites have reflected the grandeur of this part of England and brought joy to people.

But it is hard country to farm and both George and Chris are collie enthusiasts. They have little option, for they are efficient farmers and neither could ever contemplate trying to manage a flock of sheep in this rugged land without the aid of efficient collies. These men are of an honest, reliable, independent and totally committed nature, as are their dogs.

Take the 'Nipper', George's strong, black-coated Nip who, almost every day of his life, went to the high ground to do his job. In my opinion he was a great collie dog. You could not but admire his integrity, his rough, tough and wholly dependable nature. On the heights of Setmabanning, with the wind whipping at his lean wiry body, he was oblivious of the energy-sapping slopes for his one thought was of sheep. Sheep were for shepherding. They were his minions over which he ruled without malice or temper but with authority and determination. He was fit and capable and master of the flock.

I have heard visitors to trials disparage the appearance of collies, but

The 'Nipper', George Hutton's strong, black-coated Nip from the fells of Lakeland.

collies are not show dogs and their condition is a working condition. They do not carry an ounce of extra flesh, their bones are strong and their muscles are flexible.

Proof of Nip's fitness and ability was reflected in his competitive record. In his first International in 1974 he found little difficulty in mastering Kilmartin's storm-lashed conditions to finish reserve Supreme champion and win the Brace championship in partnership with his fellmate, Shona. Nip and Shona, grandson and granddaughter of Supreme champion McKnight's Gael, repeated their International Brace success in 1975, and Nip won England's Driving championship two years later.

Carrying on Nip's trials tradition, his tricolour son, Roy, ran fourth in the English National in 1978 at his first attempt. George Hutton reckoned Nip was 'one of the best hill dogs that ever lived', yet he considers the dog's father, Nap, to have been better. But Nip was such a character. Dedicated to his work, he believed that all work and no play made for a dull life, so when off duty he was very much a part of the family and enjoyed a game of football with the children. This playfulness

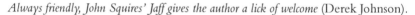

Always friendly, John Squires' Jaff gives the author a lick of welcome (Derek Johnson).

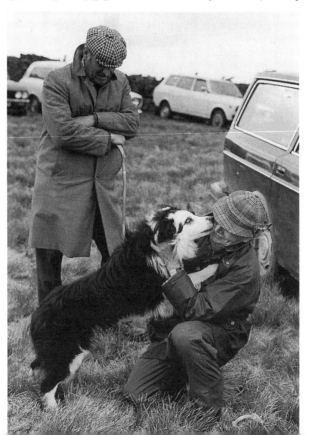

is, of course, a part of the collie temperament. Tim Longton's Nell was a great one for rabbiting, my own Rhaq was never happier than when chasing water-voles, Dick Fortune's Glen and Jill loved car riding, John Templeton's Buff loved to be petted by the children, and you can see collies playing together like puppies at any trial. Very rarely are there any shows of bad temper.

This raises the question of working collies as pets, a question put to me more and more since television made them so popular. The answer simply is that they are marvellous pets and companions for they have the right temperament to get on with people. They are mild mannered, obedient, intelligent, always interested in life and completely free from disease – provided they are fed and watered in a proper manner and given sufficient exercise, which are basically the necessities to maintain a healthy dog of any breed.

Whether or not one should take a dog which is bred to work the wide open spaces and coop it up in a town or city house is another question and really one for the individual.

If taken at weaning age the collie will adapt, as is its nature, but its minimum requirement is sufficient exercise, and whether or not that can be provided is essentially the first question a prospective owner should ask himself. On no account should anyone ignorant of the ways of sheep take an untrained dog of any breed near a flock of sheep.

I suppose the time will come when we have a Border Collie that has lost the interest to work stock, now that the breed is accepted on to the show bench, for there will undoubtedly become two distinct types: the collie as we have known it through the years, whose only yardstick of quality is the intelligence of its brain and the strength and stature of its body, and the dog whose beauty and appearance will be paramount at the expense of its thinking powers and stamina to do a day's work.

This has happened with many other types of working dogs, for fashion dictates the appearance of show dogs and fashion is fickle. Many modern show dogs bear little resemblance to their forbears, and nearly all have changed for the worse. As one who admires the almost uncanny skill of today's working collie I can but view the Border Collie of the show bench with suspicion and distrust. Shows of appearance spoil dogs and it does mean that farmers will need extra care when choosing their herding dogs to see that they are of working bloodlines.

So back to the real thing. Pete and Bob were litter-brothers and as rugged and earthy as the country they shepherded with Chris Todd from Kirkgate Farm at Loweswater near Cockermouth. Melbreak, with sheep grazings rising perpendicular to the cloud-capped summit, is where the Swaledales live and where the two dogs and their master tended them.

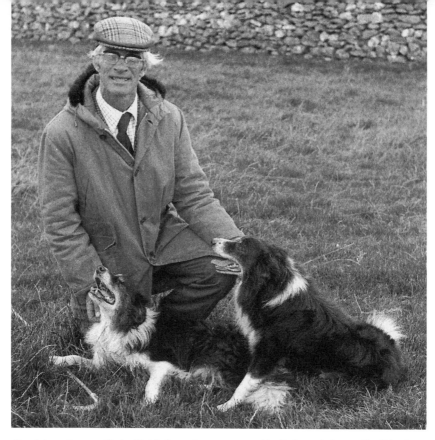

Cumbrian farmer Chris Todd from Loweswater with Bob and Pete, English Brace champions in 1976 and 1977 (Derek Johnson).

That these two nine-year-old rough-coated, medium-sized collies did their master's bidding with skill was so aptly demonstrated when they won the 1976 and 1977 English Brace championships over ground at Chatsworth and Swinhoe that must have been like running the Wembley turf in comparison to their Lakeland fell. Pete and Bob were home bred by Chris out of his Lassie, a smooth-coated granddaughter of Sam Dyson's Mac of Whitehope Nap line, and their entry to the International Stud Book was on the merit of their work, for their father was not registered. So dedicated to the craft of herding were these brothers that though Bob carried a stiff front leg, where the nerves of his shoulder had been damaged, he still insisted on doing his share of the work.

Chris likes the competition of sheepdog trials and is keen to compete at any level, whether it be at the nursery trials which are held by the Windermere and Westmorland societies in the county, or at the great open trials. He is invariably successful at all levels, and his home-bred litter-sisters, the smooth-coated Pat and the rough-coated Belle, born in May 1989, were reserve champions in the Brace class of the England

National in 1994, and also reserve champions when they represented their country in the two-strong Brace team a month later at the International at Monymusk by Pitfichie Forest west of Aberdeen.

They are paternal granddaughters of Bwlch Taff which won the Welsh championship for Glyn Jones of Bodfari in 1980 and 1981, and Chris bred them out of his own Floss. She goes back to Lassie, the mother of Pete and Bob, so that Pat and Belle are of the same hard-working strain which Chris needs to shepherd on the rough fells of West Cumbria.

Pat and Belle also represented England in BBC2's 'One Man and His Dog' trials at Tindale Tarn in north Cumbria in 1994 and won through to the final when they were beaten by the Welsh pair by five aggregate points.

Running first of 150 top dogs in intense heat at the English National of 1995 over an extensive undulating course by Rockingham Forest in Northamptonshire, the tricolour Pat set a high standard which earned her her first singles 'cap' in the 15-strong English International team.

Pat and Belle are also descendants of Fred Coward's Ken from Lindale, one of the most famous of Lakeland collies, and a bloodline which has produced many trials winners. Chris's smooth-coated Pip, which ran for England in 1984, was a son of Ken and again home bred out of Floss.

Collies are an essential part of the workforce at Kirkgate, for Chris has no other help with his sheep and beef cows. He has been interested in sheepdog trials for some 40 years, running his first competition when he was 21 years old. Chris admires the skill and intelligence of his dogs and tells many tales of their versatility. One bitch he had, fearing further disaster after an accident to one of her four pups, carried the remaining three to a hide among the rocks on Melbreak and reared them in the wild. They were later found by a passing fell-walker who saw the bitch instructing her offspring in the initial craft of shepherding.

A land which at one time had its own Cumberland sheepdog, a very old breed with a thick, heavy, water-resistant coat like the native Herdwick sheep, and whose sheep shows, sheepdog trials, hound trails and fell sports take the place of the football and cricket interests of other areas, Cumbria has had many famous sheepdog handlers and collie dogs. Yet its two International Supreme championships were won by a Highland Scot, Raymond MacPherson, who farmed with Zac at Hallbankgate near Brampton. International ruling states that a man shall represent the country in which he farms.

Just before the Second World War Jimmy Renwick's black and tan Kep from Kirkhaugh, Alston, a rough-coated grandson of Thomas Hunter's Sweep, the 1923 and 1924 International Shepherds' champion, was the best Cumbrian collie, winning the 1935 and 1938 English championships. His kennel-mate, Bet, a granddaughter of J. B. Bagshaw's 1927 Supreme champion Lad, also won the English title in 1939. Mr Renwick's Ben won the first-ever International Driving championship in 1937, and his Glen and Moss the 1947 International Brace honour. G. A. Leslie of Swinside Cottage, Portinscale, also won the International Driving championship with Spot in 1956, and this trophy went to Cumbria the following year too, with John Chapman's smooth black and white Lad, son of Joe Gorst's Shep of blue-bitch breeding.

Such handlers as John Leak of Troutbeck, Ernest Holliday of Windermere, Tom Lancaster of Ravenstonedale, Jack Mason, who started running at trials at the age of 15 and went on to represent England five times and win the 1936 National Brace event with Ken and Glen, and the great Joe Relph of Birkett Bank Farm, Threlkeld, who won two English Brace championships and whose collies were legend in the north, established a prestige which is still upheld by the men and dogs of today. Joe Relph's rough-coated black and white Fleet was the dog star in the film *Loyal Heart*, and Joe ran his dogs in three other films. The Relph tradition is carried on today by his nephew, Charlie Relph, and Charlie's son, Joseph, who herd sheep in the picturesque area of Borrowdale. Charlie has many Lakeland trophies to his credit, including the winning of the famous Vale of Rydal open championship in two consecutive years with Jeff, a smooth-coated great-grandson of Supreme champion McKnight's Gael, and Jeff won every major Lakeland honour.

August is the busy month of trials in the Lake District and 15 top events are a great attraction for the host of summer holiday visitors to the area. The Vale of Rydal 'dog-day', started in 1901, with two courses for open and novice collies, hound trails and shows for many types of working terriers, has become world renowned. Other top class trials are held at Keswick, Threlkeld, Patterdale, Hawkshead, Ravenstonedale, Crosby Ravensworth and at Ings above Lake Windermere. First-class trials outside the central holiday period include Lorton, Cockermouth, Penrith, Loweswater and Crosthwaite. Regular contestants at these trials have helped to take 10 English championships and 43 other National titles to Cumbria in the last 60 years of the International Sheep Dog Society's organisation.

Tommy Brownrigg from Newbiggin in the Upper Lune Valley below Kirkby Stephen and his bare-skinned Nap, a legend on the trials fields, won the English National championship at Rydal in August 1991. Tommy was then 69 years old and retired from active farming, and Nap was ten years old, and their experience in the ways of sheep won this most prestigious trials championship in England.

Their partnership resulted in steady and controlled shepherding of Swaledale sheep to earn 208 of 220 aggregate points from two judges in a competition of the highest order, and was two points better than their nearest rivals of 150 of the best handlers and collies in the country. Nap was always in control of the sheep, unflustered and sure in his purpose. His work, as always in the winning of 39 open championships in nine years, was good and without fuss, and he finished his test a worthy and undisputed winner. Nap represented England in International competition on three occasions, in 1986 at Beaumaris, in 1989 at Margam Park and in 1991 at Syde Farm, Carmichael, in the Scottish Borders.

A big black and white collie, born in September 1981, Nap went to Tommy when he was nine months old to help in the management of a flock of Swaledale ewes on the 1,200 ft high windy fells above the Lune Valley.

His master 'polished' him to competitive standard and, to get him used to strange places and strange sheep, ran him in the nursery season of the 1982–3 winter. He was the son of Jack Errington's Roy from Brancepeth in County Durham, bred in that county out of Mrs A. Dodd's Jess. His paternal line came from Mel Page's Welsh champion Nell and Watkins's Robbie, and in his maternal pedigree were English champions Harry Huddleston's Udale Sim, Joe Gorst's Bet and Queen from north Lancashire, and Wilson Hardisty's Jim from Cautley, near Sedbergh. Always reliable, Nap became master over sheep of all breeds, and he understood the ways of his master – and Tommy knew the temperament of the dog. Nap was in the hands of a man who understood collie dogs – and sheep – for to understand the whims of sheep is to understand the ways of directing a dog to match them.

Nap was one of the most intelligent dogs ever to run the Westmorland hills. Now retired after 36 years of farming in Upper Lunesdale, Tommy, who lives in a bungalow at Fell View, Newbiggin, a mile from his original farmhouse, was an experienced sheep farmer with Swaledales on the fells of the Lune Valley. He has always had fine collies of good breeding, for they were indispensable to his management of the sheep, and he schooled them to competitive standard.

Another English National winner from Cumbria was John Harrison, whose family farm Swaledale ewes and store cows at Thorny Bank Farm, Wet Sleddale on Shap Fells, with the smooth-coated Craig in 1990 near Dorking in Surrey. For John, then aged 28, 1990 was a good year at the National. His Craig was top by one of 220 aggregate points from two judges over 150 of the best collies in the land and his half white-headed Meg was third, only one aggregate point behind Craig.

John started 'polishing' his dogs, so essential to his daily work on the bleak moors, to trials standard when he was only 16 years of age, and he has brought them to International status, for they have run eight times for England. Indeed, he has learned so much of the ways of sheep and dogs in doing so that he has been invited to judge trials in America.

Another parallel interest of John's is showing sheep, and he has been successful at that too, particularly at the Swaledale Sheep Fair at Tan Hill on the heights of the Pennines.

His Craig, which won the English honour in 1990, is a son of John Templeton's famous Scottish Roy, and a grandson of Stuart Davidson's Ben, the 1980 Scottish National champion and the 1981 singles champion of 'One Man and His Dog'. Craig competed for England in the 1991 filming of 'One Man and His Dog' at Ennerdale Water.

Alan Leak from Gaisgill, near Tebay, is another famous Cumbrian handler who has often been in the English team. His five collies Tweed, Sally, Roy I, Roy II and Joe have represented England 11 times in the last 16 years, and in that time won over 50 open honours. All were blooded in nursery competition away from the limelight of the big occasions. In 1979 and 1989 Alan had two dogs in England's team to meet the Scots, Welsh and Irish collies.

Tweed, a grand, strong collie, patient in temperament and experienced in competitive work, and of Scottish heritage, a maternal grandson of Supreme champion Wiston Cap, ran for England four times and won 34 open championships. Sally was a lady – a black and white daughter of Tweed, who represented England in 1986 when she ran

Alan Leak from Gaisgill with Roy and Tweed at Moorcock trials, 1980.

fourth in the National at Beadnell by the North Sea in Northumberland, and won the trophy for the best outwork at the trials. Five months after leaving the nursery fields Roy I won a place in England's team, placed fourth at the first four-day National at Penrith in August 1979. Another of Tweed's pups, the tricolour Roy II, won two 'caps' and came closest of all to winning the National championship, placed second in both 1987 and 1989. And rough-coated tricolour Joe, a grandson of Scottish champion Dryden Joe and descended in his maternal bloodline from Fred Coward's Ken, earned three representative honours and won 30 open championships.

Cumbria is a county whose farmers rely particularly on dogs for their livelihood, for no other creature could manage the farm stock on the inhospitable fells. In so doing the sheepdogs of the county are well schooled and very intelligent, and England has chosen many of them in recent years to help her International cause.

Apart from the dogs of Tommy Brownrigg, John Harrison and Alan Leak, Jack Longton of Low Bank House, Barbon, youngest of the renowned Longton brothers, has run Gem, sister to Raymond MacPherson's Supreme champion Zac; Glen, son of Tim Longton's Supreme champion Ken; and Quen, a home-bred daughter of Gem and a granddaughter of Fred Coward's Ken. Wilson Hardisty of Hebblethwaite Hall at Cautley, who won the English championship with his five-year-old black and tan Jim at Windermere in 1961, has run the 4½-year-old Roy, son of Jack Gumbley's Nell. Alan Elliot, from Lowbyer Farm at Alston, winner of England's championship in 1984 with the young smooth-coated Moss, ran his home-bred Roy in 1987; Charlie Relph from Borrowdale had his tricolour Roy, the five-year-old son of John Harrison's Craig, in the 1993 team; and Peter Ellis from New Hutton near Kendal, had Cap, the brother of Charlie Relph's Roy, in the 1991 team.

From the northern part of Cumbria Josh Nixon of Hallees, Longtown, had his rough-coated Rex, born in Cornwall, and Kep, a grandson of McKnight's champion Gael, in the English team; Jack Elliot of Kirklinton with the smooth-coated Moss and Roy, a son of John Richardson's International Shepherds' champion Mirk, represented England; his son Mark Elliot was successful with the tricolour Roger in 1990 and 1992; and shepherd of 1,000 Swaledale ewes near Hadrian's Wall at Askerton near Brampton, John Calvert handled his home-bred Bess into England's team in 1994. Ken Shield, from a Blackface herding at Dandy Croft, Brampton, with Gwen, a granddaughter of the 1962 Supreme champion Lloyd's Garry, and Shep, a granddaughter of the 1967 Supreme champion McKnight's Gael, in 1974, and Derek Scrimgeour, from a Swaledale herding on land which rises to 2,000 ft towards Skiddaw at Lonscale Farm near Threlkeld, with his mother and son pair, Meg and Glen, in the 1995 team, are among the few handlers to get two collies in an International team in the same year.

With a reputation second to none for top quality dogs handled by some of the best farmers in the world, it is not surprising that England has looked to Cumbria for judges – Thomas Harper of Sedbergh, Jack Longton of Barbon, Doug Reynolds of Barbon, Raymond MacPherson of Hallbankgate, Athol Clark of Middleton, and Andrew Preston of Graythwaite, who judged the 1995 National.

One of the best sheepdog handlers in the area is Alan Foster, who farms 600 Dalesbred ewes and 60 beef cows on 300 acres of rocky grassland at Sow How on Cartmel Fell by the south-east shore of Lake Windermere. His Dart, son of Fred Coward's Ken, earned International recognition in 1979 when he also won the English Driving champion-ship, and at the International that year was the highest home-bred dog in the Supreme contest. Dart, a good all-round dog, went from strength to strength, winning the 1980 English National and Inter-national Shepherds' championships, and the reserve Supreme. His older brother, Darkie, won the 1983 English Shepherds' championship at Northleach in Gloucestershire.

'We're a great team', Dart reminds 'the boss' Alan Foster of Cartmel Fell after winning the 1979 English Driving Championship. They went on to win the 1980 English National Shepherds' honours (Lancashire Evening Post).

Alan Foster is a man who prefers to school his own dogs from puppyhood and his priority is a dog which can shepherd efficiently over the undulations of the home farm, not particularly on the trials fields, although he likes to 'polish' them for these more precise skills. He has been very successful, too, winning 203 nursery awards, including 10 nursery championships, eight novice titles, 51 open championships, three top awards in the English National trials, one International championship. He has also represented England five times in International competition.

The home-bred Dart, Alan's International champion, and a rough-coated black and white dog, strong in personality and good on any type of farm stock, was schooled on the nursery fields of the 1976–7 season where he won 11 awards. He went on to win 13 open championships, four National titles and four International 'caps'. He died in March 1988, aged 13.

Alan has schooled many good collies to nursery success, but none better than his two-year-old Flint, the star of the 1994–5 winter season. No other young collie ever started a nursery season with such dominance, he was so confident and authoritative in his work. His record of six wins in five weekends, his winning of ten awards in the first seven weeks with victories at the Trawden, Fylde, Windermere and Northern Association trials was of the realms of fiction. He completed the season with 20 awards, including six victories.

Flint was bred by Peter Ellis at New Hutton and of illustrious bloodline from Alan Leak's Tweed, four times in England's International team, Jim Cropper's Cap, the winner of the English National trials in 1986, Idris Morgan's Ianto, successful in many Welsh trials, and back to Supreme champion Wiston Cap.

One of the unluckiest of competitors at the National, when something always seems to go wrong for him, Athol Clark of Middleton-in-Lunesdale finally beat his 'jinx' in 1979 when his Rob, a half-brother to Alan Foster's Dart, earned international recognition in Lowther Park at Penrith. Athol judged the 1994 English National at Northleach in Gloucestershire and was England's judge for the 1986 International at Beaumaris on Anglesey.

If ever a man needed power and guts and brain and initiative in his collies it is Raymond MacPherson, with 2,000 breeding ewes of the Blackface × Swaledale type to manage on 4,000 acres of land in the 2,000 ft high Tindale Fell range in northern Cumbria, some ten miles east of Carlisle.

'If you put a dog out to gather sheep you expect him to go for them and bring them with purpose,' he says. 'A good all-round dog can save me a lot of work.' And Raymond should know, for he is used to hard

All go! Raymond MacPherson and Zac, 1975 and 1979 Supreme Champions, move fast to control Blackface ewes (Frank H. Moyes).

shepherding over vast tracts of hill land. Before he went to Tarn House near the village of Hallbankgate by Brampton in 1965 he farmed near Loch Treig in the Grampians, and then a 19,000 acre hill farm in the north of Sutherland.

A Scot who has competed in International trials for both Scotland and England, by virtue of residence, he has proved his belief in sound hill-breeding and practical hill experience not only by the successful farming of his land but also by taking Britain to the very top in the competition world. In 1973 he won the first American World Trials Championship with the black-coated Nap, and at the second championship in 1976 he retained the world crown with the bare-skinned Tweed.

Both collies were of Jim Wilson's Whitehope Nap line, a bloodline Raymond favours for its sheer power and authority, not forgetting adaptability and initiative, for both Nap and Tweed had quickly to master the differing American trials courses and the heat of the climate to win honours which have put them, along with their master, into the annals of Border Collie history.

Of a possible 300 points over three differing courses over three days in Pennsylvania and Maryland in 1973 Nap, then aged eight years, scored 290 to beat the best of collies from America, Canada and South Africa. Nap's fellmate at Hallbankgate, the five-year-old black and white Speed, ran third in the event and, emphasising British dominance in collie matters, John Templeton's Fleet and Cap, the 1972 Supreme champion, from Ayrshire, and Britain's other representatives, finished second and fifth.

Fortunately Nap and Speed, though overcome by smoke, survived the motel fire which climaxed the championship and in which John Templeton's Fleet died, along with two Texas collies.

In the 1976 championship, in Maryland, Tweed, a most reliable collie, scored 276 of 300 points, with his kennel-mate, Moss, son of Clarence Storey's international Roy, placed fourth.

Nap was a grandson of Whitehope Nap, and born in Cumberland out of Thomas Graham's Jill at Aglionby, sired by his master's Ben, with blood back to Hughes's Jaff and Kirk's Nell. He was a collie with a great enthusiasm for work and brains to match, and in England he won the 1971 National championship on wily Swaledales at Middlesbrough in the north-east.

Tweed, six years old when he won the American title, was by Scottish champion Gilchrist's Spot, and his mother, Jim Wannon's Bess from Freuchie, was a granddaughter of the British Supreme champion Wiston Cap and thus back to Whitehope Nap. In 1980 he won the English Driving championship and the 'One Man and His Dog' singles trophy.

World championships, though the various veterinary and quarantine regulations of the countries taking part make them difficult to stage, are great honours, but it is still the greatest ambition of every sheepman in the United Kingdom to win the Supreme championship of the International Sheep Dog Society.

This Raymond MacPherson did in 1975 with the white-headed Zac,

'The best friend I'll ever have', was how Raymond MacPherson described Zac, the 1975 and 1979 Supreme Champion.

Pedigree of ZAC (66166) 1975 and 1979 Supreme Champion with Raymond MacPherson

The numbers in brackets are the Stud Book numbers of the International Sheep Dog Society

to take his place rightfully as one of the greatest collie handlers of all time. For good measure he again won the Supreme championship in 1979, over the flat lands of Castle Kennedy near Stranraer in south-west Scotland, handling Zac on Blackface ewes in heavy rainfall into that small elite band of collies which have won the world's greatest sheepdog honour more than once.

Only the seventh collie in 63 years of International competition to earn such high distinction, Zac, a grandson of Tot Longton's old Rob and another dog of the Whitehope Nap strain, was then 8½ years old and in his fifth International. In his second International in 1975 the good-looking dog won the most keenly contested event ever on strong grey-faced Halfbreds over the expanse of York racecourse by a single aggregate point from three judges. He was then 4½ years old and, in addition to his master, had honoured the faith of another man by his triumph.

As a pup Zac, who grew into a handsome white and black, rough-coated collie, was discarded as useless until Andrew Preston of Graythwaite in the Furness Fells saw something in him that others had missed. Patiently schooling him to the basics of his craft and giving him competitive experience in nursery trials, he slowly moulded him into a proud and efficient collie. Cool, calm and easy to handle, Zac was the only collie to salvage England's shepherding prestige by twice winning the top trials award during ten years of Scottish and Welsh dominance.

Raymond MacPherson has been competing in trials for around 50

Raymond MacPherson of Hallbankgate in Cumbria, and Flint, winner of over 50 open trials, wait to compete in BBC2's 'One Man and His Dog' trials in 1990.

years, starting at Newtonmore when he was 11 years old, and he gained his first International place for Scotland in 1957 with Lark, a sister of Whitehope Nap. He has three Scottish International 'caps', including the 1957 Brace title, and has represented England 24 times in 28 years.

In International trials he has won two Supreme championships with Zac; the International Farmers' championship with Fleet, an Irish-bred collie, in 1986; and two Driving titles, in 1994 with Dolwen Chips, a son of Welsh International Glyn Jones's Taff, and in 1995 with Ben, a big handsome son of Bobby Dalziel's dual Supreme champion Wisp.

At the English National, Raymond won the National and Farmers' championship with Nap in 1971, and five Driving championships – with Supreme champion Zac in 1975; with Tweed, his 1976 American World champion, in 1980; with the powerful Spot, a son of David Carlton's international Tony, in 1985; with the tricolour Dolwen Chips in 1994; and with Ben, the son of Bobby Dalziel's Wisp and the grandson of Bobby Dalziel's Dryden Joe, in 1995.

England's National President, a tall Highlander with the natural charm and courtesy of his race, Raymond is a true contender. He always believes that he has a good chance of winning a trial and his handling of strong, hard-working collies has that decision and authority which is so essential on the fell and which must never be lost to weaker types on the trials field. His sort of collie will run all day if necessary and it is a delight to see a dog getting on with the job it knows without frills or fuss.

Raymond MacPherson, by dint of putting his beliefs to the test, has brought honour to British shepherding. He was awarded the MBE in the Queen's 1979 Birthday Honours List, in recognition of his International successes with sheepdogs.

CHAPTER THIRTEEN

Of Aristocratic Lineage

I enter the land of Old Hemp, the foundation sire of the modern working collie, discover the early history of the breed, and admire the pride and dedication which the farmers of Northumberland gave, and still give, to the breeding of wise dogs.

Northumberland smells good, the scents of livestock farming mingling on the clean fresh air with the dampness of grass heath and rich lowland pastures. The bleating of white-faced Cheviot ewes blends with the call of the curlew and the whistled commands of a shepherd to his dog ring clear in the vastness of open moorland.

Leaving behind the skills of the Tarn House collies at Hallbankgate and journeying east along Hadrian's Wall and the great ditch of Vallum, then northwards into country steeped in Roman history, I came to a land whose cultures are the most unspoiled in England. The ewes graze with their backs to the wind, and the land is rich in the shepherding craft which has played a major part in the history of the working sheepdog.

From this country came Old Hemp, the forefather of the modern dog.

Northumberland is a county of a million sheep. On the 400,000 acres of rough grazings run the hill breeds which form the nucleus for the lowland crossbreeds, seen on the better pastures. These are sheep in the care of some of the finest collies in Britain.

On the rough grass moors the Cheviot breed is the native sheep, stocky little white-faced creatures whose lambs are crossed with the Border Leicester to produce the well-known Halfbred ewes for lowland farms. The Cheviot is an old-established breed on these Northumberland hills, its centenary ram sale having been held over the Border at Hawick in September 1945, and it produces a lean class of lightweight mutton. Its wool is used mainly for weaving Scottish tweed.

On the heather hills the Scottish Blackface ewe is preferred for its hardier constitution and is crossed with the Border Leicester or Blue-faced Leicester to produce the famous Mule or Greyface sheep. As in Cumbria the Swaledale is extending its territory to the detriment of the Blackface.

This farming of the hills is a hard life and demands devotion to sheep and land by men and women whose income is wool, lambs and the draft ewes for the lowlands, and whose rewards are the tranquillity of life in unspoiled country, an independence of spirit, and a character which is entirely local and does not come from the assembly-line. See them at one of the local agricultural shows with their sheep, the women with their dairy products, baking and knitting, among the honest excitement of the sheepdog trials, the sports and wrestling, the dancing to the Northumbrian pipes, and their ways are to be envied.

Second best is no good to the Northumbrian character, and their collie dogs are consequently top class, for this is the country where the serious improvement of collie dogs for herding work really started (though Scotland will probably claim the honour). It was at Fairnley, just to the north of the A696 road which runs from Newcastle up over the Cheviot hills to cross into Scotland at Carter Bar, that Adam Telfer bred Old Hemp. So completely did Old Hemp dominate the sheepdog scene at the turn of the century that other dogs were almost ignored; all eyes and thoughts were on the handsome rough-coated collie with Adam Telfer.

Hemp humoured sheep, he let them feel his strength, and it is recorded that his concentration was so intense that he physically trembled when working them. He was the absolute master of his craft, a sheepdog genius without fault. His quality realised, his fame and influence spread. Soon he was the talk of the Borders, the most sought-after sire of his day, and his blood stamped the type of the Border Collie.

Adam Telfer was a man dedicated to the improvement of the working collie, as were his two sons, Adam and Walter, and in the process they won four International championships, five International Farmers' titles and four English National championships. In 1924 the Telfer menfolk were all three in the English team at Ayr.

Northumberland was also the birthplace of what may be termed another great branch of the collie family or, more precisely, a strong offshoot from the Old Hemp line.

Thomas Armstrong's Sweep was born a grandson of Old Hemp at Greenchesters, Otterburn in Redesdale, and he can claim to have founded three families which in turn bred International champions: Batty's Hemp in 1920, Bagshaw's Lad in 1927, and Walter Telfer's Midge and Queen in 1919 and 1932. Sweep was a big handsome collie blessed with the genius of method. He could calm sheep by his very personality and he was a cool, level-headed dog, qualities which won him the 1910 and 1912 International championships.

So with Old Hemp born at Fairnley, and William Wallace's Tommy and Armstrong's Sweep bred in the valley of the Rede, Northumberland farmers made perhaps the most important contribution of all to the history of shepherding, for Hemp, Tommy and Sweep really produced the champions.

Thomas Armstrong also won the International championship with Sweep's half-brother, Don, in 1911 and 1914 before this rough-coated black and white dog was exported to James Lillico in New Zealand.

William Wallace, a Scotsman who farmed at East Farm, Otterburn, is renowned as the man who was responsible for great improvements in the handling of collie dogs. Before Wallace – at Hawick in 1883 when he was in his early twenties – showed the ability to work his dogs quietly and without fuss, and use the power of their eye to the fullest advantage, shepherds had handled their collies with a great deal of shouting and whistling. Wallace's methods were almost gentle by comparison but the technique brought results, for he won the International championship in 1907 with Moss and again in 1922 with the 2½-year-old Meg. Moss had 11 first prizes and two seconds in 15 trials before going to New Zealand as Border Boss.

Wallace is recorded as having won 163 first prizes during his trials handling, and one of his best dogs was Glen, of Old Kep's line, whose tricolour son, Haig, won the 1921 International for Adam Telfer, and whose black and white granddaughter, Meg, after being stolen and recovered in a hectic adventure after qualifying to represent England, won the 1922 International title for Wallace.

William Wallace's son, W. J. Wallace, who moved down to Sussex around 1940 and became famous for his demonstrations with sheepdogs, upheld the family tradition, running his first trial at Kelso when he was 12 years old, winning his first English 'cap' in 1932 when he was 21 and taking the 1938 International championship with Jed. W. J. won 236 prizes, including 70 firsts.

Northumbrian farmers have won ten Supreme championships for England, more than any other county, though all the honours came before the Second World War. Yet unsuccessful in emulating their forbears at this level of competition, the post-war generation of handlers are equally skilled in the breeding and training of collie dogs and in using them where it matters most, in the management of their sheep flocks on the hills and pastures of the county. And they have always enhanced the area's reputation in competition which is today far stronger than in pre-war days.

Robert Scott Fraser, a shepherd for over 50 years, continued the earlier work of his fellow Northumbrians in improving the collie dog, and he was most successful on the trials field. In 50 years of competition – he won his first trials as an assistant shepherd when he was 16, in 1925 – he won two International Shepherds' championships, six English Shepherds' championships, and the English Driving title in 1960. His achievement was more remarkable when you consider his six English wins were with six different dogs. Undoubtedly England's top shepherd trials competitor since the war, Bob was known throughout the world for the quality of his Mindrum strain of dogs which have been sent to make their contribution to the shepherding of every big sheep-run in the world.

The Mindrum line, started in 1923 when Bob was herding at Mindrum at the foot of the Cheviots, two miles from the Scottish Border, is renowned as having the qualities of high intelligence, forceful control, virility and stamina which are the essentials of daily shepherding. It is a bloodline which is sought by men who have a job to do, and with very little 'polishing' has proved a line equally successful in trials shepherding. Bob Fraser himself showed just how good Mindrum collies are on the trials field, for all his National successes were with dogs of his bloodline.

Bob's interest in collies began when his uncle gave him a pup named Moss which carried the blood of Old Hemp and it was with Moss that he won his first trial at Kelso. Moss and Bob were great pals, but Bob once told me how Moss was never more pleased to see him than one Guy Fawkes night when the dog had fled in panic from a firework explosion. Four miles from home Bob found the frightened collie, who was so happy to see the 'boss' that he jumped up on to the petrol tank of Bob's motorcycle for the ride to home and safety.

Bob trained Moss himself and every collie that won for him followed the same pattern. His first entry to National competition was not until 1947, when he won the Shepherds' title at the first attempt with Sam, whose normal mode of travel to local trials was in a specially made box on the back carrier of a push-bike. Sam enjoyed the journey as much as the trial.

The black, white and mottled Nickey won the following year and went on to win Bob's first International title; in 1950 it was Nickey's sister, Lass; in 1955 the two-year-old Nell; Roy won at Darlington in 1968; and in 1974 the little rough-coated Betty gave Bob Fraser his sixth English National. Cap, son of the 1955 winner Nell, won the English Driving championship in 1960.

With Moss as its foundation, the Mindrum line was built on Wilson's Cap blood, for the famous hill collie was but a few miles over the Border, and Bob's first National winner Sam was a grandson of Cap.

Experienced and knowledgeable on collie matters, Bob built well, for apart from providing himself with the most efficient helpmates for his daily work, the collies he bred gave him endless pleasures on the

Bob Fraser, founder of the famous Mindrum line of collies, with Mindrum Phil at the first television series of 'One Man and His Dog' at Buttermere in 1975.

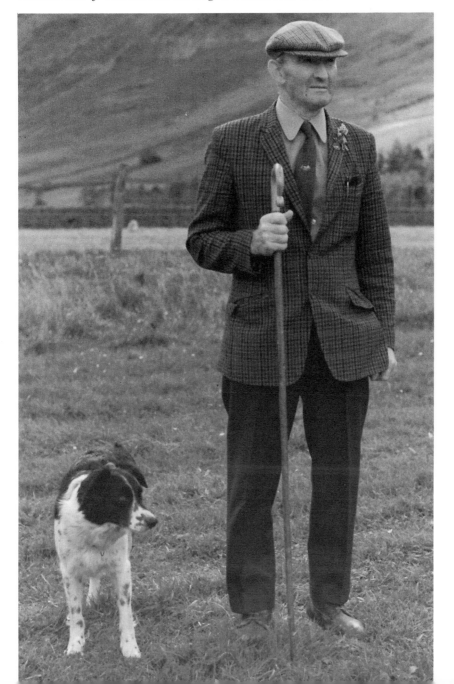

competitive fields of both England and Scotland. Twelve times Bob was in England's international team, often with two dogs, and his Phil, a bitch with a lovely temperament, was only beaten in the final of the 'One Man and His Dog' television trials by one point.

One of Bob Fraser's most satisfying victories was his winning of the 1968 International Shepherds' honour at Towyn in Merionethshire with Mindrum Corrie, for the well-marked black and white rough-coated dog got off to a poor start in life when his mother Tibbie died when he was only one day old. Fortunately a foster-mother took to him with her own litter of three pups and he thrived. Corrie was very typical of Bob Fraser's dogs for he bred for rough-coated looks, though 'the ability and brain must come first'.

Though always within sight of the Cheviots, a land remote enough to support wild goats, Bob Fraser's Mindrum collies worked the lower lands with Halfbred sheep and feeding cattle ever ready to test their strength. Their master finished his working life before retirement to Wooler with the calls of seabirds blending with the bleat of his sheep and the historic pile of Lindisfarne Priory on Holy Island ever in his view from the pasture of Fennan. Bob, for whom we all had the greatest respect, died as he would have wished – at a sheepdog trial in Coquet-dale, in August 1986.

A true Borderer, born of a Scottish shepherd father and an English mother at Bowmont Hill at Mindrum, Bob always retained that mixture of Northumbrian speech and Scottish dialect, and he was truly proud of his heritage and of the line of sheepdogs he evolved. It was one of the longest bloodlines in the history of the Border Collie breed and is renowned for its intelligence. The first Border Collie to win an obedience trial at Cruft's dog show was of the Mindrum line.

The Mindrum line has done much for Northumbrian prestige and four other champions from the county, Gordon Rogerson's black, white and tan Spot, and his mother Nell; Archie Tait's Tug; and Jack Tully's five-year-old Glen carry Fraser blood.

Northumberland's most famous collie in recent years has been Paul Turnbull's black and white Nap, a fine type of dog and a good-looking collie who likes to get on with his shepherding, from a Blackface herding on the hills of Rothbury Forest at Debdon.

His forthright and controlled shepherding of Halfbred ewes at his first English National in 1993 won the National and Farmers' championships at Cleveland's rain-soaked and wind-buffeted event, and later in the year at the International at Armathwaite, near Carlisle, the rough-coated dog was only one of 680 aggregate points from four judges from taking the Supreme championship.

In the Supreme content he was beaten by Alasdair MacRae's 3½-

year-old Nan for Scotland whose outfield work just had the edge over him, although he was more determined in the shedding ring and at the pen than the Scottish bitch. Nap, who has been the most unfortunate of collies, prone to injury, had suffered ligament trouble on both his back legs at the times of previous Nationals, so that although he was eight years old, 1993 was his first National, when he quickly showed what practical work he could do when he was fit. He won the Champion of Champions trials against the champion collies of Scotland, Wales and Ireland at the major agricultural shows, and television's 'One Man and His Dog' trials in 1994. He has earned a great reputation in the North Country where his successes have been legion.

Going to Paul Turnbull when only seven weeks old, Nap was unregistered when born in 1985 out of Mike Graham's Jess, and he earned merit-registration by the International Sheep Dog Society in 1990. He has the skills of his paternal ancestor, Thomson McKnight's Gael, which won the Supreme championship in 1967, and his maternal ancestor, Harry Huddleston's Bett, the Supreme champion of 1969. He ran for England again in 1994, when he was third at the National held on Suffolk Mule shearlings over a tricky and undulating course at Lodge Park at Northleach near Cheltenham.

The year 1993 was a good one for Northumbrian collies, Ron Bailey's 4½-year-old Pen from the Northumberland College of Agriculture winning the Shepherds' championship, and George Turnbull's seven-year-old Nickey from Melkington, Cornhill-on-Tweed, running reserve to the team, the sixteenth of 150 collies. The following year Nickey, in work with 450 Mule ewes and 50 suckler cows and a son of John Bathgate's Vic which won the 1984 Scottish Driving championship, won the Shepherd's championship, and was second in the 15-strong English team, four of 220 aggregate points behind the winner, Vic Morris's Mac from Clun, Craven Arms, in Shropshire.

Northumberland shepherds have done better than their farmer counterparts in the last ten years of National competition, and four of them have been in England's team on five occasions.

In 1987 at Byford near Hereford, remembered mainly for the perverse and unruly ways of big Welsh Halfbred sheep which made competitive shepherding almost impossible and caused 101 of 150 collies to retire over the three days, David Ogilvie's clever home-bred, merit-registered Sam from Flotterton near Thropton showed a tenacity and courage to win the Shepherds' championship under such adverse conditions. Shepherding 1,000 Blackface and Cheviot breeding ewes at Flotterton Hall, the 3½-year-old Sam won his first International representation the previous year. David had another merit-registered collie, the black and white Moss, in the 1988 team.

Also dealing with the stupid antics of the sheep at Byford in 1987 with authority and coolness, Ron Bailey's nine-year-old Chance, a son of Clarence Storey's international Blade, deservedly worked his way into the English team. In 1988 another Northumbrian shepherd, David Baxter of Harbottle in Coquetdale, ran his home-bred Cap into the English team.

With Gordon Rogerson in the management of 1,000 Blackface sheep on 1,800 acres of heather hill on the Chatton Moors, eight miles inland from the picturesque Beadnell Bay, Spot and Nell combined Mindrum 'know-how' with Rogerson handling skill to win the reserve Supreme International championship and the English Shepherds' title.

A determined little prick-eared dog with a nice nature, and in complete harmony with his master, Spot ran reserve by 13 aggregate points to Bob Shennan's Mirk in the 1978 Supreme test at Chatsworth. The previous year he had been the youngest collie in the television trials. His paternal grandsire was Davie McTeir's Ben, the white-headed collie which beat his mother Nell by four points for the 1972 International Shepherds' award.

Rogerson's Nell, a little black and white bitch, won the English Shepherds' honour in the same year when she was 5½ years old, and for the following two years was in England's team.

Ken Brehmer, then the 31-year-old shepherd-manager to the Duke of Northumberland on the Emblehope estate at Tarset, and the bare-skinned Ben formed the outstanding partnership at the English National at Welbeck in Nottinghamshire in 1978, winning the National, the Shepherds' and the Driving championships. Ben, a strong, black-coated dog, was a 'foreigner' to the district, bred in Yorkshire by Richard Haggas at the other Otterburn near Hellifield, and of Bathgate's Rock and Cropper's Bonnie line back to Wilson's Cap and Kirk's Nell. He was a very clever collie who served England well for three successive years before leaving the 2,000 Blackfaces he watched over in Northumberland to work with Ralph Pulfer in Ohio, America, in March 1979.

Export of shepherding craft is a common trait when collies are good, as in Northumberland, and the farmers and shepherds of the county have also passed on their knowledge to other countries. For instance, Jim Easton, farm manager at West Ditchburn near Eglingham north-west of Alnwick, has played a great part in improving the standard of collie handling in Europe.

British collies do not often get to work in the grounds of French châteaux but in September 1973 a Northumberland shepherd, Ron Bailey, and his two dogs from Ponteland held a knowledgeable French crowd of farmers and agricultural advisers spellbound with their demonstration of sheep herding over the parkland of the Château de la

Bastide just outside Limoges, Haute-Vienne. So good was their work on Vendeen crossbred sheep which were absolutely unused to dogs that the collies were not allowed to return to Northumberland – they were bought by the French sheep co-operative which organised the demonstration for the training of their members!

Though mechanisation can never replace the collie's skill on such terrain as the Northumbrian hills, John Davison at least mechanised himself to cover his 480 acres of moorland at Stone House Farm near Wark, and his dog Spot adapted to riding a motor-cycle. To get around his Blackface and Blue-faced Leicesters with extra mobility John changed from a pony to a 125 cc trail-bike, and the 18-month-old Spot settled on the petrol tank, clinging with his forelegs to keep balance, until he was called into action on the sheep.

Every day I see more and more of the adaptability and intelligence of working collies and the Cheviot has seen every aspect of their nature. In December 1944 a little bitch, John Dagg's Sheila, from a farm at the foot of Cheviot located the wreckage of an American Flying Fortress which had crashed into the hillside during a blizzard, and searching around with nose and ears as her only guide led her master to four surviving airmen sheltering in a nearby peat hole. For her part in the rescue of those airmen she was awarded the Dickin Medal for Gallantry. To cement the bond of friendship which grew from that act one of Sheila's pups, Tibbie, went to America, and subsequently won a first prize in a dog show at Columbia in South Carolina.

The narrow valley of the Rede has played a great part in Border history and its sheepdogs have added to its fame. It is one of the natural passages between England and Scotland, the route of the Scottish raiders in less peaceful days and of the drovers with their flocks in later times, and it was the site of the Battle of Otterburn, recorded in the ballad of Chevy Chase, where the Scots heavily defeated the English in August 1388. Modern Scots have been trying ever since to emulate their ancestors – often with success – though in a much more sporting manner on the trials fields of Northumberland, and the last time I was at Belford I met as many Scottish friends as Northumbrians.

CHAPTER FOURTEEN

Gael, A Collie Legend

I say how Gael of Glencartholme became the greatest sheep bitch of all time, remember her qualities and temperament and her record in Scotland's International cause, before travelling north to meet her contemporaries in the land of clever dogs and skilful shepherds.

'The wisest sheep bitch of all time' is an accolade which, down the years, has been given by many men to very few female collies. They have included Wallace's Loos, Kirk's Nell, Wilson's Fly and Nell, Wallace's Meg, Longton's Nell, Wilson's Peg, and you could also add Gwilym Jones's Nell, Illingworth's Fly, Worthington's Juno, and Longton's Gyp, but surely from a very elite band the title should go to Thomson McKnight's Gael.

From Glencartholme on the Scottish Border, Gael was a most willing and confident worker, a winner of trials championships, the mother of champions and the truest of companions. Born on 6 April 1957, a little smooth-coated black and white pup, she was to become a legend in her time. At six months old she saw her first sheep, for Thomson McKnight was then managing a dairy farm, Hairmyres at East Kildride on the outskirts of Glasgow, and the only sheep ever on the place were hill hoggs which arrived on the first day of October to spend the winter on the grassland.

Gael liked what she saw. She quivered in anticipation. Her blood was fired with the urge to order them. Untaught, she went to work them with an inbred skill. Sheep herding was to be her true vocation.

In the winter months which followed she grew in stature, her character blossomed, her interest never flagged, and Thomson recalled of those early days with Gael, 'She taught me such a lot about sheep.' So much in fact that Thomson became keen to extend his tuition and Gael's experience when the hoggs left the lowland and went back to

186

Thomson McKnight's Gael, the greatest sheep-bitch of all time and 1967 Supreme Champion.

their home pastures at the end of March, and so he cycled – with Gael balancing on the bike – two miles to the nearest flock of sheep on which to practise.

Life was full and the dairy cows which Gael often drove five miles between two farms tempered her courage and fired her determination to master all farm stock. It was this determination and experience with young wilful hoggs and cows which gave her the right temperament to deal with the varied types of sheep she was to meet in later years on trials fields all over Britain. If sheep were nice and workable she was patience personified, but if they wanted to play it rough, she could match them with a ruthless authority.

The farm work, more rewarding as her knowledge grew, came first and she was two years old before she was tested on the trials field. Settling to the strangeness of unfamiliar places, she won a third prize on her third outing at Drymen on the shores of Loch Lomond. 'I was a raw character with not much experience,' said Thomson about those days. But the ease with which Gael handled farm stock gave him confidence and two years later, at Stirling in 1961, they entered for their first Scottish National. They finished eighth and thus qualified to represent Scotland in the International trials.

Gael was four years old on that first Stirling visit and it was the first of her seven international 'caps'. For the next six years until her retirement she was never out of Scotland's team – a proud and unequalled record. In that time she won the Supreme championship in 1967, the reserve Supreme in 1965, the Scottish National in 1964, the Scottish Driving in 1967 and, with her daughter Dot, the International Brace championship of 1967 and three successive Scottish Brace titles – and more important for the sheep farming community as a whole, she started a bloodline which became in demand throughout the world. It can truly be said that Gael contributed an awful lot to sheep farming in general. 'Nobody is ever likely to forget old Gael – a dog and a legend' wrote my colleague in agricultural journalism, Matt Mundell of *The Scottish Farmer.*

Yet Gael very nearly went on the New Zealand sheep-runs when she was barely out of her puppyhood. Thomson had bred her out of his nice-tempered, black and white Dot, who was only four years old and competent for his farm work. So Gael was prepared for New Zealand. She stayed in Scotland because Dot died suddenly when Gael was 12 months old and had to take over her mother's duties.

Thomson and his family moved from East Kilbride in 1960 to Glencartholme, a name which Gael was to make known throughout the world. Here on the gentle timbered slopes above the famous fishing River Esk near the village of Canonbie, just four miles north of the Border in Dumfriesshire, Gael at three years old became responsible for assisting Thomson in the management of 120 Blackface ewes and a herd of milk cows over the 200 acre arable and grazing unit. Relaxation from these duties came on the trials fields of Britain where she made shepherding a pleasure, and a delight to watch.

Rightly, and almost of the realms of fiction, her trials career ended with the greatest honour a sheepdog can win: the Supreme championship, the blue riband of the heather. Further, she won that Supreme championship of the International Sheep Dog Society with the convincing margin of 35 points over her daughter Dot and 58 points in front of the third-placed collie.

To have Dot also win the Farmers' honour and to have the pair of them win the Brace title at the same event – the first time in 12 years that Scotland had won the Brace title – was a great triumph for Thomson McKnight whose ability as a handler had blossomed parallel to Gael's expertise.

Gael and Dot saved the Stirling International from being remembered – or forgotten – as one of the worst-ever for the general quality of its shepherding. Gael and Dot were superb when others were dismal. Only one other – Wyn Edwards's three-year-old prick-eared Jaff from North Wales – of the 12 collies in the final Supreme test completed the work. Gael herded the 20 Blackface sheep on the two half-mile gathers over the Supreme course with customary skill. She needed a little whistled encouragement from Thomson on the first outrun, then settled to her familiar and confident style, going back on the second gather without hesitation. She coolly mastered spreading sheep on the drive and, just when her experience was really needed, prevented what could have been a disastrous finish to her shedding test. Her final penning was almost a formality and, at ten years old, she proved herself the supreme collie. She was only the second bitch in 29 years to win the Supreme, only the eighth since the International trials started in 1906.

Herbert Worthington's Juno from Mardy, Abergavenny, won the Supreme in 1963, and since Gael's victory, Harry Huddleston's Bett from Arkholme, Tom Watson's Jen from the Borders, Tot Longton's Jess and Thomas Longton's Bess from north Lancashire, Gwyn Jones's Queen from Snowdonia and Alasdair MacRae's Nan from near Loch Levan have won the title.

At the close of Gael's weekend at Stirling she received seven trophies and the acclaim which rang out over those flat lands below the grey walls of Stirling Castle heralded a Scottish victory which has never been bettered. It was the stuff that dreams are made of.

She died rather suddenly though peacefully after a heart attack at Glencartholme on a grey day in 1968 and the whole sheepdog world went into mourning, so widely was she famed. She was 11½ years old. A truly great collie, she is buried in the garden of the old farmhouse she made famous, a quiet spot where in February the snowdrops nod their white heads around her grave and the peace is only slightly disturbed by

The famous Whitehope Nap.

David McTeir's Ben, a grand champion.

the bleat of sheep. Beside her lies her daughter, Dot, who though perhaps a little overshadowed by such greatness earned a record few others have matched, and her grandson, Drift, whose promising career after he had won the 1970 International Driving championship was tragically ended by poisoning when he was only four years old.

Simplest memories are the most lasting – Gael was always loyal to her craft and to her folk. Never was she complacent in her success. Every job of herding, whether it was the ewes and lambs up the road to fresh pasture or the dairy cows down to the byre for milking, with a bright-eyed robin or a shy roe deer the only audience, was carried out with the same degree of skill and energy that won the Supreme championship in front of thousands of spectators at Stirling.

It is always difficult to estimate accurately the effect that one dog, one bitch, indeed one animal of any kind, can leave on a breed, but Gael undoubtedly influenced the collie breed. Because she was a dam her effect had less influence than if she had been a sire, as she was unable to mate with as many dogs, but while her personal make-up stamped her own line she was also adding to and enhancing the quality of a line already proven. Few of her progeny failed to make efficient working dogs, for she always bred well and was wisely mated. In 1968, the year that Gael died, nine of her sons and daughters competed at the National trials. She mothered an International Farmers' champion, an International Shepherds' champion, an International Driving champion, and an English and a Scottish National champion.

Gael acquired much of her inbred intelligence from Jim Wilson's Cap, of whom she had at least five crosses of his blood, and her sire was the noted Whitehope Nap, Scotland's powerful dog and a most successful sire whose influence I have discussed earlier. Again we see the links in the breeding chain, for Gael was related to Ashton Priestley's Pat and Alan Jones's Roy, the 1951 and 1961 Supreme champions, to Hughes's Jaff, the greatest driving dog of all, and to Raymond MacPherson's Nap,

Pedigree of GAEL (14463) 1967 Supreme Champion with Thomson McKnight

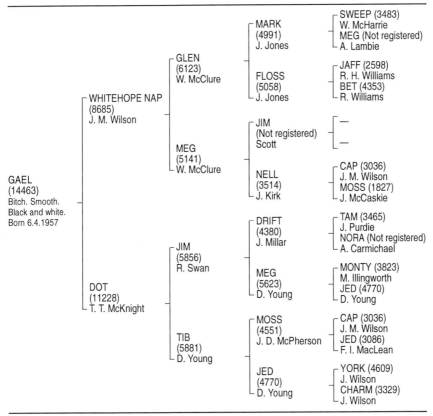

The numbers in brackets are the Stud Book numbers of the International Sheep Dog Society
— Indicates that this dog is not known

winner of the 1973 American World championship, to list but four great collies.

Thomson died suddenly while visiting his son, Ewan, in New Zealand in 1994. Thomson McKnight's Gael was the greatest sheep bitch of all time; her great-granddaughter, David Shennan's prick-eared Meg from Girvan, was the best known, for her adventurous and dominant spirit took the fancy of the four million people who watched her win the first-ever television trials in 1976. In her three tests before the cameras, Meg's inherited determination and will to win the trophy for Scotland appealed to the competitive spirit, for she was wholly professional in her attitude and so obviously enjoyed her job.

She set in behind the strong Swaledale sheep over the lakeside course at Buttermere and her skill and enthusiasm, controlled and manipulated by her master, immediately won her star rating with the viewing public so that she was invited down to London to appear in a studio 'interview'. She took it all as a matter of course and later in the year she won Scotland's National championship at Golspie near Sutherland's shoreline.

A smooth, mottled bitch who liked to get on with the job, Meg was born in April 1970, her sire, McKnight's Drift, the 1970 International Driving champion and the grandson of Gael, and her mother, Murray's Gael, the daughter of Supreme champion Wiston Cap and the granddaughter of Scottish champion Gilchrist's Spot. Such a blend of the very best of Scottish collie bloodlines gave Meg exceptional ability, a forceful personality, a good temperament, an adaptable manner and a nature that always strove to please – and she won numerous trials prizes including four international 'caps'. In addition to Scotland's National title in 1976, she won the country's Farmers' championship in 1974 and ran third in the 1975 Supreme test. In 1978 her granddaughter, Nan, won the Scottish National championship.

Sharing her work with Blackface ewes and beef cows on 1,500 acres of Knockgerran Farm in the Carrick district of south-west Ayrshire at the time of her television popularity was another great bitch of the Gael blood, the older tricolour Maid, one of the best known of Scottish collies. She won her fortieth championship on the Great Glen course near Fort William when she was 11. Maid, a collie accepted into the International Sheep Dog Society Stud Book on the merit of her work, also won the 1971 International Farmers' championship and the 1970 reserve Supreme – the closest David Shennan, who has run for Scotland 18 times, has been to the top honour.

Scotland has produced some good bitches in recent years – Alasdair MacRae's Nan, which won the 1993 Supreme championship and television's 'One Man and His Dog', Bobby Dalziel's Dot, the 1995 Shepherds' champion, Johnny Wilson's Peg, Kenny Brehmer's Bute, the 1991 International Driving champion, and I particularly liked Peter Hetherington's smooth black and white Nell of the kind nature.

Also of the McKnight's Gael bloodline and from the Carrick area of Ayrshire, Nell was a marvellous friend and worker for her master in his management of over 2,500 Grey-faced and North Country Cheviot ewes and feeding lambs and a herd of blue-grey suckler cows on 1,200 upland acres. Easy to get on with, Nell was worth her weight in gold for she was so easily adaptable to any type of farm stock. She had a particular liking for showing her skills on the trials field and a record of 39 first-prize cards and seven Scottish 'caps' in nine years proved her ability.

The greatest sheep-bitch that ever lived. Thomson McKnight's Gael, Supreme Champion of 1967, winner of two International Championships and five Scottish Championships, and in Scotland's team on seven occasions.

Nell, bred by Peter in May 1968, reached the height of her competitive career in 1973 when, herding Welsh Mountain ewes over flat, undulating ground on the banks of the River Dee outside Bala in North Wales, she won the International Shepherds' championship. In 1970 she won the Scottish National title and, with her son Hemp, the 1976 and 1978 Scottish Brace championships.

Another Nell, the smooth-coated granddaughter of John Templeton's Moss, won the 1995 International Shepherd's championship for Peter.

It is interesting to see the similarity of breeding in so many top-class collies and Hetherington's old Nell and Shennan's Meg were very alike in their make-up. Each contained the dominant blood of McKnight's Gael, Richardson's Wiston Cap and Gilchrist's Spot. Gael and Cap were of the Whitehope Nap line, and I have discussed their influence on the collie breed earlier. John Gilchrist's Spot from Roslin in Midlothian was equally famous and, though he failed to win the Supreme championship, his line has been sought for the best breeding programmes both in the United Kingdom and abroad, and his progeny have won trials in the United States.

A striking-looking dog with a white cheek and a lot of white on his

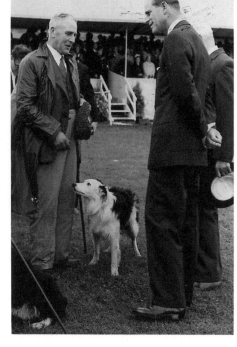

The Duke of Edinburgh asks John Gilchrist about his Scottish Champion, Spot, at Cardiff 1965 (Western Mail & Echo).

rough coat, he had a dour, determined, forceful style of work and his masterful, smooth nose-to-the-ground craftsmanship was always eye-catching. He was calm, good natured, steady and easy to handle, and became a popular sire because he bred puppies with similar qualities. He won Scotland's National championship in two consecutive years, 1965 and 1966, and was reserve Supreme in 1966. In 1966 the four-year-old Spot herded the Kilmartin ewes to the impressive total of 197 of 200 points for the Scottish honour, and he was only beaten by a half-point – by Wiston Cap – for the International Shepherds' trophy later in the same year.

He was bred by Peter McGregor Hepburn at Upper Firth, Penicuik, in Midlothian, out of Wiston Nan and sired by John Gilchrist's Bob down from his 1947 Supreme champion Spot I. He ran his first trial at Kinross in 1974, and John came to consider him a better collie than his champion ancestor.

Spot died in 1975, Wiston Cap in 1979 and Gael in 1968, and all have left a great heritage. It is a heritage, especially from the wider influence of the males, Spot and Cap, which some sheepmen view with a little trepidation, but the question of line and in-breeding has always been with us and wise out-crossing can keep the blood balance right.

Sitting by the side of old Gael's grave in the pleasant pastures around Eskdale, crossing the tops of the Southern Uplands, or walking across

Pedigree of SPOT (24981) 1965 and 1966 Scottish Champion with John Gilchrist

The numbers in brackets are the Stud Book numbers of the International Sheep Dog Society
— Indicates that this dog is not known

the rocky heather growth of the Grampians – when you really appreciate a good crook – I have often considered the variety of terrain which Scotland's collies have to run in their daily duties. Yet pick any hundred of them at random and few will fail to reflect Scotland's reputation as the land of high quality herding dogs. The country has wide agricultural interests and some of the best farmers in the world, and much of their husbandry is with sheep.

Hill ewes graze 72 per cent of Scottish farmland and are mainly concentrated in what is generally regarded as the Lowlands in comparison to the Highlands proper. The Highland sheep-runs, the farms and croftings north of the central lowland plain of Glasgow and Edinburgh, started to diminish with the Clearances at the end of the Jacobite uprising, and with the people evicted, these runs became deer forests and grouse moors and, in still later years, forestry plantations. Today the bulk of Scotland's sheep population of seven million is to be found on the Scottish Uplands – the Pentlands, Lammermuir, Moorfoot, Ettrick, Lowther, Carrick and the Scottish Cheviots – and it is in this area that the cream of Scottish collies have been and still are to be found. To date they have won 32 Supreme championships for Scotland to lead the four-country international table.

Already we have met many of them – Kep, Lad, Spot, Fly, Nell, Craig, Roy, Glen, Mirk, Nap, Gael, Cap – their very names sounding the romance of the wild places. There are others, loved and respected by the men whose lives they share in lonely places, for no shepherd could do his job without their help.

When asked by a newspaper reporter how much his dogs were worth, after winning the International Brace championship with Vic and Number at Edinburgh in 1955, the white-haired David Murray, a shepherd all his life, quietly said, 'They're beyond price to me, I couldn't earn my daily bread without them.' Simply put, it summed up the whole purpose of a collie's life, far more important to David Murray who tended 400 Blackface ewes at Glenbield in Peebles than his win-ning of five International and 13 Scottish championships on the trials field.

A grand old man, David, with Vic and Number, strong and clever father and son, were artists of the partnership, winning the International Brace title in three successive years and the Scottish title for four consecutive years.

David Murray was one of the many legendary figures in Scottish sheepdog history. Another was Alex Millar, a man of over six feet in stature, from Highbowhill at Newmilns in Ayrshire, who firmly believed that 'like breeds like', and that the aptitude to work sheep must be bred into a dog. 'A good sheepdog is like a poet – it's born and not made' was one of his comments. He proved his point with one main bloodline by winning one Supreme, three International Farmers' and three International Brace championships, and he won the Scot-tish National title nine times, for seven years from 1924 to 1930 in succession, a remarkable feat.

The fidelity of the Border dogs has been proved a thousand times. One little bitch who was close to motherhood when her master went on ahead and left her alone to fetch a drove of sheep some miles across the Scottish hills gave birth to her pups one after another along the route, yet carried her herding to a successful conclusion. Her job done she returned along the route and, carrying them in her mouth, took her pups home, making a separate journey for each. This is also a tale of a bad master – an isolated case I can assure you – who allowed her to work when she was so close to whelping, but it is a marvellous tale of a collie's devotion to duty.

Another dog huddled close to its master during a snowstorm in an unsuccessful effort to keep his frozen body alive by the warmth of its own.

And James Hogg, the Ettrick shepherd-poet, tells of his Hector who stood guard all night over a flock of lambs because he felt it his duty, even though his master had called him to rest. A true shepherd as well as a poet, Hogg recorded that 'almost any other collie would have discerned that the lambs were safe enough in the fold, but honest Hector had not been able to see through this.' So Hector, it seems, was not of the brightest, though Hogg loved him for his 'humour and whim'.

The collies of the Scottish hills were good sound workers in Hogg's day, at the beginning of the nineteenth century, and his writings show them to have had a high degree of skill, a skill which has steadily been improved until today their shepherding ability has become legend.

Part of that legend are David McTeir's trio of International Shepherds' champions, Mirk, Vic and Ben, and his Supreme winner, Wiston Bill. All were of the Border line. Mirk, the 1964 champion, was from Murray's Vic and Number on his sire's side and he was a collie who used a lot of common sense in his work; the black, white and tan Vic, in his first trials season, when he won the 1967 title, came of Wilson breeding through Bill II; and the half white-faced Ben, winner in 1972, was a son of Wiston Cap with Bill II blood on both sides of his pedigree. Wiston Bill, the 5½-year-old tricolour dog which won the Kilmartin Supreme title in 1970 was a son of his master's Mirk and, out of Walter Hetherington's Fly, was a half-brother to Wiston Cap.

All had one thing in common – they were coolly competent, capable of solving their own shepherding problems and never shirked their job on the hill. They were wise. This is so essential to a shepherd when, like David McTeir who lived at Milton in the Manor Valley near Peebles, there are 650 sheep and a suckler herd of cows to be cared for over 1,000 acres.

A good shepherd whose handling skill has won ten Scottish 'caps' since 1964, David always had a particular regard for Mirk whom he said was so reliable in a tricky situation and never once let him down in ten years. Mirk came to know sheep and their ways so intimately, respecting them while always their master. He would be gentle to a lame ewe and give her plenty of time, come strong on an awkward one that tried to outwit him, and his actions were all natural. He became one of the greatest of hill dogs and, watching him with admiration, David said: 'It was simply due to his natural working ability and honesty.'

Also one of David's favourite collies was the white-headed Ben, who won Scotland's National championship in 1972 and who was used quite extensively as a sire. Fifteen of his sons and daughters ran in the 1978 Nationals. Ben had plenty of spirit, an essential trait for a good hill collie, and despite coming out of veterinary care only a few days prior to the 1972 International, he settled immediately to the strenuous task of winning the Shepherds' title. Though of the same mould in calibre, Ben was a different type of dog to Mirk. He was big and well made, classy in his moves, well balanced and had the power to move any type of stock.

I remember Phil Drabble saying to me, after we had been involved with television's 'One Man and His Dog' series of trials for a few years, that it was so nice to work with modest countrymen who had no airs and graces, and were so proud of their craft.

Scotland's John Templeton is one of the best examples of this sentiment. He is a mild-mannered, courteous, polite and kindly man whose success as a sheep farmer and sheepdog handler has brought him worldwide respect. John has handled his dogs to the very top of International competition, has competed with success in America, has judged trials throughout the country, has been a Director of the International Sheep Dog Society since 1955, is a conscientious secretary of his local sheepdog trials and has won over 200 open championships.

From early beginnings, when he was only 12 years old, and acquiring experience by shepherding ducks on his father's farm at Blackbriggs, Mauchline, in Ayrshire, to the winning of the 1972 Supreme championship of the International Sheep Dog Society – the highest accolade in the sheepdog trials world – John has been regarded with something akin to awe by his fellow handlers, although they all regard him with affection.

John Templeton with Fleet and Cap, 1972 International Brace Champions. Cap was also Supreme Champion the same year at Newcastle. Fleet died in a motel fire after running second in the 1973 American World Championship
(Matt Mundell).

He farms Blackface ewes, Ayrshire milk cows and a small herd of Limousin beef cows at Airtnoch on the edge of Fenwick Moor, and he breeds dogs which he reckons are indispensable to the management of the stock on the farm.

Trials are a bonus, but that bonus, if it can be called such, took him in great style from his first trial when he was 12 years old to his first International 'cap' ten years later when he won the Scottish National championship with Roy, a big, smooth-coated dog which was to win 150 trials awards in his time. From that eventual 'breakthrough' to International recognition, John graced the Scottish team for 11 successive years with dogs of Roy's line and in 1972, after twice being reserve, finally won the Supreme title with Cap, a son of Wiston Cap, who the following year went to America.

John's younger Roy, son of his Moss, had remarkable success in the 1980s, winning the International Farmers' championship three times, the Scottish National championship three times, the International and Scottish Driving titles twice, the Scottish Farmers' championship three times and, partnered with Ben, three successive Scottish Brace championships and the International Brace title of 1984. Probably the most successful dog of all time in competition shepherding and famous throughout the world, Roy earned six International championships, 11 National titles and 14 'caps' for Scotland.

Every collie which is as successful as Roy comes in for a large amount of adverse criticism, because people become jealous and want to knock the dog off its perch. Roy has had his share and has been accused by

Tom Watson's 1976 Scottish Shepherds' Champion, Mirk, goes steady at the pen (Frank H. Moyes).

some farmers of lacking power. In answer I would just point to his winning of two International and two Scottish Driving championships, and his success at the Bowmont Water and the Dowhill Hill trials at the back of Glendowne House, Girvan, in Ayrshire.

Roy was a tricolour smooth-coated collie with his right ear pricked and his left ear bent. He had the drive and determination, and a will to work which was single-minded in his ordering of stock. His method was classed as genius by most handlers. He first graced the International scene at Scotland's National at Glamis in Angus in 1981 when he made an immediate impact, running second at only 2½ years old, 6½ of 220 aggregate points from two judges behind his half-brother, Harford Logan's three-year-old Star from Appin.

Born in March 1979 by his master's Moss out of Tom Stevenson's Lass, his bloodlines went back to Supreme champions McKnight's Gael and Wiston Cap, and thus to the great dogs of yesteryear. Roy has also proved himself as a breeding sire. Of his sons, John Harrison's Craig won the 1990 English National, John Bathgate's Vic won the 1984 Scottish Driving championship and was twice reserve champion at Scotland's National trials, Pat Byrne's Irish Star and Roy's daughter Dot won the International Brace championships in 1994 and 1995, and Eifion Owen's Morgan was runner-up in the 1989 Welsh National.

John Templeton has won seven International championships, 17 Scottish National championships and 40 'caps' for his country. He was born at Mauchline in 1934, only a dozen or so miles from where he

One of the most famous of modern collies – John Templeton's Roy that won six International titles and eleven Scottish Championships.

now farms, and he was so interested in farm stock that his schoolteacher used to say 'the only thing in your heid is beasts', for he had no other interest. His farm runs to 330 acres, lying about 600 ft above sea-level a few miles to the north-west of Kilmarnock in Burns country and in a 'less favoured area', bordered on the east with 18,000 acres of forestry, and rather exposed to the prevailing winds off the waters of the Firth of Clyde.

John is a good farmer, has been successful at ploughing matches, runs the local trials efficiently, and above all shows good manners and great sportsmanship in everything he does. He was awarded the MBE in 1990.

Like a lot of the top-class handlers John is never too high and mighty to come down to the grass roots, and most of his collies acquire their first taste of competitive shepherding on the nursery field. All his dogs since 1977 have got their blooding on the nursery fields of north Ayrshire, and the strong-working, determined Davy which won the English National and the Supreme championships for Sydney Price in 1987 was with John Templeton for the first two years before going to Shropshire.

John took his Fleet and Cap, the Supreme champion of 1972, and together the 1972 International Brace champions, to compete in the American World championship in 1973. The eight-year-old home-bred Fleet ran second to Raymond MacPherson's Nap, but tragically died in a motel fire after the event. Cap, the second successive son of Wiston Cap to win the British Supreme, stayed in the US, sold to Fred Bahnson of North Carolina.

Tom Watson, another shepherd who added to Scotland's glory in 40 years of trials work, bred, reared and trained his own dogs to assist in the care of one of the finest flocks of Blackface sheep on the Lammermuir Hills. His bloodlines were much akin to Bob Fraser's Mindrum family in Northumberland, and his brave and placid Jen, a medium-sized, rough-coated, black and white bitch, won the Supreme championship in 1980. She was a great-great-granddaughter of Wiston Cap.

One of the most fascinating contrasts I find in the collie dog is its ability to be strong and dominant, almost ruthless in its total mastery of a rebellious ewe at one moment, and then persuasive, kind and gentle with a tiny lamb at the next.

Drift was a typical example of this. Viewers of 'One Man and His Dog' saw him almost vicious in his determination to push reluctant Blackface ewes into the dipping trough for John Bathgate at Hallmanor Farm at Kirkton Manor – yet during lambing time he was a past master at mothering-on an orphan lamb to a foster-ewe, using authority, tact and gentleness in his task.

John Bathgate is one of the nicest blokes I know and one of the unluckiest in the International field. His Rock, like his ancestor, Wilson's Moss, who was also generally unsuccessful in International trials, won every major trial in Scotland yet never succeeded at International level.

Rock was the sire of Jim Cropper's Fleet and Clyde, International Brace champions in 1973, and the great-grandsire of Glyn Jones's Supreme champion Gel. He was such a clever collie that John could 'forget him' when working on the moor, knowing full well that the dog could carry out his task without any guidance. Having gathered a heft of sheep, John could send him home with them while he went on to gather another heft with the other dogs. Having delivered them safely to John's wife – and received a pat on the head for his cleverness – he would return to the hill for the next heft.

John told me: 'In lambing time I often sent Rock to a pen where a ewe had a dead lamb. I'd put the dead lamb in my bag and say to him "Take the ewe to the parrick man", and off he'd go, never looking at another sheep, and he'd lay at the parrick with his ewe until I arrived to foster another lamb on her. Another great skill of his was, if a ewe wouldn't let a lamb suck he would jump into the parrick beside her and wouldn't allow her to move until the lamb had sucked its fill. He was a very intelligent dog and must have had a terrific brain. He was so pleasant and friendly and was always the same.'

John Bathgate won Scotland's Driving championship with his tricolour Vic in 1984, when the collie was unflappable. A son of John Templeton's famous Roy, he mastered wild Blackfaces which were inclined to gallop like deer over the flat parched grass in Bellahouston Park at Glasgow for second placing in the Scottish team. Vic, calm and collected in work, was also in the Scottish teams in 1986 and 1990 and his son, the rough-coated Clyde, was in the 1992 team.

Repeatedly I refer to the adaptability of the modern Border Collie and as you travel northwards into the Highlands of Scotland yet another trait becomes apparent – the ability of the dog to hunt out unseen sheep from among the rock and bracken of the high mountains. Generally the collie is known for its quiet voiceless method of herding sheep, but when ewes are hidden in gullies and among rocks and loath to move, particularly in hot sunshine, the dog that can find them and chivvy them with barked authority stands a far greater chance of moving them. We often tend to think that the Huntaway type of working dog is the product of the New Zealand sheep-runs, but collies that can hunt out sheep and use their voices to encourage movement have always been used on Highland herdings.

CHAPTER FIFTEEN

A Good Dog Can Do Anything

Winter comes quickly to the Pennines and I talk of sheep rescue in snow blizzard, recall the unquenchable spirit of Len Greenwood, discuss the part of nursery trials in collie improvement, and talk of champions.

Fleeces white with driven snow, the four ewes stood bemused by the fury of the blizzard. Their eyes wide with surprise, they huddled together under the stone wall while the wind-driven snow piled around them. Loath to face the icy wind which whipped across the upland pasture with the cutting speed of an express train, they were stoically resigned to their plight. As yet they were in no real danger, but their position was worsening with every passing minute as the snow piled higher against their bodies. They were tough, hardy hill sheep, used to the rigours of winter on the high ground, but the suddenness and ferocity of the snow blizzard had surprised them. I slipped and slithered across the field, head down to protect my face from the pin-pricks of windborne ice, my crook balancing my plunging progress. Gael, the collie, was white coated at my side, her sable colouring smothered in clinging snowflakes.

The sheep had to be moved from the possibility of an icy prison. I plunged through the growing drift to reach them and Gael skipped lightly over the white barrier. The ewes were not interested; they were storm battered and apathetic, so that I had to physically push a leader to break a trail through the snow drift. Coaxing and shoving, and with Gael nosing from behind, I encouraged some action, and the sheep walked slowly, one behind the other, to ground bared by the wind.

I leaned on my crook to catch my breath. The crook is the shepherd's 'third leg' and has many uses – such as a resting prop – and it is almost as indispensable as his dog. Without mine I would feel undressed.

Gently, slowly, Gael coaxed the ewes down the hill, walking two

Playfully happy, collies have none of the farmers' worries in transporting feed-blocks to snowbound sheep in the Lakeland fells (Terry Bromley).

yards behind them as they started to trot to the safety of the lower ground. They disappeared into the flurry of dancing snowflakes and I called Gael back to me. Other ewes were down there, grouped in the shelter of high walls and the remains of an old building. The four sheep we had driven down would join them. Gael and I were the only living things on the higher hill. She was a comforting companion in the bitterness of the cold. Life on the hills could be harsh when snow and ice came, and especially with such sudden severity.

Such wintry conditions are difficult enough in the valleys – in the towns and cities, when roads and pavements are turned into skating rinks, progress becomes dangerous for both motorist and pedestrian, but few town or city dwellers can have the remotest idea of what such weather conditions are like on the hills. Up there the wind is the killer and exposure fatigue comes quickly from its probing fingers.

Always, even in the summer months, there is a wind on the hills and when in winter it carries the icy touch of frost or drives the stinging frozen snowflakes it quickly numbs the senses. Day after day of dazzling whiteness on your eyes can bring its dangers too, a sort of numbing sensation which saps the energy. Tiny black spots begin to swim around before my eyes after a day or two of walking the snow-covered hill and I have to make a physical effort to keep concentration. I suppose this is akin to snow blindness. Gael also loses some of her interest in wet snow, for the snowballs which form on the long feathering of her legs actually become so ponderous that she finds it difficult to run, and I have to break them away to keep her mobile. So the constant warnings we hear from mountain rescue teams and the like are not to be ignored. When walking the hills always be sure that you have ample protective and warm clothing with you.

This leads me to the often vexed question of the rights of others to walk our high sheep-runs. Most farmers do not object to people enjoying themselves on the hills and fells provided they behave themselves, keep their dogs under control when there is stock about, do not damage walls and fences, or leave litter all over the place. It is only when the summer visitors – we see few in winter – propound their knowledge of life in the hills, demand outrageous privileges and seek, in letters to *The Times*, to alter our ways that we get annoyed. And the hillman can never forget the large number of sheep that are savaged every year by uncontrolled dogs.

On a hill surprised by snow blizzard even the hardy sheep, usually warned by some sixth sense of impending weather threat, can become trapped. Drifting wind-whipped snow is the danger, for though the sheep can stand the cold and are good foragers, they become entombed in drifts. Then it depends on the hard and conscientious work of the farmer and his dogs to rescue them. And it is a tedious and back-breaking task searching for sheep which may have been covered by drifting snow. Slowly each drift has to be probed by crook or rod to feel for the soft resistance of a sheep's body, and then, once located, each animal has to be dug out. Some collie dogs are particularly expert at scenting sheep under snow and save hours of unrewarding probing by their skill.

Sheep can survive for quite a long time in what for humans would be an icy tomb. The heat of their bodies drives minute air holes to the surface and, having eaten bare the ground on which they are trapped, they will nibble their wool, chewing out the grease for sustenance. There is a superstition among Welsh hillmen that a buried sheep cannot live more than nine days but I have known them to be alive after 21 days.

In prolonged snowy weather, when the ground is covered, sheep may find difficulty in reaching their grass bite though they are very adaptable and able to scrape away the snow and ice with their sharp hooves. Then the best supplementary food that the farmer can provide is hay, but it has to be carted to the flock in the tractor and even humped up the hill by human effort. It is not a job for the faint hearted. Heavy and prolonged snowfall on the hills can decimate a sheep flock for, tough as all hill breeds are, they must have food. If food is cut off deaths occur and, equally serious, the ewes come to the lambing in March and April in poor condition and the lamb crop is low.

In one severe winter my old friend, Len Greenwood, a most familiar

When a good dog is needed – when the moors are snowbound and the sheep flock needs extra attention. Len Greenwood and his collies on the hills of Ramsden Farm in the Lancashire Pennines (Farmers Guardian).

name among sheepdog enthusiasts, lost 270 of his 500 ewes and the lambs from those which survived were few. Len farmed 1,500 acres of bleak and forbidding moorland to 1,300 ft in the Lancashire–Yorkshire Pennines from Ramsden Farm, Walsden, where his wife Rachel had been born. They are both dead now, but they were people for whom I had a special regard and respect. They were born of the high hills, and by dint of their skills and labours learned how to farm them successfully and happily. Moulded by the most rigorous of conditions, they were of an independent and sterling character. Always there was a welcome to the grey stone-built farmhouse perched 1,000 ft high on the hill and always there was a good warm fire with a friendly collie laid close by.

Once I struggled through 12 ft snow drifts up to Ramsden to see how Len and Rachel were faring to be told on arrival, and as expected, that 'nothing ailed them'. Outside, the scene favoured the Arctic wastes, yet in spite of being cut off from the valley for some six weeks, of having a frozen water supply and diminishing feeding-stuff, and of having to carry hay to the sheep they had managed to gather round the buildings, they were fit and cheerful.

Under such conditions – and winter always came early to Ramsden – it was not surprising that Len and Rachel had great faith in good dogs, for they were absolutely essential to the management of the farm. The ability of the dogs was the measure between success or failure in their farming. Necessity fosters efficiency and Len became known throughout the sheepdog world, for when put to the trials test his dogs found it comparatively easy work after Ramsden Moor. 'A good dog can do anything, hill work, close work, singles or doubles trialling. If the dog has the brains and the shepherd has the understanding, the dog will work efficiently under any conditions', Len always believed.

So often he proved his point and with over 50 years of experience coupled with the patience, sympathy and discipline he showed towards his dogs, he was one of the outstanding sheepdog handlers of his time. He won over 1,000 trials awards and represented England many times for he had a natural affinity towards dogs. He would meet a strange dog which had travelled down from Scotland muzzled and chained, according to the railway's regulations, at Littleborough station and, removing both muzzle and chain, would have it walk at his heel to Ramsden Farm without the slightest problem of it running away.

A little man with a big sense of humour, perhaps his greatest escapade was to appear on the BBC 'That's Life' programme as the only shepherd who'd had his teeth made to fit his whistle. He only used his false teeth to whistle commands to his dogs, never for eating!

Len took life in his stride with the philosophy of a man who had been in the trenches of Flanders when he was 18 years old, had been a successful professional boxer and had worked hard all his life. Nothing ruffled him, except perhaps the time he had to do without his smoking-twist for four days at an International, having left it at home – and twist being unheard of in the area we were visiting. My pipe tobacco was for 'little lads' and useless to him. Incidentally, whenever we were setting off for a few days to one of the big trials he used to tell my wife, 'Men and dogs were meant to roam, women were meant to stay at home.'

Len was a great sportsman and I never knew him to query a judging decision – except when I disqualified his dog for biting a sheep at the English National in 1967! He got his own back, borrowing my coat to run and win a trials during a thunderstorm. He got first prize. I got wet through.

Len Greenwood will always be remembered for his good company, his great knowledge of dogs and his sense of fun, but it must not be forgotten that he was one of Britain's finest sheepdog handlers. He had some good collies, Spot, Roy, Dot, Fleet, Cap, Moss, Bett and Sweep, all of which worked hard on the hill and won prizes on the trials field. Dot was the first collie in the country to win a prize of £50 at Nottingham in 1945.

Len favoured two bloodlines, collies of Jim Wilson's Whitehope Nap line, and collies from Thomas Roberts's 1924 Supreme champion Jaff, the rough-coated descendant of three other Supreme champions, Scott's Kep, Wallace's Moss and Telfer's Haig. The Jaff dogs, he felt, were cool, manageable and highly intelligent workers, and the Nap line gave him his most powerful dog, Moss, the 1964 English Driving champion and one of the few collies to represent England in all sections

– singles, brace and driving – of International competition. Moss also won such top trials as Longshaw, Yorkshire, Holme and Harden Moss.

In his later years his dogs brought him lasting pleasure, none more so than Sweep, a handsome black and white, rough-coated son of Michael Perring's Jen, exported to South Africa and that country's 1970 novice champion. Len handled Sweep into the English International team when the collie was only two years old and made him a television star. With Sweep in front of the cameras, Len worked him from behind them in a children's story of farming.

Sweep was devoted to his master and gave Len his last great triumph on the trials field in 1976, outrunning faultlessly and uncommanded over 520 yards of rough bog moor and climbing through 260 ft to gather hill sheep, grey dots in the distance, on the 1,450 ft contour of Deerplay Moor, to win one of the toughest trials in the North Country – for which the Len Greenwood Memorial Trophy is now the victor's prize.

Behind every successful man, it is commonly said, there is a good woman and Mrs Greenwood played a big part in all Len's successes, for it was she who took care of the dogs at home, with a knowledge of canine ailments and cures that would have done credit to a professional veterinarian.

The Deerplay Hill trial which Sweep won is a prime example of just how effective the right kind of test can be in improvement of collie ability. When the first event was run over the open moor in 1975, 30 per cent of the dogs failed to gather their sheep; today only an odd one fails.

When Len Greenwood died Sweep found a good home with Danny Wild, who respects his collies as workmates and friends, and he joined the handsome black and white Len, bred by and named after Sweep's former master and a grandson of Shepherds' champion Kyle and the older Clair, from Jack Gumbley's Meg, in the care of a flock of horned Lonk ewes on the high bleak hills adjoining Blackstone Edge above Littleborough. Here, where the wind is cold and the snow lingers long on moorland rising to 1,300 ft, he found satisfying work and another good home and still enjoyed his trips to the trials fields though age was beginning to take its toll on his stamina.

Danny Wild is England's National Vice-President of the International Sheep Dog Society, and judged the 1991 English National trials at Rydal near Ambleside in Cumbria.

Danny's first International 'cap' was with the black-coated Nicky in 1984, whose bloodlines were from the champions and great hill dogs of yesteryear, and who was a great hill dog himself with natural qualities of shepherding. In 1992 Danny won England's reserve National championship with his three-year-old good-looking Nell, a maternal granddaughter of Scottish champion Dryden Joe, and a paternal granddaughter of Robert Fielden's grand hill dog Clint. Nell also won the trophy for the best outwork at the trials on Swaledale ewes.

Danny Wild is a good farmer, wresting a living from some of the bleakest country in England, as his family has done for many years, and there is a long tradition of sound stock and good dogs in the locality. It is not very long since flocks of sheep were driven along the valley roads to the railway yards at Littleborough and the dogs were trained to go in advance of the sheep to sit at the road junctions and prevent them from straying off the route. One farmer once told me he was so thirsty during particularly hot weather that he drove a flock of 200 sheep on to the car park of a public house and left his dog in sole charge whilst he nipped inside for a pint of beer. Such was the faith of the men in their dogs, and such was the high herding skill of the dogs that this part of the Pennines on the Lancashire–Yorkshire borderland has a reputation in competitive shepherding.

The Holmes brothers, Cecil, John and Jim, represented England regularly. Ernest Dawson from Whittaker Farm above Hollingworth Lake was a winner throughout the North Country, and Jack Gumbley has bred many fine dogs at Littleborough. It is easy to think of the area as industrial, with the big manufacturing towns filling the valleys to produce cotton and woollen cloth and thriving on the fact that, in the case of wool, the raw material was close at hand.

The Pennines are great sheep rearing areas and, stretching from the Derbyshire Peak to the Cheviot, have evolved many distinct breeds of sheep. The Derbyshire Gritstone has spread from the Goyt Valley, the Lonk is a native of east Lancashire and the Swaledale is becoming a most popular breed. There is the Dalesbred, the Rough Fell, the Blue-faced Leicester and the Wensleydale. The Teeswater is renowned as the sire of the well-known Masham; the white-faced Cheviot is the favourite in the northern Pennines; and the ancient Woodland still roams the southern extremes.

Each breed has been produced to meet the particular land and weather conditions in which it lives for the most effective return of meat and wool, since the Pennine uplands are very diverse in the character of their grazings. They are of harsh vegetation, heather and moss, rough bents, starved and acid fells. Always they are bleak and desolate, vast stretches of peat moors, rocky outcrops and deep-cut cloughs. Wild by nature, they are yet full of mellowing surprises – the rich claret of heather bloom spilling over the slopes in August, the snow-white carpet of cotton-grass in June, the green swaying mantle of summer bracken.

I have lived among them all my life, lashed by their storms, frozen by their icy winds, refreshed by their rain showers, warmed by their suns, and they have a charm which no other hill land can match. Perhaps it is the hint of mystery which hangs over them, the sorcery of the Lancashire witches, the dominance of the Roman legions or the romance of the Brontë stories. Whatever, in basic everyday facts the Pennines are a hard land to farm where man needs every assistance he can get to earn a living, so that a good dog is an essential assistant to manage the sheep.

'Without this little bitch and others like her, this farm would be unworkable. This holding, by the nature of its harsh land and severe weather, is fit only for sheep and beef cows and without Sally and her kind I could not control such stock.' So said Bob Moore of the 220 acre Bradget Hey Farm in the Cliviger Gorge, and of the collies which helped him farm it – thus summarising the whole pattern of Pennine hill farming.

Sally, essentially a competent hill bitch in the herding of 100 Lonk–Swaledale breeding ewes and a small herd of suckler cows, also became renowned as a trials worker. In the Pennine nursery trials of 1973–4 she won 18 awards, including five firsts, and progressed to open victories at Quernmore, Allandale, Holme, Moorcock, Hodder Valley and Lowgill. She earned International recognition in 1979. She was the trim, smooth-coated daughter of Supreme champion Wiston Cap and, on her mother's line, from Jim Cropper's Fleet.

Bob Moore was once given a thrashing because of the efficiency of a collie. He and his brothers had been sent to gather some sheep from their father's flock with their father's bitch Meg, but boys being boys, they started to play hide and seek among the rocks on the hill, seeing no urgency in their mission. Meg thought otherwise, gathering the sheep on her own initiative and driving them back to the farm. When the boys returned later they were each given a thrashing for neglecting their job!

In a land which has recognised the value of a good dog since the great droving days in the eighteenth century, it is not surprising that sheepdog trials societies flourish and stage some of the best events in the country, like those at Fylde, Deerplay, Trawden, Moorcock and Harden Moss. I have a card advertising a sheepdog trial in Worsthorne, the next village to where I live, on 5 September 1904, informing would-be spectators, at a charge of 6d for the day, that waggonettes would run from Burnley five miles away. Other trials in the locality were held at Ingleton in August 1905, at Edgworth in 1906 and at Radcliffe in 1909.

The Pennine hills were the birthplace of nursery trials, organised by sheepmen who had a genuine interest in improving their work dogs and at the same time bettering their neighbours' skills.

Eric Halsall and Gael on the snowbound land above Cliviger in the Lancashire Pennines (Associated Newspapers).

Starting after the end of the open trials season in October, they now take place each Saturday throughout the winter months until the restart of the opens in April. Their purpose is simply to give a young collie – and very often a young or raw handler – some experience of trials shepherding over modified courses, yet including all the tests of the opens. They are held on host farms where sheep, usually wintering hoggs, are available and they have come to play an important part in the rising standards of the hill dogs for they have demonstrated the value of an efficient dog in the quiet handling of farm stock and have awakened an interest in breeding. Nursery trials have over the past 20 years led to the better handling of sheep flocks in the Pennines.

The nursery scene is very different from the glamour of the big trials where spectators applaud good effort, the colourful trade stands brighten a summer's day and we all wear our best clothes. Working clothes and waterproofs are the nursery scene; we huddle in the shelter of a Land Rover and try to treat the inevitable rainstorms as though they never existed. Reward for a good trial is a simple 'well done' from a friend, and the satisfaction of having another good youngster on the bottom rung of the status ladder.

Nursery trials, and we now have puppy and beginners trials too, are held in Scotland, throughout Wales, the north-east dales, the fells of Lakeland, on the Yorkshire moors and in the Vale of York, in the Derbyshire–Cheshire area and in the south of England, enabling more and more young collies to acquire trials experience before facing the keener competition of the summer opens. Many youngsters thus blooded have gone on to International recognition.

One of the best was Jim Cropper's Fleet, who learned his basic craft with 500 Lonk and Gritstone ewes and 40 beef cows on the 1,000 high

Jim Cropper's Fleet and Clyde, power dogs and International Champions of the high sheep-runs of east Lancashire.

acres of Turn Hill Farm in the Forest of Rossendale. Of Scottish breeding, the son of John Bathgate's Rock and John Bonella's Trim, he went to the Lancashire Pennines when he was only a pup and at 18 months old, in October 1966, started his nursery trials experience. Before the end of the season he was the talk of the area. A big black and white, smooth-coated dog of eye-catching appearance and extreme intelligence, the ideal hill dog, he was immediately among the awards and by the end of the season had created a record of 23 awards, including eight victories, in 31 trials. In his second season in open trials, in 1968, Fleet reached international status, winning the English Driving championship at Darlington and giving Jim Cropper his first International 'cap'.

Misfortune overtook the big hill dog when he lost the sight of an eye after being kicked by a cow, but he still went his winning way – for sheer guts there was never a more determined collie than Fleet. He again won a place in England's team in 1969, and in 1970, in spite of further injury which made him run lame, he repeated his winning of the English Driving championship.

When Fleet was three years old his younger brother and sister, Clyde and Bonnie, of the same Rock–Trim litter, went to Turn Hill and made almost the same impact on the trials scene. Sadly Bonnie was to go blind but she left her mark on the sheepdog world, being the grandmother of

Ken Brehmer's Ben, the 1978 English National champion, which went to America.

Clyde, a keen, prick-eared, smooth-coated dog, smaller than Fleet in size, however, followed the pad-marks of his older brother and first won the honour to run for England in 1970, the year in which he won 22 awards in open competition, and in his first International at three years old he was the best of England's dogs in the Supreme championship, finishing third.

Two strong hill dogs to honour English prestige with their decisive and workmanlike shepherding, Fleet won six successive International 'caps' and Clyde four, and they left the International scene with a flourish at Bala in 1973, finally winning – and together – a richly deserved International championship, the Brace title. Clyde also won the reserve Supreme honour, but for Fleet, one of the truly great canine characters in the sheepdog world, this International Brace championship was the final accolade to an illustrious working career.

A tall, long-striding, sandy-haired hill farmer, and so obviously a 'natural' in the art of collie handling, Jim Cropper respects the power and stamina of collies which are tough and strong enough to work over the rugged terrain that he farms. On this count he had a great respect for Fleet, Clyde and Bonnie, who had the courage and 'stickability' for endless work. They never gave up their tasks on the moor. Fleet, Clyde and Bonnie were products of the Pennine nursery trials, which I believe have a major purpose in improving the efficiency of general stock handling, provided they are used as intended – as training grounds for

John Holliday with Moss, 1957 Supreme Champion, from Pateley Bridge in Nidderdale (R. Ackrill).

young collies and not as highly competitive events, a danger with their increasing popularity.

Jim Cropper, a master handler of sheepdogs, won the English National and Farmers' championships in 1986 at Beadnell by the North Sea in Northumberland with his young hill dog Cap, and with Cap partnered by his older fellmate, also named Cap (although we in Lancashire called him Fonsie, to differentiate the two), ran second in the Brace contest. Cap II and Fonsie were also Brace champions in television's 'One Man and His Dog' in 1987. The older Cap was also sixth in the English team in 1986, to give Jim a National event to be remembered.

Sam Dyson's Mac, a smooth-coated, black and white son of Jim Wilson's Whitehope Nap and a litter-brother of Len Greenwood's Moss, was another collie which really left his mark in the Pennine area and his reputation as a breeding sire earned far more renown in the farming world for Ponden Hall, the 'Thrushcross Grange' of Emily Brontë's *Wuthering Heights*, than ever it got from the famous novel. From Ponden Hall at Stanbury near the famous Brontë village of Haworth, Mac was in-dispensable in the management of Lonk × Dalesbred ewes over 3,000 acres of wild bleak moorland rising to Withins Heights at 1,500 ft.

On the trials field his successes were constant rather than outstanding, though he won a place in England's 1961 International team, but it was as a sire of strong, intelligent and courageous workers that Mac was written into the history of Pennine shepherding. Throughout his life, and he lived to the ripe old age of 16, he probably served more bitches than any other collie in the area and all his progeny were sound working dogs. One of his sons was the blue and white Sam, who won the 1965 International Shepherds' title for Tom Leedham, and of his last litter was Adrian Bancroft's Anne, the winner of two English Shepherds' championships.

One of Mac's party tricks, or if he had to cross the water of the Ponden reservoir by the farm buildings to reach sheep, was to swim to the whistled commands of his master, turning left and right just as though running the land. 'The best dog that ever lived' was Sam Dyson's opinion of Mac – so often the opinion of every sheepman of his favourite collie and rightly so. But it is a bold man who would set one against another – apart from competitive contest. Recalling Mac's water prowess, my good friend John Lever, former chairman of Lancashire county branch of the National Farmers' Union and a great humorist, used to tell the tale of how a prospective buyer, having seen the collie in question jump the stream on its way to the sheep, asked for a repeat run, and on the collie again jumping the stream refused it because 'it can't swim'.

They take as much pride in their dogs as in their cricket in Yorkshire

Allan Heaton orders Belle round to stop a breakaway ewe at Stoneleigh in 1976 (Coventry Evening Telegraph).

and for me, a mere Lancastrian, even with strong Dales ties, to denigrate Yorkshire's greatest collies is tantamount to committing 'hara-kiri'.

Sufficient to recall Mark Hayton's Glen, the 1926 Supreme, and Pat, the 1936 International Farmers' champion; and his son Arthur's Pattie, Jock, Paddy and Barney, winners of two International Shepherds' championships and one International Brace title, collies which brought honour to Wharfedale. And as considered earlier there were the clever collies handled by Michael Perrings and Adrian Bancroft. Then there was Moss with John Holliday at Knott House, Pateley Bridge, in Nidderdale. Moss was a strong, rough-coated dog of controlled and determined power who went one better than his father, Roy, the winner of the 1951 English championship, by winning the Supreme championship at Loughborough in 1957.

John, a Cumbrian by birth, was one of the calmest and least ruffled handlers ever, and he conveyed his quiet confidence in his skill to his collies. One of nature's gentlemen, he was wise in collie ways, the best of counsellors on trials matters, and the finest judge of a sheepdog trial I have been privileged to sit with. He had confidence in his breeding of dogs, starting with the 1950 success of Roy in winning the English Driving championship at Bakewell, through to Moss II, a grandson of the Supreme Moss, winning the 1968 English National at Darlington. Roy's lines were from his master's Roger and Meg through Holmes Brothers' breeding to Wilson's Supreme champion Craig.

Nidderdale has another good handler in John Suttill, whose herding comprised 1,200 Swaledales over 2,600 acres of Heathfield Moor, the

Mary Heaton from Brandsby in Yorkshire, one of the most competent of lady handlers, works Moss over the Penrith National course in 1979. (Marc Henrie).

vast expanse of bleak and exacting land to the west of the dale. He has represented England on many occasions and in 1956 won the English Brace title with Wylie and Jaff. His Trix, a confident black and white, rough-coated bitch, was a regular merit choice for England.

One of John's best dogs was the father of Trix, Shep, who at 7½ years old showed true hill stamina and courage to win the first Deerplay Hill trials in June 1975 with a gather of Gritstone ewes over 520 moorland yards. A son of Supreme champion Wiston Cap, and a good-looking, rough-coated dog, Shep was the typical proven hill collie whose skills were reflected with many trials victories, including Barnard Castle, Alston, Barbon, Harden Moss, Ryedale, Husthwaite and Denton. Shep was to meet an unusual death from one of the many hazards a hill dog faces. He was bitten by an adder on Heathfield and though John rendered first-aid and carried him across the moor, he failed to reach veterinary treatment in time.

Half-sister to John Holliday's champion Moss was the trim little Fly who, at 4½ years old, won the 1957 International Shepherds' championship for Mark Illingworth of Askrigg. Two of Yorkshire's finest collies, Moss and Fly, had the same sire, John Holliday's champion Roy.

Fly was a delightful little bitch, black and white and sturdy, keen and interested in her work, and inheriting the power of her Wilson's Cap line she was completely masterful with sheep. But though she never gave ground and never faltered in facing up to the most truculent ram, she was also the gentlest of creatures in her dealings with lambs. She reached the ultimate in animal trust when she was so well accepted that a ewe would allow her to lick clean its first-born of twin lambs.

Wise and reasoning in all her actions, she overcame her small stature by running to the top of a peat bank to increase her range of vision over the moor. At the time of her International championship win she was assisting her master with 750 ewes on the bare fells above Semer Water by Wensleydale, and she also won the English Shepherds' championships of 1956 and 1959.

She was of champion stock, her dam, Meg, and her grandsire, Monty, together winning the 1949 English Brace title, and she passed on her skills to her two sons, Moss and Jim, who together won the 1963 International Brace championship.

Two International Brace championships have gone to Yorkshire's vast sheep-runs since the war. In 1981 Norman Darrell, farming on the edge of Dalby Forest at Thornton Dale, handled Pat and Cap to victory; and 30 years earlier, in 1951, Maurice Collin with Cap and Kep took the title to the Vale of York. Norman Darrell also won the English Driving championship in 1993 with Flynn, a rough-coated collie whose bloodline went back to Gilchrist's Spot.

At the Blackpool International Maurice Collin, at 20 years old, was the youngest handler and he had worked hard for his title. Being the manager of only a small farming unit at Skeeby he had to train his collies on borrowed sheep flocks, loaned by the friendly farmers of Swaledale.

After a lapse of many years Maurice returned to the trials field, in 1974, and soon showed that he had lost none of his handling skill,

Mark Illingworth and the trim little Fly from Semer Water, International Shepherds' Champions in 1957.

winning the Thirsk championship 12 months later with a faultless run from his 3½-year-old Spot. He handled Spot into England's International teams in 1976 and 1977, Roy in 1979, Derk twice, and Shep in 1984. The third generation of Maurice's breed to get into the English team, the home-bred black and white Shep, which went back in bloodline to Wiston Cap, Gilchrist's Spot, Bosworth Coon, Longton's Gyp and Whitehope Nap, won television's 'One Man and His Dog' singles trophy at Ullswater in 1985.

A granddaughter of Maurice's old Cap took the English National championship to Yorkshire in 1967, judged by Ashton Priestley and myself as the best of the 122 collies over the Dovedale course in Derbyshire. She was Maid, daughter of McKnight's Gael from the Cleveland Hills who gave Miles Cook of Park Farm, Kildale, his first National trophy, and she was only the second bitch in ten years to win England's top honour.

Two Yorkshiremen have represented Britain in the New Zealand World championships, Allan Heaton from Brandsby in the Howardian Hills in 1975, and Clarence Storey of Delph in 1973. Both competed to the honour of Yorkshire collies.

Allan, who won the 1963 English Brace title with his home-bred Bob and five-year-old Garry, is head of a family whose interest and knowledge of working collies is profound. His wife, Mary, regularly runs her dogs at trials and his son, Mark, died tragically after training a team of collies to New Zealand requirements during an 18-month shepherding work-tour of that country.

Clarence Storey is one of the very few non-farmers to have made the International grade in trials work. A heating engineer before retirement, though he farms Gritstones at Pack Horse on 90 acres of the Yorkshire–Lancashire borderland near Standedge Moors, and has farming interests in Wales which give him the 'feel' for sheep, his greatest success was in the winning of the English Brace championship at Alnwick in 1964 with the white and black Moss partnered by the blue-coated Ben, which commendably he graded up from 11 awards in Pennine nursery trials. Failure to pen after the best outfield work of the International at Drymen later in the year lost him the greater honour.

Clarence has handled some good collies, none better than the big tricolour Roy, one of the most respected collies in Britain, and Cass, the two dogs he took to New Zealand. Cass stayed in New Zealand to be used as a stud-dog by Vic Cook at New Plymouth, but Roy came home to grace England's trials courses and to sire some fine dogs which were to make their mark both in Britain and in America. One of the best was Blade, twice the conqueror of the Deerplay Moor test, and winner of over 30 open victories.

Roy and Cass, both with Wiston Cap blood, were bred by Tommy Anderton at Longridge near Preston, a man who knew how to breed working collies as well as anyone and better than most. A quiet, soft-spoken man of few words, he had the knack of blending the right ingredients, the skills and the temperaments, with the touch of the cordon bleu chef.

Storey's Roy came from his direct use of Wiston Cap on Jill, a bitch by Tot Longton's famous Rob; and Cass, just three days younger than Roy, was from a litter of five sired by Rock, John Bathgate's great Scottish worker, out of Nell, the daughter of Wiston Cap.

Clarence sent Roy back to Tommy so that the old dog could spend his last days in pleasant retirement – a contradiction to the odd and better publicised instances of working dogs being 'put down' when they have lost their usefulness.

One collie bitch for whom I always had a great regard was Bet, whose gentle but firm qualities were not always reflected in trials prizes though she represented England three times. A rough-coated, black and white collie with a distinctive white face, she worked with John Squires on a 46 acre holding at Meltham near Huddersfield, and mothered the blue-coated Mirk, England's choice on three occasions and winner of such top championships as Hornby, Bodfari, Bamford, Hope and Fylde twice.

CHAPTER SIXTEEN

From Sheer Guts to Quiet Intelligence

❦❦❦❦❦❦

Memories of the early days in north Derbyshire, of the important work of the Peakland farmers in evolving their efficient workmates of today, dogs which have set the standard for the shepherding of the Midlands and southlands.

The southernmost point of the Pennines brings me to a land – the open windswept Derbyshire Peak and its attendant dales – where sheep and grouse vie for priority, where the sheep flocks are large and scattered, and where the dogs have to be fit and strong to watch over them.

I have more than a passing interest. In sheep terms, I suppose I'm a bit of a crossbred with Lancashire Lonk and Yorkshire Swaledale, and further, as former secretary and honorary member of the Derbyshire Gritstone Sheepbreeders Society, into Derbyshire. And my wife's folk came from the Hayfield area. So I know the Derbyshire northland where collies handled by such men as John Thorpe, Ernest and Ashton Priestley, Ray Ollerenshaw, Eric Elliot, Cyril Bostock and Chris Furniss have stamped their quality on English breeding. Derbyshire is synonymous with the famous Longshaw trials, the most important pastoral event held in the county and claimed to be the oldest trials event in the country, supported down the years by the ducal families of Rutland and Devonshire.

Today, during the early days of September, when the trials are held over three days, a big crowd of townspeople gather on the pastures before Longshaw Lodge, once the stately shooting lodge of the Dukes of Rutland. They come mainly from the big industrial areas of Sheffield and Manchester and their wondering attention far outweighs the technically expert view of the farmers who gather from Scotland and Wales as well as England.

But apart from the added interest and attraction of a multitude of people whose sole purpose is to enjoy the spectacle of clever dogs at work in pleasant country surroundings, Longshaw still holds to the original aim of the shepherds and gamekeepers who watched the first official trials in March 1898 – that of testing the working collie by competition. And such is the strength of that competition that the open championship is one of the most coveted in the world.

When it all began you could buy a good sheepdog for 'half-a-crown and a pint of beer'. Today a top class dog would command £1,000 or more.

The first Longshaw dogs were of no fixed breeding or qualities so that some were good and others were bad. Their major assets were their loyalty, their tremendous stamina and their unquenchable spirit. It was said that they would work the hills until their pads were raw and bleeding. They were far removed from the quiet, intelligent, speedy workers which have graced Longshaw in post-war years – dogs such as Ashton Priestley's Pat, the 1951 Supreme International champion; Eric Elliott's three National Driving champions Tess, Queen and Bill, or his Maid which won Longshaw in 1987; Ray Ollerenshaw's experienced Tweed, the Longshaw champion in 1977; or Mike Northwood's black and white Turk, the Longshaw champion of 1994.

Ashton Priestley's Pat, seven years old when he won the 1951

Ashton Priestly's Pat, 1951 Supreme Champion, from the Derbyshire Peak District
(Sheffield Telegraph).

Supreme championship at Blackpool, was a medium sized, smooth-coated, black and white dog whose intelligence made hard work look easy. He was quick to act to the wiles of sheep and he had an extraordinary turn of speed to outmanoeuvre the fastest ewe. Most important, he had the perfect understanding with his master, for before he went to assist Ashton in the management of 1,400 sheep on 5,000 upland acres on Bamford Edge he had been spurned by at least two other competent handlers.

Discussing dogs in general during our three-days judging stint together at the National at Dovedale, Ashton told me that Pat was one of those dogs gifted with the skill to scent buried sheep. 'Wandering across the packed snow drift he would suddenly put his nose down and there, when we dug, would be a buried sheep. . . . In the bad winter of 1947 he assisted in the rescue of some 500 sheep from beneath the snow.'

Of Wilson's Cap line, Pat was of Cumbrian stock, the son of Joe Relph's Fleet, reserve Supreme champion and the star of the film *Loyal Heart*, and he was bred by Ernest Warwick out of Tib near Penrith. Ashton acquired him in 1946 from the well-known Welsh handler, R. O. Williams, on Anglesey for £200. 'The best £200 I ever spent' he

Ashton Priestly of Bamford in Derbyshire, and Pat, before their International Supreme winning trial at Blackpool in 1951.

Ashton Priestly with Eric Halsall, the judges of the 1967 English National trials at Dovedale (Lancashire Life).

said, for Pat took the well-respected name of Priestley to the very top with his Supreme success.

The Priestley family have been handling dogs and winning competitions for years, indeed it is the accepted version of the start of Longshaw that it was a Priestley who got things going. It was Ashton's father, Ernest, a great man with a dog and the Duke of Rutland's head shepherd, who threw out a challenge to the shepherds and gamekeepers of the estate to a trial, offering a fat wether sheep as the prize. Only two dogs competed in March 1894 and Sam White's steadier Gyp beat Ernest's somewhat erratic Tinker – though all enjoyed the prize – served up at a supper held the following night! The Duke of Rutland gave a gold cup to start Longshaw properly.

Ernest Priestley, who lived in the remote farmstead of Overstones, a former coaching hostelry at the head of the desolate Cupola Valley on the 2,000 ft high borderland where Derbyshire and Yorkshire meet, won the English National three times, in 1922 and 1923 with the rough-coated, black and white Moss, and in 1930 with Hemp, the grandson of Moss who went back in blood to Dickson's Hemp.

Moss had a great reputation in the Peak where it was said that he would turn a lion, such was his power, but one of Ernest's best dogs was Jet, a daughter of the champion. She was a rough-coated, black and white bitch and home bred out of a daughter of the 1924 International Shepherds' champion, Hunter's Sweep. Wise herself, she became the mother of champions – two dogs, Hemp and Lad, and a bitch, Wylie, born on 1 March 1926 – from her mating with Dickson's Hemp. Hemp won the 1930 National at Welbeck for Ernest Priestley, and Lad and Wylie, in Ashton's hands, won the International Brace title the same year, and in singles competition they shared over 20 first prizes in succession. They won the Longshaw Brace championship three times in succession.

Ashton also handled Lad and Hemp to victory in the 1933 English Brace contest and, after his father's tragic death, he handled Hemp to the old dog's final trials victory at Cawthorne in 1937. 'I was so overjoyed at the old dog's success I hugged him to me at the end of that run,' he told me. Hemp was then 11½ years old and it was a sentimental finale to his career. Ernest Priestley was killed in a motor-cycle accident in 1936 while travelling to a trial.

Ashton actually started working collie dogs when he was only eight years old and, blessed with the inherent skill of his family tradition, it was not surprising that at 17 years of age he became the youngest handler ever to represent England in an International contest.

On the International scene his Pat won the International Farmers' and reserve Supreme championships in 1950 and the 1951 English Driving title in addition to the 1951 Supreme. His Jim in 1955 and Sweep in 1960, both smooth-coated dogs with very similar bloodlines to John Jones's Midge, the daughter of Jim Wilson's Scottish International Moss, won the English National championship. Ashton gave me some idea of the improvement in collie efficiency in the 30 years between his father's Moss and his own Pat when he said: 'Pat was streets in front of Moss in ability and intelligence.'

Ten dogs were included in the work force of the International Sheep Dog Society's former Chairman, Ray Ollerenshaw, in the management of around 5,000 sheep over the high ground above the Derwent Valley, cradle of the Ladybower reservoir where the Dambusters trained for the famous raid during the war. The dogs were essential to obtain the fullest and most efficient farming use of over 10,000 acres which climb in energy-sapping slopes to 2,000 ft of picturesque yet demanding countryside in the High Peak.

They were handled by Ray, who was Chairman of the International Sheep Dog Society for 12 years, his brother Stuart, and three farm workers in a unit which went into action like a well-oiled machine and enabled 5,000 sheep to be gathered from around 20 square miles of moor and put through the dipping bath in just over three days. Such efficiency – which would frighten any work-study engineer to death – depended on men and dogs working slickly as a team, each dependent on the other for 100 per cent effort. It was not a job for the faint hearted.

Old House, Derwent, the homestead, was aptly named when Ray took the 35 acres which went with it in the early 1940s, but a most enterprising and successful hill farming programme of moor management which over the years reclaimed 100 acres of heather and bilberry into productive grassland supported probably the biggest self-contained flock of sheep in Derbyshire, together with a suckler herd of 40 Welsh Black cows. A wholly commercial flock, the main sheep breeds were Dalesbreds and Swaledales, which suited the land and climatic conditions, and these were mated to various types of rams including Derbyshire Gritstone, Woodland, Blue-faced Leicester and the German Oldenberg.

Efficient sheep farming – and Ray Ollerenshaw was awarded the OBE for his services to agriculture – and efficiency in handling collies are inseparable, so that Ray became a most respected competitor on the trials field with many International appearances.

In 1972 he was England's reserve National champion with the handsome black and white Ken, beaten only on his outfield work after finishing on the same score as the champion, Harry Huddleston's Udale Sim. Ken, a prick-eared son of Tim Longton's 1966 Supreme champion Ken, also won his 'cap' in 1971 and went on to the Supreme championship in which he finished seventh.

Ray won Longshaw open twice, in 1952 and in 1977. In 1977 it was the big long-legged Tweed, then with nine years' experience of sheep work, which gave Ray the coveted award. A good strong, black and white collie, Tweed, who ran for England in 1975, went to New Zealand in 1978 with Ray to compete in the Rotorua International championships and, though scarcely acclimatised and a stranger to the type of tests 'down under', finished a most creditable fifth in the finals. Of the line from Wilson's Cap and Kirk's Nell, Tweed, who stayed in New Zealand as a stud-dog, was bred on Salisbury Plain out of Coward's Bess and sired by Chris Winterton's international Spot.

Ray Ollerenshaw did much by example to improve hill farming in Britain and was one of the International Sheep Dog Society's most efficient administrators. For many years – up to her marriage in 1968 – Ray was assisted in his farming by his daughter Janet, the fourth of his five daughters, who worked her first collie when she was only three years old and won the novice classes at Longshaw and Hope when she was 11.

Janet had a way with dogs, and as the chief ingredient in the recipe for a successful partnership between handler and dog is the mutual respect of each for the other, perhaps female intuition scored, for the bond between Janet and her dogs was founded on affection. The proof was in their easy and confident work on the hill and in their successful trials performances.

In 1966 at Blackpool she came very close to becoming the first lady to win a place in England's International team – the honour which eventually went to Jean Hardisty in 1977.

Winter in the High Peak is hard and unrelenting. The peat hags drip silver icicles in the cold light, the wiry grasses lie flat under the screaming wind and the bareness is polished by its own exposure. And these conditions have taken their toll on men, dogs and sheep.

In March 1969 Ray Ollerenshaw's Sam went through the ice to his death when bringing sheep to safety off the frozen reservoir.

One of the most remarkable instances of collie fidelity was that of Tip, a 12-year-old bitch, who guarded her master's body for 15 weeks on high snowbound land. Joseph Tagg, an 86-year-old shepherd of Bamford, went missing during a visit to his sheep, and such is the vastness of the hills that in spite of repeated searches his body was not discovered for about four months. Tip stayed by his side all that time, living it was assumed on what she could catch in the way of rabbits and birds, though she was very weak when found. Ben Eyre, one of Joseph Tagg's oldest friends and one of the most experienced sheepdog men in England, called Tip's loyalty to her dead master 'the most amazing story I have heard about sheepdogs'.

Remembering the brains of the Derbyshire dogs, the old smooth-coated cur dogs which lingered in the Edale area, Ben Eyre told me his father had one which could be trusted to take a flock of sheep along the dales roads entirely on its own. Further, when a horse and trap approached, the dog would herd the sheep to the roadside to let the vehicle pass by.

At Old House, Derwent before Ray Ollerenshaw, John Thorpe trained collies which won many prizes at Longshaw; indeed, he was so successful that the officials handicapped him in 1932 with an extra hurdle to negotiate. He was a very quiet handler and the only other Derbyshire handler to Ashton Priestley to win the International Supreme. This was in 1931 with Jess, a daughter of Mark Hayton's 1926 Supreme champion Glen. The tricolour-marked Jess also took part in the winning of one International Farmers', one International Brace and two National Brace championships.

A near neighbour of Ray Ollerenshaw was Eric Elliott, who has won three International and four English Driving championships, two English Brace titles, and in 1973 the English National with his Scottish-bred Bill. Eric had many good collies at Crookhill Farm, Ashopton, none better than Coon who had a cheerful disposition to any amount of work and won his International 'cap' on each of the four successive years he entered the English National.

In Nottinghamshire by Sherwood Forest Willie Bagshaw was the

Chairman of the International Sheep Dog Society for six years until February 1968. He won well at Longshaw and at the other big Derbyshire trials in Dovedale which are equally long standing, and he won three English Nationals. His Jess, who was one of England's best ever with eight International appearances and the daughter of the 1924 Supreme champion Roberts's Jaff, won in 1928 and 1932, and the rough-coated Mac, of Mark Hayton's breeding, won in 1946. But best known of Willie Bagshaw's dog was Glyn, the canine star of the sheepdog film of Alfred Ollivant's book *Owd Bob*. Glyn was bought for under £4 at ten months old and was insured for £200 when the film was made.

I am more familiar with the black and white faced Gritstones or the horned Lonks foraging quietly like grey ghosts in the mirk across the high lands of the Lancashire Pennines than with the heavier ewes whose lambs fatten readily on the downs, wolds, heaths and commons or in the folds of the arable lands of the southlands and Midlands. Once the farms of Britain were set out to suit the sheep, the four-footed muckspreaders which fertilised the land for the crops. This has changed with advancing agricultural technology and sheep are diminishing in numbers on the lowland farms in the face of mechanised cultivations.

But among the downland and longwoolled sheep are breeds which have made Britain famous throughout the world, quality meat producers like the blackfaced Suffolk, the Southdown, Hampshire, Dorset, Oxford and Ryeland, and the longwools of the West Country, the Devon and the Dartmoor, and from what is probably the largest area of lowland grass in England, the famous sheep of Romney Marsh which have pioneered many lands to create their breed society's slogan of 'the sun never sets on Romney sheep'. These sheep are herded by sheepdogs whose lives are generally not quite so arduous as those of the high country, though they have matched hill dogs in competition and, commonly not as good, have yet been found capable.

Bosworth Coon proved the best collie in Britain in 1968 by winning the Supreme championship for Llyr Evans, the cheery Welshman who left Wales in 1938 to farm beef and sheep in Leicestershire, and who produced grey-faced lambs and fed bullocks at Lordsfields Farm, Whittlebury, near Silverstone motor-racing track in Northamptonshire. Llyr never represented Wales in International competition though, under the now somewhat outdated rule of the International Sheep Dog Society which compelled him to represent the country in which he lived, he was in England's team 12 times.

Of fairy-tale romance was his return to his birthplace at Towyn in 1968, for over the flat land between the mountains, where he shepherded as a boy, and Cardigan Bay he handled Coon, four years old and handsomely black and white and home bred, to his greatest-ever sheepdog honour, the Supreme.

And Llyr won many honours. The year after his Supreme, Coon was reserve Supreme and won the International Farmers' title at Chester, and he earned the best-ever trials record of any English collie from the Midland counties, winning at all their leading trials and making his presence felt on his visits to North Country events.

Coon won 50 open championships in seven years, represented England four times and won the National and Farmers' titles on stubborn Halfbred sheep over the downlands of Berkshire in 1969; he was third in the Dovedale National in 1967, and was used extensively as a stud-dog to leave his mark in collie improvement. Born in April 1964 out of his master's Fly, he was sired by his master's Bosworth Scot, the winner of the 1962 International Driving championship, and he was of breeding to Scotland's Whitehope Nap, England's Mindrum Nickey and Welsh champion Hughes's Jaff.

His son Chip ran an impressive trial on Mule ewes over the Chatsworth parkland in 1976 to win England's National and Farmers' championships, and another son, Lad, with timberman John Russell from Seaford in Sussex, surprised everyone with his skill in mastering rather fast and flighty grey-faced Halfbreds for the Farmers' honour at the York International in 1975. In 1974 another son of Bosworth Coon, George Reed's 4½-year-old Patch from Boring House Farm, Vines Cross, Sussex, won the English Driving title.

Llyr Evans and Bosworth Coon, 1968 Supreme Champions from Whittlebury in Northamptonshire.

It is interesting that of the relatively few National and International titles that have gone south, most have been for driving successes. Perhaps it is because the southern collies are used to pushing around the heavier breeds of sheep.

Graham Parsons's six-year-old Frank from the Wiltshire Downs, and Edwin Powles's black and white Sweep from the Forest of Dean won the English Driving championships in 1963 and 1966, and Sweep went on to win the International championship at Chester. They were the son and grandson of John Evans's 1953 Supreme champion Roy. In 1955 at the International at Edinburgh, Scotland swept the board in all but one section, the driving contest, and it was Norman Seamark's smooth-coated tricolour Kep from Warwickshire which salvaged English prestige on that occasion. Kep, a five-year-old descendant of Wilson's famous one-eyed Roy, won the English Driving title at Darlington for Norman who now farms at Wilstead in Bedfordshire, and who is the Chairman of the International Sheep Dog Society.

One of the best-known dogs in Britain was Brocken Robbie with Mrs Barbara Carpenter at Pastors Hill House at Bream in the Forest of Dean. A quiet, almost gentle dog, but with power to move the most obstinate of sheep, Robbie became famous as a sire of champions rather than for his own trials successes. Well bred by Worthington's Hemp, the son of the 1953 Supreme champion Roy, and from Hughes's Jaff,

The North Berkshire trials committee: Betty Corley, Ron Webb, Jimmy Ogston, Bill de-Grey, Bill Smith (chairman), Barbara Houseman (secretary) and Alan Walters (Oxford **Mail** *Times).*

Robbie added to their qualities in his breeding and such renowned workers as McKnight's Jaff, Ollerenshaw's Taffy and Watkins's Robbie were his sons. Mated to John James's Fly, he sired Dick Nicholl's Moss and Gordon Lewis's Jim, Welsh National and Farmers' champions.

Famous for his sheepdog demonstrations at the big agricultural shows, John Evans was one of the most successful of International competitors, winning honours for both Wales and England, depending on which side of the Border, he was farming at the time. Learning his craft in the valleys of his native Monmouthshire, John won the Supreme championship for Wales with Roy, his favourite of many good dogs and a grandson of Hughes's Jaff, and after moving some 12 miles into Gloucestershire to farm 200 acres at Tidenham, he won the 1958 Supreme with Tweed, the tricolour son of Wilson's Moss, for England. He won both the Welsh and English National titles and six International, four Welsh and seven English titles.

Originally designed to cut down travelling distances in attending National trials, it is surely time to scrap the International Sheep Dog Society ruling that a man shall represent the country in which he farms rather than the country of his nationality. Can you imagine all the Scottish stars in the English football leagues being told they had to play for the English International team!

A great showman and a very clever dog trainer, John Evans showed me, while waiting to compete at the English National at Windermere in 1961, how Ben could walk the top of a five-barred gate, turn round on command, and even straddle it and balance with all four paws close together.

John Evans with Roy, Tweed and Moss (Mrs W. J. Evans).

Collie dogs are adaptable to changing situations and have blended into even the most modern attempts at improving sheep farming techniques. Where it is possible for their masters to use motor-cycles to speed their flock inspections on the less rough ground, some dogs have learned to ride pillion or across the petrol tank, and in north Devon Charles Trace's Mac joined his master in the passenger seat of a light aeroplane when Charles made an aerial survey of his 400 scattered acres at Sheepwash. But always in the final job of herding the sheep the dog is indispensable.

The West Country with its wild tracts of Exmoor and Dartmoor, Bodmin Moor, and the Quantock and Blackdown Hills, is sheep country and there is a calendar of some 50 sheepdog trials in Cornwall, Devon and Somerset.

It is recorded that the first sheep which came to Exmoor were Scottish Blackface ewes brought down from the Highlands by kilted shepherds and their dogs as part of the Knight family's efforts to put the land to good use. Many of the descendants of those Scottish shepherds are still on the moor. No doubt the blood of their dogs is still in the make-up of the present generation of collies which now have a wider variety of sheep to deal with, the descendants of those original Blackfaces together with imported Cheviots and Swaledales and the heavier native breeds and resultant Halfbreds.

Competent in their daily work, West Country collies have had sparse success in the National and International competitive sphere though Harry Thomas, one of the best-known competitors in the area, won the English National, Farmers' and Driving titles in 1982 with his immaculate Bess; and an Exmoor shepherd, Fred Land, won the 1958 English Shepherds' championships with his black and white Fleece.

Gwyn Jones's white-headed Shep, winner of the 1976 Supreme championship, was bred in Cornwall by Harry Thomas at Penpell Farm, by St Austell Bay; but the bells of Staindrop church rang the omen of Harry's greatest success when he handled his clever and precise Bess to the English championship at Raby Castle in County Durham in August 1982. As the chimes pealed over the rich farmlands of lower Teesdale, Harry, who rings the bells at his local church at Par, took Bess in a commanding partnership to 204 of 220 aggregate points – the only collie of 133 to top the 200 points mark – to win the most coveted of English trophies. A match-ploughman and a stick-dresser of repute, Harry bred Bess from Cap and Gael with bloodlines to Supreme champions Bosworth Coon and Wiston Cap. Cornwall county champion, the 'Champion of Champions' of the Devon, Cornwall and Exmoor societies, and the 1981 South of England champion, the 4½-year-old Bess had quite a reputation in the West Country.

Harry Thomas of Par in Cornwall with Penpell Bess, the 1982 English National Winners (C.H. Barrett).

Harry Thomas's next success in International competition came in 1995 when he handled his home-bred Penpell Lucky, daughter of his Tweed and Bess, to fourteenth placing in the English team.

Careful but dominant mastery of five heavy Suffolk Halfbred ewes, which were somewhat lethargic in the extreme heat over an extensive undulating course by Rockingham Forest in Northamptonshire, won the National and Farmers' championships for Dick Roper and his six-year-old Cap from Eastington in Gloucestershire at the 1995 English National. Dick, who is farm manager to more than 2,000 sheep at Lower End Farm over 2,000 acres of the Cotswolds, also had the black and white Cap, a strong, jaunty-looking collie with left ear pricked and right ear flopped, in the 1992 and 1993 English teams. Cap is a paternal grandson of John Thomas's Don, the 1984 English Shepherds' champion whose father was John Thomas's Craig, the 1977 Supreme champion.

Similarly bred, Sweep, who loved to play with children but was wary of grown-up strangers, ran third in the 1988 English National at West Heslerton and won through to the Supreme contest at the International; and Sweep's son, Dick, a medium-coated upstanding collie, was sixth for Dick Roper in the 1992 English National in Cumbria.

In 1983 the English National title was won in the cool of the second morning by Derek Lloyd's six-year-old Jim from the Welsh Borders before a relentless sun made life hard for both dogs and Halfbred sheep over the rich Gloucestershire farmlands by the village of Eastington. A practical, all-round farm dog, as happy behind his master's suckler cows as with the flock of 250 crossbred ewes at Menalls Farm, Kimbolton, near Leominster in Herefordshire, Jim was a handsome tricolour Welsh-bred grandson of Wiston Cap.

Sheepdog trials have become very popular in the Sussex area in spite of the fact that, with changing farm patterns on the Downs, much of the shepherding is now so-called mechanised with farmers on motor-bikes or in four-wheel drive vehicles, although they still call upon a collie dog for the final gather. Shepherding by vehicle cannot be done as well or as thoroughly as it was when flocks were walked round by a shepherd and dog, and flocks have suffered. But there are still some farmers who believe that the old ways were best.

One of these is Ray Edwards, a natural dog handler, who farms with his wife Ros at Partridge Green north of Brighton in the Vale of Sussex. He looks for power in his dogs to move big lowland sheep, but this trait has to be coupled with natural ability and calmness. The dog has to be used to this type of work, for it is no good if it loses its patience and temper when things go too slowly for its liking.

As we've seen, on the various breeds of sheep in various conditions, a collie dog has to be wise to use its inbred intelligence to the best advantage on whatever it is faced with.

Ray likes to breed his own dogs. They have never let him down in his daily work, and they have brought him success, not only locally, but at International level on the trials fields. Although a relative newcomer to the International scene, he has represented England eight times since 1985.

His first success at international level was to earn a place in the English team with Spick, a Scottish-bred collie, in 1985 at the Peterborough National, although he perhaps has a particular regard for a Welsh-bred bitch called Bet. Although she didn't win much on the trials field she was a good breeder, the mother of the tricolour Glen which won the English Shepherds' championship in 1990 when Ray was at West Grinstead, and also the mother of Taff whom Ray got into the 1986 team.

Ray was in the English International team for five years from 1985 to 1990 when his rough-coated Rob, a home-bred son of Spick, won the English Driving championship at Dorking. Spick was again in the English team in 1987, the rough-coated Glen in 1989, and Bracken, a tricolour daughter of Taff, in 1994 and 1995.

Ray's wife Ros, who assists him in the farm duties, has also been successful in handling collie dogs. She was fourth with the 9½-year-old Don in the English National at Moorsholm in 1993, and has featured in 'One Man and His Dog' trials.

CHAPTER SEVENTEEN

Sheepdogs in Harmony

*I discuss the sheep and dogs of Brecknock, investigate the claims
of the Welsh collie, applaud the staging of the first sheepdog
trials in Britain, and pay tribute to some of the finest working
dogs in the world.*

It was lambing time on the hills of the Eppynt in Brecknock and the
bright sunlit fields were busy with the happy frolics of well-grown
handsome lambs whose faces were speckled with black and white
markings. The weather was mild, it was mid-April and for once running
to the calendar with the still air vibrant to the joyful bleating of lively
lambs. A cuckoo called from a distant patch of trees and a dunnock sang
cheerful notes from the hedgerow.

I watched the sheep with interest, leaning on the field-gate that
closed the only gap in the neatly laid and impenetrable hedges bounding the field which are such a feature to the district. My host, Thomas,
a little weather-tanned Welsh farmer whose wrinkled face showed
obvious pleasure at my interest, stood at my side.

The Beulah Speckled-face breed of sheep is not unlike the Derbyshire Gritstone which I knew so well and it was because of their similar
characteristics, size, colour conformation and wool, and also the fact
that the Beulah is a hornless breed of hill sheep, that I was interested.
The rams from both Beulah and Gritstone have been used on the Welsh
Mountain breed to improve progeny size and wool quality, and it was
in Wales that the Derbyshire Gritstone first showed its potential as an
improver.

So my Welsh friend and I argued the merits of our breeds. His were
the best lamb producers and easier managed; mine had better jackets
and a hardier constitution. And of course we agreed to differ – and
switched our discussion to his dogs.

They were a real motley crowd. There were two smallish black and white collies of the old Welsh type, a big wall-eyed dog with a smooth coat and roguish grin, a red and white, rough-coated bitch who flagged her tail whenever she was spoken to, and a long-muzzled dog with a hint of blue in his coat and sharply pointed ears. Thomas had lambed 500 ewes with this bunch, and the roguish dog which looked as though it would enjoy lamb for supper any day of the week had the year previously hung on to the nose of a stampeding bull to save Thomas from almost certain death.

But I shuddered at the amount of stress put on the ewes and lambs when he put two of the dogs, the red bitch and the long-snouted dog, round the flock. They sped to their job in double-quick time, but then dashed hither and thither with no pattern, they snapped at ewes and bowled lambs over, and as we say in the North Country, 'sammied them up' with no messing. The sheep arrived at our feet with flanks heaving, mouths gaping, amid a torrent of bleats and in a cloud of steam.

After seeing the quality of his sheep and his obvious pride in them I was somewhat flabbergasted by the dogs. Thomas must have read my thoughts. 'None of your fancy trials dogs here,' he said. I groaned inwardly, 'Here we go again.' But I bit my tongue.

Thomas had been the perfect host and so it was with a deal of patience that I thumped the tub of pedigree. 'You have just been arguing how important it is to keep your sheep pure for performance, does not the same apply to your dogs?' I concluded. I do believe I convinced him for, as his dogs have died, they have been replaced by more recognisable collies of the modern type.

But the Welsh are proud and if some of the letters Phil and I received while doing the commentaries on 'One Man and His Dog' are to be believed, the only working dog of any moment is the Welsh Collie and not the Border Collie. It's a pity some of the more scathing letters with reference to our ignorance were unsigned.

Wales did indeed have its own sheepdog and a very ancient breed it was, referred to by Hywell Dda in the Ancient Welsh Laws of the tenth century, about AD 920, as the herdsman's dog and classed as indispensable to the 'summer resident' with a value equal to that of an ox. Down the years pastoral history in Wales leads one to consider the herdsman's dog to have been not unlike the corgi cattle dog, and refers to the Gellgi, a hound, as the ancestor of the Black and Tan Sheepdog and of the Hillman Sheepdog, a handsome golden-coloured dog. The third stock dog to be found in Wales was the Old Welsh Grey, a smaller dog than the other two and, being taken by immigrant Welsh farmers to the Argentine, became the ancestor of the Barbucho or Patagonian Sheepdog.

It is said that the first Border Collie to go into Wales was a mistake, a white bitch leaping from a train while travelling from Scotland in the 1820s and finding a home with a farmer named Lewis in Rhayader in mid-Wales. Today, in spite of the sentimentalists who would have us think differently, there is no doubt that the Border Collie is dominant in Wales and is confidently meeting the demands for increased efficiency to counteract the declining numbers of shepherds on the country's vast acres of sheep grazings which stretch the whole length of the Cambrian Mountains from Snowdonia in the north to the hills of the Rhondda in the south. And it has proudly taken Wales to the very top in International competition.

Of the sheep the tough little active Welsh Mountain sheep is easily the most popular, with a breed society membership of around 700, because of its hardy ability to thrive on the poorest land. I have heard trials competitors speak of these ewes as 'Welsh bolters that go like express trains', but much depends on the sheep lore of the handler and the intelligence of the dog.

Other sheep breeds to be found in Wales are the Beulah Speckled-face in the midland, with the spritely tan-faced Radnor and the docile broad-backed Ryeland of great productivity, and the soft-woolled Llan-wenog to be seen grazing between the Teifi Valley and Banc Sion Cwilt around Llanybyther. The smart-looking black-nosed Kerry Hill is the grassland sheep of the Montgomeryshire–Shropshire border, together with the full-bodied Clun Forest of the region by Offa's Dyke in the more hilly areas of Shropshire, Montgomeryshire and Radnorshire.

And so with countless sheep to be harvested from bleak lands, Welsh collies have to be good and have built a reputation second to none. On the competition fields they won six successive Supreme championships in the 1960s, nine since the Bala centenary trials in 1973, and in 62 Internationals have won the team shield 24 times – more than any other country.

If England and Scotland can claim to have evolved the modern type of shepherding dog, Wales can certainly claim to have staged the first sheepdog trials. In September 1973 the International Sheep Dog Society held its International trials at Bala to mark the 100th anniversary of the first sheepdog trials ever held. The International trials were held on a course by the River Dee, very near to the original rock and bracken-strewn field of Garth Coch where the trials were held in October 1873. Mr R. J. Lloyd Price of Rhiwlas, Bala, organised the first trials in conjunction with the Rhiwlas Field Trial Committee, and he declared it 'open to the world'.

It is interesting to note that the editor of *The Field* commented before the event: 'We fear that there are few dogs in the south which would properly bring a flock of sheep off a Welsh mountain.' This does not speak highly of the dogs he expected to take part, but it is more than likely that the worthy editor was getting his dogs mixed up for it was about that time that show collies were coming into being and the working collie was virtually unknown outside the farming community.

For historical interest the first competitor at the trials, and thus the first handler ever to run in a trial, was a 16-year-old boy called Roberts from Panteronym with his dog, Boy. The first sheep used in trials were Welsh Mountain ewes, and the winner of that first trial was a Scotsman, Jamie Thomson, with a Highland-bred dog, the small black and tan Tweed. Fittingly, to honour the Welsh pioneers, the Bala centenary in 1973 was won by Glyn Jones and his clever Gel from Bodfari in North Wales.

Following the editor of *The Field*'s somewhat adverse comment on the quality of dogs at the time of the first Bala trial, it is equally interesting to note, when considering the growth in proficiency of Welsh handlers and dogs, that even in 1930 they were still not considered very efficient by some.

'As a handler the Welshman is apt to be a little tempestuous and his dog is inclined to be a little reckless' wrote W. T. Palmer in *Things Seen in North Wales*. But the criticism seems harsh for in 1930 Wales had been competing against England and Scotland in the International trials since 1922 and had won one Supreme championship: Thomas Roberts, who farmed at Ty Cerris, Brynyreglwys, Corwen in North Wales, took the 1924 honour at Ayr with his little Scottish-bred Jaff. The Welsh have since done more than hold their own and for a period of six years from 1959 to 1964 – the longest successive dominance of any country – were unbeatable.

Quality has indeed risen since 1930. Take a Welsh sheepman nowadays and give him a sound dog and he will give you a contest. Take Wyn Edwards and Bill from their mixed farm herding, Gwyn Jones with either Bill, Shep or Queen from their Welsh ewes, or Glyn Jones and Gel from the mountainside above the Vale of Clwyd, and they would have given you the Supreme championship! And they would have done it with a fervour and national pride that shames we more conservative English, Scottish and Irish. The spontaneity of song that greets a Welsh victory at the International is truly moving – 'Land of My Fathers', 'Cwm Rhondda', sung with all the emotion of a victorious Welsh contingent.

They can be a bit odd in Wales, of course – and that's my passport confiscated! But I cannot quite understand a national fervour that can on occasion get near to bitterness between north and south. They even have their own method of trials in the south – a test known as the

'South Wales style' which incorporates a different hurdle layout and a maltese-cross, a narrow fenced passage through which the sheep have to be driven.

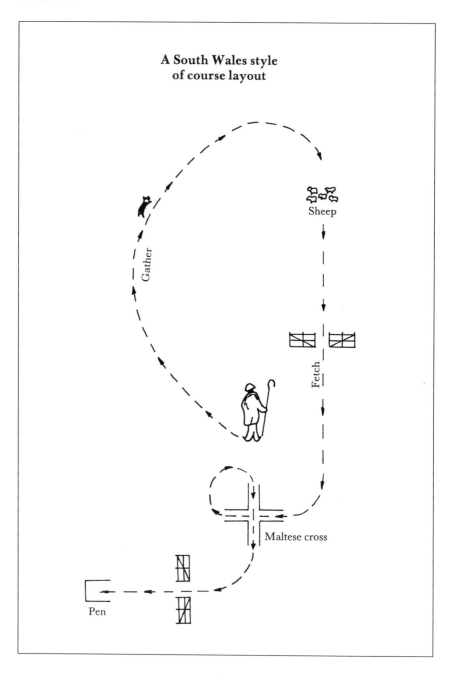

A South Wales style of course layout

Mervyn Williams, from Speckled-face country at Gladestry, but 1½ miles from the English Border, has been a regular Welsh team member, three times with two dogs in the team, has represented Wales in the 'One Man and His Dog' series and has judged the International – and he thinks that the South Wales style is a stiffer test of a collie's ability. He has thrived on the style ever since he started running at trials in 1947 at Rhos Goch when he was 15 years old and his dogs have proved their basic training by honouring him and Wales in the top flight of competition. His smooth blue-touched Dan at four years old set the remarkable record of seven first prizes – one each day – in a week of trials in 1966. His medium-coated Nell, which ran for Wales in 1987, 1989 and 1990, was a great-grandson of Craig which won the Supreme championship in 1977 for John Thomas.

Mervyn's Dan was the grandson of Allan, the good-looking and successful trials worker who won the 1958 International Farmers' championship and 21 first prizes in one season for David William Daniel. David William and his son, Eurwyn, worked and bred the most famous family of collies in South Wales at Henglyn Farm, Ystradgynlais in the country of the Black Mountains.

Never do I expect to see a better example of shedding 15 unwanted sheep from the bunch of 20 to leave the five marked sheep at the

David Daniel's Chip, winner of the 1949 and 1952 Supreme Championships.

International than that by Eurwyn Daniel and his clever tricolour Chip in the 1968 International at Towyn. So good was their work that the packed grandstand broke into spontaneous acclaim – breaking the unwritten law of no applause until the end of the trial. The first cut of sheep Eurwyn and Chip made was five and, to be used as 'bait' to draw off others, they were driven no further away than 25 yards, kept from rejoining the larger flock by the power of Chip's eye. Then we saw shedding to perfection. Facing each other across the gap between the two packets of sheep, Eurwyn and Chip persuaded, guided or allowed unmarked sheep to drift across to the unwanted flock. When a marked sheep tried to cross the forbidden boundary line Chip immediately answered Eurwyn's command to turn it back, until the job had been completed for maximum points in probably the most practical manner ever seen at an International. Chip won the reserve Supreme championship, having dropped points on his fetching which finally put him behind Llyr Evan's Bosworth Coon, and lost him the chance to emulate the success of his sire Ken eight years previously.

Chip, reserve Supreme champion of 1968, was the son of Ken, 1960 Supreme champion, who was the son of the black and white Chip,

Eurwyn Daniels of Ystradgynlais who won the Supreme Championship of 1960 with Ken, the 1992 Welsh National title and the Welsh Farmers' Championship of 1994 with Fly (pictured)
(Austin Bennet).

1949 and 1952 Supreme champion. Such was the bloodline of the Daniel dogs.

The older Chip was the best dog that David William Daniel ever worked during his trials career of 63 years from 1910. He was medium sized, had a good head with plenty of brain space and a warm eye, and he was the dog for the big occasion, strong and powerful yet very cool. His first victory at Ayr was almost classic after a hesitant first gather.

Chip's son, Ken, handled by Eurwyn Daniel to the 1960 Supreme title at muddy Blackpool, was home bred, mothered by Floss, a fast agile bitch with the ability and stamina to run all day and descended from Jim Wilson's famous one-eyed Roy. As he showed in his championship run, Ken was a collie whose enjoyment in his work was obvious. He was intelligent and always willing – a big factor in his success – and his skills were quietly reliable. A strong, good-looking black, white and tan dog, he was always happy at work either on the hill or the trials field, and he was four years old when he won his Supreme – two months after his father had died. He was one of the many good dogs sired by Chip whose progeny made quite an improvement in the quality of stock handling in South Wales.

Eurwyn's collies learn their trade on the hillsides of the Black Mountains above the town of Ystradgynlais where, at Henglyn Farm, they assist him with the management of Welsh Mountain ewes and beef cows. Eurwyn now farms with his son David, who is also an accomplished handler in trials and has represented Wales in International competition and been on 'One Man and His Dog'. It is on the mountain slopes that Eurwyn says the dogs get their experience of the ways of sheep, for he believes that 'the dog that grows up with you is the best' and he buys few, and then when they are only just showing ability, for he prefers his own breeding whenever possible.

He has a particular regard for the smooth-coated Fly, the daughter of Scottish champion Bobby Dalziel's Dryden Joe, with which Eurwyn won the 1992 Welsh National and Farmers' championships, the Welsh Farmers' championship in 1994, and which has been 'capped' for Wales six times in seven years. She is one of the collies he has bought, liking her when she was one of a litter of seven bred by Dai Jones at Llanilar near Aberystwyth. Just how highly Eurwyn rates Fly is reflected in his lilting South Wales brogue when he says, 'She'd drop before she gave in. She'd die for me; no two ways about that. If the going gets tough she's with you all the way. I look for stamina and a will to work in a dog.'

Fly, a black and white bitch born in April 1986, is well bred. She has Fortune's Glen, Gilchrist's Spot, McKnight's Gael and Wilson's Moss in her paternal pedigree, and Davie McTeir's Garry, Scotland's Driving

Eurwyn Daniels' Fly which won the Welsh National Championship in 1992, the Welsh Farmer's title in 1994, and in seven years earned six representative honours. (Austin Bennett) .

champion in 1980, on her maternal side.

Eurwyn enjoys going to trials and he's not right bothered about winning them. 'I go for the love of it. I enjoy meeting people which I probably enjoy more than winning.' As is obvious, and like most farmers who depend on them in their daily work, Eurwyn has a great respect for his collies. 'They are wholly faithful, they never let you down, and they never leave your side.'

This faithfulness has been the theme at every successful herding on our journey through the collie country of Britain.

They still yarn in Wales of the little dog who, having spent most of his days on the hill with his master, laid by his master's bedside during his last illness, laid by his coffin until burial and then refused to leave his graveside. The little dog would not be comforted at the loss of his beloved master and was in danger of dying himself – until after a week some sheep strayed into the graveyard. Suddenly the herding instinct was roused in the dog and, almost as if bidden, he left the grave and gathered the sheep, faithful not only to his master but to the craft his master had taught.

They also talk in South Wales of little Nell, whom the rest of the world forgets, though she came within a whisker of winning the 1965 Supreme championship – and then Wiston Cap might never have been heard of! The whole story of sheepdog competition, indeed of any competitive sport, is filled with 'ifs' – but we too easily forget that had

Nell, handled by Gwilym Rhys Jones of Brechfa, completed her final penning on that last day at Pontcanna in Cardiff she would have taken the Supreme title – and she was in her eleventh year.

To the pen she was nine points better than Wiston Cap and we tend to forget in that gasp of wonder at Wiston Cap's second outrun that Nell's overall outrunning and gathering had been 4½ points better. But Nell had taken too long in the shedding ring and had only one minute of time left to pen. She failed – and the Wiston Cap legend was launched. But Nell, with Speckled face ewes in Carmarthenshire, and the granddaughter of Whitehope Nap, shepherded so well that in spite of losing 30 points at the pen she still finished fourth, adding to the Farmers' championship, and the Brace title, taken in partnership with her 2½-year-old son, Sweep, at that International gathering.

I wrote at the time of Nell that she was a bitch of immense wisdom, experience and initiative, gentle but firm in her work. She was bred by J. H. Davies over the hill at Llanfynydd of a litter of six and went to Brechfa to be trained from puppyhood by Gwilym – a handler who has been most successful in the Brace section of International competition, winning the title on five occasions.

From later work on the same farm where her master, Mel Page, was the shepherd, another bitch called Nell was one of my favourite collies. Often I saw her at work and on many different types of sheep, and I never failed to admire her. I saw her push strong wilful Lonk ewes to victory in my home county of Lancashire, skilfully persuade Swaledale ewes that the place for them was in the pen in the 'One Man and His Dog' Loweswater trials, and use her wise authority to master difficult mountain sheep to win the Welsh Shepherds' championship for the third time at Beaumaris in 1978.

Nell, who was the Welsh National champion in 1973, learned that controlled aggression was often the way to complete mastery of either sheep or cows. She was a good, strong, medium-sized bitch from the best of breeding with Supreme champion Wiston Cap as her paternal grandsire and Supreme champion Alan Jones's Roy her maternal grandsire. Bred by John James at Kingsland in Herefordshire out of his international Fly, Nell's father was Clarence Storey's Roy, a collie who quietly left his own legacy of quality on the breed.

Another bitch from South Wales which earned the respect of all who saw her win the 1963 Supreme championship over York racecourse was Herbert Worthington's black and tan Juno, for she was strong and masterful on Dalesbred ewes and worked with a method that was convincing and confident. From duties with Welsh ewes on the mountainsides around Mardy, Abergavenny, she was the first bitch for 25 years to win the Supreme title. Ever since 1938, when Willie

Wallace and his black and white Jed won the honour, dogs had been successful.

At York Juno was only young in years, at 3½, but wise in experience, and she set about toppling the male dominance in no uncertain manner. She finished her work well within the time limit and dropped only 17 of 225 aggregate points. It was a worthy victory for both Juno and her master, whose great satisfaction was that the young bitch was home bred and of a line of collies which he had bred down the years.

Juno's mother and father, Fly and Hemp, were half-brother and sister, both out of Floss. Together they won two International and one National Brace championship, and Fly won the 1959 International Shepherds' title, with Hemp winning the 1959 National Shepherds' award.

Fly's sire – Juno's grandsire – the smooth, black, white and tan Moss, had a great competitive career with a record of two International and four National Shepherds' championships in six years, and established his master as a handler of international repute.

Juno followed her Supreme victory with other top successes, the National and Farmers' championships in 1967 and the National Driving honours in 1964 and 1965. Herbert Worthington had six International and 16 National titles between 1946 and 1968 with bloodlines that stem from two great Welsh dogs, Dick Hughes's Jaff, of driving fame, and Tom Roberts's 1924 Supreme champion Jaff.

Both Jaff dogs were products of North Wales, though Roberts's black and white dog was bred in Scotland of Dickson's Hemp line.

Hughes's Jaff was a true Welshman and one to grace the annals of Welsh shepherding history. A big three-coloured dog, he was born at Tyddyn Isaf, Rhewl, near Ruthin in the Vale of Clwyd in July 1938, the son of T. O. Jones's Nell and Lord Mostyn's Coon, of Brown's Spot and Dickson's Hemp lines. He grew into a good-natured, broad-headed, clever collie but like many dogs that do not find their true human partner until after many 'divorces', Jaff took four years to find Dick Hughes who farmed sheep and milk cows in the centre of the Isle of Anglesey. Then he settled down to show the sheepdog world just what he was worth.

With Dick Hughes at the helm there blossomed a unique partnership and in 1946, when Jaff was eight years old, they won the National, Driving and – joined by Jaff's son Ben – the Brace championships at the Welsh trials at Llanfairfechan, and a month later, the International Driving championship at Edinburgh. In the next three years Jaff was to become one of the greatest driving dogs ever seen, the secret of his success being in his natural balance, his strong concentration and, of course, his power to move sheep as he desired.

At this shepherding task he was in a class of his own, able to put sheep together in a bunched flock and drive them without stress or upset to wherever his master commanded. He won three Welsh Driving and three International Driving championships as well as two Welsh National titles. More important, he was able to pass on his qualities to his sons and daughters, and fortunately that was recognised so that he was well used before he was gored to death by a cow. A sad end for a great collie but he died as he lived, simply carrying out his daily task of herding stock. The list of famous collies who owe some of their skills to his influence runs into three figures and includes many Supreme champions.

One of the best was Alan Jones's tricolour Roy. In 1961 Roy, then in his fifth year with Welsh ewes on the lowland pastures of Lleuar Bach Farm at Pontllyfni, created the record of winning the Supreme, the International Farmers', the National, the National Farmers' and the National Driving championships, and in partnership with his kennel-mate Spot, the National Brace championship − one year's record of trials successes running into the realms of fiction. I watched and judged Roy often and considered him one of the best ever, a dog with power and method, stamina and speed, and the intelligence to use his inbred qualities to the best advantage. He went about his work in a relaxed manner which gave confidence to his sheep, keeping them content to follow his lead. He won the Supreme on Ayr racecourse with solid practical work which only dropped below classic standard in the shedding ring, and he won the Farmers' championship the day before with a loss of only one point per judge.

Bred by John Evans out of his Jill, a daughter of Jim Wilson's Moss, he was sired by John Evans's Roy, the 1953 Supreme champion and the

One of the best-ever Welsh collies, Alan Jones' Roy from Pontlyfni, winner of the Supreme Championship and four Welsh National titles in 1961 (Daily Express).

Pedigree of JAFF (4313) 1946, 1947 and 1949 Welsh and International Driving Champion with Dick Hughes

The numbers in brackets are the Stud Book numbers of the International Sheep Dog Society
— Indicates that this dog is not known

grandson of Hughes's Jaff. He won the Welsh National championship for the first time in 1959 and, partnered by the Scottish-bred Glen, won the National and International Brace championships of 1964 and the National Brace title of 1962.

Roy was, of course, in the hands of a master at the art of collie handling, for Alan, tall and smart, quiet and confident, stills the crowds to rapt attention whenever he walks on to the trials field. He stole the show in the 1977 series of 'One Man and His Dog' with the easy blend of his own guiding personality with that of the two black and white collie dogs, Spot and Craig, which took them to victory in both the singles and brace competitions.

Pedigree of ROY (15393) 1961 Supreme Champion with Alan Jones

The numbers in brackets are the Stud Book numbers of the International Sheep Dog Society
— Indicates that this dog is not known

'Concentration is the thing that wins Supreme championships,' Alan told me when we were sitting under the grey stone wall at Austwick during the filming of that series. 'Your dog must be intelligent and have the right temperament and the fitness to get to the final test, but then in addition, he must have the stamina to concentrate in absolute harmony with you for half an hour without any lapse of thought.'

Farmer of 600 Welsh ewes and 200 Welsh Black cows producing lamb and beef on 300 lowland acres on the Lleyn Peninsula, across which blow the sea breezes from Caernarfon Bay, Alan has served the Welsh International sheepdog cause better than any man. Since his first trial in 1945, when he was 16 years old, Alan has won over 800 first prizes and 36 Welsh International 'caps'. He has nine International titles and 22 Welsh titles.

He has very definite likes and dislikes in his dogs. He prefers to work with young dogs, about two or three years old, and he does not like working bitches. Usually he buys his dogs rather than breeds and puts the 'polish' on them himself. Two of his most successful and certainly best-known dogs, because of their television successes, were Spot and Craig.

Craig was a striking prick-eared black and white collie who won the International Farmers' championship in 1977 and in 1979 and the Welsh National title at Talsarnau in 1976. He was a powerful dog who needed handling. 'He fights against you all the time and keeps you on your toes, but he's good,' Alan said of him. Remember Glyn Jones telling me almost the same thing about his champion Gel? It was Craig's controlled power that won three National and two International Driving championships in three successive years. And he was a great-great-grandson of old Roy.

The younger Spot – he was three years old, and 2½ years younger than Craig, when he won the television singles championship – took the rock-strewn hillside at Austwick in his stride for his moment of glory, and showed that it was no 'flash in the pan' by winning a Welsh International 'cap' the following year and going through to the Supreme where he finished third at his first attempt. Bred in Lanarkshire in June 1974 out of J. M. Orr's Fly, an unregistered bitch, Spot soon proved his worth in stock management and earned merit registration. In his first year of trials work with Alan he won eight open trials, but the television event was his first big test, and viewers had the privilege of seeing a champion in the making. Craig and Spot won the 1980 International Brace title. Alan's most recent success at National level have been two Driving championships in 1985 and 1986 with two home-bred collies which were half-brothers. His rough-coated Vic, the winner in 1985, and his smooth-coated Lad, the 1986 victor, were both out of Alan's Nell. The mottled Lad was the great-grandson of Alan's collie of the same name which won the 1971 Welsh National and the 1973 International Farmers' championships. Lad ran again for Wales in 1989.

In 1992 Alan was in the Welsh team with the tricolour Taff, a son of Bwlch Taff which won the Welsh Nationals of 1980 and 1981 for Glyn Jones. Alan Jones is known throughout the sheepdog world as a master handler, a reputation he has worked hard to earn. He is a modest and unassuming man who gives most of the credit for his success to the ability of his collies.

'Land of My Fathers' was never sung with more feeling than

on Ely racecourse on the outskirts of Cardiff at the close of the 1959 International, for, of the six championships, five were won by Welshmen, and Meirion Jones from Llandrillo and one of the youngest members of the team won the Supreme with his young Ben. Only Lancashire farmer Tot Longton with his clever black and white Nell, winners of the Driving championship, prevented a Welsh 'grand slam'. For three days, in perfect shepherding conditions, the Welshmen destroyed the English and Scottish challenge with the forthright and determined handling of their collies on well-behaved Garth mountain ewes. Herbert Worthington from Mardy and his Fly and Hemp placed first and second in the Shepherds' championship; Ivor Hadfield from Prestatyn, master of the skills of working two dogs, handled his home-bred Jean and the rough-coated Roy to the Brace honour; Meirion Jones also won the Farmers' championship with Ben; and together the Welshmen won the team shield.

A quiet, soft-spoken hill farmer who ran sheep and beef cows above the Vale of Clwyd in North Wales, Meirion Jones gave confidence to his dogs with his ease of manner, and his winning of the Supreme championship on that Cardiff weekend was a triumph for the cool, unflustered method of sheepdog handling. His coolness in the face of trouble in the shedding ring with so much at stake was to be admired. It

Meirion Jones and Ben, Supreme Champions at Cardiff in 1959 (Sport and General).

was his first International success and it gave particular satisfaction to his father, John Jones, who won the coveted award in 1935 with the smooth-coated Jaff, son of the 1923 winner Brown's Spot. Meirion's Ben, a rough-coated 3½-year-old dog, was a grandson of Hughs's Jaff, and among his later successes was the Longshaw championship.

Meirion started trialling his dogs when he was 12 years old in 1945 and from that time onwards was a regular member of the Welsh team. A good handler of the working collie, he gave demonstrations of the supreme intelligence of the Border Collie for working farm stock at the leading agricultural shows.

In 1988 he won his second Supreme championship, proof of his understanding of working dogs, with the clever, handsome Spot at Blair Atholl on a course below the Grampian Mountains in Scotland. This highest accolade in competitive shepherding was worthily won by a collie which showed both strength and restraint when needed on Blackface ewes, guided by a man whose knowledge of stock was profound and whose quiet, precise way of control earned the respect of the sheepdog world. And on that Tayside pasture, the temperamentally sound Spot also won the Farmers' championship. Registered on merit, Spot is a happy dog, bred at Bala and mainly of Welsh breeding though his paternal pedigree includes Fred Coward's Ken from Cumbria, and Allan Heaton's Stonewalls Ken from Yorkshire.

Meirion was good at working two dogs together in trials, and he won the International Brace championship with the black and white Bill, his 1984 International Farmers' champion, and the smooth-coated Cap in 1986 after they had won the Welsh Brace championship. He also won the Welsh Brace championship in 1995 with the merled Mac and the tricolour Glen.

Meirion's near neighbour Wyn Edwards farms in the Vale from Cefn Coch, south of Ruthin. Winner of 20 Welsh 'caps', eight Welsh titles and five International titles, Wyn has a distinction held by only three other men in the first 75 years of International history − that of having handled a collie to successive Supreme championships.

In 1981 his Bill, a strong and forceful dog from daily work with Welsh ewes and beef cows, herded Swaledales to victory over Armathwaite's fellside, and again in 1982, he ordered Blackface ewes to his bidding at Blair Atholl in Perthshire's Glen Garry. Bill's record then was that of being only the second collie in 60 years to have won the Supreme twice in successive years, and only the eighth in history to have won more than once.

Making history and enhancing his reputation as a handler of collie dogs, Gwyn Jones of Penmachno won his third Supreme championship in 1990 to earn his place in the annals of the International Sheep Dog

Three great handlers: Tom Bonella of Scotland, and Harry Greenslade and Ivor Jones of Wales.

Society. Apart from Scotsman Jim Wilson, who won the Supreme championship a record nine times, Gwyn, who farms Welsh ewes and milk cows at Cae Llwyd Farm at Penmachno, near Betws-y-Coed, is the only person to win the Supreme title more than twice. This he did in 1974 with the tall-standing Bill at Kilmartin, in 1976 with the white-headed Shep at Lockerbie, and in 1990 with the handsome black and white Queen at Alnwick.

The 1974 International over Kilmartin's course of waterlogged bog, dyke and trees truly tested the modern collie, assessing its standards of stamina, vigour and adaptability, and Gwyn Jones's Bill, cool and clever in every situation, was a great Supreme champion. A son of Wiston Cap, his mother's line went back to David Murray's International Vic, and he showed such heritage with controlled power and natural balance on strong Blackface ewes. At the same event he won the Driving championship, and his son, Johnny Wilson's prick-eared Scott from Ashkirk, won the Shepherds' championship for Scotland.

In 1976 Lockerbie was also a good test for the International and the big, white and black, rough-coated Shep, a grandson of Wiston Cap, won the blue riband of the sheepdog world with work that was solid, purposeful and well managed.

Working over Alnwick pastures in Northumberland, Gwyn and the 8½-year-old Queen showed a rapport and expertise in their craft that was almost perfect, to control Mule ewes to a 36-point victory.

Queen was bred by C. Lloyd at Caerws in South Wales, the daughter of J. M. Evans's Lad, and her bloodlines were from Alan Jones's Craig and Roy, Griffith's Craig and Dick Nichol's Moss which won the 1972 Welsh National championship and 50 open championships. Apart from winning the 1990 Supreme, Queen also won the International Farmers' championship and the Welsh Driving championship in 1990, the Welsh National and Farmers' championships of 1987, and television's 'One Man and His Dog' in 1988.

Gwyn, who was 29 years old when he won the Supreme in 1974, has very definite views on what he wants from a dog. Essentially it must be positive in its work for he says that a dog – or a man – who hesitates usually gets into trouble. 'I want a dog with plenty of power, a good pace, and able to balance sheep from any distance. Most dogs can balance sheep close at hand,' he says. 'I look for beauty also, for you don't see a good ugly dog.'

Thoroughly at home in front of the International crowds, Gwyn Jones has few peers on the big occasion. He enjoys showing the skill of his dogs just as much as he enjoys working with them on the mountain grazings in the Mignaint range of Snowdonia.

Welsh sheepmen have been particularly good at handling two dogs in unison in brace contests. At International level they have won 22 brace titles since the contests started in 1929. Ivor Hadfield of Prestatyn and G. R. Jones of Brechfa won the trophy five times each; Herbert Worthington of Mardy, Alan Jones of Pontllfni and Meirion Jones of Pwllglas won twice each; and in recent years John Griffith from the slate quarrying area of Snowdonia at Talysarn won the 1992 and 1993 International Brace titles, and the 'One Man and His Dog' event in 1993 at Buttermere in Cumbria. Wyn Edwards from Cefn Coch at Ruthin in the heart of the Vale of Clwyd has won the Welsh National Brace championship four times.

Colin Gordon from the Gower Peninsular, about ten miles from Swansea, who won television's 'One Man and His Dog' Brace trophy in 1986 in the Wye Valley with his brother and sister team, the smooth-coated Robbie and the prick-eared Nell, and who in 1990 at Bassenthwaite in Cumbria swept the board in the 'One Man and His Dog' trials, winning the Brace trophy with his home-bred Meg and smooth-coated Cap, a grandson of John Templeton's Roy, the Welsh National Brace winners in 1989, has won Wales's Brace championship twice. The tricolour Meg, a granddaughter of Gwyn Jones's Supreme champion Bill, won the 'One Man and His Dog' singles championship at Bassenthwaite.

Thinking of 'One Man and His Dog' and the dominant role of Welsh Brace handlers, Glyn Jones's clever pair Gel and Bracken from the mountainside at Bodfari above the Vale of Clwyd were unbeaten after five television trials. They were the 1974 Welsh Brace champions.

Glyn's younger pair, the tricolour Taff and the rough-coated Cap, won the television trials in the Peak District of Derbyshire by the Ladybower reservoir in 1989. Taff went back in bloodline to Alan Jones's Craig, the 1976 Welsh National champion. Cap was sired by Glyn's Bwlch Taff which won the Welsh National in 1980 at 16 months old, and the Welsh National again and reserve Supreme championship the following year. Taff and Cap also won the Welsh Brace championship at Llandinam in 1993.

One of the most successful of Welsh farmers has been Aled Owen from Penyfed, Ty Nant, whose stock of Welsh Mountain and Halfbred ewes and crossed Welsh Black cows run on the slopes of Foel Goch in North Wales. Aled had represented Wales 12 times in the last 16 years, and in competition has won the 1985 Welsh National and the Driving championships of 1987, 1992 and 1994, and his collies have been most successful in local trials.

Two young men who have done much for Welsh prestige in sheepdog circles are Meirion Owen from Rhos-yr-Hafod, Llanarthne, in Dyfed, and Hefin Jones from Dolgellau in Gwynedd.

Meirion is Welsh National Vice-president, a Council member of the International Sheep Dog Society, has been Chairman of the South Wales Sheepdog Trials Association twice and is on their executive committee, is Secretary of the Carmarthen Nursery Trials, and was the local secretary for the Welsh National at Landsawel, Llandeilo in 1981. In competition he won the 1989 Welsh National trials championship with the faithful old Rock, a grandson of Johnny Templeton's Roy and Bobby Dalziel's Dryden Joe.

Hefin, who farms Welsh Mountain sheep at Llwynsarn, Rhydymain, has shepherded for Gwilym Humphreys, secretary of Montgomeryshire FUW on Cader Idris and has sheared sheep in New Zealand.

I particularly admired his Meg who was one of the most intelligent, adaptable and good-tempered little dogs I have known. Fully trained when she was only eight months old, she efficiently tended both sheep and cows in her daily work, and went on to win in competition four 'caps' for Wales. In her four appearances in the Welsh team she was first twice, third and seventh, and reserve in 1991 – a remarkable performance.

She was most reliable. The first time that she entered the Welsh National at Talsarnau, in the heart of Welsh-speaking Wales in 1986, she ran seventh of 149 collies, only 7½ aggregate points from two judges behind the winner, Hugh Owen's Spotan from Anglesey. In the International at Beaumaris the next month she qualified for the Supreme contest and finished 11th. That proved to be good competitive experience for her in the top flight, and she went on to win the Welsh

Hefin Jones with Meg, one of the most intelligent and good-tempered of collies, from Rhydymain, near Dolgellau, the Welsh National Champion in 1988 and 1990.

National championships of 1988 and 1990, and the Welsh Farmers' championships in the same years. In 1988 in the International at Blair Atholl in Scotland, she worked Blackface ewes to third placing in the Supreme test, such was her cleverness.

Hefin put a lot of thought into mating her, and eventually chose Glyn Jones's Bwlch Taff which had won the Welsh championships of 1980 and 1981 as her partner. To say that she was a good mother makes her one in a million, but she was, and her daughter, also named Meg, won the Welsh National and the Welsh Driving championships in 1995.

We tend to think of the North Wales countryside as somewhat remote but during the Second World War Ivor Jones of Rhuallt, who was 21 times in the Welsh International team, had a champion bitch called Betsy who was so scared of the noise of the bombs falling on Liverpool that she had to be sent as a canine evacuee to Cecil Holmes in my part of the Lancashire–Yorkshire borderland.

CHAPTER EIGHTEEN

Ireland Comes of Age

◦⟫◦⟨◦◦⟫◦⟨◦◦⟫◦⟨◦

I acclaim the untiring efforts of Lionel Pennefather in his quest for International recognition for Ireland, meet Jim and Sweep who go to their shepherding by boat and their handler who has won top honours in both Ireland and Scotland, and reflect on the rising status of the best of Irish collies.

Irish farmers breed some top quality livestock in a country which is mainly agricultural, but had been content to order their animals with home-bred dogs which, while adequate, had not quite the polish of the collies on the mainland. It was not until 1961 that Irish farmers took part in the trials of the International Sheep Dog Society, and then it was mainly due to the efforts of one man, Lionel Pennefather, who was Chairman of the Northern Ireland Sheepdog Association, and who had led a delegation to put the Irish case to a Directors' meeting at Carlisle in 1950. In spite of being told quite often that he was wasting his time, because Ireland would never reach the required standard, he felt otherwise and persisted, and his dreams were eventually fulfilled.

Ireland was granted a full team of 15 singles, two brace and one driving entry in 1993 at the International trials held at Armathwaite in Cumbria, and in 1997 the International is to be held at Thurles racecourse in County Tipperary, some 65 miles south of Dublin.

More satisfying is the fact that the first team of three Irish dogs – then classed as Northern Ireland – in 1961 at Ayr, Lyn McKee's black and white Snip and his rough-coated Whitehope Corrie from County Down, and Jim Brady's tricolour Whin from County Antrim, were bred from collies imported from England and Scotland while the recent teams of Irish dogs have been bred in Ireland – which shows the strides that Irishmen have made to improve the standard of their working collies.

But the road has been bumpy, for the International Sheep Dog

Society – rightly so – intended to keep the International, which is regarded as the best trials test in the world, on top and not brought down in standard by inferior dogs taking part.

Ireland – still Northern Ireland – held their first National Trials in 1961 at Castle Demesne, Glenarm, in County Antrim. In 1965 Northern Ireland amalgamated with Eire to form what has since been known as the Irish team, but the International Sheep Dog Society only allowed them four singles and one brace entry. In 1966 the first Irish National was held in Eire at Glenealy in County Wicklow, and in 1969 Ireland had their first driving dog, Ronnie Kinrade's red-marked Hemp, a son of Alan Jones's Supreme champion Roy, competing in the International.

At the 1973 centenary trials of the International Sheep Dog Society, Ireland's President, Lionel Pennefather, was on the Trials Committee for the first time. In 1979, at the Stranraer International, the Irish singles entry was put up to eight.

In 1984 Ireland had a judge, Caldwell Hemphill of Castlederg, at the International for the first time; and in 1987 at the Woburn International they had their own Course Director, D. Forsyth of Coleraine.

The country had its singles entry increased to 12 in 1990, and in 1993 was granted full status and deemed to be on a par with the other three countries. Thus Ireland 'came of age' and her emergence as a competitive force was due mainly to the untiring efforts of Lionel Pennefather, her National President for 15 years and the finest ambassador Ireland could have had.

Lionel set his sights on International recognition for Ireland after his first sheepdog trial in 1926, and he finally achieved his aim after 35 years. Though he failed to win a place in Ireland's three-strong team to their first International in 1961, Lionel, who was then in his early fifties, made Irish sheepdog history the following year when, after winning the Irish National with Bess, she became the first Irish collie to win through to the final Supreme contest where she finished eighth. This made her, in fact, the eighth-rated collie in Britain in 1962.

Bess was a trim little black and white bitch, bred by Edward Metcalfe at Tebay near Penrith in the county where Lionel spent his farming apprenticeship, and she won two Irish National championships and was twice runner-up in the five years 1962 to 1966.

Lionel, now retired from farming 2,000 hill acres in County Londonderry to Coolbeg near Carrigaline in the south, was a pioneer in other ways. He took the first demonstration team of collies to South Africa in 1936 and opened a tour of the country at the Rosebank Show in Capetown before a crowd of 35,000 people. His skill and that of his dogs, in particular Spy, son of English champion Bagshaw's Moss and a

G.L. Pennefather's Bess, Irish Champion in 1962 and 1966.

courageous and strong collie, made South African sheepmen think about improving their own dogs, and Lionel was again invited to tour the country in 1968.

Originally Ireland imported quality blood, one of the most noteworthy dogs being Whitehope Corrie whom Lyn McKee took to Hillsborough in County Down from the Scottish Borders. Apart from winning the 1963 National championship and six Irish 'caps', Corrie started a strong Irish line which included Jim Brady's red-coated Buff, twice Ireland's champion; Buff's daughters Moy and Gyp, 1968 and 1970 champions; and John McSwiggan's Rock, the 1971 champion. Corrie was a clever blend of bloodlines which included Wilson's Cap, Purdie's Tam, Anderson's Garry and Illingworth's Monty.

Perhaps the most unusual requirement of a collie dog is that it be a good sailor, yet Jim and Sweep, two good-looking, rough-coated collies which shepherded an offshore island for Harford Logan, had to acquire 'sea-legs' to get to their job. Their duties were on the grazings of Copeland Island two miles off the Irish mainland in Strangford Lough and their journey to work was by boat. Jim particularly liked sailing, but then Jim liked anything that got him to sheep for he was dedicated to his work and, in his prime at six years old, when he showed his skills to the viewers of 'One Man and His Dog', he had won the Irish National twice, the Irish Driving, and the Irish Brace championships in competition.

His regular beat was unusual in that it was divided by water: on one side was 50 acres with Friesian dairy cows and a small pedigree Border Leicester flock at Millisle, and over the water another 350 acres.

Thus another duty which was not on a collie's normal itinerary was

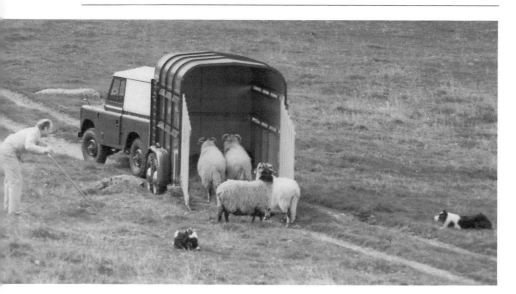

A tense moment in the television trials at Austwick as Harford Logan from Ireland, with Jim and Sweep, puts sheep into the trailer (Derek Johnson).

expected of him. When the flock of Blackface ewes and lambs was gathered for grading and the lambs were taken for Ballyclare market he had to help load the boat, driving reluctant sheep from a rocky jetty on to the bobbing deck of the boat. It was tricky work and with the waves bouncing, the salt spray flying and the sea birds screaming to the bleat of sheep, gentle chivvying was necessary to persuade the ewes to embark. A slip meant a ducking and with sheep prices to £50 a head a rescue had to be successful, either Jim or Sweep following them into the water for a bit of aquatic shepherding. So fond of the seaman's life did Jim and Sweep become that they had to be watched for sneaking aboard any ship which tied up in the harbour.

At lambing time the dogs were Harford's only companions for three to four weeks at a stretch, for it was then that he lived with his flock on the island.

Harford moved to Scotland, to Legnaha Farm, at Duror in Appin in 1951 where his dogs managed 900 breeding ewes and 520 hoggs, and he immediately made his presence felt on the trials fields. At the Scottish National at Glamis in August 1981, best remembered for the blue-painted holding-pen, he beat the best of 160 Scottish handlers with his young tricolour Star, and handled his eight-year-old Sweep into the 15-strong Scottish team.

Star, a rough-coated collie which had grown up in Ireland with

Harford Logan and Jim from County Down make the art of penning look easy at the 1978 Chatsworth International (Marc Henrie).

Harford, was Scottish-bred by J. McGregor at Lesmahagow. Harford bought the dog from Davie Gibson of Dalquhandy Farm at Lesmahagow when he was five months old, and schooled him to win his first of six open trials in Ireland when he was only nine months old. Star also ran for Ireland in the Brace contest in 1980. When he moved to Scotland, he won the Great Glen open championship. Star again proved his quality, and Harford's good handling skills, by running fifth in the singles and, with Sweep, second in the Brace contest at the Scottish National the following year at Strathaven in Lanarkshire.

Harford moved to farm at Wellhouse, Kirkcowan, at Newton Stewart, and then at Foreside Farm, Neilston, in Renfrewshire, before returning to Ireland, to Newtonabbey, to handle his home-bred rough-coated Dick, out of his Jean by his Micky, into the 1992 Irish team when the country had the maximum entry of 150 at Baronscourt in County Tyrone. The black and white Dick was one of Harford's most successful dogs, representing Ireland for four consecutive years from 1992, and winning Ireland's Driving championship in 1994. In 1980, while representing Ireland, Harford, coming into the contest at the last minute when Jim Brady's Meg was missing, won the International Driving championship with Sweep.

Harford Logan has won five Irish National, five Irish Brace and one Irish Driving championship, and one Scottish National and one Scottish Farmers' title in the past 35 years, becoming one of Ireland's most successful sheepdog handlers. The high quality of his dogs reflects the standard which the top Irish collies have now reached.

It was not always so, and though the majority of Irish working dogs are below the standards of those of England, Scotland and Wales, the present quality of the top flight shows just how far Ireland has travelled in improving its shepherding standards in the past 35 years – really since entry to the International set-up in 1961.

At that first Irish National at Glenarm in County Antrim there were only 15 single and four Brace entries in a one-day programme, and the top three single entries went to the International. The 1995 National at Blessington in County Wicklow had 150 single and nine Brace entries in a three-day programme, and the Irish team for the International had 15 singles, two Brace and one Driving competitor. Such is the interest now in working collies that the Irish membership of the International Sheep Dog Society is approaching that of Wales in numbers.

In 1972 at the International at Newcastle in England, Ulster farmer Jim Brady from Ballyclare made history by winning Ireland's first International championship, taking the Farmers' honour with his good-tempered Bosworth Jim, a four-year-old son of Llyr Evans's Bosworth Coon; and the following year at Bala, Bosworth Jim added the Driving honour for Ireland's second International championship.

In 1976 Martin O'Neill, whose clever Nell from Summerhill in County Meath had been such a stalwart in the Irish cause, won the International Farmers' championship with her grandson, Risp, a tireless, medium-coated collie; and in 1977, John McSwiggan of Gortin Glen in Tyrone won the International Brace title with his brother and sister partnership of Chip and Jess.

In 1985 Willie Watt, a shepherd to over 1,000 Grey-faced and Halfbred ewes at Mountjoy West, Omagh, County Tyrone in Northern Ireland, won the International Driving championship with Chip, back to Whitehope Nap on both sides of his pedigree, the same year that his son, Barton, won the Young Handler contest with Chip's half-sister Moy.

Barton's brother, Gordon, won the first Young Handler competition of the International Sheep Dog Society at Armathwaite with Chum in 1981. Gordon showed outstanding ability as a handler when Chum, a nice-tempered, medium-coated bitch which he had schooled since his father bred her in 1975, was reserve Irish National champion in 1979 at Clonmany in County Donegal. Gordon was then only 15 years old, and just two aggregate points from two judges behind the far more experienced Tim Flood.

It was Gordon who led to us changing the rules for television's 'One Man and his Dog'. We had no time limit on the trials, but after Gordon had spent an hour – and we were running short of film while he was waiting – quite rightly – for the right opportunity – in the shedding ring at Loch Lomond in 1983 we did put a time limit on subsequent trials.

The first young handler to win the section at the International in 1981. Gordon Watt representing Ireland with Chum. (Marc Henrie).

In 1985 Ireland also had another success in the International trials at Lockerbie when Denis Birchall won the Brace contest with the little prick-eared Kate and the black and white Mist from Blackhill, Dunlavin, near the Wicklow Mountains. The dogs' quiet and sensible approach to the North Country Cheviot ewes at the lift set the seal for a good trial which, although at fault in fetching, was concluded with a faultless second pen. Ireland were also second in the team shield contest that year.

The tricolour Kate and the rough-coated Mist won the Irish Brace championships of 1982, 1983 and 1985 for Denis Birchall. Kate was a reliable and independent little bitch, the daughter of Tim Flood's Scott which won the Irish National championship in 1978, which Denis had trained from 15 months old. Mist, the granddaughter of Lionel Penne-father's Nell, was trained by Denis from six months old.

Denis, who farmed Cheviot and Blackface ewes, and had spent his life with farm stock, has been one of Ireland's most reliable handlers at trials. He has won one Irish National championship with the speedy little Eve, three Brace titles with Kate and Mist, and one Irish Driving championship with Jan.

Tim Flood, who farms around 150 mixed acres on the flat land in the Clonroche area of County Wexford, and who is one of the most cheery of Irish handlers, won the 1989 International Brace championship with his home-bred pair Pip and Flash, and the 1988 International Driving

Tim Flood of County Wexford, with Cosy, Ireland's Driving Champion in 1975 and 1977.

championship with Pip. Tim has won more 'caps' for Ireland than any other handler and he has taken 16 National titles.

Pip, one of the most lovable little dogs in the Emerald Isle, was a very placid friendly collie who would work for any member of Tim's family. Fast in his work and with lots of concentration, he was the son of what Tim calls 'the favourite', Scott, who in his competitive career won the Irish National championship and the Irish Driving title twice.

Pip suffered a bad accident in 1983, but after he had spent some time at the Dublin Veterinary College, such was his courage that he came back to the competitive field to win two International championships, three Irish National championships, one Irish Brace title and two Irish Driving championships. He was a true Irishman, out of his master's Midge, and his paternal grandsire was Jim Brady's Risp which won the 1970 Irish Driving championship.

In the 1990s, to date, Ireland has won four International championships.

George Graham of Portglenone in County Antrim won the International Driving championship in 1992 with the merled Jess, bred in Wales by Colin Gordon, after a most successful National at Baronscourt when Jess was second in the team and won the Irish Driving championship.

A carpenter by trade who runs his own joinery business at Ballymore-Eustace in County Kildare as well as farming sheep and beef cows on the Wicklow Hills, Pat Byrne has won the International Brace championships of 1990, 1994 and 1995, and has been Ireland's most successful handler in recent years, particularly in the brace contests. Handling such collies of the calibre as his half-brother and sister Star and Dot, both of which were sired by John Templeton's Roy, Pat is a force to be reckoned with.

Star, a smooth-coated black and white dog, goes back to Supreme champion Wiston Cap on the paternal side of his pedigree, and to Stuart Davidson's wise old Ben, which won Scotland's National championship in 1980 with the highest points for four years, on his maternal side.

Dot is a friendly and good-tempered bitch, but is very forceful when she gets behind sheep. She has the same bloodline as her younger partner Star, and her maternal line, although of a different route, also goes back to Wiston Cap.

Jim Brady, who was probably one of the best-known Irish handlers at the Internationals, had won three National championships with Buff when he took Bosworth Jim from Llyr Evans's champion Coon to win two more in 1972 and 1973, as well as Ireland's first two International championships. Bosworth Jim was a black and white mottled tan dog who enjoyed a game with the children when work was done and he won many trials, though a car accident when he was six years old took a lot of the speed out of him. He added his aristocratic line to Irish progeny.

Now Ireland had its own stud-dogs, and National champions Brady's Buff, McSwiggan's Rock, Tim Flood's Scott and Pip, Lutton's Glen and Irvine's Shep were all bred in Ireland.

One of the best known of Irish collies, because he took the opportunity to raise national prestige before a large television audience in his

Jim Brady and Buff.

winning of the second 'One Man and His Dog' trophy, was Martin O'Neill's black and white Risp, the winner of the 1976 International Farmers' title. Bred by Tim Flood – who entertained us all on 'One Man and His Dog' with tunes on his mysterious nose-whistle – at Clonroche in County Wexford out of his Fly, a daughter of Martin's Nell, Risp was by Jim Brady's Risp, the son of Scottish champion Gilchrist's Spot. Working with Suffolk × Cheviot ewes and 300 beef cows at Curraghtown, Summerhill, he was good tempered, placid and quiet by nature, yet strong and powerful when it came to moving awkward sheep or tetchy bullocks.

Martin, a tall, happy fellow, told me how he nearly made the biggest mistake of his life when Risp was just three years old. The dog was not suiting him and he offered it for sale at £60. No one took Risp and later

Pedigree of RISP (61527) 1976 BBC 'One Man and His Dog' Champion with Martin O'Neill

RISP (61527) Dog. Rough. Black and white Born 14.1.1970

RISP (45699) J. Brady

FLY (51822) T. Flood

SPOT (24981) J. Gilchrist

SNIP (21772) J. J. Thompson

SPOT (38147) N.F. Deacon

NELL (43414) M. O'Neill

BOB (12684) J. Gilchrist

NAN (9896) P. McG. Hepburn

JIM (12967) W. Hardisty

FLY (11362) W. Hardisty

BUFF (23069) J. Brady

JILL (22018) J. Brady

FLASH (19291) N. F. Deacon

LASSIE (9971) M. Flood

SPOT (7320) J. Gilchrist

NELL (10141) G. Hunter

MOSS (5176) J. M. Wilson

ANN (4545) W. S. Hetherington

LADDIE (8049) W. Goodfellow

MERRIE (6880) J. Warwick

LADDIE (8049) W. Goodfellow

MIST (9025) G. Stainton

WHITEHOPE CORRIE (13706) J. W. L. McKee

LASS (12974) J. Brady

JIM (12967) W. Hardisty

MEG (19190) T. R. Harper

LAD (10676) H. J. Persse

MEG (15613) H. J. Persse

JIM (6198) J. Evans

NELL (6199) J. Evans

The numbers in brackets are the Stud Book numbers of the International Sheep Dog Society

in the year, as if to prove Martin wrong in his judgement, he won a place in Ireland's team. When Risp won the television trophy in 1976 he was worth more than ten times that asking price.

Included in the Irish section of the International Sheep Dog Society for administration and team purposes are the collies of the Isle of Man. In 1970 the island was host to the Irish National event for the first time and two local dogs, the home-bred brother and sister Bob and Gyp, won the Brace championship for Arthur Quayle from Cronkdhoo on the slopes of Greeba mountain near St Johns, with G. S. Quirk's Chum and Teresa from Ballaquine second. Like the Irish, Manx collies have improved greatly from the import of good bloodlines and from the growing interest in competitive trials.

The Isle of Man championship, which is held annually with around 25 entries in July, has been a major factor in this improvement for, based on the qualifying and Supreme double-gather tests of the International trials, the event has truly tested collie skills and encouraged competitors to raise their standards.

Only one collie from the Isle of Man has won the Irish National, Matthew Graham's five-year-old black and white Gay, a Lancashire-bred bitch working with one of the first pure Charolais herds in Britain. From an upland farm on the lower slopes of the South Barrule on the island, Gay, a daughter of Supreme champion Wiston Cap and a grand-daughter of Jim Cropper's champion Fleet, won both the Manx and the Irish championships in 1976.

The only Manxman to have earned regular inclusion in the Irish singles team is Ronnie Kinrade, whose collies assist in the management of Black-face and Dorset breeding ewes and beef and milk cows over the flat lands of the sheading of Ayre between Bride and Ramsey in the north of the island. A number of Ronnie's dogs have represented Ireland. Hemp, a son of Alan Jones's Supreme champion Roy, ran for Ireland in 1969 and 1970; Cap, a son of Supreme champion Wiston Cap, in 1975 and 1979; Ben, a grandson of Wiston Cap, in 1976; Bill, a great-grandson of Wiston Cap, in 1982; the four-year-old Fly in 1986; and the Welsh-bred Nan in 1988. Hemp won the Irish Driving championship in 1969.

Television took a lot of interest in sheepdogs in 1971. Lionel Pennefather working. (Derek Johnson).

CHAPTER NINETEEN

British Collies Shepherd the World

From visiting the sheepdogs of Belgium, I record the skills of British collies which have taken them to work in almost every sheep rearing area of the world, and detail the dogs which stamped their qualities on the bloodlines in New Zealand, Australia, America and South Africa, finally considering the possibilities of a World championship trials event.

Hanging on the walls of a château at Groenendael on the outskirts of Brussels are faded pictures of the black sheepdogs of Belgium. I looked at them with interest, for they were pictures of dogs that had all the requirements of good herding dogs – sturdy limbs, weatherproof coats, broad heads and intelligent eyes – but in the flesh I sought them in vain.

The Groenendael and its kindred spirits, the Malinois and Tervueren, I could not find in work on any Belgian farms, and the trials I found were those for police type of work. The intelligent traits of the Groenendael have been utilised by the police for their requirements, and in many countries the breed has been evolved for the show bench. This is the fate of many West European working dogs.

There are no longer professional shepherds in Belgium, so there is a dearth of good herding dogs in the country. The Belgian Border Collie Club, which is only ten years old, is interested in helping local farmers who are looking for good working dogs.

Only once on the Continent, in the Black Forest of Germany, have I seen a dog – an Alsation or German Shepherd Dog – in action with a flock of sheep.

One of the great successes of the International Sheep Dog Society has been the inauguration of the European Continental trials, built mainly on the pioneering work of Jim Easton of Eglingham in Northumberland, who since 1976 has given Dutch handlers a lot of advice and encouragement.

The first event was held at Genthod, just outside Geneva in Switzerland in November 1985, and broke new and exciting ground for the International Sheep Dog Society. The Society's Chairman, Ray Ollerenshaw, the secretary, Philip Hendry, and Jimmy Easton, who judged the competition on the British-type course, gave the European competitors plenty of encouragement and advice.

Six European countries participated in the first trials, which were organised by Odette Lieber of the Swiss Sheepdog Society, which then had 84 members. Eleven Continental trials have now been held in Switzerland, France, Holland, Germany and Belgium, and the officials of the International Sheep Dog Society have always been there to offer suggestions.

When the eleventh Continental trials were held at Achel in Belgium, some 40 miles north of Antwerp, in 1995, there were 53 competitors from Belgium, France, Germany, the Netherlands, Denmark, Finland, Switzerland, Sweden and Austria. Rising in standard as the years have gone by, with mainly Border Collies (though not always), they have been placed by British judges.

Jim Easton of Northumberland, Norman Seamark of Bedfordshire, Ron Fitch of Northamptonshire, Raymond MacPherson of Cumbria, John Templeton of Ayrshire, Johnny Wilson of Selkirkshire, Glyn Jones of Clwyd and Tim Flood of County Wexford in Eire, have been among those who have placed the awards. Increasingly, British judges have been invited to judge trials in various countries in recent years.

Nowadays the Border Collie is entering the Common Market in ever-growing numbers. British dogs have gone to Belgium, France, Germany, Finland, Holland, Denmark and Sweden for work with farm stock. And in the post-bag of the International Sheep Dog Society are letters from many parts of the world – from Australia, Argentina, New Zealand, South Africa, Rhodesia, Italy, France, Germany, Denmark, Luxembourg, Norway, Sweden, Finland, Canada, Greenland, Columbia, the United States – all wanting to know about British collies.

Britain has long been regarded as the stud-farm of the world and for centuries has supplied many countries with the best of livestock. No longer can this be generally claimed, however, for in many instances we have been the importers, bringing the cattle and sheep breeds of the Continent to Britain in an effort to increase our own farming efficiency. The Charolais, Limousin, Simmental and other breeds of cattle have entered Britain; the Landrace, Ile de France and Texel breeds of sheep have also come here. But Britain can still claim the stud-farm title in regard to working collies.

Puppies romp in the comfort of a Welsh farm building before leaving for Bulgaria. Part of a 35-strong exportation by Glyn Jones in 1976.

The demand for British collie bloodstock is increasing and since James Reid, secretary of the International Sheep Dog Society, said in 1935 that British collies had gone to work in Australia, New Zealand, Tasmania, Canada, America, South Africa, Japan and the Falkland Isles, exports have increased a hundredfold and to such places as Switzerland, Austria, Latvia and even Alaska. Falkland bloodlines were infused with new British blood in September 1983, as I discuss in the next chapter.

Scotland's John Templeton, British Supreme Champion in 1972, works Fleet in the American World Championship at Maryland, Delaware in May 1973. They finished in second place.

World sheepdog trials championships, in spite of the great difficulties of organisation, have highlighted British superiority. Raymond Mac-Pherson from Cumbria won both the American World championships of 1973 and 1976 with Nap and Tweed. Collies imported from Britain or their progeny are regular winners at National championships trials, particular in America. Seeing Raymond and Nap win the first American title, one Texas stockman said, 'That is what I came 1,800 miles to see.'

There are around 2,000 million sheep in the world, the big populations in Australia with 140 million, Africa's 188 million and New Zealand's 70 million, with 141 million in America, over 23 million of which are in North America and Mexico. Of Europe's 141 million, 43 million are in the United Kingdom and 31 million in the rest of the European Community. Russia rears around 140 million sheep and China 99 million. The remainder are in Asia and scattered thinly round other parts of the world, but numbers fluctuate so much in each country that they are difficult to assess. Management methods vary greatly and are dependent on purpose, terrain and weather conditions, but wherever sheep require herding, dogs of one sort or another are necessary.

New Zealand sheepmen have acknowledged their dependence on the sheepdog by erecting a monument on the edge of Lake Tekapo in Mackenzie Country, South Canterbury, in the South Island, which depicts a collie dog with the inscription 'Without the help of the collie dog, the mustering of this mountainous country would be impossible.' Similarly, the foreword to the first edition of the first volume of the *New Zealand Working Sheepdog Stud Book* of 1940 contains this tribute to the sheepdog: 'That wonderful animal that has made possible the conquest of the grazing country of this Dominion.' These two citations say it all. Without the collie dog the sheep flocks of the world would be unmanageable and much of the earth's surface would be valueless.

The Border Collie is highly valued in New Zealand, for both terrain and climatic conditions are in many respects akin to those of the United Kingdom. Gatherings, though, are immense and James Lillico, who left Scotland to farm near Invarcargill in the South Island at the turn of the century, wrote of the mustering of 20–40,000 Merino sheep – 'as wild as the birds of the air' – from possibly half a million acres of country varying from rich river flats and sheltered glens, up bare shingle faces, over rough gullies of scrub and fern right up to the land of everlasting snow.

James Lillico was one of the first importers of British-bred dogs and under his name in volume one of the International Sheep Dog Society's Stud Book are many well-known collies including Thomas Armstrong's Don, 1911 and 1914 International champion, Thomas Brown's Lad,

1913 International champion, and William Wallace's Moss, 1907 International champion, who was renamed Border Boss in New Zealand. He also imported Yarrow and Jed, the father and mother of Dickson's Hemp; and another importer, J. B. Armstrong brought in Wilson-bred collies Sprig, Roy III and Pink. The progeny of these dogs, blessed with the intelligence of their heritage, adapted readily to the specific requirements of the New Zealand sheep-runs and did much to set the standard for the Border Collie on the other side of the world.

In 1934, during the Depression, Dick Fortune, shepherding in East Lothian in Scotland, left his job and sailed for New Zealand to train collies for James Lillico. Like so many Scots he was a man of vision, with the courage of his convictions, and when he sold up and returned home to Edinburgh in 1957 he left behind a 2,500 acre sheep station producing the famous Canterbury lamb, and a reputation as one of the finest sheepdog handlers in New Zealand.

During his years in New Zealand he imported well over 100 collies from Britain, the first, he told me, at a freight charge of £7. Very different from today's £300! The dogs he imported he used in New Zealand and Australia in demonstrations the aim being, as reported in the Timaru local newspaper, 'to improve the standard of working sheepdogs in the two countries, and Mr Fortune asserts that a trainer blessed with the necessary patience can bring his dogs to a standard of efficiency which will make them worth their weight in gold on the farm'.

Dick won most of the leading trials in both countries and became a regular judge of trials, and on his return to Scotland he won the 1975 National Farmers' and the 1977 National Brace championships and five

Well-trained collies show their paces in rehearsal at Sydney's Show. They were handled by Dick Fortune, known world-wide for his prowess as a sheepdog trainer.

International 'caps'. With his wide experience of shepherding in Scotland, New Zealand and Australia, Dick had forgotten more about sheep and dogs than most of us will ever know.

Telling me about the trials of the New Zealand Expo-International championship which, like their American counterparts, were an attempt at staging a world event with New Zealand, Australian and British dogs competing, he said that all New Zealand trials were vastly different from trials in the United Kingdom. The home dogs would be difficult to beat, he said, though no doubt our dogs could do just as well provided they arrived there in time to get used to the conditions.

Thus acclimatisation is another difficulty against a genuine World championship, and Dick was right, though British dogs have never let the side down and though without material success have been highly praised for their sound workmanlike and quiet methods in strange and exacting conditions. So much so that half of those that made the trip never returned – the New Zealanders bought them for stud purposes.

It is the proud boast of New Zealand sheepmen that they handle larger mobs of sheep more skilfully than their counterparts in any other country in the world due to the efficiency of their dog teams. The 'team' for each shepherd will include one Border Collie type of dog, known as a heading dog, which attends to all the gathering jobs and the finer work, as at lambing time, and at least two and often more Huntaway dogs – the specialist dogs for which New Zealand is renowned.

Huntaways have a special job to do – to hunt out the sheep from rough country – and they do it by foreceful manner and vigorous barking. They are also used in sheep-yards to harry sheep into drafting races or dipping chutes.

While New Zealand, by virtue of its mountainous terrain, in South Island particularly, has developed this type of dog to the extreme, Huntaways have a similar function to the noisy dogs of certain parts of Cumbria and the Scottish Highlands, whose job is exactly similar. Trials are held for both types of working dogs and it was in the heading trials that the British dogs competed at the Expo championships.

British sheep have also been found good for New Zealand farming and the Romney breed, the native of the marshlands of Kent, is the most popular breed in North Island with two Romney crossbreds, the Perendale from the Cheviot and the Cooperworth from the Border Leicester growing in popularity. In South Island the Merino is found on the hills with the Corriedale on the large farms of the plains.

As in New Zealand, British breeders supplied the nucleus of Australia's sheepdog stock and here again we see the adaptability of the Border Collie, for Australia's climate and terrain are vastly different from either Britain or New Zealand. Sheep stations in Australia are so extensive that aeroplanes and motor-cycles are used to cover the ground, and at the musterings collies travel great distances, often in intense heat. They drive sheep across country that can vary from lush grazing pasture to barren, stony plains and the demands on their stamina and courage defy anything that can be found in their homeland.

For many years I wrote for an Australian sheepdog magazine and came to admire the versatility of these collies, and of their compatriots the Kelpies, whose exploits were recorded in those pages.

As in New Zealand, the blood of Britain's Old Hemp was used in the foundation of Australia's collie dogs, and one of the first breeders to assess its importance was J. L. Moore of Melbourne with one of his best imports being Moss from C. B. MacPherson of Kingussie in Inverness-shire. Moss was a rough-coated black and white son of George Brown's Spot, the 1923 International champion, and Thomas Hunter's Fly, and mated with the imported bitch Caley, daughter of the 1908 and 1909 International champion James Scott's Kep, produced pups which founded the aristocratic line of Australia. This bloodline was also mingled with Kelpie blood. Edgar Ferrier of Queensland imported Wilson's Nickey, the 1933 Scottish National champion; and Gyp, a daughter of Wilson's triple Supreme champion Roy, went to Australia.

The working Kelpie of Australia is rival to, or complementary to the Border Collie, for both are excellent stock herding dogs. A great

Three Kelpie puppies from Tim Austin's well-known Elfinvale stud at Coleraine, Victoria, Australia, show interest in Merinos.

A good Kelpie bitch at work in the stockyard. Tim Austin's Elfinvale Daffy backing Comeback (Merino-Polworth) *sheep at Coleraine, Victoria, Australia.*

shepherding dog in its own right, the Kelpie suffered in popularity down the years because of its dubious origin and because of its introduction to the show bench.

Originally it was alleged that Kelpies came from either a cross between the wild fox and a domestic Scottish collie or the bushman's idea of a cross between the dingo, the native wild dog, and a domestic dog, and some of the leading canine authorities in Australia held one or other of these views. Now it is generally accepted that the 'great red dogs' were evolved from smooth-coated black and tan Scottish sheepdogs which were imported into Australia around 1869. From them the Kelpie was bred to cope with stock in extreme conditions and probably much on the same lines of trial and error as the original British dogs before Old Hemp.

Such men of New South Wales and dogs of Scotland as Elliott and Allen of Yeraldra station with Brutus and Jenny, George Robertson of Warrack station and J. Rutherford of Yarrawonga each with two unnamed collies were the pioneers. Their stud-dogs were good workers and Brutus and Jenny produced Caesar who, mated to a black and tan bitch from Robertson's breeding, produced King's Kelpie, winner of the first sheepdog trial ever held in Australia, at Forbes in 1873, who became the 'mother' of the breed. King's Kelpie mated to the black-coated Moss, son of Rutherford's two imports, bred Clyde who in turn was the sire of Coil, the 1898 Sydney trials winner who became known as the 'Immortal' Coil.

Bred to withstand the high extremes of temperature in Australia and to travel long distances, often without water, the Kelpie has natural initiative to control large numbers of sheep without constant command. It is a smooth-coated, long-legged, lithe and active dog, alert and good to look at, and it is proficient at its job. Indeed, Kelpies dominated the important Sydney trials in the early years, though Border Collies have gradually overtaken them in this proficiency. (Trials in Australia, run mainly on Merino sheep, are popular with upwards of 300 entries for the National championships.)

Old Hemp spread his influence to America as to Australia through George Brown's Spot, the 1923 International champion and great-grandson of Herdman's Tommy, who went out in 1923 to Sam Stoddart, a Scottish shepherd who had emigrated to Bradford in New Hampshire. Sam Stoddart imported many other quality dogs from his homeland, including the outcrossing bloodline of James Scott's Kep through J. R. Robertson's Cheviot, a grandson of William Wallace's Moss, the 1907 International champion who, as we have seen, was exported as Border Boss to James Lillico in New Zealand.

A canine genius – George Brown's Spot, the 1923 Supreme Champion, that went to America to Sam Stoddart and was the founder of many American champions and registered Number 1 in the American Society's stud book.

Pedigree of SPOT (308) 1923 Supreme Champion with George Brown

SPOT
(308)
Dog. Rough.
Black and white.
Born 1920

(Transferred to
Sam Stoddart,
America,
and registered
No 1 in the North
American Sheep
Dog Society
Stud Book)

BEN
(249)
G. P. Brown

RUBY
(207)
G. P. Brown

DON
(217)
C. Hardisty

FAN
(208)
G. P. Brown

SKIP
J. McKnight

MOSS
A. Harrison

DON
(17)
T. Armstrong
1911. 1914 Int Champ.

MEG
(27)
J. Renwick

TOMMY
(16)
I. Herdman

NELL
(205)
T. P. Brown

DON
W. Burns
TRIM (37)
T. Armstrong

SWEEP
Hall
MAID
Bell

TWEED (246)
W. Wallace
GYP
(daughter of
OLD HEMP)
W. Wallace

DON
A. Renwick
MAID (1)
A. Brown

The numbers in brackets are the Stud Book numbers of the International Sheep Dog Society
— Indicates that this dog is not known

These imported dogs, their progeny and their herding qualities brought home to American stockmen the value of top class collies. For many years Sam Stoddart and Spot gave demonstrations, 'charmed audiences wherever they appeared' and won at trials which became established in America around 1925. Spot could be classed as a canine genius. He was brainy and quick to learn his craft so that he allied experience with intelligence. His eyes were gentle, yet commanding, and he was lithe and faster than any sheep that tried to outwit him. He was medium coated and feathered and typical of the Scottish dogs of his age. On his mother's side were ten collie generations of the Browns of Oxon.

On the formation of the North American Sheep Dog Society in 1940

Sam Stoddart became its first President and Spot was registered Number One in the Society's Stud Book. Numbered 308 in the International Sheep Dog Society's Stud Book, Spot was a clever dog who conquered a continent.

Dewey M. Jontz, when President of the American International Border Collie Registry, told me that in the early 1920s Border Collies were almost unknown in America, though during those years many Scottish and English shepherds who went to America with sheep and cattle importations took Border Collies with them. Crossed with resident dogs, the progeny became known as English Shepherds. The United States is vast, and this made trials growth a slow procedure with competitors having to travel great distances. Ralph Pulfer from Maplewood, Ohio, says he averages 1,000 miles round trip for each trial he attends today.

The first record of a trial being held in America, however, is as early as September 1880, as a part of Philadelphia's centennial year celebration. Thirteen dogs competed in adult and puppy classes and the winner was a dog called Tom handled by Charles Pugh of Philadelphia, with Fannie, under T. S. Cooper, the puppy champion. This was obviously a 'one-off', for in 1928 a report states that '1,500 people from all over New England gathered at Fillmore Farms in old historic Bennington, Vermont, on 16 August 1928 to witness the first sheepdog trials ever held in the United States', in which seven dogs competed. The winner

One of America's leading handlers, Clifford Parker of Pearland, Texas, works Fay at the 1977 Lexington trials.

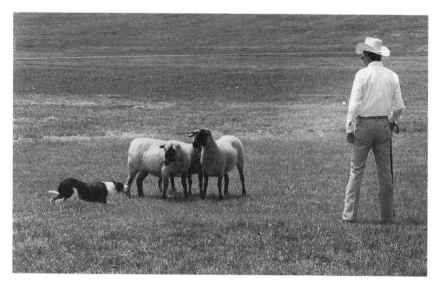

was Preston J. Davenport of Colrain, Massachusetts with Spottie, a son of Sam Stoddart's Spot. Spot himself was fourth on that occasion.

Spot's influence was boosted by later importations, notably Cullen's Sam, the sire of Jim Wilson's famous Cap, and William Wallace's tricolour Moss, a superior worker, to Luke Pascoe at Powling, New York in the early 1930s; Anderson's Wull, a descendant of Spot, of Dickson's Hemp, and of Batty's Hemp, the 1920 International champion, to Dewey M. Jontz in the 1940s; and as the years passed more and more British dogs crossed the Atlantic, including Jim Wilson's 1955 Supreme champion Bill in 1957 to Ray Parker, and the 1972 Supreme champion John Templeton's Cap who stayed in America after running fifth in the 1973 World championship.

British dogs were riding the crests of the Atlantic waves and men as well as dogs went to show their skills.

One of the best was Ashton Priestley of Bamford in Derbyshire who took his 1951 Supreme champion Pat along with Jim, Lark, Mac and Moss to demonstrate their qualities. Coming out of the enforced quarantine on his return to Britain, Jim showed that a collie never forgets his craft by winning the 1955 English National championship.

Quoting Dewey M. Jontz, 'The 60s and 70s witnessed an increase in imports and there is a ready market for quality Border Collies in America today. British Border Collies are still looked upon as the source of quality and seed-stock for the superior Border Collie.'

A champion team sail on the Queen Elizabeth to give demonstrations in America. Ashton Priestly from Bamford in Derbyshire and his Jill, Lark, Mac, Pat and Moss.

Ray Ollerenshaw, when he was Chairman of the International Sheep Dog Society, was invited to judge the eighteenth International Stock Dog Classic trials in America and was interested to see that the organisers, the Southern Arizona International Livestock Association, were keen to run their trials under the same rules and principles as in the United Kingdom. Ray was also interested to discover that while the Americans were breeding their own working dogs they were not as good as the imported ones – of the 67 entries 46 were imported.

Collie interest in America – and Canada – has never been higher. Canada held its first National championship at Bond Head, Ontario in 1967 and Brian Nettleton, a veterinary surgeon from Yorkshire living in Nova Scotia, judged. He also organised the importation of 1,450 breeding ewes to Nova Scotia in 1970, and has also imported British dogs for work and trials competition.

'There seems to be no record of the first sheepdog imported to South Africa but there is little doubt that they have been here since the last century,' Ron Philip of the South African Sheepdog Association told me. He said that during this century Border Collies had been imported from Britain, many Kelpies had come from Australia, and some dogs had been brought from New Zealand. The first dog he owned was a Kelpie named Snoggs. 'The art of handling and training seemed to have remained with a few isolated enthusiasts until the South African Sheep Dog Association was formed in Graaff Reinet on 11 July 1961 when the first National championship trial was held. The first National champion was Tess owned by Billy Kingwill of Coloniesplaats, Graaff Reinet, and the Junior champion was my 20-month-old Tracer.'

News of these trials spread and requests for demonstrations came from agricultural shows so that handling has now become more sophisticated, with trials held regularly in the Eastern Cape, Border, Midlands and Western Cape areas. Annual courses for handlers are held at the Elsenberg College of Agriculture in the Western Cape and at Grootfontein College of Agriculture, Middelburg in the Karoo. 'Farmers throughout the country are eager to learn the art of training and handling,' Ron Philip said.

South Africa is one of the biggest fine wool producing countries in the world, with 34 million sheep. Until recently rural labour was plentiful, but with the rapid industrialisation of the country it is now becoming scarce and sheepdogs are filling the gap in both sheep and cattle handling, and even in ostrich farming.

In 1973 and 1976 a South African team took part in the American world trials and Ron told me that the experience of competing against the British, American and Canadian teams was of the greatest value.

I particularly admire the action which the South African Sheepdog

African herdsmen are beginning to realise the value of a trained dog. A Xhosa tribesman in the Eastern Cape Province with his Border Collie (Ron Philip).

Association took against the threat of the Kennel Union registering Border Collies on breed standards as bench dogs. They evolved a comprehensive scheme whereby sheepdogs are registered on working ability. A recognised breeder is obliged to become a member of the Association and must own at least one dog with a 'certificate of working ability'. Ron told me that the scheme was popular and most successful. He also said that a recent development was the participation of Africans with sheepdogs. 'Traditionally they have dogs which hunt hares, buck and jackals. The use of sheepdogs has been foreign to them. But with the influence of the Association the value of trained sheepdogs has filtered through to these tribesmen and, being natural stockmen, they are apt pupils and are capable of working sheepdogs with considerable skill.'

Ron Philip, who farmed sheep and cereals at Bredasdorp in the winter rainfall region of the Cape, relied on British blood for many of his sheepdog successes on the trials fields which included the South African National championship six times with four dogs. His Tracer, the 1961 Junior champion, was bred from Jim Wilson's British Supreme champion Craig and went on to win the 1964 and 1965 South African National championships. He was adjudged 'dog of the year' in 1963, 1964 and 1965. His Flick, of Whitehope Nap breeding, won the 1963 National title, and his home-bred Shadow, from Tracer and Flick, won

Ron Philip, chairman of the South African Sheepdog Association, with Zap and his flock of Dohne Merinos at Bredasdorp (Ron Philip).

the National in 1968. Tracer mated to Tweeny, from John Evans's English champion Don, produced the alert little Tag who won the 1972 and 1973 National championships and went to the American World championships as a member of the South African team.

With Ron Philip at the 1973 American World championships was Rodney J. Miles from a 2,700 acre property with 600 Merino ewes and 100 Friesland cows at Glencairn, Imvani in the Cape Province. He took Guy, the 1971 South African champion, and Sally, South Africa's 'dog of the year' in 1968. The 1976 South African representative to America were Chipper Kingwill and Bennie Strydom. Chipper took two imported collies, Jen, a daughter of Supreme champion Wiston Cap, and Drift, a son of Scottish champion Gilchrist's Spot.

South Africans have always been grateful for any advice on improving their dogs. In May 1980 Lionel Pennefather, of Irish fame, made his third trip to South Africa, where he was to give 14 demonstrations, hold symposiums on training and judge the top trials, including the South African Royal Show. He first went out in 1936, when he was 29 years old, as we saw earlier, at which time the modern sheepdog was almost unknown in South Africa and no one knew of any trials. Since the influence of people like Lionel Pennefather South Africa now has a Sheepdog Association over 20 years old, the Department of Sport and Recreation recognises sheepdog trials, and trials are run regularly but sparsely by many organisations. Lionel took the black and white Fay,

Roy and Ben, a two-year-old son of Bob Fraser's Moss to South Africa with him in 1936.

Perhaps the home-bred dogs are not as good as those imported from Britain, for the 1978 and 1979 Royal South African champion and 'dog of the year' in 1980 was Benny Strydom's rough-coated Spot, a two-year-old son of Jim Gilchrist's Mirk which won the 1970 Scottish Farmers' championship. His daily work was with fine-woolled Merino sheep, Dorper mutton sheep and Angora goats in the South African Karoo, a hard, dry veld which was a little different from his home country of grassy Peeblesshire hills.

In 1982 it was also a British-bred dog which won the South African championship, Bennie Strydom's four-year-old Floss from Grahamstown in the Karoo, a daughter of Tom Watson's Mirk, British International Driving champion of 1977. That was the year that the

Allan Heaton from Brandsby in Yorkshire with Chad who showed South African farmers just how good British collies are in 1982 (J. H. Pieterse)

South African Society, then with only 250 members in its twenty-first year, invited two British International handlers, Allan Heaton from Brandsby and Alasdair Mundell from the Cowal Hills of Argyllshire, and their dogs to compare them with their home dogs, most of which had been bred from stock imported from the United Kingdom.

Both the 2½-year-old Chad and the 20-month-old Ken, a son of his international Ken, with Allan Heaton, and Ben, a grandson of Davie Shennan's Meg, and Roy with Alasdair showed the South Africans that they still had a fair way to go before they could better their imported dogs.

The good-looking, balanced, cool and precise, black and white Chad was truly amazing and upheld British prestige under the most trying circumstances. She journeyed 6,000 miles to compete in five trials in ten days, and came very close to winning this first-ever International contest. In competition with 16 home-based dogs, all Border Collies from imported stock except for two Kelpies, Chad finished second – a remarkable performance in strange company, under exacting climatic conditions and on unfamiliar sheep. Between the five trials from Bredasdorp in the Cape to Johannesburg in the Transvaal there was often a 500-mile journey.

The four British dogs stayed in South Africa, Chad going to Ron Philip of Bredasdorp for work with Dohne Merino sheep. She was a rough-coated bitch bred by Brian Hope in the Hambleton Hills of Yorkshire with maternal bloodlines going back to Supreme champion McKnight's Gael. Her sire was Tony Iley's international Goss, back to Supreme champion Bosworth Coon and Tot Longton's Gyp.

Guarding sheep from a pack of wolves is not a job undertaken by Border Collies in Britain, but this is one of the tasks with which they are faced in Latvia. Here the dogs to guard the Latvian Darkhead ewes are really guard-dogs, but a recent correspondent with the International Sheep Dog Society wanted more capable dogs, which could put his sheep into the barn to protect them during the night.

Can there ever be a true World championship? Neither the American nor the New Zealand events were such, for neither were open to the world and only Britain had collies at both. The problems of a single accepted championship are many, with such obstacles as differing judging standards and rules, tests to individual country requirements and, perhaps most of all, rigid quarantine regulations against disease. Nor can the problem of collie acclimatisation, and the stress and strain of long journeys be discounted in order to give equal chances to all.

Three pertinent comments on World competition came from my journalist colleague, Matt Mundell; Archie McDiarmid, Chairman of the International Sheep Dog Society at the time of the first American event; and Clarence Storey, British representative at the first New Zealand event.

Matt said, 'If an event is to have a "World" prefix, then surely the countries asked to participate should have a say in arrangements. We cannot accept the method used in the American contest of reaching points decisions, there must be judges, and the courses must be better laid out.'

According to Archie, 'I for one will not be satisfied with any World championship unless it is a real one embracing every country willing to take part in such a competition properly organised. . . . It must give every competitor a fair and equal chance.'

Clarence philosophically commented, 'We were the pioneers, we did not know what to expect, and our experiences will be of tremendous value to future British representatives.'

Rules and regulations as to the running of the events can be overcome but every collie that enters Britain, either coming to or returning from an envisaged World contest, must spend six months in quarantine. This is right, and as farmers with livestock at risk we cannot in all honesty ask for a waiving of the rules which protect that livestock – and our livelihood – for the holding of a contest which has only competitive value.

Each country already uses trials for the practical purpose of upgrading its working dogs whose true vocation, after all, is the shepherding of the world's sheep population.

CHAPTER TWENTY

Practical Shepherding Counts

Watching the black-coated Nicky enjoying his craft in shepherding the high Pennines, I applaud the practical nature of modern testing grounds, eulogise over two great collies, and recall a most popular Supreme victory.

Nicky, as black as coal about his wise young head, drifted silently through the cotton-grass to the left, and the ewes turned to his bidding to come in a packed, jostling flock down the hillside.

The moor was cold and bleak on Blackstone Edge in the Lancashire Pennines. The wind tugged at Nicky's long hairs. Body low in a crouch, muscles taut, gaze fixed solidly on the ewes, he slunk through the rough herbage to order the sheep to his master's bidding. A squall of raindrops buffeted his body and pricked at his eyes. He ignored this sudden flurry of the weather's wind-whipped fury, his mind solely concentrated on his job, his senses alert only to the whistles of his master.

Danny Wild ordered his helpmate with equal concentration. He was master to Nicky. Friend also, for theirs was an understanding of mutual respect. The harmony between them was something special, which few outside the hill country would ever comprehend. Nicky relied on Danny's guidance when at hand; Danny depended on Nicky's wisdom when the big collie was beyond his ken. Together they were able to manage 470 ewes to turn this bleak Pennine moor into viable production.

Crouched from the rain beneath sheltering rock, I watched and admired their partnership in the gathering of strong self-willed Lonk sheep, over which Nicky had to show respectful mastery.

Nicky, from Rakewood on the Lancashire–Yorkshire borderland, was one of the collie dogs which, in the early 1980s, brought the importance of his daily work in the management of farm stock to the understanding of people in the towns and cities. Shepherding before the

Champion of the Pennine Hills, Danny Wild's black-coated Nicky on the home moor.

television cameras in the BBC's 'One Man and His Dog' programme, he took his skills into four million homes. As never before, his urban audience came to realise his contribution to their way of life, his role in the management of the creatures which provided their 'daily bread', the meat on the dinner-plate, the woollen clothes on their backs.

After years of television exposure, in programmes that have gone round the world, after numerous popular newspaper and magazine articles, the sale of sheepdog mugs, T-shirts and the like, an ever-growing number of published books and crowds of trials spectators, the working collie has become a star – but never should its fame cloud its purpose in life, which is the herding of stock.

Publicity can be good. Apart from the most important aspect of recognition for its vital role in British – and world – agriculture, the collie's inbred wisdom has come to the notice of the police and rescue organisations. The collie's scenting ability and sense in tricky situations is put to good use in the search for explosives, drugs and even dead bodies; and collies form the bulk of dogs in the search for people lost in the mountainous wilds of Britain.

Though perhaps not of ideal size, and long coated, it is also used for guiding the blind. In tracking tests it is at the top, and in obedience trials it is unsurpassed.

Even some farmers who have accepted its intelligence for generations have finally realised its true potential. Yet never have I been more surprised than to see a young man walk some 100 yards to an 8 acre field, and then proceed to run round 50 milk cows to bring them home for milking at an agricultural college – and in the north-east of all places – where students were taught the practical aspects of farming.

At the International trials at Mostyn in September 1995 I chatted with visitors from America, France, Switzerland and Sweden, and all

Tested at the pen at the famous Longshaw trials, Danny Wild's Nicky moves in with confidence to counter the break of an awkward ewe (Sheffield Newspapers Ltd).

were keen to know more of Britain's working collies. While the rest of the sheep-rearing world has made great strides in evolving dogs for the management of their flocks, British is still best. When the Falkland Isles were able to recommence their main industry of sheep farming, they sent to the United Kingdom for a consignment of working collie pups in order to re-establish and strengthen their bloodlines. In September 1983 Glyn and Beryl Jones of Bwlch Isaf at Bodfari sent 26 pups to the Islands.

In 1983 a German television crew came to Loch Lomandside where we were running 'One Man and His Dog', in order to show their viewers the workings of the British collie dog. Breakfast television, 'Blue Peter' and 'In at the Deep End' programmes have featured sheepdogs, and Welsh television regularly 'covers' the North Wales championship.

However, publicity can also do harm. Popularity can take the collie into the worst of environments.

When Nicky completed his work at Rakewood he ran to Danny for a customary word of praise, then he came to me for a fuss. When he had finished work he was as soft and playful as any household dog and he liked to be petted and spoiled. He had the right temperament for this change of role, but work was first and foremost. He would have had it no other way for he was a craftsman, and his craft was shepherding sheep with authority and care. He had been bred and reared for shepherding and that was his prime purpose in life.

Sadly, fame has made the Border Collie the most popular dog in Britain – sadly, because it has become the most popular of pets. I have written earlier of collies being marvellous pets, but have stressed – and I make no excuses for stressing again – the importance of the right people and the right environment. These essentials are being overlooked, and the most unsuitable people are taking the Border Collie into their homes.

Friends who deal with the rehabilitation of collies have fearful tales to tell of abandoned dogs, damaged dogs and traumatised dogs. Advertisements, quoting 'One Man and His Dog', are regularly persuading the wrong people to buy Border Collies. This is the unhappy result of the Border Collie becoming so well known by an urban public. The popularity of the working collie – or Border Collie – has regrettably taken it on to the show bench, a step which over the years will mean two distinct types, as with other working dogs.

The labradors, golden retrievers, springers and cocker spaniels of the show bench are not workers, and indeed many of their adherents have cast aside any pretence that their show dogs will work. This sad state of affairs will inevitably come to the Border Collie.

Breeders of the one-time gundogs tried for what I suppose can be classed as a dual-purpose dog, one which retained its working qualities while taking on the false elegance of 'fine feathers'. It didn't work, and resulted in the dog being reduced from the status of companion and helpmate in the field to that of ornament and pet dog. The Border Collie is a bonny dog and, as I have written elsewhere, its beauty was developed along with its brain power. But looks were incidental, intelligence paramount, for no shepherding dog could hope to earn a living on looks alone. Soon – sadly – it may well be able to do so.

Throughout this book I have emphasised the value of good breeding in all aspects of livestock production. It is of paramount importance in producing the best of everything.

Fred Coward's rough-coated black and white Ken, the son of Tot Longton's Rob, and from Fraser's Mindrum Nell and Gilchrist's Spot, had seven sons and two daughters qualified to compete in the 1984 English National, and four of them, Richard Fawcett's Bute, Chris Todd's Pip, Ron Bailey's Ed and Alan Foster's Dart, won through to the International trials.

Dart won the International Shepherds' championship and the English National title in 1980, and Ken was also the sire of Alan Foster's Darkie, the 1983 English Shepherds' champion, and of Raymond MacPherson's Zac, Supreme champion of 1975 and 1979.

Coward's Ken, who will best be remembered for his powerful control of sheep and for his good gathering qualities, was a consistent sire of top class collies. In addition to four of his offspring in the 1984 English team, he had two in the 1983 team and four in the 1982 team. Ken was also a prime example of the character and temperament of his kind, for he spent most of his life with two steel pins in his jaw. When he was two years old he had his jaw broken while working cows, an injury which required the insertion of the pins and over 40 stitches. He wore the pins for eight years.

There are no guarantees of the right way to choose a winner from a litter of puppies, but start with the breeding because it will give a guide to ability and temperament. See that the bitch who mothers the pup is well done-to so that she can pass on her strength to her offspring. Choose a bold pup when you go to select, and see that the physical make-up, broad skull, clear eye, open nostrils, healthy coat and strong bone are right.

Danny Wild's Nicky was a son of one of Scotland's most famous dogs, Bobby Dalziel's Dryden Joe, 1986 National, Shepherds' and Driving champion, winner of 50 open trials, and the son of Dick Fortune's international Glen who went to Clifford Parker in Texas. His line was from Supreme champion McKnight's Gael. Nicky was born of Queen, with Bobby Henderson at Heriot in Midlothian in October 1979. She was half-sister to Bobbie's 1983 International Shepherds' champion Craig, and her line was from Davie McTeir's champion Ben and John Richardson's Sweep and Wiston Cap.

Taken by Danny Wild at 11 months old for schooling to work his flock of Lonks, Nicky was easy to teach because of his good temperament and inbred ability to handle any type of stock. I saw him grow from juvenile ways to compete in the Pennine nursery trials of 1981–2 where he won 13 awards. He earned his first trials victory over the Trawden Society's snow-covered course at Gisburn Hall by a decisive ten points in January 1982, and the following week on the misty heights above Whitworth, near Rochdale, at the Holme Association's event, he took his second victory on Gritstone ewes.

He was predominantly a hill-dog who enjoyed work in the wide open ranges, yet he could control his far-reaching exuberance to the relative confines of a trials course. He graduated with open victories; he was successful in the publicity of the 'One Man and His Dog' spotlight on Loch Lomondside; he won International recognition for England by mastering unpredictable hill ewes over the undulating lands of Mottram Hall near Macclesfield in Cheshire. Inbred intelligence and the right master made Nicky into the perfect shepherding tool, the extension of his master's arm in reaching sheep on distant land.

Such efficiency from sensible breeding programmes was seen to good effect on the trials fields from 1990 to 1995. The International Sheep Dog Society set some really testing trials.

Searching work on strong Mules in fine weather conditions probed every shepherding quality over the undulating half-mile course by the castle at Alnwick in 1990.

Pedigree of NICKY (118269) 1984 English International with Danny Wild

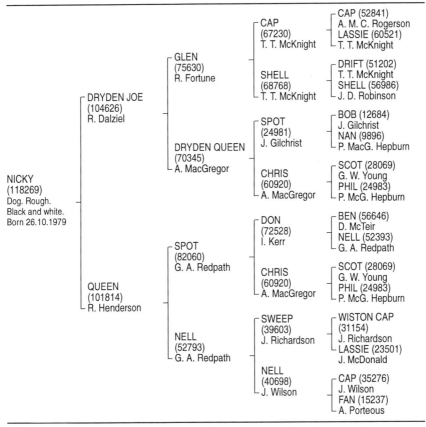

The numbers in brackets are the Stud Book numbers of the International Sheep Dog Society

Truculent Blackface gimmer shearlings proved a real test of collie stamina in cold, showery and dull weather conditions in the double-gather test over the extensive grassy hillside rising to 1,000 ft and cut by the infamous 'death valley' in the Borders between Biggar and Lanark in 1991.

In 1992 collies were faced with a real test of initiative to overcome the vicious conditions of blustery wind which demolished part of the grandstand at Aberystwyth by Cardigan Bay.

Over the rough hillside at Armathwaite in Cumbria in 1993 collies came through a most gruelling shepherding test on Swaledale ewes with flying colours.

Monymusk west of Aberdeen in 1994 was a contrast, on uneven but mainly flat extensive land, and tested immediate reaction to command by collies on Scottish Mule ewes.

Concentration, never wavering for a second in half an hour of tests, and stamina to run two very steep hillside gathers marked the winner of the 1995 International at Mostyn in North Wales as a very great collie indeed.

The sites over which the television trials were run for the 'One Man and His Dog' programmes demanded perhaps even more in thinking power and quick decisions from collies and their handlers.

Collies had to cope with bog, stream, screening bracken, rocks and steep slopes at Rannerdale in the Lake District in 1979 to herd Swaledale ewes successfully.

Initiative was required of collies to work Halfbred ewes through tree-fringed lines out of sight of the handlers, in combination with stamina to gather the steep slope of mountainous land at the head of the valley outside the village of Cilycwm by Llandovery in Wales in 1980.

On the good fertile farmland of the Rhiwlas Estate at Bala in 1981 the work was a very practical piece of shepherding, with immediate and close co-operation required between man and dog to manage strong Welsh Mountain ewes which were always prepared to test a dog's calibre.

Similarly, with driving tests screened behind foliage, the work on Kelburn's hillside above the Clyde in 1982 also required initiative from dogs, while the Loch Lomond site produced a testing piece of work amid the bracken on windswept land above the famous water in 1983.

Chatsworth in 1984, over more mellow countryside, often in heavy rainfall, was tight and demanded quick partnership between man and dog, while the work on typical Lakeland fellside of a boggy nature at Ullswater near Patterdale in 1985 required careful herding to negotiate all the tasks.

At Tarn House at Hallbankgate near Carlisle in 1994 the site was set over the open moor, often the terrain that collies are asked to work over.

We realised that the conventional trials course of geometrically set lines for fetching and driving had not necessarily to be laid out in such formal order as long as they were incorporated. Hillmen want initiative in their working collies. The very nature of their farming demands that dogs should be able to look after themselves – and the sheep in their care – when they are out of sight and working independently of any human guidance. So competitive trials, if they do the job they were designed for, should be tough and testing to ensure that collies are capable of carrying out proper hill work.

It is essential that 'local trials' organisers follow the lead taken by the

International Sheep Dog Society in more recent years when setting up their courses, for the testing of collie health, strength and stamina to run the hill is vital for the future of the working breed. Societies must not fall into the trap of setting easy courses in order to get through a large entry of dogs. This does happen more in the North Country, where entries are fuller, than in the southern areas. Rather should the entry be limited than the tests set to accommodate too many entries. I make no excuses for stressing this point, for it happens all too often – and the working collie will eventually suffer.

Proof that breeding does indeed count is the fact that eight of the 'One Man and His Dog' winners were all of Gilchrist's Spot bloodline, and it must be significant that the winners of the 1982, 1983 and 1984 television series were all from John Thomas's black and white Craig, the 1977 Supreme champion. Evan Hopkins's impressive Fly, winner on Lomondside in 1983, was a daughter of Craig; Dick Nicholls's mottled Rod, winner of Kelburn, and John Wilson's gentle but sure Peg, the Chatsworth winner, were grandson and granddaughter of the Supreme champion. In addition to this remarkable incidence of successful breeding, the finalist at Chatsworth in 1984 was John Thomas's Don, the

John Thomas' Craig, the 1977 Supreme Champion, and the sire of champions.

1984 English Shepherds' champion, and the 6½-year-old son of Craig.

A strong, rough-coated black and white collie, Craig was a very practical dog. Shepherding was a job of work to be done, and enjoyed, and it was his confident nature and well-tested stamina from the daily routine with 1,500 Speckled-face ewes over high grassland in the Mynydd Epynt of South Wales which gave him victory in the 1977 Supreme championship at Libanus. It was sound, clever and practical expertise at the collie-craft which worked strong Welsh ewes over a course of natural obstacles to win the coveted championship. It was work which really enhanced the reputation of the modern working dog, for the trials ground in the Brecon Beacons was tricky and testing under a squally, buffeting rainstorm, and Craig was often out of sight and instruction from his master.

A quietly efficient, unassuming collie, who liked nothing better than to be shepherding sheep, but a dog of strong character, Craig was one of the great champions of recent years. When he peaked in trials competition in 1976 and 1977, he won three Welsh titles and three International titles, and full credit for his rise to the Supreme when he was 7½ years old goes to his master, John Thomas, who schooled him from the age of nine months.

Craig came before the public eye because of his trials successes, and his name lives on because of his breeding successes. Craig had many capable sons and daughters, and the extent of his influence is not truly recognised in shepherding circles.

The six-year-old black and white Bill from Pencoed Farm at Pwllglas, above the Vale of Clwydd, handled by Meirion Jones, one of the best handlers in Wales, won the International Farmers' championship over the Knavesmire at York in 1984, the best of the 53 competitors in the qualifying trials. Bill was out of Lassie, the 1980 Welsh Shepherds' champion, and bred by I. B. Jones of Goginan, Aberystwyth, who handled another of Craig's sons, the tricolour smooth-coated Chip, to the 1981 Welsh Shepherds' championship over the big flat course at Llansawel in hot sunshine.

Craig had an Irish-born son in Tim Flood's Craig who helped the twinkle-eyed Irishman in the care of both sheep and dairy cows in the Clonroche area of County Wexford, and who proved to be one of the best working dogs in the country. He had the Welsh Craig's courage and sagacity, and he had his mother's forceful method in ordering stock, plus his maternal grandsire's reputation as the best dog in Ireland. Tim's Cosy, Irish champion in 1977, and three times Driving champion, was his mother, and Tim's Scott, the cool and friendly expert in the ways of sheep, was his grandsire. Craig of Ireland, born in March 1978, represented his country continuously from 1981.

Two of Supreme champion Craig's sons, the smooth-coated, prick-eared, home-bred Cap, and the younger Don who ran before the television cameras at Chatsworth, continued their sire's run of successes for John Thomas, who went to shepherd 1,000 crossbred Cluns at Colesbourne on the edge of the Cotswolds. Though born in Wales, John represented England in International competition by virtue of his address, and Cap won the 1981 and 1983 English Driving championships, the

John Thomas, a shepherd in the Cotswolds, with Cap, the 1981 International Driving Champion, and England's Shepherds' Champion in 1982 (Kenneth C. Ward).

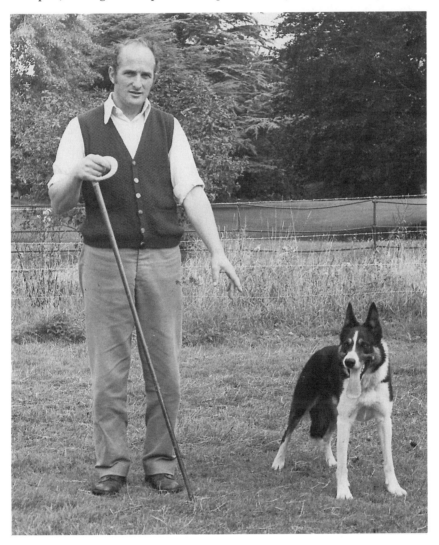

1982 English Shepherds' championship and the 1981 International Driving championship.

Don won the 1984 English Shepherds' championship on hill ewes at Mottram Hall, and was second for the top national award to Alan Elliot's three-year-old Moss, a smooth-coated youngster with similar determination and attitude, from fell-work at Lowbyer Farm, Alston, on the Cumbria–Northumberland border. Don, who had the unworried nature and forceful trait of his father, represented England three times in successive years, and was one of the best of British collies. He had the best 'gear-box' in the whole business, and with John handling him could interpret commands to varying speeds in moving his sheep.

On his maternal line, he was a grandson of Willie Welsh's big tricolour Don who won the 1978 Scottish Shepherds' title and the 1979 International Shepherds' championship while plying his craft on 500 Blackfaces on 1,000 acres at Minnivey, Dalmellington, in Ayrshire. A fearless and sensitive collie, well built with a bare tricolour coat and prick ears, Don started to work when he was only 11 weeks old, running his first trials in 1979, and won over 50 premier awards in competition.

Fortunately, no collie is perfect – or there would be no further competitions, with their fun and upsets. For some inexplicable reason, best known to himself, Thomas's Don failed to lift Mule ewes in his customary forthright manner in the 1984 'One Man and His Dog' final at Chatsworth, leaving the championship to his kin, John Wilson's clever little Peg, his niece in human terms. So the Welsh shepherd, John Thomas, won two International championships, including the great Supreme, and three Welsh titles with the Welsh Craig.

When John came to live in England, at Brampton Abbotts near Ross-on-Wye in 1979, and subsequently ran in the English National trials, he handled the progeny of Craig, one of the most famous of collies, to 13 championships. John's first English National was at Penrith in 1979 when he ran Dilwyn Lad II and Cap, both sons of Craig. In 1981 he made his presence felt in English sheepdog circles, winning the International and National Driving championships with Cap when the dog was six years old.

The white-headed Cap was a quietly efficient home-bred son of Craig out of John's Maid which was a granddaughter of Supreme champion Wiston Cap. He went on to win the English Shepherds' championship in 1982, and the English Driving championship in 1983.

The black and white Moss won the International Driving championships of 1986 and 1989, the English Driving championships in the same years, and the English Shepherds' championships of 1985, 1986 and

1989, and was bred by W. H. Duggins at Pontarddulais near Swansea out of his Jan, a daughter of Craig.

Jos, a tricolour smooth-coated collie, by Dilwyn Lad II, a son of Craig, out of R. C. Barwell's Dell from Cottesbrooke, won the English Shepherds' championships of 1988, 1991 and 1992, and the 1988 English Driving title for John.

A granddaughter on her paternal side of Craig, John Wilson's Peg, a medium-sized black and white bitch, normally of good temperament, was so forceful that she gripped to disqualification in the 1984 Supreme championship, but she enjoyed her competitive work that year. With John Wilson in the management of 700 Halfbred ewes at Hallrule, Bonchester Bridge, in the Borders, Peg was always a willing partner, eager to please, wise in the ways of sheep and successful in competition.

Her baptism in National contests was on her own ground at Hallrule House in 1983 when she was 2½ years old, but it was in 1984 on the flat drought-stricken grassland of Bellahouston Park in central Glasgow that she really showed her quality in mastering wild, bouncy Blackfaces, which turned the trials into a mad chase. Further tested on flat grassland in the International at York, Peg ran fifth on strong Swaledale ewes in the qualifying contest to take the International Shepherds' title, but then

Always willing to please, and seen as a worthy champion by four million people, John Wilson's clever little Peg from the Borders, the winner of 'One Man and His Dog' 1984/85.

she lost her temper – not without reason – to disqualification in the final Supreme contest.

At Chatsworth, for 'One Man and His Dog', the confident little Peg really showed her mettle, and her adaptability, for there she ran strong Mule ewes over the tricky course. In three contests she powered her way to victory, not losing a single point in the three shedding tests, and dropping only four at three different penning demands.

Peg was trained by John Wilson from ten months old and by his breeding and schooling of her son finally produced what was reckoned the greatest collie in the land – the Supreme champion. That was in 1991, at Syde Farm, Carmichael, in the Scottish Borders when Spot, the

Pedigree of PEG (125220) 1987 Scottish Shepherds' Champion; 1984, 1986, 1987 International Shepherds' Champion; 1986, 1987 Reserve Supreme Champion; 1984 BBC 'One Man and His Dog' Champion with John Wilson

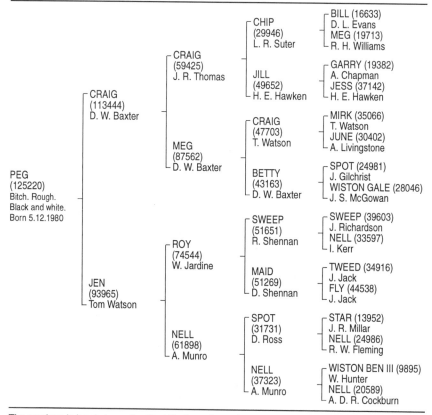

The numbers in brackets are the Stud Book numbers of the International Sheep Dog Society

5½-year-old handsome black and white son of Peg, herded 20 truculent Blackface gimmer shearlings to victory over the half-mile course in a double-gather test. To prove that this was no 'flash in the pan', and that John had got the right sire, Raymond Macpherson's tricolour Cap, for the clever Peg, the rough-coated Spot won the Supreme test again as well as the Shepherds' championship three years later at Monymusk near Aberdeen. Sound method with the black and white collie just using the right amount of power and not putting undue stress and strain on his sheep showed that he was indeed a world-beater.

As I have often said, there is of course no perfect collie – they all have their 'off days', like we human beings – although I thought that John Wilson had got as near to it as possible with Peg who won three International Shepherds' championships, one Scottish Shepherds' championship, was reserve Supreme in 1986 and 1987, and won the television trophy of 'One Man and His Dog' in 1984. In three Internationals she was placed second twice and once third to qualify for the Supreme test, and in the four Supreme championships she ran, she was second twice. The Supreme championship was to elude her, but she did the next best thing – she got her son to win it!

I judged Spot into fourth placing at Scotsheep '95 over the lush grasslands of the Lammermuir Hills above Westruther in May 1995. Spot was representing the Ashkirk area for the Border championship when his master was shepherding for T. D. Hogg and Partners, herding a flock of Blackface and North Country Cheviot ewes producing Halfbred lambs from Headshaw.

John's first success at International level came when he was 25 years old in 1974, when he won the International Shepherds' championship in Kilmartin's downpour in the Highlands of Argyll with his tricolour Scott. He was the five-year-old prick-eared son of Gwyn Jones's Bill, Supreme champion of the same International. In 1982 John won the Scottish Shepherds' championship with the son of another Supreme champion, his five-year-old Cap, the black and white rough-coated son of Wyn Edwards's dual Supreme Bill, who mastered a real tough test of shepherding at Braehead in Strathaven.

So John believes in well-bred collies – for example, his Peg is grand-daughter of Supreme champion Thomas's Craig on the paternal side, and the daughter of the 1980 Supreme champion Tom Watson's trim and self-assured Jen from hill work in the Lammermuirs – only the fourth bitch in 40 years to win the greatest accolade.

It was one of the most popular wins of the International scene when Jen and Tom Watson won the Supreme, for the 67-year-old shepherd had been competing with honour in Scotland's cause for around 40 years. It was his fourteenth International, but it was the number 13

Tom Watson and Jen, the 1980 Supreme Champions from the Lammermuir Hills of Scotland (Marc Henrie).

which proved the lucky one. Tom and Jen were drawn thirteenth in the qualifying test to muster the Welsh ewes which were proving touchy, flighty and somewhat skittish over the flat course by the River Dee at Bala. They managed their task, for Jen was cool and easy in her manner, and Tom was calm and experienced in reading the ways of sheep. They scored 296 of the 300 aggregate points from the three judges to finish in fourth placing, and ensure a place in the final test.

Fourth to run in the championship, the five-year-old Jen first mastered the blustery wind conditions, then the ewes, with outfield work which set the seal on victory. She took the first 800 yd gather and fetch without trouble, and went back on command for the second batch of ten sheep. Spreading sheep were quietly and efficiently put through the drive gates, and when she came into the shedding ring she had dropped 42 of the 390 aggregate points. In the closer partnership of the sawdust ring, Tom was able to help Jen with the cool manner and skill of years of experience. Together, without haste, and awaiting the right opportunity, they cut out eight ewes at the first shed, then two, a further three, and finally with a nice touch of co-operation, the last two were cut away. The penning was quick, simple and faultless for a final marking of 429 of 480 aggregate points, and Tom Watson had finally succeeded in a lifetime's ambition.

Everyone, irrespective of national pride, was pleased. A practical shepherd with one of the finest Blackface flocks in the Borders, a man who was respected throughout the world, had won with a practical collie whose boldness and assurance in her craft had blended to prove the perfection of the herding partnership.

Jen, who showed her shepherding potential when she won the 1978 International Shepherds' championship over the Chatsworth layout, was of Whitehope Nap's line. She was sired by Willie Jardine's Roy, a great-grandson of Supreme champion Wiston Cap, and she was out of Nell, a good breeding bitch with Alistair Munro, of Dell of Inches,

Balanced control with a measured stalk – Tom Watson's Jen brings Blackfaces down the hill.

Inverness. Mated to Supreme champion Wiston Cap in 1972, Nell mothered two good championship contenders from the same litter in John Campbell's Spot, fourth at Kilmartin in 1974, and David Shennan's Fly, second at Lockerbie in 1976 and eighth at Libanus in 1977.

Wiston Cap was the grandsire of the Farmers' champion in 1980, Tim Longton's red-coated Tweed from north Lancashire, in an International at Bala that will be remembered for top quality shepherding. Tweed had a bold nature, and was of the right temperament to work the high sheep-runs of Clougha Fell at the head of the romantic Trough of Bowland in the Lancashire fells, where Tim Longton farmed Dalesbreds. He liked work, he was reliable in all conditions – and it could be very rough on the heights – and he was brave and strong. He was a sound champion who, after winning 13 awards and two championships in the 1977–8 winter nursery season, went on to win 27 open championships and six International 'caps' in the following seven open seasons. He was champion of both Lancashire and Yorkshire in 1982, and he won the English National championship in 1981.

Similarly reliable on high ground, Alan Foster's Dart, from assisting with Dalesbred and Swaledale ewes over 300 acres of rough grazing above Lake Windermere in Cumbria, showed his North Country grit and courage to win the Shepherds' championship, and work to within only five aggregate points of the Supreme honour.

CHAPTER TWENTY-ONE

Shepherding to Stardom

I recall some outstanding victories in the trials fields, tell of one of the greatest collies of all time, think of the bravery of working collies, and consider publicity.

One of the best victories of 1981 was that of Irishman Harford Logan who had moved to farm in Appin and thus competed in the Scottish National trials at Glamis – and won with Star to show the Scotsmen just how good the Irish collies had become.

While the rough-coated Star was taking Scotland by storm, another youngster was making the headlines in Wales, the two-year-old Bwlch Taff winning the National title for Glyn Jones from Bodfari for the second successive year, and beating the 'supreme-to-be', Wyn Edwards's 8½-year-old Bill from Ruthin.

When the two youngsters got to Armathwaite for the International the following month, the old dog really did his stuff and won the coveted prize, with Taff challenging strongly on fifth marking, and Star failing to get through the qualifying test.

Bill won the Supreme championship with an understanding of his master's ways: victory was brought about by the perfect partnership which existed between them. Attentive, courageous and strong to react to counter any possible slip in the ordering of the 20 Swaledale ewes, Bill was master of his shepherding. He won the best marks of any collie for four years of International competition, and earned every one of them with a devotion to his craft that held his watchers spellbound.

With power from a maternal line to Jim Cropper's Fleet, Jim Wilson's Bill II and Whitehope Nap, Bill was the son of the 1974 Supreme champion, Gwyn Jones's Bill, and the paternal grandson of Wiston Cap.

The following year at Blair Atholl, Bill again won the top award of the sheepdog world to work himself into the history books – the second

301

collie in 60 years to win successive Supreme titles; and only the eighth in 68 years to win more than once.

Bill was one of those rare characters whose shepherding was as competitively near-perfect as it is possible to get, yet the best trial which I ever saw him run was not for the judges' eye, but for the camera's lenses. He ran the only perfect trial I think I have ever seen over the North Wales championship course at Ruthin while we were setting up cameras for BBC Wales transmission.

Another sound piece of shepherding before the Welsh television cameras was worked by Bwlch Taff, a collie whose brains and stamina put him among the great dogs of all time. I commentated on his victory work under Glyn Jones over the interesting Devils Bridge course in the North versus South Wales contest – a gathering of the elite – which was transmitted by the BBC from one of the loveliest places in Wales, among the smooth sheep mountains above the beautiful Vale of Rheidol in May 1984.

Wales has continued to produce the best of collies down the years, and I have been privileged to meet many on their home ground where their prowess really counts in day-to-day farmwork.

I must admit, though, that it was the beauty of the Welsh mountains which made me play truant during the Welsh National at St Asaph in 1982. With my Gael, I wandered the mountainside of Bwlch Isaf above the Vale of Clwyd while in the distance I could see the reflected sunlight from the windscreens of the cars parked by the trials course in Llanerch

Master of his craft, Glyn Jones' Bwlch Taff, twice the Welsh National Champion and the 1982 reserve Supreme Champion (Ceri Jones).

Park. With the freshness of clean wind in my face, the bleat of contented sheep in my ears as they walked quietly away from Gael's approach, I trod the land on which champions had perfected their craft.

On that distant trials field, the latest of the Bwlch Isaf champions, the clever prick-eared Bwlch Taff was winning his third successive International 'cap'. Taff in action was a delight to watch. He respected sheep, he had them willingly to his wishes, and he had the genius of method. With the blend of Wiston Cap on both sides of his pedigree, he had all the good traits in the hands of a master-handler. Home bred, by Glen, a grandson of Wiston Cap, and out of Bwlch Bracken, the energetic daughter of Cap, Taff won two Welsh Nationals and the reserve Supreme before he was 3½ years old.

The Wiston Cap line was well to the fore in the 1981 International. Every one of the collies which won the five championships had the 1965 Supreme champion in their pedigree. Supreme and Farmers' champion, Wyn Edwards's Bill, was a grandson of Cap; Jim Dyson's tricolour Glen from a herding above the Vale of Llangollen, the Shepherds' champion, was a 8½-year-old son of Wiston Cap; Driving champion John Thomas's Cap, the prick-eared son of his Craig, was the great-grandson of Cap; and the winning Brace pair, Norman Darrell's decisive Cap, and Pat, the outstanding collie of the 1978–9 northern nursery season, were both from Wiston Cap. The Brace championship was England's first success in this section for six years, and Darrell's Cap and Pat served their country regularly and well in the four years 1981 to 1984. They won the National Brace title three times and ran second on the other occasion.

One of the most outstanding collies which had Wiston Cap in its breeding was John Templeton's Roy, the smooth tricolour son of his master's Moss who ran second to Raymond MacPherson's white-headed Zac with less efficient outwork in the 1979 Supreme test at Stranraer. Bred by Tom Stevenson at Broombrae Farm, Kilmarnock, in March 1979 out of Lass, of McKnight's Gael line, Roy was under 12 months old when he went to John Templeton to learn his job in the herding of Blackface ewes and pedigree Ayrshire milk cows at Airtnoch on the edge of Fenwick Moor.

Always ready to listen and learn, with a retentive mind, he was easy to train. In the hands of a man who has respect for collies and a trials reputation second to none, Roy matured to win three International Farmers' championships, two International Driving titles, three Scottish National victories, three Scottish Farmers' championships, two Scottish Driving championships, and the Scottish heat of 'One Man and His Dog' at Kelburn in 1982. Partnered by his workmate, Ben, he won one International and three Scottish Brace titles.

Scotland's 'first-team', John Templeton with Ben and Roy, International Brace Champions in 1984, and Scottish Brace Champions for three successive years.

Entering the Scottish National for the first time in 1981 at Glamis, he had a remarkable four years of success in the keenest competition in the world. In 1981 he ran second in the National and third in the Supreme championship of the International; in 1982 he won the Scottish title at Strathaven and finished third in the Supreme contest at Blair Atholl; in 1983 he again won the Scottish honour and was fifth over the storm-tossed Supreme course at Aberystwyth where he won International Driving honours; and at the 1984 Scottish National in Bellahouston Park in Glasgow he missed the Scottish team selection for the first time, finishing his work on flighty Blackfaces in sixteenth placing.

In the five Internationals to 1989 he qualified to run in all of them, and won through to the Supreme four times, so consistent was his shepherding. In 1985 he ran to the top of the 150 entrants by an easy five points to become the Scottish National and Farmers' champions for the third time in four years, moving five Grey-faced ewes around the course like clockwork at Monymusk, and at the International at Anandale near Lockerbie in Dumfriesshire, after winning the qualifying trials, a slip at the pen put him down to second in the Supreme test.

Just recovering from injury, Roy mastered strong Mule ewes for sixth placing at the National at Eddleston near Peebles in 1986, and in the

International coped with most unruly ewes over extensive grassland on Baron Hill by Beaumaris Castle on Anglesey for fifth placing in the qualifying trials and tenth place in the Supreme test. He won Scotland's Driving championship as well as second place in the National at Doune in Perthshire in 1987, and went on to win the International Farmers' and Driving championships on rising parkland at Woburn a month later.

A pin could have been heard dropping on the wet turf of Loanes Field at Troon when Roy and Stuart Davidson's 5½-year-old Moss from Sandbank were called upon to rerun after both had earned equal 198 of the 220 aggregate points at the 1988 Scottish National. Roy's five Blackface gimmers skipped round the fetch gates and his master conceded victory to Stuart.

In the International that year at Blair Atholl Roy was unplaced in the qualifying trials.

In 1989 Roy was ninth in the Scottish team chosen at the National at Dumfries, and that year at Margam Park, in South Wales, Roy was one of three Scottish collies to enhance the reputation of their kind for stock herding when he won the Farmers' championship and ran second in both qualifying and Supreme contests.

Three of the greatest collies in the land vied for the top International honour – Roy, Bobby Dalziel's Wisp from the Ettrick Valley and John Wilson's great-hearted Peg from Bonchester. All met and conquered the gruelling half-hour shepherding test with confidence, facing the natural hazards of hillock and valley, often unseen by their handlers, over the rough half-mile undulating course to pick up on the hillside and to shepherd strong and testing Lleyn crossbred ewes in the worst of conditions. The younger Wisp, at 3½ years old, was adjudged the winner; Roy, then 10½ years old, was second; and Peg at 8½ was third.

Margam Park was Roy's finale on the International field, and his work over the difficult course in such foul conditions proved just how great a collie he was. He had shown the world how good British collies were at herding, and he certainly left the competitive International field with his head held high and his movement as jaunty as ever in the gloom of South Wales. Although the Supreme title eluded him throughout his illustrious competitive career, he had been reserve for the title twice, third twice, fifth twice, and tenth once in eight Internationals.

Prick-eared, alert and attentive to the wishes of his master, Roy was one of those collies whose method of working sheep was akin to genius. He had the inbred wisdom to assess the mood of sheep, and he had the good sense to respond to the quiet and highly skilled guidance of his master. He matched his pacing to the sheep under control, geared them to compliance with his will, and his precision and judgement were a joy to watch. He enjoyed his work and was ever-willing to please his master.

Perhaps even more remarkable was his marvellous understanding with Ben, 12 months his junior and his partner at Airtnoch Farm. Together on the trials field for the first time over a demonstration course on Shetland in 1982, they won the Scottish Brace title for three successive years, in 1982, 1983 and 1984, and in 1984 over the Knavesmire at York they smashed the Welsh dominance of five Brace titles in six years to take the International Brace honour, Scotland's first for eight years.

Ben, a rough-coated black and white collie who ran successfully in the 1981–2 Scottish nursery competitions, had blood ties to Roy, his mother, John Barr's Jen, being sister to Templeton's Moss.

Moss was a dog of good temperament and nature, well built and strong, and he passed these traits to his offspring. Himself of aristocratic line from Supreme champions Wiston Cap and Tim Longton's Ken, he sired some grand collies, including Scottish champions Roy and Logan's Star.

Jane McDonald's red-coated Roy, the winner of the junior television trophy in 1983, was a son of Moss; and Nell, the winner of the 1984 International Sheep Dog Society young handler contest at York with John Templeton Junior, was his granddaughter.

Despite the obvious success of well-set courses, sheepdog trials still have their critics, and rightly so, for only under controversy do things

Of aristocratic line, John Templeton's Moss.

improve. Cynics of trials accuse them of not being fully able to test the true character of a dog when it is constantly under command, its health, and particularly its stamina and speed for work on the hill. I simply refer such doubters to recent Supreme contests. A half-mile double-gather of 20 sheep over testing ground with all the necessary aspects of outrunning, fetching, driving and close work to assess a collie's worth is not for the faint hearted.

'Why does a collie which is used to running and shepherding great distances in its daily work leave the comparatively smaller course of the Supreme trials field panting?' is a question I am often asked. The answer simply given is because it has to concentrate and shepherd more precisely than it does at home. It doesn't matter a hang if a collie which may be sent out over a mile to gather sheep at home brings them down the hill without keeping them in a perfectly straight line – and it has no obstacles to negotiate as on a trials field.

In the Supreme test a collie – and the person who handles it – has to concentrate for half an hour, and think of nothing else but keeping the sheep on the right lines, while going through all the tests of outrunning, gathering, leaving the first packet and returning for another small flock, fetching, driving, shedding and penning the sheep precisely – tasks which it can do more leisurely and often more or less in its own time on the home farm.

When running the Supreme trials test both dog and handler have to concentrate in absolute harmony, without any lapse of thought, for half an hour, the dog ever on the alert to take the instructions of its handler immediately while also having the intelligence to act on its own initiative, and the handler thinking of nothing else but helping the dog to be precise. The dog must have the right temperament and the fitness to do this. It expends more energy in half an hour than it does all day at home. Such concentrated work can take its toll on both dog and handler.

As much a triumph for collie courage and stamina as for intelligence and skill, the big medium-coated six-year-old Ben, with Brian Hall on fell land at Ainstable in Cumbria, took the Farmers' title over the Blair Atholl layout in September 1982 while barely free from the mending of the broken hind-leg sustained at lambing time.

Talking of guts, could any dog be braver than Evan Evan's clever Glen from the Ministry of Agriculture's Trawscoed Home Farm near Aberystwyth? Four months after a serious accident which resulted in an operation to save his life, and the installation of a plastic hip-joint in his right hind-leg, he was back in action helping with the management of 1,000 breeding ewes. Hit by a Land Rover in April and operated on early in May, Glen won nine open trials in South Wales in August and September.

'That dog showed real guts to have worked to that standard while it must have been in severe pain' commented the veterinary surgeon, after seeing John Campbell's white-headed Roy work big strong Welsh Halfbreds into fourth Supreme marking over the storm-blown Aberystwyth course in 1983. Roy had displaced the lens in his left eye, and it formed a cataract, thought to have been caused by a rough heather stem on the home moors in Ross-shire, but not apparent until the night before he had to compete in the Supreme championship.

After the necessary veterinary treatment, Roy, one of Scotland's finest working dogs and the 1982 International Shepherds' champion, ran the tricky Loch Lomondside course two weeks later in the 'One Man and His Dog' television trials. Overcoming, indeed ignoring, the problem of his defective eye, he partnered his workmate Moss to win the television Brace trophy.

One of the happiest and friendliest dogs I ever knew, Roy, at 7½ years old, was broad headed and wise, good natured and affable and, even with his eyesight so badly impaired, he had the easy grace of greatness. He represented Scotland for four successive years from 1980 with John Campbell whose handling skills complemented his sheep wisdom.

John and Roy were the first pair to run in the gale of Aberystwyth, and they set a high standard of simple courage and sound shepherding which no cynic would ever dare to criticise as lacking in practical work-quality or collie wisdom or stamina. Blowing from off the waters of Cardigan Bay, the wind-storm wrecked tents, marquees, caravans and grandstands, and made it impossible for the dogs to hear the commands of their handlers. Collies needed integrity to face the gale, initiative to overcome the problems it set and wisdom to work unguided. To win such a contest was the ultimate, and it was the forthright style, knowledge in the ways of sheep, the simple thinking-out of problems and the obvious pleasure in her work which gave victory to the little mottle-legged Jess, with Tot Longton from north Lancashire.

She became Britain's top collie with the sure knowledge and easy confidence of method, and an experience derived from daily work in the herding of Dalesbred ewes and black and white milk cows at Lee End Farm in the Conder Valley at Quernmore, near Lancaster. Sound practical work won the day, for there was no chance of copybook shepherding and high pointings under the conditions.

Running thirteenth, Jess was unanimously marked top by the three judges, scoring 347 of 480 points, 23 aggregate points better than her closest rival, John Thomas's eight-year-old Cap. Faulted mostly on her first fetch of ten sheep, she settled to the best outfield work of the day, balanced in her driving of the Welsh Halfbreds round the 600 yd triangle, and her shed and penning were faulted 21.

Persuasive and quick, Jess was rising ten years old, a medium-coated, black and white bitch, and the Supreme title was her 28th championship. Never showy, but quietly confident and sure, she had won such

Tot Longton and Jess (Marc Henrie).

Pedigree of JESS (88627) 1983 Supreme Champion with Tot Longton

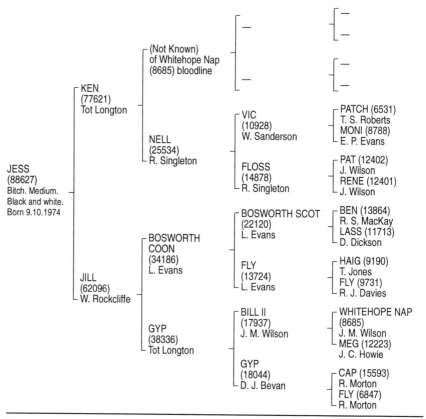

The numbers in brackets are the Stud Book numbers of the International Sheep Dog Society
— Indicates that this dog is not known

high honours as Longshaw, Fylde, Hope, Penton, Barbon, Chipping, and the championships of Lancashire and Derbyshire. The following year she was the top collie at both the Lancashire and Yorkshire championships.

By her master's Ken, of Whitehope Nap line, Jess was bred by Bill Rockcliffe at Kendal out of Jill, the daughter of Supreme champion Bosworth Coon and Tot Longton's Gyp.

Even greater than all her trials successes, however, was her indispensable role on the home farm in the Conder Valley. 'She's been a great friend to me. I'm never stuck with any stock when she is around,' Tot said of Jess. That is the greatest compliment that any man can pay to his dog.

International Sheep Dog Society Supreme Champions, 1981–95

Wyn Edwards with Bill, the 1981 and 1982 Supreme Champion, only the second collie in 60 years to win successive supreme titles (Marc Henrie).

Eric Halsall with Tot Longton and Jess from Quernmore in North Lancashire, the winners of the 1983 Supreme Championship.

A forthright style, an easy confidence and sure knowledge in the ways of sheep gave Tot Longton's mottle-legged Jess the 1983 Supreme Championship (Ron Duggins).

Wilfred Reed and Turk, the 1984 Supreme Champions (Marc Henrie).

John Pirie MacKenzie and Don, Supreme Champions 1985 (Marc Henrie).

Thomas Longton and Bess, Supreme Champions 1986 (Marc Henrie).

*Sydney Price and Davy, Supreme Champions International
Sheep Dog Society 1987.*

Meirion Jones's White-faced Spot, 1988 Supreme Champion at Blair Atholl (Austin
Bennett).

Bobby Dalziel's Wisp, winner of the 1989 and 1992 Supreme Championships (Austin Bennett).

Gwyn Jones and Queen, Supreme Champions 1990 (Marc Henrie).

Gwyn Jones's Queen (Austin Bennett).

John Wilson and Spot, Supreme Champions 1991 and 1994 (Marc Henrie).

Bobby Dalziel and Wisp, Supreme Champions 1992 (Marc Henrie).

Alisdair Macrae and Nan, Supreme Champions 1993 (Marc Henrie).

John Wilson and Spot, Supreme Champions 1994 (Marc Henrie).

Stuart Davidson and Craig, Supreme Champions 1995 (Marc Henrie).

One of the greatest of brace handlers, Gwilym Rhys Jones, who farmed beef and sheep on 250 acres of marginal land in the Carmarthenshire Hills of South Wales, won his second successive, and Wales's nineteenth Brace championship at Aberystwyth with the immaculate mother and son team of Queen and Glyn. Three successive National Brace championships in 1982, 1983 and 1984, the International victories of 1982 and 1983 added to previous successes totalled five National and three International Brace titles and made Queen and Glyn one of the top partnerships of all time. Under Gwilym Jones, Queen and Glyn worked with absolute understanding of each other, adaptable and strong to keep sheep moving at the leading point of a triangle.

Queen was extremely well-bred and clever, a striking black, white and tan smooth-coated daughter of Captain Grant-Jones's Tos, the 1974 Welsh National champion, and her immediate paternal line included Elwyn Griffith's Craig, Gilchrist's Spot and Wiston Cap. Her mother was the Scottish Maid from Dalkeith, the daughter of Davie McTeir's International Shepherds' champion Ben, the son of Wiston Cap. Maid was also a granddaughter of Pat, one of Eric Elliott's Brace-winning pair in 1965 and 1967.

Glyn was Queen's son by Thomas's black and white Mac, son of

A champion partnership in Wales, Gwilym Jones' Queen and Glyn, the mother and son duo which won five National and three International Brace Championships, on the home pastures at Brechfa (Tim Fearon-Jones).

David Young's Dusk, 1965 International Driving champion, and grandson of Supreme champion McKnight's Gael. His 'party trick' after penning his sheep was to stand up and, resting his chest against the gate, walk forward and close it.

Of Queen, Gwilym had nothing but unashamed affection and praise, 'She was quick and easy to train, and she knew all about the job of herding sheep,' he said. Queen and Glyn had a 46-point lead over their nearest rivals, John Templeton's Roy and Ben, winners the following year, at Aberystwyth with a polished performance on Welsh Halfbred sheep. Gwilym won the Welsh Brace championship in 1988 with Lystin Flash and Lystin Roy, sister and brother of Glyn and mothered by Queen.

Another Welsh pair, Ben and Tip with Ivor Hadfield, a Cheshire man resident in Prestatyn, ran three successive National Brace championships in 1966, 1967 and 1968, and won the International Brace title twice.

David Murray's Vic and Number, an artistic father and son partnership from a Blackface herding near Peebles, won the Scottish National Brace contest for four consecutive years, starting in 1951 at Inverness, and they won the International Brace championship on three consecutive occasions.

The legendary one-eyed Roy and little Nell with Jim Wilson had a great partnership to win three successive Scottish and two successive International Brace contests between 1936 and 1938.

With a flock of Halfbred ewes on hill land in Snowdonia, John Griffith's black and white Sweep partnered his son, the tricolour Moss, to win the 1992 and 1993 International Brace championships.

The York International in 1984 was cold and blowy over the wide expanse of the Knavesmire on the outskirts of the city, and collies had to earn their successes. The Swaledale sheep on which the trials were run were so uniform in stature and nature that success or failure was entirely dependent on man and dog. Every one of the 15 collies in the final got round the big course, and the winner, Wilfred Reed's upstanding 4½-year-old Turk, did it in style.

Wise and strong, he was in complete mastery of the 20 Swaledales over the half-mile vastness of the flat Knavesmire, and he reflected all that is best in the modern working collie. Yet another Supreme champion of proven line, Turk from the Wye Valley in Monmouth was temperamentally suited to his partnership with Wilfred Reed. His work was simple yet decisive, and he controlled stock with an easy concentration. Big and bonny to look at in smooth-coated black and white markings, he was well coupled and lithe.

First to run on the final day at his first International after third-placed

Decisive in his shepherding and the 1984 Supreme Champion, Wilfred Reed's 4½-year-old Turk.

qualifying work, he was acclaimed top by four judges in a contest of first–class standard in cold and damp weather conditions.

A son of his master's Jasper, the 1978 International and Welsh Driving champion, Turk was bred by Harold Lewis out of Meg at Pontywaun near Cross Keys, and his maternal line was from Gilchrist's Spot and Irish champion Whitehope Corrie. His paternal mould went back to legendary Welsh collies in the line of Harry Greenslade's Glen, the Welsh champion of the 1950s. Taken to Duffield's Farm at Upper Redbrook as an eight-week-old puppy, Turk was schooled to work with 350 Welsh Mountain ewes over 76 acres on the fringe of the Forest of Dean on the banks of the Wye. Prior to his Supreme triumph, Turk had won at such top events as Cirencester, Evesham and Ruardean.

Reflecting the overall quality of the collies in the National teams which go to the International, the team prize has been won 24 times in 62 years of competition by the Welsh collies, one more than Scotland, although perhaps a better yardstick of the quality of the present teams is Scotland's success of 12 times in the last 20 years. Wales have won seven team shields in the past 20 years; England only once in 1983 when the team of 15 comprised such handlers as Tot Longton, Alan Foster, John Thomas, Raymond MacPherson, Tony Iley, Eric Elliott, Tim Longton and Ron Bailey.

'One Man and His Dog' has provided the best possible stage for the Border Collie to show off its talents, and there have been many memories from the programmes, now having completed 20 series. Winning trophies has not been important, putting up a good show has,

Pedigree of TURK (118169) 1984 Supreme Champion with Wilfred Reed

The numbers in brackets are the Stud Book numbers of the International Sheep Dog Society

and the reputation of the finest working breed of dog in the world has blossomed.

Remember Evan Hopkins's impressive little Fly from Aberystwyth, the tricolour Driving champion of Wales in 1983, giving her tail the luxury of a wag after a faultless driving over the most difficult terrain of bracken and burn on Loch Lomondside? Or the 'old headed' wisdom of Raymond MacPherson's clever Tweed when faced with a rebel ewe at Cilycwm; and the delightful and effective showmanship of John Angus MacLeod from the highlands of Ben Lawers in coaxing Cap and Ben to shepherd out of trouble to the Brace victory over Chatsworth's tight course in 1984?

Remember the controlled driving of Maurice Collin's six-year-old

Scotland's television trials contestants with Eric Halsall and Phil Drabble on the shores of Loch Lomond in September, 1983; John Campbell with the white-headed Roy, International Shepherds' Champion 1982; Bobby Dalziel and Dryden Joe, Scotlands' Shepherds' Champions 1979; and David Moodie with Hope, a collie with great personality (BBC).

Shep, of Whitehope Nap line, over Lakeland's rough fellside at Ullswater in 1985; the good line of Thomas Longton's little Bess with Welsh Mountain sheep under perfect control on the cross-drive between the trees on the bank of the wide River Wye at Doldowlod Hall in 1986; or the relaxed way in which Gwyn Jones's Queen took Swaledale ewes round the field by Esthwaite Water in 1988?

The close harmony of the tricolour Gel and her son Cap with Timothy Longton impressed us all when working in the Brace contest over that course by Esthwaite Water. Remember Katy Cropper's half white-faced Trim, of Wiston Cap heritage, never losing a point in three outruns at Derwent Dale by the Ladybower reservoir in 1989; and the near-perfect shepherding of Herdwick ewes by Alasdair MacRae's Supreme champion Nan at Buttermere in 1993?

Commentating at most of these trials, I often became so engrossed in the work of the dogs that I came out with such comments as 'Oh calm down . . . the bitch is getting too excited' which pleased the critics. One critic doubted if David Coleman, Harry Carpenter or Bill McLaren could get away with such unorthodox remarks . . .

Remember Dick Nicholls's strong young Rod, barely two years old, calming his impetuosity after dropping five quick points at the lift to settle to a steady control of Blackface ewes to earn the victory pointing on Kelburn's hillside near Largs? It was a distant relation to Rod, Tim Flood's four-year-old Pip, which nearly made much greater history for Ireland than having a representative in the judging corps for the first time at the 1984 International.

Both Rod and Pip were descended from Dick Nicholls's Moss, the 1972 Welsh National champion and winner of 50 first prizes at trials, and Pip made a redoubtable effort to win Ireland's first Supreme cham-

Jack Burke of Llandinam Hall and collies Jaff, Glen and Hemp.

pionship on the final run of the 1984 International contest. He finished second to Wilfred Reed's Turk. Ireland's National champion for the year, Pip was a prick-eared smooth-coated, four-year-old home-bred son of Scott and Midge from 140 acres of mixed farming on the flat fertile lands of County Wexford.

Pip was of collie blood which Tim Flood had proved with many successes, and another handler who stuck to a strain he particularly liked was Jack Burke, an Englishman who shepherded 1,200 ewes on 800 acres in the upper valley of the River Severn at Llandinam Hall south-west of Newtown. Jack always bred his own collies and stuck to his own lines in search of what he called the 'super dog', and one of his particular fancies was the blue-merle colouration. From his blue Jess he bred Hemp and Topsy in March 1976, sired by Jim Dyson's Glen, the

A jump for joy — 17-year-old David Bristow from Murton in the Vale of York and his 3½-year-old Tweed, winners of the first television trophy at Cilycwm.

1981 International Shepherds' champion and a son of Wiston Cap. Hemp won the Welsh Shepherds' championships in 1983 and 1985, and Topsy's son Glen, by Peter Miller's English Farmers' champion Sweep, won the 1984 Welsh National, Shepherds' and Driving titles.

Hemp, who had no qualms about facing the flooded river to gather either sheep or cows at home, won the Welsh heat of 'One Man and His Dog' at Chatsworth in 1984 with controlled pacing of the Mule ewes and decisive close work for 102 of 110 points, the best of all scores in the four National heats. Jack won the Welsh Shepherds' championship in 1989 with his rough-coated Jaff.

From knocking in the posts and tying up the hurdles, letting out the sheep at the bottom of the field, to course directing for England and judging the top trials in a lifetime's involvement with sheepdogs, my most satisfying job was to present the prizes at the first young handlers' competition on television in 1980. (The International Sheep Dog Society ran their first young handlers' competition at Armathwaite in 1981.)

David Bristow of Rose Farm, Murton, in the Vale of York, and his 3½-year-old Tweed were the recipients of the BBC's award in 1980, but it was far more important that the other three contestants, Willie Welsh from Lanarkshire with Craig, Ceri Jones from Bwlch Isaf, Bodfari with Gel II, and Gordon Watt from County Tyrone with Chum, had also enjoyed their trials and had made their reputations.

Since that first year of 1980 Meirion Jones from Conway with Jill for Wales, 17-year-old Liam Marley and Glen from Lifford in County Donegal, the irrepressible Janie McDonald and the red and white Roy from Argyll, and Lancashire's 15-year-old Mark France and Flash, have won the television event.

In 1985 19-year-old Mark Owen with the placid Silver from Llandrindod Wells won the trophy, young James Gill and his forceful Ben from Emley in Yorkshire won it for England in 1986, Janet Mason from Gaisgill and the easy-going Slade also gave England the honour the following year, Wales came back in 1988 when Graham Powell and his Jill from a hill farm on the Welsh–English Border in Powys won the trophy, and Ireland were successful in 1989 with David O'Sullivan from County Tipperary and Bin, four years later Ireland's Shepherds' champion. Schoolboy Robert Ellis and Roy from Port Talbot won in 1990, 15-year-old Vanessa Reed from Slaggyford, who has since won open honours with Jen, were the winners in 1991, and Martin Doherty and Moss for Ireland, Kevin Evans and Maid for Wales, and Ross Watson and Joy for England have won the television event.

Ireland's Gordon Watt with Chum, and John Murphy and Lassie; David Bristow and Tweed for England; and John G. Templeton with

Nell for Scotland have won the International Sheep Dog Society trials. Barton Watt with Moy equalled his brother's success in 1985, and Martin Doherty with Moss, and Martin Feeney with Nell have also won the International Sheep Dog Society Young Handler award for Ireland. Wales have had three successes with Robert Edwards and Max, Graham Powell and Jill, and Robert Ellis with Roy; Scotland three from John Templeton and Nell, Miss Fiona McMillan and Garry, and Barry Common and Jaff; and England four with David Bristow and Tweed taking the honours in 1983, Miss Janet Mason and Slade in 1988, Miss B. Benn and Glen in 1990, and Ross Watson and Joy in 1995.

The high quality throughout, and such encouragement of junior handlers, augurs well for the future of sheepdog trials, and at the end of the 1995 open season working collies have never been more efficient at their job. As my friend, Eurwyn Daniel, 1960 Supreme champion from South Wales, says: 'No machine will ever take their place, bless them.'

Trials must always be regarded as a means to an end, never as an end in themselves.

The end is with the practical shepherding qualities of such collies as Danny Wild's black-coated Nicky on the Pennine hills, and the maintenance, and wherever possible, the improvement of such qualities is

Eric Halsall explains the course for television's 'One Man and His Dog' trials to Tot Longton, John Thomas and Charlie Relph at Chatsworth in 1984 (BBC).

Winners of the 'One Man and His Dog' television trials at Derwent Valley in Derbyshire in 1989 with the Duchess of Devonshire who presented the trophies, and programme presenters Eric Halsall and Phil Drabble, Brian Dodd, Glyn Jones, Katy Cropper and Willie Cormack (BBC).

the only true reason for trials, though there is some justification for staging trials as an educational spectacle. Any other reason is really a myth, and can do the working collie no good at all – can indeed actually harm the breed with false impressions. As the premier stock-herding dog in the world, the Border Collie has a vital role in agriculture, and we must maintain those skills by proper trials which test to the full the qualities of the various bloodlines.

Never must we reduce these qualities by inferior testing.

CHAPTER TWENTY-TWO

Breeding Counts

*The glory of the Supreme championship of the International
Sheep Dog Society which I have recorded for almost 40 years. I
maintain that practical shepherding dogs win trials, that breeding
counts, that although nerves in the handlers play a part at the
major events, and a lot of water has gone under the bridge since
1906, the qualities of collies has certainly been maintained.*

Coat sleeked by the fierce wind, the hairs of his rough-coated body flat
as if plastered to his skin, the handsome white-bibbed Wisp only has
eyes for the sheep he musters on the high hill.

This rough land which rises to over 2,000 ft towards the top of
Ettrick Pen above the Ettrick Valley in the Scottish Borders is Wisp's
land, far from the public eye and the trials fields where he has won two
Supreme championships to become world famous. This is where he
earns his keep in the everyday tasks in which he excels, shepherding
around 1,000 Blackface and South Country Cheviots for his shepherd-
master Bobby Dalziel from Potburn in the Ettrick Valley on the borders
of Selkirkshire and Dumfriesshire.

This is where Wisp's true value is realised, for Bobby could not
manage his sheep without the aid of the purpose, authority, practicality
and knowledge of sheep ways shown by the big dog, and this is where
his value is worth his weight in gold.

It is harsh land, far above the tree line, that he covers in his daily work
away from the admiring crowds of the trials field, which to some extent
are respites from the rigorous conditions of the hills. When he comes
down from the hills of home to the trials fields to concentrate all his
skills in winning competitions, his work should silence forever the
sceptics who say that 'a trials dog is not a work dog'.

Wisp showed that he could concentrate the skills he had learned on
the hills into one half-hour of precise shepherding when, with classic

Bobby Dalziel from the Ettrick Valley, with Wisp, the Supreme Champion 1989 and 1992 (G. Gibbs).

work, he won his first Supreme at Margam Park in South Wales in 1989.

He is not a prima donna of the trials field, but a true work dog, and in 1992 he formed the perfect partnership with his master to work 20 strong Halfbred ewes with barely a blemish and again win the Supreme championship at Aberystwyth. That victory put him among the elite, only the ninth collie in 76 years to win the title more than once. To win one Supreme championship is the stuff that dreams are made of. To win it twice is of the realms of fiction.

Bobby Dalziel is a good handler, one of the best in the world, make no bones about it, but he is genuinely self-effacing and gives much of the credit for his successes to his dogs. And they have earned it for they are his indispensable colleagues, essential to help with his work on the home farm where they get their work ability. Bobby believes that practical work should be the basis for all considerations in successful collies. For him, breeding, training and all aspects of competitive shepherding should stem from roots bound in general work ability.

Wisp, a clever prick-eared collie, big in stature and eye catching with his white face, was 3½-years-old when he won his first Supreme championship at Margam Park, enthralling his audience of thousands of knowledgeable spectators with workmanlike and practical shepherding which mastered the Lleyn crossbred ewes to his bidding over the rough hillside. He was guided by the whistled commands of his master over the undulating terrain, but often had to use his own intelligence and anticipate Bobby's wishes when out of sight, and with unflinching assurance he finished his tests to a great roar of Scottish appraisal. He was master throughout his trial and finished 24 aggregate points from four judges in front of his nearest rival, John Templeton's famous Roy.

The month previously at the Scottish National trials at Barony College in Dumfries he had won the National Shepherds' championship, and before that had won Jedforest without losing a point.

Wisp got his initial schooling with Mark Hallam in Teesdale, and going to Bobby Dalziel when over two years old finished his education on the Scottish Borders. He was bred by John Barr at Eaglesham out of Nell and his sire was Norman Rutter's Gunner Keele from Gunnerside in Swaledale, Yorkshire.

Keele got his name by being from a mating on the motorway service station of that name when his mother was stranded while going down south to John Thomas's Don, and the dog had to come north to fulfil his obligation. Don is therefore Wisp's grandsire, which also makes him the great-grandson of John Thomas's Craig which won the 1977 Supreme championship.

About four generations back in Wisp's paternal pedigree is the blood of the 1965 Supreme champion Wiston Cap and Willie Welsh's Don, winner of the 1979 International Shepherds' championship. On Wisp's maternal side is John Templeton's Ben, a son of Templeton's Glen and John Barr's Jen, which was by one of the finest practical working collies, and Sandy Campbell's powerful Hemp. Also on Wisp's female side are Alistair Munro's noted Nell genes, and other big collie names include Andrew Chapman's Garry, John Richardson's Mirk and Sweep, and John Gilchrist's Spot. So the striking Wisp has a bunch of good work dogs in his ancestry.

This he showed when he was 6½ years old and won his second Supreme championship for Scotland over the pastures of Tany-Y-Castell Farm by Aberystwyth in 1992. Displaying the teamwork that had made them famous, Bobby Dalziel and Wisp were undisputed winners, for good partnership was necessary for precision work to gauge the obstacles over flat land in weather conditions of blustery wind which, funnelled off Cardigan Bay, wrecked part of the grandstand. With Bobby plotting the way and the clever Wisp responding immediately to his wishes they worked immaculately together and all four judges had no hesitation but to put them at the top for their second Supreme championship.

Bobby Dalziel thinks the world of Wisp, but perhaps has a soft spot for Dryden Joe who, although he never won the Supreme championship, is perhaps better known, and who figures in so many pedigrees of successful collies. Joe, who won well over a hundred open championships as well as the Scottish National and was a natural worker and easy to school, was born in September 1977 and died in 1992. He was of medium size, rough coated, black and white with tan colouring on his

Pedigree of WISP (161487) 1989 and 1992 Supreme Champion with Robert Dalziel

The numbers in brackets are the Stud Book numbers of the International Sheep Dog Society

legs, and very adaptable. He had a good temperament, and was very affectionate with the family.

Joe's outrunning was good and he could spot sheep at a distance and plot his way accordingly; he always kept good control of sheep; and though his driving was never spectacular, it was plain and purposeful and very practical. He was bred by Alistair McGregor at Roslin out of Dryden Queen. His sire was Dick Fortune's Glen, which went to America, and his forbears included Mindrum Corrie, Whitehope Corrie, McKnight's Drift, Gilchrist's Spot, Wilson's Moss, and Supreme champions McKnight's Gael and Jim Gilchrist's 1947 champion Spot.

Showing an interest in sheep when he was only nine weeks old, he took part in competitive trials in 1978, and immediately showed that he was made of something good, winning the Berwick, Roxburgh and Selkirk nursery league. His first Scottish National was at Kilmartin in August 1979 when he was the youngest dog in the trials, at 20 months old, and Bobby was 24 years old and looking after 600 Halfbred and Suffolk cross ewes at Horsley. He finished in third placing, beating 130 of the best collies in the country, and went on to represent Scotland on two other occasions, in 1982 and 1984, but 1986 was his finest year. He won the National, Shepherds' and Driving championships on a big sloping field at Easter Deans Farm, Eddleston, near Peebles, herding fit Mule ewes in a firm, unruffled way. His trial started in sunshine but finished in a downpour, but unflappable to the end, his only thought was of putting the sheep where his master asked.

In his time he won over 100 open championships, ran for Scotland four times, won the Scottish National championship in 1986, the Scottish Shepherds' trophy twice, and Scotland's Driving title once, but he is best known for having passed on his skills to numerous offspring.

Both Wisp and Dryden Joe were practical work dogs, and another practical work dog that proved it could gear its working skills to trials competition was John Wilson's Spot, which also won two Supreme championships to make history. The handsome black and white Spot won the Supreme title on Blackface gimmer shearlings over the extensive hillside course in the Borders between Biggar and Lanark in 1991, and won on Scottish Mule ewes at Monymusk by Pitfichie Forest west of Aberdeen in 1994.

Both times it was with very practical work, which gave the lie to the thoughts which we of the 'older end' tended to think. Often we who saw many of the dogs of yesteryear tend to think that collies have deteriorated in skill in recent years. But then we often tend to embellish the skills of the earlier days just as we think, for instance, that the old football teams were much better than those of today.

I think this is wrong thinking, for the collies which have won the Supreme championship, say in the last five years, were every bit as good, perhaps better, as the dogs which were winning the honour in days gone by. No one can decry the prowess of the earlier winners, albeit that the competition was not as fierce as it is today.

Only ten collies have won the Supreme championship trials more than once, from 1906 to 1995, two of them in recent years.

James Scott's Old Kep from Ancrum in Scotland, a cool, well-balanced collie which won 45 prizes in trials competition, won in 1908 and 1909; Thomas Armstrong's rough-coated Don from Otterburn in Northumberland, who was subsequently exported to New Zealand, won in 1911 and 1914; Sweep, a half-brother to Don, won in 1910 with Adam Telfer of Cambo in the Morpeth area of Northumberland, and in 1912 with

Thomas Armstrong of Otterburn; Jim Wilson's famous one-eyed Roy of Whitehope Farm fame, a shepherding genius if ever there was one, won the Supreme in 1934, 1936 and 1937; and his fellmate, the brisk and confident Glen won in 1946 and 1948.

David Daniel's medium-sized Chip from Ystradgynlais near Swansea, won the Supreme championship in 1949 and 1952; Raymond Mac-Pherson's good-looking Zac from Hallbankgate in Cumbria won in 1975 and 1979; Wyn Edwards's forceful Bill from the Vale of Clwyd in North Wales won in 1981 and 1982; Bobby Dalziel's upstanding prick-eared Wisp from the Ettrick Valley in Scotland won in 1989 and 1992; and Johnny Wilson's black and white Spot from a herding of Blackface and Cheviot ewes in Ettrick Forest won in 1991 and 1994.

The clever Spot with John Wilson worked every day in the Borders, for his master was a shepherd responsible for the well-being of Black-face and Cheviot ewes at Headshaw in Selkirkshire, and the dog was his helpmate.

The two gathers at Syde Farm, near Carmichael, in 1991 were to land which rose to 1,000 ft and was notorious for 'death valley', a deep gully when the sheep and dog were lost from sight of the handler and the dogs had to work on their own initiative. This, coupled with all the other work of outrunning, lifting, fetching, driving, shedding and penning in the half-hour test made the winner a very capable dog indeed.

Spot was equal to the task and throughout worked with confidence and surety of purpose, faulted to competitive standard mainly on his first fetch while he tussled a bit with the Blackface gimmers, and in the shedding ring. In spite of being downpointed to the tune of 96 aggregate points in these stages, he finished his test with a laudable 530 of 680 aggregate points, just 3½ more than Roddie MacDiarmid and Cap, another shepherd's dog from Cairndow in Argyllshire.

At Monymusk he used his brains to know when to put on pressure in sound method, thereby not putting undue stress and strain on 20 Scottish Mule ewes, to win the 1994 Supreme. The rough-coated Spot was then eight years old, and had had lots of experience in sheep ways – so much so that his experience and intelligence also won the Shepherds' championship, top shepherds' dog in the qualifying tests.

In December 1994, Wilson's Spot ran for the Scottish team against the Northumberland team at Debdon, and won the individual honour. In all his trials he showed calm assurance, he was assertive on his sheep, quickly reacted to his master's commands, and moved well to enhance the reputation of the modern Border Collie, to prove that it is still the best dog in the world for herding farm stock.

The ideal working collie and handsome to the eye, Spot was home bred out of his master's clever Peg which won three International

Shepherds' championships, the 1987 Scottish Shepherds' championship, and the television trials at Chatsworth in 1984, showing that breeding really does count.

His sire was Raymond MacPherson's Cap, which worked daily on 4,000 acres in the Tindale Fells of Cumbria, and his bloodline went back to former Supreme champions Tom Watson's Jen, John Thomas's Craig, John Richardson's Wiston Cap and Jim Wilson's Mirk. Also in his line were previous champion collies, John Richardson's Mirk, the 1975 International Shepherds' champion, and John Gilchrist's Spot which won the Scottish championships of 1965 and 1966.

The Supreme championship of the International Sheep Dog Society is recognised throughout the world as the highest accolade in the working sheepdog competitive world. To win it means that the collie is virtually the finest in the world. Admittedly one needs a little luck to take the honours, but this element is cut to a minimum as a collie has to come through three stages of trials successfully to take this award.

It has to finish in the top 15 of 150 dogs at the National to earn representative honour, has to finish in the top 15 of 60 of the best collies from the four countries in the qualifying trials at the International, and then has to finish at the top in the gruelling Supreme contest.

Also – and often forgotten – the handler is keyed up for these big events, and nerves in the handler can be transmitted as uncertainty in the collie. The handler is more on edge at a National – the first stage – than at other trials. He wants to get his collie into the team of 15, and he has only one chance each year. At other trials there is 'always next week' if he makes a 'cock up' of it.

At the International, too, the pressure is great. The handler has to go out to the post in front of a teeming grandstand, he has the extra onus of having to get as many points as he can for his team, and he naturally wants to join that elite company of having won the greatest accolade in the sheepdog world.

Being honest, there is little excitement in sheepdog trials – although BBC2's 'One Man and His Dog' has perhaps proved me wrong – but the Supreme competition that had us all on the edge of our seats was at Armathwaite, near Carlisle, in 1993. Only one of 680 aggregate points from four judges decided the issue between Scotland's 3½-year-old Nan with Alasdair MacRae, and England's Paul Turnbull and the eight-year-old Nap. It was the closest Supreme contest ever held, and we watched enthralled as the two collies showed their skills in shepherding 20 Swaledale ewes over the rough hillside.

The tricolour Nan just had the edge in the outfield work although Nap was more determined in the shedding ring and at the pen, and the judges collectively gave the decision to the bitch.

Both Nan and Nap had recovered from veterinary attention for ligament injuries in their daily work – Nan, with a flock of Blackface ewes and North Country Cheviots at Fossoway near Kinross, for the three main ligaments in one hind-leg, and Nap, who shepherded Blackface ewes in the Rothbury Forest area of Northumberland, in both hind-legs – but neither showed any ill effects in their competitive shepherding.

Nan, delightful to look at, tricolour in rough coat, with one ear cocked and the other half drooped, and of medium stature, won television's 'One Man and His Dog' trials a week later at Buttermere in the Lake District. The black and white Nap had won England's National championship over 150 dogs earlier in the year in Cleveland, and a year later, in 1994, won the International Society's 'Champion of Champions' contest.

Both Nan and Nap were work dogs, earning their keep by shepherding their master's flocks. Another collie that proved the 'knockers' of trials wrong was John Pirie Mackenzie's medium-sized smooth-coated Don from Oldshoremore in the Highlands of Sutherland, the Supreme champion of 1985.

Used to herding large flocks of Cheviot sheep over 3,000 hill acres on the north-western seaboard of Britain, the five-year-old Don put the brashness which he sometimes had to use on these flocks aside and geared his shepherding to the speed of 20 North Country Cheviot ewes with skill and composure to win the most testing of trials over the level pastures of Annandale in Dumfriesshire. Reared and schooled from puppyhood by his master, Don also showed that breeding does count for he was a descendant of Cap, Jim Wilson's great hill dog, and to Hughes's Jaff, one of the greatest driving dogs ever seen.

I remember my old friend Len Greenwood, who farmed in the Lancashire Pennines, telling me that 'a good dog can do anything'.

One of the most difficult dogs we, as agricultural journalists, had to

John Pirie MacKenzie's Don, Supreme Champion International Sheep Dog Society 1985.

photograph was Sydney Price's six-year-old Davy from Shropshire who won the Supreme and English championships in Bedfordshire and Herefordshire in 1987. He just would not stand as we wanted him, although put some sheep on his nose and he showed the right attitude, head low and commanding, his whole body like a tensed spring ready to leap into action. Davy was a very practical collie, big, strong and very determined, and he showed his prowess in both his big trials.

At Woburn to win the Supreme he went about his job of shepherding Mule ewes with a calm and methodical stint of work over the rising parkland, and at Byford in the English National his good solid shepherding of the most wild and unruly Welsh Halfbreds on their own hard and bare ground won the title. His quick and ready understanding of sheep put him in control, for sheep knew immediately that he was too strong for them, and that he intended to be the boss. Initially schooled in Scottish nursery trials under John Templeton, he came to Sydney Price when he was two years old and won 13 open championships for the semi-retired farmer from Cressage, including the North Wales championship of 1984. Well-bred of Scottish lines, his ancestors were Wiston Cap and Whitehope Nap.

Another collie the merit-registered Spot which calmly and purposefully worked sheep, Blackface ewes, over undulating Tayside pasture by Blair Atholl below the Grampian Mountains in 1988 won the Supreme title the following year for Meirion Jones and Wales. A happy dog, most of his ancestors were Welsh although Fred Coward's Ken, one of the most famous of Cumbrian collies, was in his paternal make-up. Wales triumphed again in 1990 when the 8½-year-old black and white Queen from Cae Llwyd Farm in Snowdonia gave Gwyn Jones his third Supreme championship. In 1974 at Kilmartin Gwyn had handled Bill to

Meirion Jones's Spot, Supreme Champion 1988 (Barbara Collins).

victory, and in 1976 at Lockerbie he handled Shep to the Supreme title.

Queen's victory in 1990 made Gwyn the only handler, apart from Jim Wilson, to win the coveted title more than twice. She was a lovely little bitch who delighted in shepherding sheep. She was good too. She won the International Farmers' championship the same year that she won the Supreme, the Welsh National in 1987, and television's 'One Man and His Dog' championship in 1988.

Bred in South Wales with an illustrious pedigree that went back to Alan Jones's 1961 Supreme winner Roy, and to Dick Nichols's Moss which won the 1972 Welsh National championship and 50 first prizes, she was schooled by Gwyn on Welsh Mountain breeding ewes on high grazing near Betws-y-Coed.

I particularly remember the 1986 International on two counts. First, because the International Sheep Dog Society kindly awarded me the Wilkinson Sword, presented annually to a person who has made an outstanding contribution to sheepdogs, and second, and more importantly, because little Bess deservedly won the Supreme title. She was a particular favourite of mine, and headed my column of writings on sheepdog matters in the *Farmers Guardian* for many months.

Hers was the most convincing win of the Supreme championship in recent years. With Thomas Longton, the little Bess from Quernmore won the title by a massive 46 aggregate points with quietly efficient, confident shepherding of the most unruly ewes over extensive rising grassland on the island of Anglesey. Forthright throughout and most

Thomas Longton and Bess from Quernmore in North Lancashire, winners of the 1986 Supreme Championships of the International Sheep Dog Society – the greatest accolade in the sheepdog world (Marc Henrie).

practical in its method, hers was a stint of shepherding to grace the International, and she won the blue riband of the trials field.

This Supreme accolade was no more than she deserved to crown an illustrious career. Almost ten years old, she had spent her days herding the hill ewes and black and white milk cows of Lee End Farm in the Conder Valley of north Lancashire, and her weekends winning trials awards in every part of the country. Intelligent, dominant and with a mind of her own in stock control, she was the only bitch in 20 years to have won the Supreme title and the National title.

English National and Farmers' champion in 1985, England's Brace champion in 1979 and 1982 with her Lee End partner Lassie, England's Brace champion in 1985 and 1987 with her daughters Maggie and Gem, and winner of more than 20 top trials awards, including Longshaw, the Royal Lancashire and the Royal Welsh, Bess was so assured in her work by the castle at Beaumaris that even the most unpredictable of sheep acknowledged her authority with grace. In the greatest of all competitive tests, the full acclaim was for the little tricolour Bess, and her young master Thomas Longton, who since their first International in 1979 had served England so well.

Together at Baron Hill, Beaumaris, they concentrated on winning further honours for England, unruffled when things got a little tough in qualifying, and seemingly nerveless in taking the Supreme honour by a very clear points margin. Bess's victory emulated the success of her kennel-mate at Lee End Farm, near Lancaster, for Jess had won the Supreme championship with Thomas's father, Tot, who bred Bess, three years previously.

Going to Lionel Pennefather when she was weaned, to be reared and initially schooled by him, Bess went back to Lee End for more advanced training. Again we see in her good-looking appearance and sound ways with sheep the value of proven breeding. Bess was a granddaughter of Supreme champion Wiston Cap, and her line included Supreme champions Bosworth Coon and Alan Jones's Roy, going back to Jim Wilson's Whitehope Nap.

Bess was one of only 14 bitches to have won the Supreme championship since 1906; most of the winners have been dogs, and that is how the majority of handlers like it. The winning bitches were Walter Telfer's Midge from Cambo, William Wallace's Meg from Otterburn, Jim Wilson's Fly from Holmshaw, John Thorpe's Jess from Derwent, W. B. Telfer's Queen from Cambo, W. T. Wallace Jnr's Jed from Otterburn, Harry Worthington's Juno from Mardy, Thomson McKnight's Gael from Canonbie, Harry Huddleston's Bett from Arkholme, Tom Watson's Jen from Lauder, Tot Longton's Jess from Quernmore, Thomas Longton's Bess from Quernmore, Gwyn Jones's

Queen from Penmachno and Alasdair MacRae's Nan from Fossoway.

As my mate, the bluff Ernest Dawson once told me, 'A dog can earn a lot of money in stud-fees, a bitch is only a bellyful of pups twice a year.'

But sheepdog success cannot be judged on financial grounds – the value of a good collie to a farmer in shepherding a moor is beyond price. The working sheepdog is the wisest dog in the world, and its value cannot be classed in mere pounds, shillings and pence.

What price the winner of the last Supreme championship – Stuart Davidson's Craig? What sort of money do you put on a dog that is indispensable to his master in the daily farming of Blackface sheep on Loch Fynside in Argyll?

In competition, the 5½-year-old Craig extended Scottish victories in

Pedigree of BESS (101142) 1986 Supreme Champion with Thomas Longton

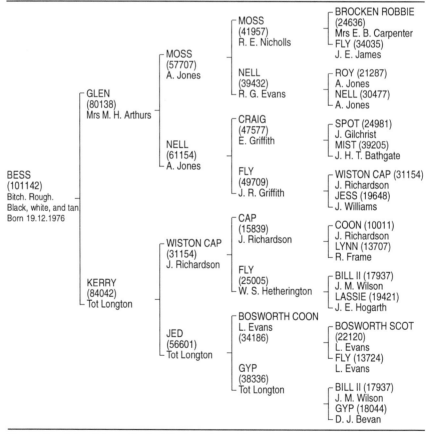

The numbers in brackets are the Stud Book numbers of the International Sheep Dog Society

Thomas Longton and Bess, Supreme Champions 1986 (Marc Henrie).

the great Supreme to five in succession over a layout of steep gathers and generally difficult terrain overlooking the Dee estuary at Mostyn in North Wales which, coupled with the general organisation, resulted in probably the best International trials ever held in the 90 years of the International Sheep Dog Society's history. The black and white Craig was authoritative throughout his test, and after fetching the first ten sheep down the field on his left-hand gather without trouble, and after a sound return for the second packet of sheep on the right, only then did he need a little whistled encouragement from Stuart to take the right line to the top of the extensive hill.

He was bred at Newton Stewart by John Paterson out of Scot and Gell, and his ancestry takes in many Scottish champions, including John Templeton's Moss, Dick Fortune's Bill, and Supreme champions McKnight's Gael and Richardson's Wiston Cap.

Since I wrote the first edition of this book in 1980 a lot of water has gone under the bridge. I have resigned my Directorship of the International Sheep Dog Society after 21 years; I have relinquished my work as secretary with the Derbyshire Gritstone Sheepbreeders Society after 15 years; been appointed secretary of the Lonk Sheepbreeders Association; and after commentating on 14 series have finished on the television scene of BBC2's trials of 'One Man and His Dog' – the best publicity that sheepdogs ever had, for it took them into the homes of 'lay people'. Ray Ollerenshaw, a former Chairman of the International Sheep Dog Society, was my successor for the commentaries, and when he sadly died after doing three, his place was taken by Gus Dermody, whose sheepdog demonstrations are well known. My mate and partner, Phil Drabble, who presented the series during my time, resigned from the programme after 17 series and his place was taken by Robin Page.

During this time the working Border Collie has proved to me that it is indispensable in the management of sheep, and is not just a trials dog. All the 68 collies which have won the 79 Supreme championships since the International Sheep Dog Society came into being in 1906 were in regular daily work with sheep, and most of them were of proven bloodlines.

Pedigree of CRAIG (188525) 1995 Supreme Champion with Stuart Davidson

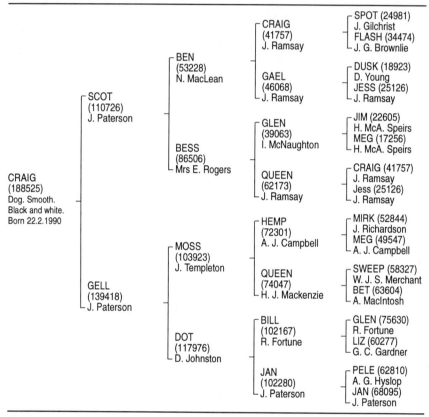

CRAIG
(188525)
Dog. Smooth.
Black and white.
Born 22.2.1990

SCOT
(110726)
J. Paterson

BEN
(53228)
N. MacLean

CRAIG
(41757)
J. Ramsay

SPOT (24981)
J. Gilchrist
FLASH (34474)
J. G. Brownlie

GAEL
(46068)
J. Ramsay

DUSK (18923)
D. Young
JESS (25126)
J. Ramsay

BESS
(86506)
Mrs E. Rogers

GLEN
(39063)
I. McNaughton

JIM (22605)
H. McA. Speirs
MEG (17256)
H. McA. Speirs

QUEEN
(62173)
J. Ramsay

CRAIG (41757)
J. Ramsay
Jess (25126)
J. Ramsay

GELL
(139418)
J. Paterson

MOSS
(103923)
J. Templeton

HEMP
(72301)
A. J. Campbell

MIRK (52844)
J. Richardson
MEG (49547)
A. J. Campbell

QUEEN
(74047)
H. J. Mackenzie

SWEEP (58327)
W. J. S. Merchant
BET (63604)
A. MacIntosh

DOT
(117976)
D. Johnston

BILL
(102167)
R. Fortune

GLEN (75630)
R. Fortune
LIZ (60277)
G. C. Gardner

JAN
(102280)
J. Paterson

PELE (62810)
A. G. Hyslop
JAN (68095)
J. Paterson

The numbers in brackets are the Stud Book numbers of the International Sheep Dog Society

In the last ten years, up to 1995, Johnny Wilson's black and white Spot had such former champions as Wiston Cap, John Thomas's Craig and Jim Wilson's Mirk in his line; Alasdair MacRae's little tricolour Nan went back to what I consider to be the most famous of all sheepdog bitches, Thomson McKnight's Gael; Bobby Dalziel's white-faced Wisp was a descendant of Wiston Cap and John Thomas's Craig. Gwyn Jones's rough-coated Queen had Alan Jones's Roy in her pedigree; Meirion Jones's white-faced Spot was a great-grandson of Glyn Jones's Glen and Beryl Jones's Bwlch Bracken; Sydney Price's rough-coated Davy was from Wiston Cap and McKnight's Gael; Thomas Longton's clever little Bess was of the Whitehope Nap line; and Stuart Davidson's black and white Craig had Supreme champions McKnight's Gael and

Richardson's Wiston Cap in his bloodline.

Today's collie dog has indeed proved itself to be the premier stock-herding dog and the wisest dog in the world.

Pedigree of SPOT (161819) 1991 and 1994 Supreme Champion with John Harvey Wilson

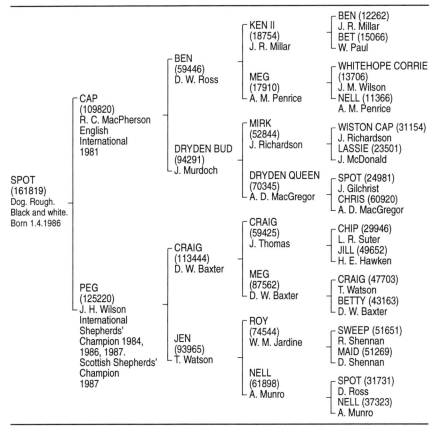

The numbers in brackets are the Stud Book numbers of the International Sheep Dog Society

Appendix

Winners of the Supreme championship of the International Sheep Dog Society – the greatest sheepdog honour in the world.

The numbers in brackets are the Stud Book numbers of the International Sheep Dog Society.

Year	Handler	Dog	Age	Sire	Dam
1906	Richard Sandilands, South Queensferry, Scot	Don (11)	–	Kep J. Scott	Jet G. Gilholm
1907	William Wallace, Otterburn, Eng	Moss (22)	–	Tommy (16) I. Herdman	Ancrum Jed J. Scott
1908	James Scott, Troney Hill, Ancrum, Scot	Kep (13)	–	Spot R. Snowdon	Cleg J. Turner
1909	James Scott, Troney Hill, Ancrum, Scot	Kep (13)	–	Spot R. Snowdon	Cleg J. Turner
1910	Adam Telfer, Fairnley, Cambo, Eng	Sweep (21)	–	Sweep J. Oliver	Trim (37) T. Armstrong
1911	Thomas Armstrong, Greenchesters, Otterburn, Eng	Don (17)	2	Don W. Burns	Trim (37) T. Armstrong
1912	Thomas Armstrong, Greenchesters, Otterburn, Eng	Sweep (21)	–	Sweep J. Oliver	Trim (37) T. Armstrong
1913	T. P. Brown, Oxton, Berwickshire, Scot	Lad (19)	–	Tommy (16) I. Herdman	Old Maid (1) A. Brown
1914	Thomas Armstrong, Greenchesters, Otterburn, Eng.	Don (17)	5	Don W. Burns	Trim (37) T. Armstrong
1915–18	Trials not held				
1919	Walter Telfer, Cambo, Morpeth, Eng	Midge (152)	1	Don (17) T. Armstrong	Nell T. Armstrong
1920	S. E. Batty, Kiveton Hall, Sheffield, Eng	Hemp (307)	8	Sweep (21) T. Armstrong	Meg (27) J. Renwick
1921	Adam Telfer, Fenwick, Stamfordham, Eng	Haig (252)	3	Glen W. Wallace	Maddie J. A. Reid
1922	William Wallace, Otterburn, Eng	Meg (306)	2½	Tip W. Amos	Nell J. Hedley
1923	George P. Brown, Oxton, Berwickshire, Scot	Spot (308)	3	Ben (249) G. P. Brown	Ruby (207) G. P. Brown
1924	Thomas Roberts, Corwen, Wales	Jaff (379)	3	Leader (666) T. Gilholm	Lille (26) T. Gilholm
1925	Alex Millar, Highbowhill, Newmilns, Scot	Spot (303)	4½	Cap (237) W. Telfer	Fan (230) R. Douglas
1926	Mark Hayton, Clifton, Otley, Eng	Glen (698)	2½	Moss (454) C. B. McPherson	Meg (57) G. Lauder

1927	J. B. Bagshaw, Blyth, Rotherham, Eng	Lad (305)	7½	Hemp (307) S. E. Batty	Jed II (250) J. B. Bagshaw
1928	J. M. Wilson, Holmshaw, Moffat, Scot	Fly (824)	2½	Hemp (153) T. M. Dickson	Loos (435) W. Wallace
1929	S. E. Batty, Letwell, Worksop, Eng	Corby (338)	9½	Hemp (181) B. Murray	Nell B. Murray
1930	J. M. Wilson, Holmshaw, Moffat, Scot	Craig (1048)	3	Hemp (153) T. M. Dickson	Mist (332) A. Craig
1931	John Thorpe, Old House, Derwent, Eng	Jess (1007)	4	Glen (698) M. Hayton	Meg (362) A. Watson
1932	W. B. Telfer, Fairnley, Cambo, Eng	Queen (533)	7½	Ben (75) T. Glendinning	Maddie (69) J. Scott
1933	George Whiting, Mawr, Aberdare, Wales	Chip (672)	8½	Don T. Hunter	Maid (489) T. Hunter
1934	J. M. Wilson, Holmshaw, Moffat, Scot	Roy (1665)	3½	Craig (1048) J. M. Wilson	Loos (435) W. Wallace
1935	John Jones, Tany-y-gaer, Corwen, Wales	Jaff (2199)	2	Jaff (1267) J. Jones	Queen (149) J. Morris
1936	J. M. Wilson, Whitehope, Innerleithen, Scot	Roy (1665)	5½	Craig (1048) J. M. Wilson	Loos (435) W. Wallace
1937	J. M. Wilson, Whitehope, Innerleithen, Scot	Roy (1665)	6½	Craig (1048) J. M. Wilson	Loos (435) W. Wallace
1938	W. J. Wallace, Otterburn, Eng	Jed (1492)	8	Moss (1009) W. Wallace	Maddie II A. Heslop
1939–45	Trials not held				
1946	J. M. Wilson, Whitehope, Innerleithen, Scot	Glen (3940)	3	Glen (3510) W. Hislop	Nell (3514) J. Kirk
1947	John Gilchrist, Haddington, Scot	Spot (3624)	4½	Tam (3465) J. Purdie	Trim J. Purdie
1948	J. M. Wilson, Whitehope, Innerleithen, Scot	Glen (3940)	5	Glen (3510) W. Hislop	Nell (3514) J. Kirk
1949	David William Daniel, Ystradgynlais, Wales	Chip (4924)	3½	Moss E. Elliott	Tib D. Dickson
1950	J. M. Wilson, Whitehope, Innerleithen, Scot	Mirk (4438)	6½	Spot (3369) J. McDonald	Chris (4065) J. Cole
1951	Ashton Priestley, Bamford, Eng	Pat (4203)	7	Fleet (4555) J. Relph	Tib E. W. Warwick
1952	David William Daniel, Ystradgynlais, Wales	Chip (4924)	6½	Moss W. Elliott	Tib D. Dickson
1953	W. J. Evans, Magor, Wales	Roy (7696)	4½	Mac (5498) J. Evans	Meg (6782) G. W. Jones
1954	Jack McDonald, Lauder, Berwicks, Scot	Mirk (5444)	8	Reed W. Corbet	Madge (5449) W. Cowan
1955	J. M. Wilson, Whitehope, Innerleithen, Scot	Bill (9040)	4	Garry (4915) J. Anderson	Queen (8279) J. Kirk
1956	G. R. Redpath, Jedburgh, Scot	Moss (6805)	8	Sweep (3834) W. Hislop	Jed (3403) J. Swinton
1957	J. H. Holliday, Pateley Bridge, Eng	Moss (11029)	4	Roy (5406) J. H. Holliday	Bess (7936) M. Kay
1958	W. J. Evans, Tidenham, Glos, Eng	Tweed (9601)	6	Moss (5176) J. M. Wilson	Trim (8859) R. Anderson
1959	Meirion Jones, Llandrillo, Wales	Ben (13879)	3½	Jaff (8228) H. Herbert	Meg (11130) E. Jones
1960	Eurwyn Daniel, Ystradgynlais, Wales	Ken (13306)	4½	Chip (4924) D. W. Daniel	Floss (11400) D. W. Daniel
1961	Alan Jones, Pontllyfni, Wales	Roy (15393)	4½	Roy (7696) W. J. Evans	Jill (7742) W. J. Evans
1962	A. T. Lloyd, Builth Wells, Wales	Garry (17690)	2½	Garry (11742) H. Greenslade	Nell (16024) A. T. Lloyd

Year	Handler	Dog	Score	Sire	Dam
1963	H. J. Worthington, Mardy, Abergavenny, Wales	Juno (17815)	3½	Hemp (13132) H. J. Worthington	Fly (12570) H. J. Worthington
1964	Leslie Suter, Cross Keys, Wales	Craig (15445)	7½	Glen (7690) H. Greenslade	Floss (10217) C. Cook
1965	John Richardson, Lyne, Peebles, Scot	Wiston Cap (31154)	2	Cap (15839) J. Richardson	Fly (25005) W. S. Hetherington
1966	Tim Longton, Quernmore, Lancaster, Eng	Ken (17166)	6	Chip (12270) P. Mason	Spy (13755) Tim Longton
1967	Thomson McKnight, Canonbie, Scot	Gael (14463)	10	Whitehope Nap (8685) J. M. Wilson	Dot (11228) T. T. McKnight
1968	Llyr Evans, Whittlebury, Eng	Bosworth Coon (34186)	4	Bosworth Scot (22120) L. Evans	Fly (13724) L. Evans
1969	Harry Huddleston, Arkholme, Eng	Bett (40428)	6½	Roy (14152) J. K. Gorst	Unregistered bitch
1970	David McTeir, Manor, Peebles, Scot	Wiston Bill (36391)	6	Mirk (13296) D. McTeir	Fly (25005) W. S. Hetherington
1971	John Murray, Sanquhar, Scot	Glen (47241)	4½	Wiston Cap (31154) J. Richardson	Katy (20820) J. Murray
1972	John Templeton, Fenwick, Scot	Cap (50543)	4½	Wiston Cap (31154) J. Richardson	Moira (19110) R. S. Carr
1973	Glyn Jones, Bodfari, Wales	Gel (63023)	3	Craig (47577) E. Griffiths	Nell (43755) W. T. Williams
1974	Gwyn Jones, Penmachno, Wales	Bill (51654)	6½	Wiston Cap (31154) J. Richardson	Nan (21068) W. Kinstrey
1975	Raymond MacPherson, Hallbankgate, Eng	Zac (66166)	5	Ken (47143) F. Coward	Queen (56602) J. G. Hadwin
1976	Gwyn Jones, Penmachno, Wales	Shep (73360)	4½	Shep (49061) S. H. Thomas	Tamsin (66472) S. H. Thomas
1977	John R. Thomas, Llandovery, Wales	Craig (59425)	7½	Chip (29946) L. R. Suter	Jill (49652) H. E. Hawken
1978	Robert Shennan, Turnberry, Scot	Mirk (67512)	7½	Mirk (52844) J. Richardson	Jan (39653) J. Nelson
1979	Raymond MacPherson, Hallbankgate, Eng	Zac (66166)	8½	Ken (47143) F. Coward	Queen (56602) J. G. Hadwin
1980	Tom Watson, Lauder, Scot	Jen (93965)	5	Roy (74544) W. M. Jardine	Nell (61898) A. Munro
1981	Wyn Edwards, Ruthin, Wales	Bill (78263)	8½	Bill (51654) G. Jones	Fly (59282) Mrs M. K. Jones
1982	Wyn Edwards, Ruthin, Wales	Bill (78263)	9½	Bill (51654) G. Jones	Fly (59282) Mrs M. K. Jones
1983	Tot Longton, Quernmore, Eng	Jess (88627)	9½	Ken (77621) Tot Longton	Jill (62096) W. Rockcliffe
1984	Wilfred Reed, Upper Redbrook, Wales	Turk (118169)	4½	Jasper (79280) W. D. Reed	Meg (94933) H. R. Lewis
1985	John Pirie Mackenzie, Oldshoremore, Scot	Don (122367)	5	Mac (115030) P. Ross	Gyp (93692) P. Ross
1986	Thomas Longton, Quernmore, Eng	Bess (101142)	10	Glen (80138) Mrs M. Arthurs	Kerry (84042) Tot Longton
1987	Sydney B. Price, Cressage, Eng	Davy (131049)	6	Bobby (119815) T. Bowey	Sandie (122755) J. Wilson
1988	Meirion Jones, Pwllglas, Wales	Spot (152290)	6	Jaff (128552) D. Jones	Dovey (127125) H. M. Roberts
1989	Bobby Dalziel, Ettrick Valley, Scot	Wisp (161487)	3½	Gunner Keele (148409) N. Rutter	Nell (143510) J. L. Barr
1990	Gwyn Jones, Penmachno, Wales	Queen (152483)	8½	Lad (91117) J. M. Evans	Jill (110568) M. Knight
1991	John Wilson, Ashkirk, Scot	Spot (161819)	5½	Cap (109820) R. C. MacPherson	Peg (125220) J. H. Wilson

1992	Bobby Dalziel, Ettrick Valley, Scot	**Wisp** (161487)	6½	**Gunner Keele** (148409) N. Rutter	**Nell** (143510) J. L. Barr
1993	Alasdair MacRae, Fossoway, Scot	**Nan** (186565)	3½	**Craig** (125319) K. Brehmer	**Fly** (131379) W. McAllister
1994	John Wilson, Ashkirk, Scot	**Spot** (161819)	8	**Cap** (109820) R. C. MacPherson	**Peg** (125220) J. H. Wilson
1995	Stuart Davidson, Sandbank, Scot	**Craig** (188525)	5½	**Scot** (110726) J. Patterson	**Gell** (139418) J. Patterson

Further Reading

Ashcroft, Patricia N., *The Border Collie*, Times Longbooks, 1965.

Billingham, Viv, *One Woman and Her Dog*, Patrick Stephens Ltd, 1984.

Billingham, Viv, *Tweedhope Sheepdogs*, 1990.

Carpenter, Barbara, *The Blue Riband of the Heather*, Farming Press, 1989.

Carpenter, Barbara *The Border Collie: Basic Training for Sheep Work,* W.S.N. Publications, 1982.

Carpenter, Barbara, *National Sheepdog Champions of Britain and Ireland*, Farming Press, 1994.

Cavanagh, Rod, *Australian Sheepdogs*, 1990.

Combe, Iris, *Border Collies*, Faber & Faber Ltd, 1978.

Combe, Iris, *Collies Yesterday and Today*, 1972.

Combe, Iris, *Herding Dogs*, Faber & Faber Ltd, 1987.

Combe, Iris, *Shepherds, Sheep, and Sheepdogs*, Dalesman Books, 1983.

Cropper, Katy, *A Dog's Life in the Dales*, Smith Gryphon Ltd, 1992.

Drabble, Phil, *One Man and His Dog*, Michael Joseph, 1978.

Drabble, Phil, *One Man and His Dog*, Pelham Books, 1989.

Grew, Sheila, *Key Dogs from the Border Collie Family*, Working Sheepdog News, 1981.

Halsall, Eric, *Border Collies – Meine Treuen Freunde*, German by Gunter Piepenbrock, 1989.

Halsall, Eric, *Sheepdog Trials*, Patrick Stephens Ltd, 1982.

Holmes, John, *The Farmer's Dog*, Popular Dogs Publishing Co. Ltd (Hutchinson Group), 1960.

Hubbard, Clifford L. B., *Working Dogs of the World*, Sidgwick & Jackson Ltd, 1947.

Compiled by Hunter, H. G., *Sheepdog Training Explained: Training Methods of H. G. Hunter,* Adams & Sons (printers), Hereford 1983.

Iley, Tony, *Sheepdogs at Work*, Dalesman Books, 1978.

Jones, H. Glyn and Barbara C. Collins, *A Way of Life*, Farming Press, 1987.

Longton, Tim and Edward Hart, *The Sheep Dog – Its Work and Training*, David and Charles, 1976.

McCaig, Donald, *Eminent Dogs – Dangerous Men*, Harper Collins, 1991.

McCulloch, John Herries, *Sheep Dogs and Their Masters*, The Moray Press, 1938.

Mundell, Matt, *Country Diary*, Gordon Wright Publishing, 1981.

Philip, Ron, *Training Sheepdogs*, South African Sheepdog Association, 1980.

Quarton, Marjorie, *All About the Working Border Collie*, Pelham Books Ltd, 1967.

Robertson, Pope, *Anybody Can Do It*, Rovar Publishing Co., Texas, 1979.

Templeton, John with Matt Mundell, *Working Sheepdogs*, The Crowood Press, 1988.

Vernon, Jim, *Because of Eve*, Eve Publishing Co., America, 1986.

Vidler, Peidje, *The Border Collie in Australasia*, Gotrah Enterprises, Australia, 1983.

Wentworth-Day, J., *The Wisest Dogs in the World*, Longshaw Sheepdog Trials Association, 1952.

Wimhurst, C. G. E., *The Book of Working Dogs*, Frederick Muller Ltd, 1967.

Articles, Guides, Newsletters etc.

Pennefather, Lionel G., *Sheepdogs*, 'Independent' Newspaper Ltd, 1967.

The newsletter of the International Sheep Dog Society – a mine of information – is published twice yearly by the Society, from 47 Bromham Road, Bedford.

Working Sheepdog News is published by Delia Sturgeon, The Enterprise Centre, St Thomas Road, Launceston, Cornwall; and *Freedom of spirit* magazine is published by Barbara Sykes, Highfield Farm, Darlton, Newark, Nottinghamshire. Current news of working sheepdogs, mainly trials reports, appears weekly in the *Farmers Guardian,* The Scottish Farmer and the *Yorkshire Post.*

Videos *Come Bye! and Away!, That'll Do!,* and *Take Time!* by H. Glyn Jones can be obtained from Farming Press, 2 Wharfedale Road, Ipswich, Suffolk, IP1 4LG. Tel. 01473 241122.

General Index

Index of Sheepdogs and
Their Masters

❖⊃○⊂❖❖⊃○⊂❖❖⊃○⊂❖

Pedigree Index

FARMING PRESS BOOKS & VIDEOS

If you have enjoyed this book, you may be interested in other books and videos on similar subjects.

For more information or for a free illustrated catalogue of all our publications please contact:

Farming Press Books & Videos
Miller Freeman Professional Ltd
Wharfedale Road, Ipswich IP1 4LG, United Kingdom
Telephone (01473) 241122   Fax (01473) 240501